Mediterranean Spain

Costas del Sol & Blanca

RCC PILOTAGE FOUNDATION

Graham Hutt

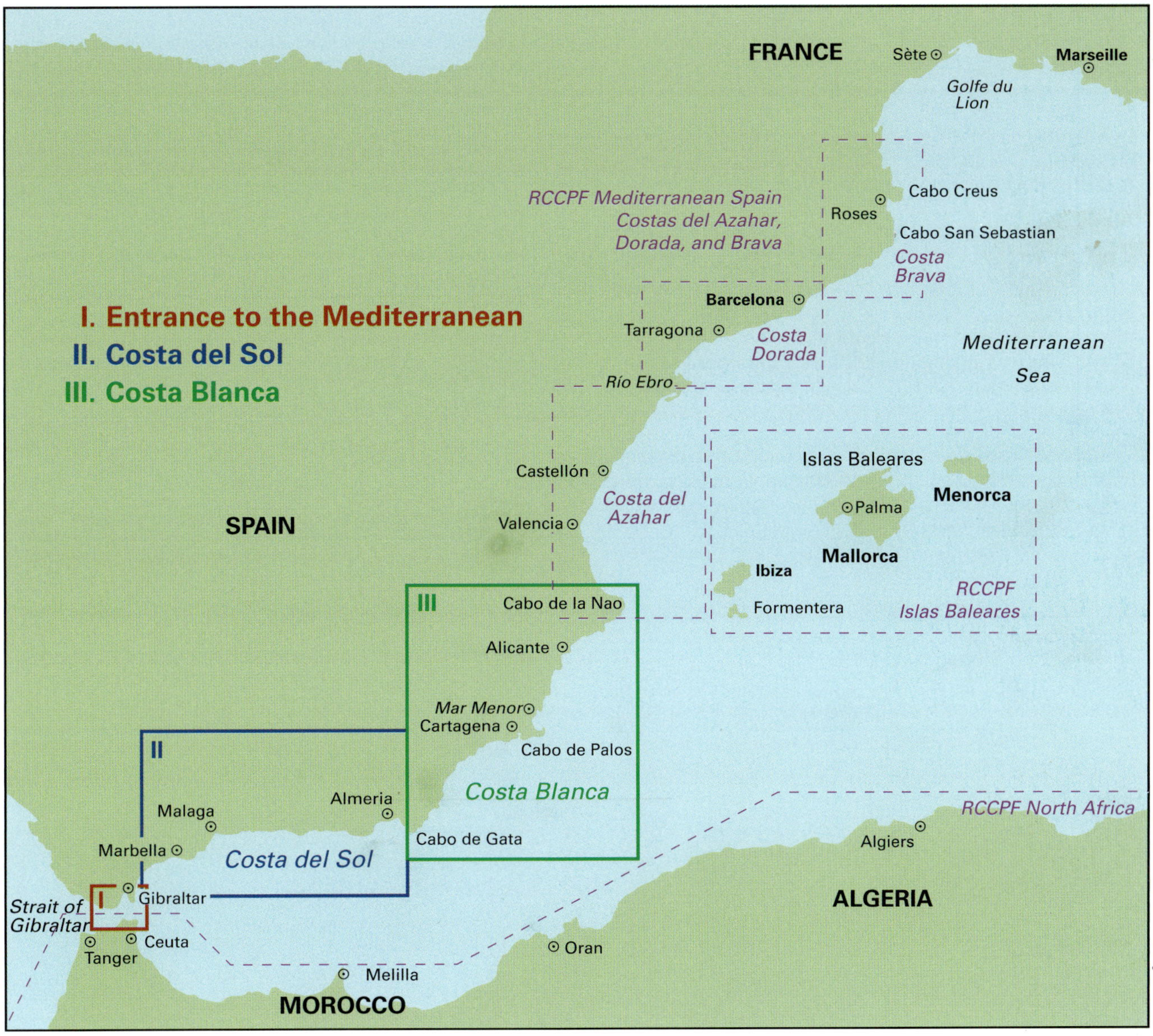

Imray Laurie Norie & Wilson

Published by
Imray Laurie Norie & Wilson Ltd
Wych House The Broadway
St Ives Cambridgeshire PE27 5BT England
✆ +44 (0)1480 462114 *Fax* +44 (0) 1480 496109
Email ilnw@imray.com
www.imray.com
2014

1st edition 1989
2nd edition 1995
3rd edition 1998
4th edition 2001
5th edition 2005
6th edition 2009
7th edition 2014

ISBN 978 184623 526 9

British Library Cataloguing in Publication Data.
A catalogue record for this title is available from the British Library.

This work, based on surveys over a period of many years, has been corrected to January 2014 from visits to the ports and harbours, from contributions by visiting yachtsmen and from official notices.

Printed in Croatia by Zrinski.

Updates and Supplements

Any mid-season updates or annual supplements are published as free downloads available from www.imray.com. Printed copies are also available on request from the publishers.

Find out more

For a wealth of further information, including passage planning guides and cruising logs for this area visit the RCC Pilotage Foundation website at www.rccpf.org.uk

Feedback

The RCC Pilotage Foundation is a voluntary, charitable organisation. We welcome all feedback for updates and new information. If you notice any errors or omissions, please let us know at www.rccpf.org.uk

CAUTION

Whilst the RCC Pilotage Foundation, the author and the publishers have used reasonable endeavours to ensure the accuracy of the content of this book, it contains selected information and thus is not definitive. It does not contain all known information on the subject in hand and should not be relied on alone for navigational use: it should only be used in conjunction with official hydrographical data. This is particularly relevant to the plans, which should not be used for navigation. The RCC Pilotage Foundation, the authors and the publishers believe that the information which they have included is a useful aid to prudent navigation, but the safety of a vessel depends ultimately on the judgment of the skipper, who should assess all information, published or unpublished. The information provided in this pilot book may be out of date and may be changed or updated without notice. The RCC Pilotage Foundation cannot accept any liability for any error, omission or failure to update such information. To the extent permitted by law, the RCC Pilotage Foundation, the author and the publishers do not accept liability for any loss and/or damage howsoever caused that may arise from reliance on information contained in these pages.

Positions and Waypoints

All positions and waypoints are to datum WGS 84. They are included to help in locating places, features and transits. Do not rely on them alone for safe navigation.

Bearings and Lights

Any bearings are given as °T and from seaward. The characteristics of lights may be changed during the lifetime of this book. They should be checked against the latest edition of the UK Admiralty *List of Lights*.

Contents

THE RCC PILOTAGE FOUNDATION

The RCC Pilotage Foundation was formed as an independent charity in 1976 supported by a gift and permanent endowment made to the Royal Cruising Club by Dr Fred Ellis. The Foundation's charitable objective is 'to advance the education of the public in the science and practice of navigation'.

The Foundation is privileged to have been given the copyrights to books written by a number of distinguished authors and yachtsmen. These are kept as up to date as possible. New publications are also produced by the Foundation to cover a range of cruising areas. This is only made possible through the dedicated work of our authors and editors, all of whom are experienced sailors, who depend on a valuable supply of information from generous-minded yachtsmen and women from around the world.

Most of the management of the Foundation is done on a voluntary basis. In line with its charitable status, the Foundation distributes no profits. Any surpluses are used to finance new publications and to subsidise publications which cover some of the more remote areas of the world.

The Foundation works in close collaboration with three publishers – Imray Laurie Norie & Wilson, Bloomsbury (Adlard Coles Nautical) and On Board Publications. The Foundation also itself publishes guides and pilots, including web downloads, for areas where limited demand does not justify large print runs. Several books have been translated into French, Spanish, Italian and German and some books are now available in e-versions.

For further details about the RCC Pilotage Foundation and its publications visit:

www.rccpf.org.uk

PUBLICATIONS OF THE RCC PILOTAGE FOUNDATION

Imray
The Baltic Sea
Norway
Arctic and Northern Waters
North Brittany and the Channel Islands
The Channel Islands
Isles of Scilly
Atlantic France
South Biscay
Atlantic Islands
Atlantic Spain & Portugal
Mediterranean Spain:Costas del Sol & Blanca
Mediterranean Spain: Costas del Azahar, Dorada & Brava
Islas Baleares
Corsica and North Sardinia
North Africa
Chile

Adlard Coles Nautical
Atlantic Crossing Guide
Pacific Crossing Guide

On Board Publications
South Atlantic Circuit
Havens and Anchorages for the South American Coast

The RCC Pilotage Foundation (www.rccpf.org.uk)
Supplement to Falkland Islands Shores
Argentina
Cruising Guide to West Africa
South Georgia
Supplements
Passage planning guides

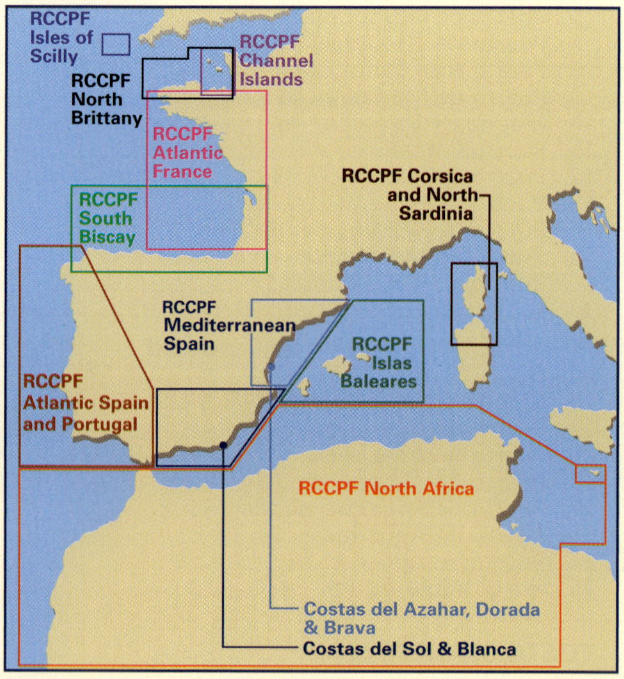

Foreword

The RCC Pilotage Foundation is very grateful to Graham Hutt for taking on the task of editing this seventh edition of Costas del Sol and Blanca. Graham is also author of RCC Pilotage Foundation *Islas Baleares* and RCC Pilotage Foundation *North Africa*. Based in Gibraltar, Graham is very familiar with these coastlines, which he now cruises in his 43ft Westerly Ocean, *Java Pearl*.

Having sailed the full length of this coastline from Gibraltar to Cabo de la Nao in recent years, reading through this edition has been an enjoyable reminder of all that the region has to offer. There is sometimes a tendency to treat the Costas del Sol and Blanca as passages to be endured, rather than enjoyed. But those, like Graham Hutt, who are familiar with the coast, know that there are many places to stop, and plenty of hidden gems ashore. The region has a rich history, nowhere better demonstrated than in the wonderful museum complex in Cartagena where the layers of time have, literally, been peeled back and revealed.

The Parque Natural de Cabo de Gata-Nijar is described in *Lonely Planet Andalucía* as one of the highlights of the whole of Spain. Certainly a highlight for me, etched in my brain, is a vivid image of a squadron of bright pink flamingos, in tight formation, flying between us and the cliffs as we rounded the cape. Cabo de Gata is the driest place in Europe, and the bones of the mountains poke up under a very brown and barren looking skin. But, if you can, take time to pause and get a little closer to this extraordinary wilderness.

The secret to a happy cruise in these waters is to monitor forecasts of wind and of swell height and direction. These do not always marry in the way you might expect, but are increasingly well predicted.

The Pilotage Foundation is very grateful to Hilary Keatinge and to Willie Wilson's team at Imray for all of their hard work in bringing this edition to completion.

We always welcome any comments, photographs and updates, either via Imray or direct to the Pilotage Foundation.

Jane Russell
Director
RCC Pilotage Foundation

Cartagena looking S towards the entrance *Jane Russell*

Preface

FOREWORD TO THE SEVENTH EDITION

I have lost count of the number of times spent transiting the Mediterranean coastline since the 1960s, especially since coming to live here over 30 years ago. The first 10 years were spent in the eastern Mediterranean with my family and four children around Cyprus, Syria, Lebanon, Turkey and the Greek Islands, with the 25m schooner *Arwen Palantir*. I downsized to a beautiful 9m Stella sloop for a while and then found a ferro cement 14m *Hartley Fijian* which became home for 18 years. After moving to Tunisia and later to Spain and the western end of the Mediterranean in 1990, I visited every port between Malta and Gibraltar, looking restlessly for a place to put down roots. Changing yachts again, I purchased a 12m Orion sloop to continue my search with a bit more speed, finally ending up with a larger Westerly Ocean Lord which gives me the extra headroom I wanted. This now serves as home for much of the year.

After several trips as far west as the Canary Islands and down the Atlantic west African coast, returning to winter in Spain, Italy, Tunisia and Malta, I finally settled on a house in Sotogrande overlooking the Strait of Gibraltar at the western end of the Costa del Sol. This turned out well for many years before I became restless again and started a new search. But I never got bored with the incredible wealth of beauty and history in Andalucia, especially inland.

Usually in a hurry to get to – or from – Gibraltar to Italy or the Baleares Islands, or to cross over to North Africa, it is only in the past 10 years that I have spent time visiting the sights inland along the Costa del Sol and realised how easy it is to miss them.

In 2013, I visited just about all the yacht facilities with sufficient depths for my Westerly between Gibraltar and Puerto de Denia. Few of the marinas themselves have anything different to offer, but there is a huge wealth of history along the coast and magnificent sights to visit for those interested in more than just sailing. I hope, with the indications of what is to be seen locally, that yachtsmen will make use of the excellent transport system throughout Spain to visit these sites and cities.

At the western end of the Costa del Sol lies the closest point to North Africa just 12 miles across the Strait. Morocco seems to have eluded the troubles of the Arab World, so this is another nearby ancient world to explore, along with the enclaves of Ceuta and Melilla on the Moroccan side.

The recession is not all bad. It has brought with it a further incentive to cruise the Costa del Sol: marina prices are, on the whole, tumbling, having formerly increased every year. Many excellent deals can be brokered, especially in the low season.

This has been a thorough revision which included reading hundreds of notes, gathering and assessing information from different websites, including the Cruising Association, of which I am also a member.

Graham Hutt, Winter 2013

ACKNOWLEDGEMENTS

Many thanks to all those who have contributed notes and photos and who have assisted with this volume. Particular thanks to Maria Kanayama for her help in updates, and to Di Stoddard for her careful checking of the text. Also to Jane Russell who contributed to this area from her trips and encouraged me to take on the project.

Alan and Sue Douglas of *Ticketeeboo* talked through some of the ports and wrote with enthusiasm about Mar Menor. Tony Bolingbroke assisted with his insights.

There is a long history of distinguished authors covering the Costa del Sol and Blanca over nearly 40 years, so it is a great honour to have been asked to take on a revision of this section of the Spanish coastline.

Graham Hutt

Introduction

Overview of the region

The Costa del Sol and Blanca conveniently link with all points of the compass at their west end, where the Rock of Gibraltar is adjoined to the Spanish town of La Línea by a short low-lying sand spit.

To the NW, the huge Bay of Gibraltar hosts the Spanish commercial port of Algeciras and Spanish marinas located within the bay. Just 12 miles south is the continent of Africa and the Spanish enclaves of Ceuta and, further east, Melilla. Looking east, the entire Mediterranean lies ahead, with the Costa del Sol giving way to the Costa Blanca around Cabo de Gata and Cap de la Nao. Added to this is the spectacular Rock of Gibraltar rising majestically between the bay and the entrance to the Mediterranean, with its own two marinas.

This volume includes coverage from the Bay of Gibraltar into the Mediterranean following the coast of Spain to Cap de Nao, where it links to the RCCPF *Costas del Azahar, Dorada and Brava* which takes you via Valencia and Barcelona to the French border. It also links to the RCCPF *Islas Baleares*, for those heading east through the Islands from Denia. With Morocco just 12 miles from Gibraltar, a link is made to the RCCPF *North Africa* which covers all the ports in North Africa on the Mediterranean coast and the West African Moroccan coast to Mauritania. West of Gibraltar is covered by RCCPF *Atlantic Spain and Portugal*.

The differences in culture, language, religion and lifestyle within a 50 mile radius of the west end of the Costa, taking into account the close proximity of Morocco, make this an attractive and interesting cruising area with plenty to see, and a logical departure point wherever you are heading.

Although the Costa del Sol is in some places overdeveloped, there are many quiet bays in which to anchor, especially between Cabo de Gata and Cabo de la Nao. Good restaurants, great repair and haul out facilities in many ports and modern marinas all contribute to a good sailing experience. Not forgetting, of course, the average 300 days of sunshine every year.

The cultural heritage left by the Moors, who occupied Spain for 800 years, and the early Christians, is mentioned in the text along with interesting places to visit – often using local transport.

Sailing throughout the year is possible in the area. In the extreme west of the Costa del Sol, weather patterns are stable and, for the most part, predictable several days ahead. Further east the development of sudden adverse conditions between March and May – as the earth and sea warm after winter – are more of a hazard, but ports are close to each other.

History

There are many traces of prehistoric inhabitants but recorded history starts with a group of unknown origin, the Ligurians, who came from N Africa and established themselves in southern Spain in about the 6th century BC; with the Carthaginians at Málaga and the Phoenicians, who had been trading in the area since the 12th century BC, and living in various small colonies dotted along the coast.

In 242BC a force of Carthaginians under Hamilcar Barca, who had previously been driven from Sicily by the Romans, captured and held the south of Spain until 219BC when the Romans took over occupation, which lasted until the Barbarian invasion in the 5th century AD. This period was one of development and construction when many of the towns were first established. The Barbarians – the Suevi, Vandals and Alans – were, in turn, overrun by the Visigoths who held the area from the 5th to the 8th century AD.

In 711AD a huge force of Moors and Berbers under Tarik-ibn-Zeyab crossed the Strait of Gibraltar and captured the whole of Spain except for a small enclave in the N. The Moors took over the S and the Berbers the N. By the 10th century AD huge strides had been made in education and development and Cordoba, which had become independent, was renowned throughout Europe as a seat of learning.

By the 13th century, the Moors and Berbers had been driven out of the country by a long series of wars undertaken by numerous Spanish forces who were supported by the armies of the nobles of France. Granada alone remained under the Moors until 1491 when they were finally driven out by Isabella of Castile and Ferdinand of Aragon who united Spain under one crown.

Then followed a period of world-wide expansion and, when the crown went to the house of Hapsburg in the 16th century, of interference in the affairs of Europe, which continued when the house of Bourbon took over in the 18th century.

Over the years the country has been in constant turmoil. Wars and rebellions, victories and defeats, sieges and conquests were common occurrences but none were quite as terrible as the Civil War which started in 1936 and lasted for two-and-a-half years, leaving nearly a million dead. Since then the country has moved away from a dictatorship into the different turmoils of democracy and the European Union, but the Civil War has not been forgotten. Though the country is governed centrally from Madrid, provinces have considerable local autonomy.

Local economy

Tourism has been the most obvious and significant factor in the Spanish economy along the Costa del Sol for many years. Some areas are overdeveloped, but inland little has changed, with small 'white' (painted) villages not much changed over hundreds of years.

Further East, the hydroponic farming with thousands of square kilometres of plastic sheeting force-growing farm produce is very evident from Motril to beyond Cabo de Gata, helping the economy, which is currently in crisis. As with most of Europe, the Spanish economy is in severe recession and relying on 'bail-outs' from its EU partners (late 2013). This has had a drastic effect on the expatriate population, which has been returning to its roots in droves. This is partly due to the austere tax regimes imposed on those living here. Spain has begun to regularise the tax situation for many expatriates who in the past were able to remain under the radar, relatively unscathed. Whereas before, the local authorities relied on the income generated from those living and spending on the Costa, income has switched to the government through taxes. Unemployment is high amongst Spaniards – especially the young workers – and the government is squeezing those who are earners.

This downturn, coupled with a particular tax imposed on yachts – matriculation tax – has in fact led to marinas being far less full and offering better prices than they have for years, when they hyped them up every year.

Matriculation tax

Nothing has damaged the Spanish yacht tourism industry more than the application of matriculation tax. An estimate by the Baleares Islands Tourist office calculates that Spain has lost tens of thousands of yachts since its implementation some five years ago. Most left for Portugal, Italy, Sardinia, Malta, the UK and North Africa. Representations have been made to the government by those most affected – the marina and tourist operators in the Baleares Islands – and marinas along the Costa del Sol and Blanca.

The tax itself is nothing new, but its application and interpretation is so wide and varied in different areas of Spain, that it has simply scared many of those who are perfectly entitled to have their yachts in Spain without having to pay the 12% tax based on the yachts valuation by a customs official, plus all the legal fees involved and change of flag at a later stage.

In brief, if you do not own or rent property in Spain and do not spend more than 183 days in any year here, then there is no liability. If the above applies, then the tax is required. This should be followed by re-registration of the yacht to a Spanish

flag and changing your yacht qualifications for Spanish paperwork. A similar procedure as is required for road vehicles. However, these latter two items are not as yet being enforced in some provinces. Plans are afoot to scrap the tax in 2014 for charter yachts over 16m in order to win back the many super-yachts who left Spain with the associated financial loss. There are many articles on this tax online if more information is required.

Currency

The unit of currency in Spain is the Euro. Major credit cards are widely accepted, as are Eurocheques. Bank hours are normally 0830 to 1400, Monday to Friday, with a few also open 0830 to 1300 on Saturday. Most banks have automatic telling machines (ATM).

Gibraltar uses the Sterling Pound but also prints its own Pound currency, which carries the same value as Sterling – but ONLY in Gibraltar.

Language

There are many differences in the Spanish language between regions. Along the Costa del Sol, you will usually hear Andalusian. Castilian is, however, considered the 'proper' Spanish and is usually taught in language classes. Further East, there is a mixture of French, Italian and Spanish in the Catalan language, which is used from Valencia to the French border. The Islas Baleares has its own brand of Catalan with differing words and accents even on islands only a few miles apart.

Communication, however, is rarely a problem. This is partly due to the fact that there are many guest workers from all over the EU, most of whom – unlike most Spanish – speak English along with their native languages. They work in bars, restaurants, offices etc and are more often encountered in some places than Spanish nationals.

Place names used in this book are, where possible, Castilian, which is also used on British Admiralty charts.

Time zone

Spain keeps Standard European Time (UT+1), advanced one hour in summer to UT+2 hours. Changeover dates are now standardised with the rest of the EU as the last weekends in March and October respectively.

Unless stated otherwise, times quoted are UT.

National holidays and fiestas

There are numerous official and local holidays, the latter often celebrating the local saint's day or some historical event. They usually comprise a religious procession, sometimes by boat, followed by a fiesta in the evening. The Fiesta del Virgen de la Carmen is celebrated in many harbours during mid-July. Official holidays include:

1 January	*Año Nuevo* (New Year's Day)
6 January	*Reyes Magos* (Epiphany)
19 March	*San José* (St Joseph's Day)
	Viernes Santo (Good Friday)
	Easter Monday
1 May	*Día del Trabajo* (Labour Day)
early/mid-June	*Corpus Christi*
24 June	*Día de San Juan* (St John's Day, the King's name-day)
29 June	*San Pedro y San Pablo* (Sts Peter and Paul)
25 July	*Día de Santiago* (St James' Day)
15 August	*Día del Asunción* (Feast of the Assumption)
11 September	Catalan National Day
12 October	*Día de la Hispanidad* (Day of the Spanish Nation)
1 November	*Todos los Santos* (All Saints)
6 December	*Día de la Constitución* (Constitution Day)
8 December	*Inmaculada Concepción* (Immaculate Conception)
25 December	*Navidad* (Christmas Day)

When a national holiday falls on a Sunday it may be celebrated the following day.

Practicalities

FORMALITIES AND DOCUMENTATION

All yachts calling at any Spanish port are required to report to the marina administration office – usually located close to the arrival or waiting berth. A form is then completed which asks for yacht information, crew nationalities, insurance details and passport information. This form is in Spanish and English. Though insurance information is required, third party insurance is sufficient. If there are foreign (non EU) personnel on board, or if the yacht is non EU flagged, border agencies police or customs officials may visit, but this is rare. If the stay is for no longer than 24 hours, payment is usually made to the duty marinero if the office is closed. Credit / debit card facilities are available in most marinas. The same routine is applicable in Gibraltar, where forms are filled out in the marina offices or in advance online – see note on page 28.

Certificates of competence are rarely asked for and are only mandatory for skippers whose countries issue and demand them.

Spain is a member of the European Union. Other EU nationals may visit the country for up to 90 days with a passport but no visa, as may US citizens. EU citizens wishing to remain in Spain may apply for a *permiso de residencia* once in the country; non-EU nationals can apply for a single 90-day extension, or otherwise obtain a long-term visa from a Spanish embassy or consulate before leaving home.

In practice the requirement to apply for a *permiso de residencia* does not appear to be enforced in the case of cruising yachtsmen, living aboard rather than ashore and frequently on the move. Many yachtsmen have cruised Spanish waters for extended periods with no documentation beyond that normally carried in the UK. If in doubt, check with the authorities before departure.

Under EU regulations, EU registered boats are not required to fly the Q flag on first arrival unless they have non-EU nationals or dutiable goods aboard.

OFFICIAL ADDRESSES

See Appendix VIII

USEFUL WEB PAGES

Spanish Tourist Office www.tourspain.co.uk
British Airways www.britishairways.com
Iberia Airlines www.iberia.com
Andalucía www.andalucia.org
Murcia www.murciaturistica.es
Valencia www.comunidadvalenciana.com
Weather websites on page 16
Port websites at each port

Temporary import and laying up

A VAT paid or exempt yacht should apply for a *permiso aduanero* on arrival in Spanish waters if intending to stay for an extended period. This is valid for twelve months and renewable annually, allowing for an almost indefinite stay. Possession of a *permiso aduanero* establishes the status of a vessel and is helpful when importing equipment and spares from other EU countries.

A boat registered outside the EU fiscal area on which VAT has not been paid may be temporarily imported into the EU for a period not exceeding six months in any twelve before VAT is payable. This period may sometimes be extended by prior agreement with the local customs authorities (for instance, some do not count time laid up as part of the six months). While in EU waters the vessel may only be used by its owner, and may not be chartered or even lent to another person, on pain of paying VAT (*see Appendix VIII for further details*). If kept in the EU longer than six months the vessel normally becomes liable for VAT. There are marked differences in the way the rules are applied from one harbour to the next, let alone in different countries – check the local situation on arrival.

The author's yacht - a Westerly Ocean

Chartering

There is a blanket restriction on foreign-owned and/or skippered vessels based in Spain engaging in charter work. See Appendix VII for details.

Light dues

A charge known as *Tarifa G5* is supposedly levied on all vessels. Locally-based pleasure craft (the status of a charter yacht is not clear) pay at the rate of €5 per square metre per year, area being calculated as LOA x beam. Visiting pleasure craft pay at one tenth of that sum and are not charged again for ten days. Boats of less than 7m LOA and with engines of less than 25hp make a single payment of €30 per year. In practice this levy appears to be added to the marina or mooring charges on a daily basis. In many years sailing in Spanish waters, I have only ever been asked to pay this in the Baleares Islands. However, it may be included in marina fees without note.

Charts

See Appendix II for a detailed list of Imray charts. Current British Admiralty information is largely obtained from Spanish sources. The Spanish Hydrographic Office re-issues and corrects its charts periodically, and issues weekly *Notices to Mariners*. Corrections are repeated by the British Admiralty, generally some months later.

Many yachtsmen are turning to electronic charts. Apps developed by Imray and Navionics, amongst others, cover the Mediterranean. These have the advantage of frequent updates and are generally accurate.

Pilot books

Details of principal harbours and some interesting background information appear in the British Admiralty Hydrographic Office's *Mediterranean Pilot Vol 1 (NP 45)*. *NP 291, Maritime Communications* will be found useful.

For French speakers, *Votre Livre de Bord – Méditerranée* (Bloc Marine) may be helpful.

Positions and Waypoints

All positions in this pilot are to WGS 84 and have been derived from C-Map electronic charts. If plotting onto paper charts then the navigator is reminded that some source charts of this area remain at European 1950 datum (ED50) and appropriate use of offsets may be necessary.

This pilot includes waypoints: note the caution on page ii. A full list is given in Appendix I.

Coastal waypoints are indicated there in bold and are shown on the plans at the beginning of each chapter. However, it is essential to keep a good look out at all times while making a coastal passage.

Waypoints which are not listed in bold, have been selected as close approach waypoints for all but the most minor harbours. The detail is shown in the data section at the beginning of each port and on the associated harbour plan. They have not been proven at sea and should be used with caution. Where scale permits they have been plotted on the harbour plan. The track line from waypoint to harbour mouth may be given on these plans to help orientation. Where the waypoint has been positioned more than 0·1M from the harbour the bearing and distance from waypoint to harbour is given with the port data.

The numerical sequence of the waypoint list does not indicate that port waypoints may be grouped together to form a route from one harbour to another. The navigator will need to plot them on a chart in order to plan a hazard-free route.

Magnetic variation

Magnetic variation is noted in the introduction to the coastal sections.

Traffic zones

There are traffic separation zones in the Strait of Gibraltar, off Cabo de Gata, Cabo de Palos and Cabo de la Nao.

Navigation aids

Lights

The four-figure international numbering system has been used to identify lights in the text and on plans – the Mediterranean falls in Group E. As each light has its own four figure number, correcting from *Notices to Mariners* or the annual *List of Lights and Fog Signals*, whether in Spanish or English, is straightforward. Certain minor lights and all buoys with a five figure number are listed in the Spanish *Faros y Señales de Niebla Part II* but are not included in the international system.

Harbour lights follow the IALA A system and are normally listed in the order in which they become relevant upon approach and entry, working from Gibraltar eastwards.

It should be noted that, whilst every effort has been taken to check the lights agree with the documents mentioned above, the responsibility for maintaining the lights appears to rest with the local *capitanía* and, depending on their efficiency, this can mean some lights may be defective or different from the stated characteristics at times.

Buoyage

Buoys follow the IALA A system, based on the direction of the main flood tide. Yellow topped black or red rusty buoys 500m offshore mark raw sewage outlets. Many minor harbours, however, maintain their own buoys to their own systems. Generally, yellow buoys in line mark the seaward side of areas reserved for swimming. Narrow lanes for water-skiing and sailboarding lead out from the shore and are also buoyed.

Hazards

Restricted areas

Restricted areas are outlined in the coastal sections.

Night approaches

Approaches in darkness are often made difficult by the plethora of background lights – fixed, flashing, occulting, interrupted – of all colours. Though there may be exceptions, this applies to nearly all harbours backed by a town of any size. Powerful shore lights make weaker navigation lights difficult to identify and mask unlit features such as exposed rocks or the line of a jetty. Do be aware that unlit and unmarked nets are often stretched across the entrance of harbours after dark. Look out for flashing lights of a torch and listen out for any shouting as you enter. Lights are rarely used to mark the nets and the boats, fishing illegally, often have no lights displayed. This is a particular hazard in Garrucha, where I have run into nets after dark, with no signs of them being there. Spanish fishermen also occasionally lay nets at night from the detached mole to the S mole of Gibraltar harbour. Keep well clear if you see flashing lights and police activity as this is a disputed area.

If at all possible, avoid closing an unknown harbour in darkness.

Gibraltar marina hazards

Note that Queensway Quay marina stretches a barrier across the harbour entrance from 2000 (winter) and 2100 (summer) every night to 0830. This prevents ingress of oil from bunkering spills and acts as an effective security barrier. It is also deployed in the event of an actual oil spill in the Bay.

Marina Bay / Ocean Village has a similar barrier, but it is only deployed in the event of an oil spill.

There is also a permanent barrier stretched across the military and S harbour area (between Queensway Quay and the S mole), which is only opened to allow vessels accessing the dockyard and military facilities adjoining Queensway Quay.

Skylines

Individual buildings on the coast – particularly prominent hotel blocks – are built, demolished, duplicated, change colour, change shape, all with amazing rapidity. They are not nearly as reliable as landmarks as might be thought. If a particular building on a chart or in a photograph can be positively identified on the ground, well and good. If not, take care.

Tunny nets and fish farms

During summer and autumn these nets, anchored to the sea bed and up to six miles long, are normally laid inshore across the current in depths of 15–40m but may be placed as far as 10 miles offshore. They may be laid in parallel lines. The outer end of a line should be marked by a float or a boat carrying a white flag with an ‘A’ (in black) by day, and two red or red and white lights by night. There should also be markers along the line of the net.

These nets are capable of stopping a small freighter but should you by accident, and successfully, sail over one, look out for a second within a few hundred metres. If seen, the best action may be to sail parallel to the nets until one end is reached.

Many *calas* and bays have fish farms proliferating. These are often lit with flashing yellow lights but great care should be taken when entering small *calas* at night.

The positions of some fish farms are indicated on the latest charts but be aware these farms change position frequently. Fish farming is developing along this coast and navigators must be prepared to encounter ones not shown on plans and charts. Where there are no buoys marking these farms, vessels can transit through or close, but stopping, anchoring or fishing is prohibited.

Commercial fishing boats

Commercial fishing boats should be given a wide berth. They may be:

- Trawling singly or in pairs with a net between the boats.
- Laying a long net, the top of which is supported by floats.
- Picking up or laying pots either singly or in groups or lines.
- Trolling with one or more lines out astern.
- Drifting, trailing nets to windward.

Do not assume they know, or will observe, the law of the sea – keep well clear on principle.

Small fishing boats

Small fishing boats, including the traditional double-ended *llauds*, either use nets or troll with lines astern and should be avoided as far as possible. At night many *lámparas* put to sea and, using powerful electric or gas lights, attract fish to the surface. When seen from a distance these lights appear to flash as the boat moves up and down in the waves and can at first be mistaken for a lighthouse.

Speed boats etc

Para-gliding, water-skiing, speedboats and jet-skis are all popular, and are sometimes operated by unskilled and thoughtless drivers with small regard to collision risks. In theory they are not allowed to exceed five knots within 100m of the coast or within 250m of bathing beaches. Water-skiing is restricted to buoyed areas.

Scuba divers and swimmers

A good watch should be kept for scuba divers and swimmers, with or without snorkel equipment, particularly around harbour entrances. If accompanied by a boat, the presence of divers may be indicated either by International Code Flag A or by a square red flag with a single yellow diagonal, as commonly seen in north America and the Caribbean.

In summer, swimmers are protected by lines of (usually yellow) buoys parallel to the shore. It is illegal to anchor or sail within these buoys. The coast is patrolled and fines are high.

Preparation

THE CREW

Clothing

Summer sunburn is an even more serious hazard at sea, where light is reflected, than on land. Lightweight, patterned cotton clothing is handy in this context – it washes and dries easily and the pattern camouflages the creases! Non-absorbent, heat retaining synthetic materials are best avoided. When swimming wear a T-shirt against the sun and shoes if there are sea-urchins around.

Some kind of headgear, preferably with a wide brim, is essential. A genuine Panama Hat, a *Montecristi*, can be rolled up, shoved in a pocket and doesn't mind getting wet (they come from Ecuador, not Panama, which has hi-jacked the name). A retaining string for the hat, tied either to clothing or around the neck, is a wise precaution whilst on the water.

Footwear at sea is a contentious subject. Many experienced cruisers habitually sail barefoot but while this may be acceptable on a familiar vessel, it would be courting injury on a less intimately known deck and around mid-day bare soles may get burnt. Proper sailing shoes should always be worn for harbour work and anchor handling. Ashore, if wearing sandals the upper part of the foot is the first area to get sunburn.

At the other end of the year, winter weather may be wet and cold. Foul weather gear as well as warm sweaters, etc. will be needed.

Shoregoing clothes should be on a par with what one might wear in the UK – beachwear is not often acceptable in restaurants and certainly not on more formal occasions in yacht clubs.

Medical

No inoculations are required. Minor ailments may best be treated by consulting a *farmacia* (often able to dispense drugs which in most other countries would be on prescription), or by contact with an English-speaking doctor (recommended by the *farmacia*, marina staff, a tourist office, the police or possibly a hotel). Specifically prescribed or branded drugs should be bought before setting out in sufficient quantity to cover the duration of the cruise. Medicines are expensive in Spain and often have different brand names from those used abroad.

Apart from precautions against the well recognised hazards of sunburn (high factor sun cream is recommended) and stomach upsets, heat exhaustion (or heat stroke) is most likely to affect newly joined crew not yet acclimatised to Mediterranean temperatures. Carry something such as *Dioralyte* to counteract dehydration. Insect repellents, including mosquito coils, can be obtained locally.

UK citizens should carry a European Health Insurance Card (EHIC) application for which can be obtained at a Post Office or online at www.ehic.org.uk. This provides for free medical treatment under a reciprocal agreement with the

National Health Service. Private medical treatment is likely to be expensive and it may be worth taking out medical insurance (which should also provide for an attended flight home should the need arise).

THE YACHT

A yacht properly equipped for cruising in northern waters should need little extra gear, but the following items are worth considering if not already on board.

Radio equipment

In order to receive weather forecasts and navigational warnings from Coast Radio Stations, a radio capable of receiving short and medium wave Single Sideband (SSB) transmissions will be needed. Do not make the mistake of buying a radio capable only of receiving the AM transmissions broadcast by national radio stations, or assume that SSB is only applicable to transmitting radios (transceivers).

Most SSB receivers are capable of receiving either Upper Side Band (USB) or Lower Side Band (LSB) at the flick of a switch. The UK Maritime Mobile Net covering the Eastern Atlantic and Mediterranean uses USB, and again it is not necessary to have either a transceiver or a transmitting licence to listen in, just a receiver. All Coast Radio Stations broadcast on SSB – whether on USB or LSB should be easy to determine by trial and error.

Digital tuning is very desirable, and the radio should be capable of tuning to a minimum of 1kHz and preferably to 0·1kHz.

Ventilation

Modern yachts are, as a rule, better ventilated than their older sisters though seldom better insulated. Consider adding an opening hatch in the main cabin, if not already fitted, and ideally another over the galley. Wind scoops over hatches can be a major benefit.

Awnings

An awning covering at least the cockpit provides much relief for the crew, while an even better combination is a bimini which can be kept rigged whilst sailing, plus a larger 'harbour' awning, preferably at boom height or above and extending forward to the mast.

Fans

Harbours can be hot and windless. The use of 12V fans for all cabins can have a dramatic effect on comfort.

Cockpit tables

It is pleasant to eat civilised meals in the cockpit, particularly while at anchor. If nothing else can be arranged, a small folding table might do.

Refrigerator/ice-box/freezer

If a refrigerator or freezer is not fitted it may be possible to build in an ice-box (a plastic picnic coolbox is a poor substitute), but this will be useless without adequate insulation. An ice-box designed for northern climes will almost certainly benefit from extra insulation, if this can be fitted – 100mm (4in) is a desirable minimum, 150mm (6in) even better. A drain is also essential.

If a refrigerator/freezer is fitted but electricity precious, placing ice inside will help minimise battery drain.

Hose

Carry at least 25 metres. Standpipes tend to have bayonet couplings of a type unavailable in the UK – purchase them on arrival. Plenty of five or 10 litre plastic carriers will also be useful.

Deck shower

If no shower is fitted below, a black-backed plastic bag plus rose heats very quickly when hung in the rigging. (At least one proprietary model is available widely).

Mosquito nets

Some advocate fitting screens to all openings leading below. Others find this inconvenient, relying instead on mosquito coils and other insecticides and repellents. For some reason mosquitoes generally seem to bother new arrivals more than old hands, while anchoring well out will often decrease the problem.

Harbours, marinas and anchorages

In spite of the growth in both the number and size of marinas and yacht harbours there is still a chronic shortage of berths in summer. A recent expansion of many marinas has eased the situation. One must check in advance whether a berth is available and note that mobile phones are replacing VHF for this function.

Harbour organisation

It is not difficult to become thoroughly confused regarding marina nomenclature throughout Spain. The port authority is basically concerned with the harbour itself and the safe navigation within, under the direction of the *Capitan de Puerto*. His office is the *Capitania*. Within the port, however, may be several yacht facilities, which are all autonomous but under his overall supervision.

Most harbours host a *club real*, or *club real de regattas*. These are private yacht marinas for club members and are often (though there are exceptions) not at all welcoming to visitors. This is indicated in the text. Then there are the *club nauticos* and marinas. Usually a 'marina' is open to visitors. There is also the *puerto deportivo*. These are indicating recreational facilities and can be applied to marinas and *club nauticos* and often indicate a cheaper rate.

Some marinas are handled by the *Junta de Andalucîa*. These are run by the local authority or leased by them and almost always offer a much lower rate than the clubs.

Adding to the confusion, many of the clubs above also have their own *capitania* and *capitan de puerto*!

Many ports have three facilities – a *club nautico*, a *club de regatta* and a marina or *puerto deportivo*.

Calling up on the VHF Ch 9 using just the harbour name can bring in several responses, so try to ascertain exactly the right designation from the book before calling.

For the best rates try heading to '*la marina*' or '*puerto deportivo*.'

It is also helpful to note that in Spanish, the use of the word port, marina or harbour on a local chart does not necessarily refer to anything grander than a cove, a natural feature, or, sometimes, even a stretch of beach where it is possible to anchor!

Harbour charges

All harbours and marinas charge on a scale depending on the month of the season. May to September are usually considered the 'high' season and increases in cost every year have been usual for years. Usually, VAT (at 21%) is not included in the price lists. Often water and electricity are also added either on a flat rate or metered – plus VAT. The difference between summer and winter rates are often double.

With the demise of the economy, along with the matriculation tax, however, many marinas are trying to attract yachtsmen by offering cheaper rates, especially if you are prepared to pay six months or a year in advance.

Although some indications are given in the text, actual pricing is best found on the internet for the marina concerned as prices change so frequently – and not always upwards these days!

Berthing

Due to the vast numbers of yachts and limited space available, berthing stern-to the quays and pontoons is normal.

For greater privacy berth bows-to. This has the added advantages of keeping the rudder away from possible underwater obstructions near the quay and making the approach a much easier manoeuvre. An anchor may occasionally be needed, but more often a bow (or stern) line will be provided, usually via a lazyline to the pontoon though sometimes buoyed. This line may be both heavy and dirty and gloves will be useful. Either way, have plenty of fenders out and lines ready.

Most cruising skippers will have acquired some expertise at this manoeuvre but if taking over a chartered or otherwise unfamiliar yacht it would be wise both to check handling characteristics and talk the sequence through with the crew before attempting to enter a narrow berth.

Detailed instructions regarding Mediterranean mooring techniques will be found in *Mediterranean Cruising Handbook* by Rod Heikell.

Mooring lines – surge in harbours is common and mooring lines must be both long and strong. It is useful to have an eye made up at the shore end with a loop of chain plus shackles to slip over bollards or through rings. Carry plenty of mooring lines, especially if the boat is to be left unattended for any length of time. Steel springs or rubber shock absorbers in the lines help enormously.

Gangplanks – if a gangplank is not already part of the boat's equipment, a builder's scaffolding plank, with holes drilled at either end to take lines, serves well. As it is cheap and easily replaced it can also be used outside fenders to deal with an awkward lie or ward off an oily quay. A short ladder, possibly the bathing ladder if it can be adapted, is useful if berthing bows-to.

Moorings

Virtually all moorings are privately owned and if one is used it will have to be vacated should the owner return. There are generally no markings to give any indication as to the weight and strength of moorings so they should be used with caution. Lobster pot toggles have been mistaken for moorings.

Laying up

Laying up either afloat or ashore is possible at most marinas, though a few have no hardstanding. Facilities and services provided vary considerably, as does the cost, and it is worth seeking local advice as to the quality of the services and the security of the berth or hardstanding concerned.

In the north of the area, the northwesterly *tramontana* (*maestral*) can be frequent and severe in winter and early spring, and this should be borne in mind when selecting the area and site to lay up. Yachts with wooden decks and varnished brightwork will benefit with protection from the winter sun.

The paperwork associated with temporary import and laying up is detailed on page 4.

Yacht clubs

Most harbours of any size support at least one *club náutico*. However the grander ones in particular are basically social clubs – often with tennis courts, swimming pools and other facilities – and may not welcome the crews of visiting yachts. Often there is both a marina and a club, and unless there are special circumstances the normal first option for a visitor is the marina. That said, many *club náuticos* have pleasant bars and excellent restaurants which appear to be open to all, while a few are notably helpful and friendly to visitors. The standard of dress and behaviour often appears to be somewhat more formal than that expected in a similar club in Britain.

Excellent and cheap seafood along the Costas *Graham Hutt*

General regulations

Harbour restrictions

All harbours have a speed limit, usually three knots. There is a five knot speed limit within 100m of coast, extending to 250m off bathing beaches.

In most harbours anchoring is forbidden except in emergency or for a short period while sorting out a berth.

Harbour traffic signals

Traffic signals are rare, and in any case are designed for commercial traffic and seldom apply to yachts.

Storm signals

The signal stations at major ports and harbours may show storm signals, but equally they may not. With minor exceptions they are similar to the International System of Visual Storm Warnings.

Flag etiquette

A yacht in commission in foreign waters is legally required to fly her national maritime flag; for a British registered yacht, this is commonly the Red Ensign. If a special club ensign is worn it must be accompanied by the correct burgee. The courtesy flag of the country visited, which normally is the national maritime flag, should be flown from the starboard signal halliard. The flag for Spain is similar to the Spanish national flag but without the crest in the centre.

Insurance

Many marinas require evidence of insurance cover, though third party only may be sufficient. Many UK companies are willing to extend home waters cover for the Mediterranean, excluding certain areas.

Garbage

It is an international offence to dump garbage at sea and, while the arrangements of local authorities may not be perfect, garbage on land should be dumped in the proper containers. Marinas require the use of their onshore toilet facilities or holding tanks.

Large yachts

Many harbours are too small, or too shallow, for a large yacht, which must anchor outside whilst its crew visit the harbour by tender. It is essential that the skipper of such a yacht wishing to enter a small harbour telephones or radios the harbour authorities well in advance to reserve a berth (if available) and receive necessary instructions.

Scuba diving

Inshore scuba diving is strictly controlled and a licence is required from the *Militar de Marina*. This involves a certificate of competence, a medical certificate, two passport photographs, the passport itself (for inspection), knowledge of the relevant laws and a declaration that they will be obeyed. The simplest approach is to enquire through marina staff. Any attempt to remove archaeological material from the seabed will result in serious trouble.

Spearfishing

Spearfishing while scuba diving or using a snorkel is controlled and, in some places, prohibited.

Water-skiing

There has been a big increase in the use of high powered outboards for water-skiing over the past decade, accompanied by a significant increase in accidents. In most of the main ports and at some beaches it is now controlled and enquiries should be made before skiing. It is essential to have third party insurance and, if possible, a bail bond. If bathing and water-skiing areas are buoyed, yachts are excluded.

Security

Crime afloat is not a major problem in most areas and regrettably much of the theft which does occur can be laid at the door of other yachtsmen. Take sensible precautions – lock up before leaving the yacht, padlock the outboard to the dinghy, and secure the dinghy (particularly if an inflatable) with chain or wire rather than line. Folding bicycles are particularly vulnerable to theft, and should be chained up if left on deck.

Ashore, the situation in the big towns is no worse than in the UK and providing common sense is applied to such matters as how handbags are carried, where not to go after the bars close etc., there should be no problem.

The officials most likely to be seen are the *guardia civil*, who wear olive green uniforms and deal with immigration as well as more ordinary police work, the *Aduana* (customs) in navy blue uniforms, and the *Policía*, also in blue uniforms, who deal with traffic rather than criminal matters.

It is not uncommon to be stopped by the *guardia civil* at sea. They are courteous and wear sailing footwear, not boots. It is their duty to prevent smuggling of drugs and human trafficking.

Anchorages

There are a large number of attractive anchorages in *calas* and off beaches, even though many have massive buildings in the background and crowds in the foreground. Where known, particular hazards are mentioned but an absence of comment in the text or on the sketch charts does not mean there are no hazards. There are always hazards approaching and anchoring off the shoreline. The plans are derived from limited observation and not from a professional survey; depths, shapes, distances etc. are approximate. Any approach must be made with due care. Skippers are advised that in season anchorages near hotels and towns may be cordoned off with small floating buoys, to protect swimmers and therefore not be suitable. It cannot be assumed that anchorages listed in this book are always available for use by cruising yachtsmen.

The weather can change and deteriorate at short notice. During the day the sea breeze can be strong, especially if there is a valley at the head of an anchorage. Similarly a strong land breeze can flow down a valley in the early hours of the morning. If anchored near the head of a *cala* backed by a river valley, should there be a thunderstorm or heavy downpour in the hills above take precautions against the flood of water and debris which will descend into the *cala*.

Many *cala* anchorages suffer from swell even when not open to its off-shore direction. Swell tends to curl round all but the most prominent headlands. Wash from boats entering and leaving, as well as from larger vessels passing outside, may add to the discomfort. If considering a second anchor or a line ashore in order to hold the yacht into the swell, take into account the swinging room required by yachts on single anchors should the wind change.

In a high-sided *cala* winds are often fluky and a sudden blow, even from the land, may make departure difficult. This type of anchorage should only be used in settled calm weather and left in good time if swell or wind rise.

Whatever the type of *cala*, have ready a plan for clearing out quickly, possibly in darkness. It is unwise to leave an anchored yacht unattended for any length of time.

Note: Some formerly free anchorages have been overrun with buoys in an attempt to gain income locally. Sometimes the buoys are removed during the winter months, along with the swimming exclusion zone marker buoys. Other *calas* may become military zones with little or no notice. It is impossible to keep on top of what is going on, so a degree of circumspection and preparedness to weigh is needed wherever one anchors. In some ports the local authorities will insist that anchoring is prohibited in order to have another customer in the marina. We try to keep abreast of the situation as regards the anchoring facilities and post regular updates on the website: www.imray.com.

Choice of anchor

Many popular anchorages are thoroughly ploughed up each year by the hundreds of anchors dropped and weighed. At others the bottom is weed-covered compacted sand. Not without good reason is the four-pronged grab the favourite anchor of local fishermen, though difficult to stow. A conventional fisherman-type anchor is easier to stow and a useful ally. If using a patent anchor – Danforth, CQR, Bruce, Fortress etc. – an anchor weight (or chum) is a worthwhile investment and will encourage the pull to remain horizontal.

Anchoring

Once in a suitable depth of water, if clarity permits look for a weed-free patch to drop the anchor. In rocky or otherwise suspect areas – including those likely to contain wrecks, old chains etc. – use a sinking trip line with a float (an inviting buoy may be picked up by another yacht). Chain scope should be at least four times the maximum depth of water and nylon scope double that. It is always worth setting the anchor by reversing slowly until it holds, but on a hard or compacted bottom this must be done very gently in order to give the anchor a chance to bite – over enthusiasm with the throttle will cause it to skip without digging in.

Supplies and services

Fresh water

Good drinking water (*agua potable*) is available almost everywhere. Price is usually included, as with electricity, as part of the mooring fee for yachts of 12m and under, but often metered for larger yachts. Known exceptions to this are Gibraltar, where a charge is made per litre in both marinas. Marina del Este and Denia's Club Nautico also meter all usage.

Quality is usually good, though sometimes over chlorinated. I find it useful to ask other long stay yachties for their opinion. Bottled water is always available from supermarkets.

Ice

Block ice for an ice-box is widely obtainable – use the largest blocks that will fit; chemical ice is sometimes available in blocks measuring 100 x 20 x 20cms. The latter must not be used in drinks, the former only after inquiring of those who have tried the product. Cube or 'small' ice is obtainable and generally of drinks quality, particularly if bought in a sealed bag.

Fuel

Diesel (*gasoleo, gasoil* or simply *diesel*) is sold in two forms throughout Spain, *Gasoleo B* which attracts a lower tax and is only available to fishing craft, and *Gasoleo A* which is available to yachts. Not all harbours sell *Gasoleo A*, particularly the smaller fishing harbours. A more limited number also have a pump for petrol (*gasolina*). *Petróleo* is paraffin (kerosene). Credit cards are widely, but not universally, accepted – if in doubt, check first.

Bottled gas

Camping Gaz is widely available from marinas, supermarkets or *ferreterias* (ironmongers), in the 1·9kg bottles identical to those in the UK.

REPSOL/CAMPSOL depots will no longer fill any UK (or any other countries') Calor Gas bottles even with a current test certificate. It is therefore essential to carry the appropriate regulator and fittings to permit the use of Camping Gaz bottles. Yachts fitted with propane systems should consult the Calor Gas Customer service agent (✆ 0800 626 626).

Almost all gas bottles can be filled just over the water in Marina Smir, Morocco – if you happen to be going that way. The blue 'camping gas' bottles are less than €5 to fill/ exchange. (See Mohammed in the boatyard.)

Electricity

Marina standard electrical supply is 220v at 50Hz. This is fed via a blue 3-pin socket which comes in three amperages, depending roughly on berth size, with the smaller sockets being available for 12m and under. The plugs are often the same as those used with caravans mains cables and may be cheaper from hardware suppliers than chandlers. It is useful to have a selection of short flexes made up with the common sizes to attach to the end of the yacht mains cable, though, most marinas keep suitable connecting plug/sockets which they lend for a deposit for the duration of your stay. Larger yachts using berths of 20m and over often use 380v which is also catered for.

Food and drink

There are many well stocked stores, supermarkets and hypermarkets in the larger towns and cities and it may be worth doing the occasional major stock-up by taxi. As a rule, availability and choice varies with the size of the town. Most older settlements (though not all tourist resorts) have a market with local produce at reasonable prices. Alcohol is cheap by UK standards with, unsurprisingly, good value Spanish wines. Spanish gin and vodka are also good value; Scotch whisky can only come from Scotland but the genuine article is often lower in price than in the U.K. Shop prices generally are noticeably lower away from tourist resorts.

Most shops, other than the largest supermarkets, close for *siesta* between 1400 and 1700 and remain closed on Sunday though some smaller food shops do open on Sunday mornings. In larger towns the produce market may operate from 0800 to 1400, Monday to Saturday; in smaller towns it is more often a weekly affair. An excellent way to sample unfamiliar delicacies in small portions is in the form of bar snacks, *tapas* or the larger *raciónes*. Tapas once came on the house but are now almost invariably charged – sometimes heavily.

Repairs and chandlery

There are many marinas equipped to handle all aspects of yacht maintenance from laying up to changing a washer. Nearly all have travel-hoists and the larger have specialist facilities – GRP work, electronics, sailmaking, stainless welding and so forth. Charges may differ – widely so – if practicable, shop around.

The best equipped chandleries will be found near the larger marinas. Smaller harbours or marinas are often without a chandlery, though something may be found in the associated town. Basic items can sometimes be found in *ferreterias* (ironmongers).

Telephones and fax

Telephone kiosks are common, both local and *teléfono internacional*, and most carry instructions in English. Both coins and phonecards, available from tobacconists (*estancos*), are used. If no kiosk is available marina offices have telephones and many have faxes. Most bars and hotels have metered telephones and the latter usually have faxes, though these are seldom metered. Wi-Fi is widely available.

- When calling from within Spain, dial the whole code (beginning with the figure 9) whether or not the number you are calling from has the same code. In some areas the number of digits to be dialled is nine, in others eight. To make an international call, dial 00 followed by the relevant country code (44 for the UK). If calling the UK do not dial the first figure of the number if it is 0.
- To reach the international operator dial 025. A telephone number beginning with the figure 6 indicates a mobile telephone which will have no area code and its own code for calling its international operator. The main emergency number throughout Spain is 112. Sea Rescue services are on 900 202202.
- To call Spain from abroad, dial the international access code (00 in the UK) followed by the code for Spain (34), then the area code (which begins with 9 except for mobile phones) followed by the individual number.

Warning Apart from a major re-organisation of area codes, individual numbers in Spain change surprisingly often.

Mail

Letters may be sent *poste restante* to any post office (*oficina de corréos*). They should be addressed with the surname (only) of the recipient followed by *Lista de Corréos* and the town. Do not enter the addressee's initials or title: that is likely to cause misfiling. Collection is a fairly cumbersome procedure and a passport is likely to be needed. Alternatively, most marinas and some *club náuticos* will hold mail for yachts, but it is always wise to check in advance if possible. Uncollected letters are seldom returned.

Mail to and from the UK should be marked 'air mail' (*por avión*) but even so may take up to ten days, so if speed is important communicate by fax or email. Post boxes are yellow; stamps are available from tobacconists (*estancos*), not from post offices though the latter will accept and frank mail. Almost every town has a Post Office; ask – *donde esta el Correo*?

Tourist offices

There is at least one tourist office in every major town or resort. Their locations vary from year to year – ask at the port or marina office.

Transport and travel

Every community has some form of public transport, if only one *autobús* a day and many of the coastal towns are served by rail as well.

Taxis are easily found in the tourist resorts though less common outside them, but can always be ordered by telephone. Car hire is simple, but either a full national or international driving licence must be shown and many companies will not lease a car to a driver over 70 years old.

Air – Alicante, Barcelona and Valencia have year round international flights and seasonal charter flights; Gibraltar has year round connections with the UK. Other airports, Málaga, Murcia, Alicante and Tarragona, have international scheduled and charter flights in summer and year round connections within Spain.

Western Mediterranean weather

The weather pattern in the basin of the western Mediterranean is affected by many different systems. It is largely unpredictable, quick to change and often very different at places only a short distance apart. See Appendix III for Spanish meteorological terms.

WINDS

Winds most frequently blow from the west, northwest, north and east but are considerably altered by the effects of local topography. The Mediterranean is an area of calms and gales and the old saying that in summer there are nine days of light winds followed by a gale is very close to reality. Close to the coast, normal sea and land breezes are experienced on calm days. Along the Costa Brava, northwest, north and northeast winds are most common, especially in winter, though winds from other directions frequently occur. This area is particularly influenced by the weather in the Golfo de León and is in the direct path of the northwesterly *tramontana* (see below), making it particularly important to listen to regular weather forecasts. Further W on the Costas del Sol and Blanca, these winds translate to an E or W airstream, following the coast near Gibraltar.

The winds in the Mediterranean have been given special names dependent on their direction and characteristics. Those that affect this coast are detailed below.

Northwest – *tramontana*

This wind, also known as the *maestral* near Río Ebro and the *mistral* in France, is a strong, dry wind, cold in winter, which can be dangerous. It is caused by a secondary depression forming in the Golfo de León or the Golfo de Génova on the cold front of a major depression crossing France. The northwesterly airflow generated is compressed between the Alps and the Pyrenees and flows into the Mediterranean basin. In Spain it chiefly affects the coast to the north of Barcelona, the Islas Baleares, and is strongest at the northern end of the Costa Brava.

The *tramontana* can be dangerous in that it can arrive and reach gale force in as little as 15 minutes on a calm sunny day with virtually no warning two to three days before a storm. Signs to watch for are brilliant visibility, clear sky – sometimes with cigar-shaped clouds – very dry air and a steady or slightly rising barometer. On rare occasions the sky may be cloudy when the wind first arrives although it clears later. Sometimes the barometer will plunge in normal fashion, rising quickly after the gale has passed. If at sea and some way from land, a line of white on the horizon and a developing swell give a few minutes' warning. Warnings are given by radio from Marseille and Monaco, but these can also be seen on the internet and are increasingly accurate in their predictions. *See page 15 for transmission details.*

Levante cloud over Gibraltar creates gloomy conditions in the town *Graham Hutt*

'Flying Saucer' clouds: Indication of strong E winds to come in 2–3 days *Graham Hutt*

The *tramontana* normally blows for at least three days but may last for a week or longer. It is frequent in the winter months, blowing for a third of the time and can reach Force 10 (50 knots) or more. In summer it is neither as strong nor as frequent.

West – *vendaval*

A depression crossing Spain or southern France creates a strong southwest to west wind, the *vendaval* or *poniente*, which funnels through the Strait of Gibraltar and along the south coast of Spain. Though normally confined to the south and southeast coasts, it occasionally blows in the northeast of the area. It is usually short-lived and at its strongest from late autumn to early spring.

East – *levante*

Encountered from Gibraltar to Valencia and beyond, the *levante*, sometimes called the *llevantade* when it blows at gale force, is caused by a depression located between the Islas Baleares and the North African coast. It is preceded by a heavy swell (*las tascas*), cold damp air, poor visibility and low cloud which forms first around the higher hills. Heavy and prolonged rainfall is more likely in spring and autumn than summer. A *levante* may last for three or four days.

South – *siroco*

The hot wind from the south is created by a depression moving east along or just south of the North African coast. By the time this dry wind reaches Spain it can be very humid, with haze and cloud. If strong it carries dust, and should it rain when the cold front comes through, the water may be red or brown and the dust will set like cement. This wind is sometimes called the *leveche* in southeast Spain. It occurs most frequently in summer, seldom lasting more than one or two days.

Clouds

Cloud cover of between 4/8 and 5/8 in the winter months is about double the summer average of 2/8. The cloud is normally cumulus and high level. In strong winds with a southerly component, complete cloud cover can be expected.

Precipitation

Annual rainfall is moderate and decreases towards the north from about 760mm at Gibraltar to 560mm at Barcelona. The rainy season is predominantly in autumn and winter and in most areas the summer months are virtually dry. The Costa Brava, however, usually manages about 25mm of rain during each summer month, as does the Costa del Sol. Most of the rain falls in very heavy showers of 1–2 hours.

Thunderstorms

Thunderstorms are most frequent in the autumn at up to four or five each month, and can be accompanied by hail.

Water spouts

Water spouts occur in the Strait of Gibraltar in winter and spring, usually associated with thunderstorms.

Snow

Snow at sea level is very rare but it falls and remains on the higher mountain ranges inland. Snow on the Sierra Nevada is particularly noticeable from the sea. This can cause strong catabatic winds along parts of the Costa del Sol in winter and early in the season.

Visibility

Fog occurs about four days a month in summer along the Costa de Sol but elsewhere is very rare. Occasionally, when the wind is a very light easterly and humidity high, a very thick fog can descend around 0900 and may not lift before around 1400. This is particularly a problem between Gibraltar and Estepona. Sometimes dust carried by the southerly *siroco* reduces visibility and industrial areas such as Valencia and Barcelona produce haze.

Temperature

Winter temperatures at Gibraltar average 10–15°C, rising steadily after March to average 20–29°C in July and August. Afternoon (maximum) temperatures may reach 30–33°C in these months. At Barcelona, summer temperatures are much the same as at Gibraltar but winter temperatures are lower, 6–13°C, as they are further west along the Costa del Sol.

Humidity

The relative humidity is moderate at around 60% to 80%. With winds from the west, northwest or north, low humidity can be expected; with winds off the sea, high humidity is normal. The relative humidity increases throughout the night and falls by day.

Local variations

Towards the E end of the Costa del Sol, the common winds blow between northwest and northeast. Gales may be experienced for 10% of the time during the winter, dropping to 2% in July and August, sometimes arriving with little warning and rapidly building to gale force.

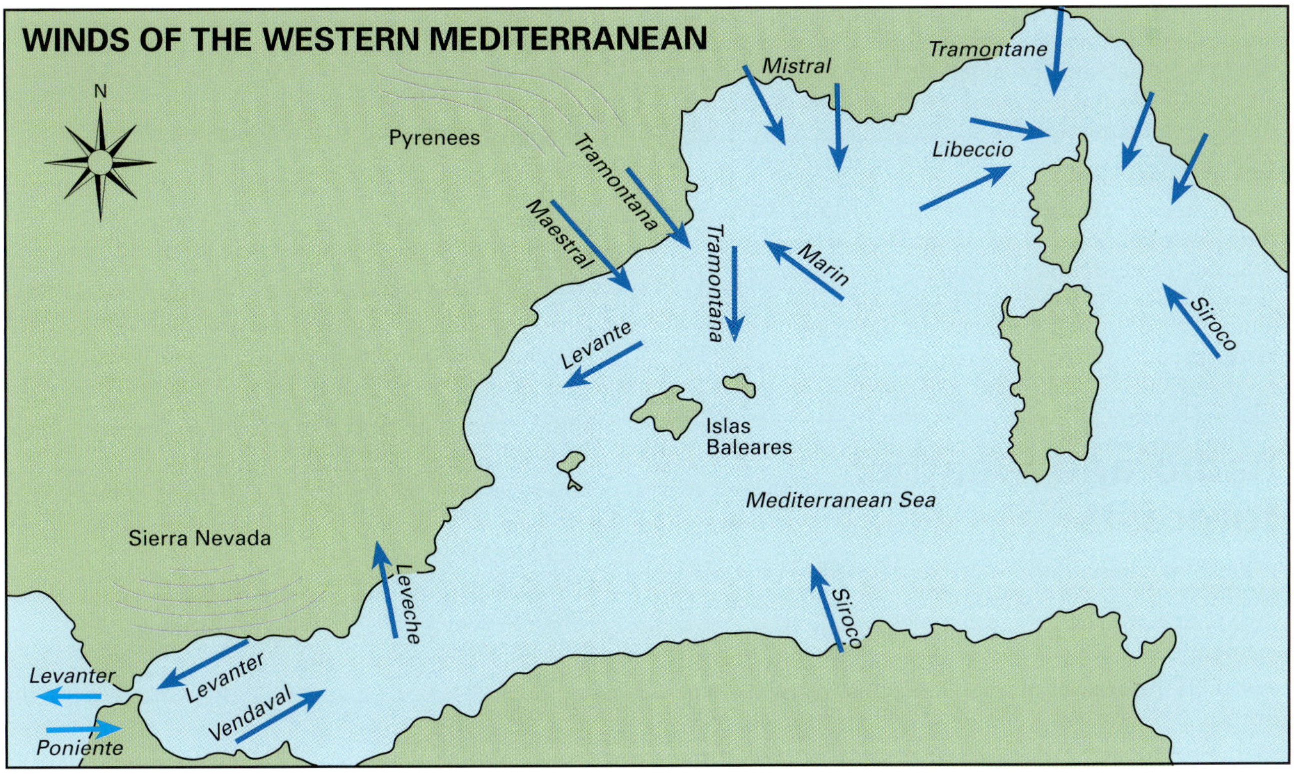

The sea

Currents

There is a constant E-going surface current of one to two knots, passing in to the Mediterranean through the Strait of Gibraltar between the Costa del Sol and the African coast to replace water lost by evaporation. Northeast of Cabo de Gata up to the border with France, a significant inshore counter-eddy runs roughly SSW at one to 1½ knots. The shape of the coast produces variations in both direction and strength, especially around promontories.

It should be noted that prolonged west winds increase the E-going current, whilst E – *levante* – winds will reverse the surface current – often creating steep seas.

Tides

Tides should be taken into account at the west end of the Costa del Sol and are noted in the introduction to that section. From Alicante to the border with France, the tide is hardly appreciable.

Swell

Strong winds – sometimes in a different part of the Mediterranean basin and from a different direction to local winds, can set up a large confused swell.

Swell has a nasty capability of going round corners and getting into *calas*.

Internet forecasts are now helpful in predicting swell height and direction as well as information on wind patterns.

Scouring and silting

Many harbours and anchorages are located in sandy areas where depths can change dramatically in the course of a storm or a season. Dredging is a common feature but there is no certainty that depths will be maintained. Charts and drawings give no sure guide. When approaching or entering such areas, it is of great importance to sound carefully and to act on the information received.

Sea temperature

Sea temperatures in February are around 14°C on the Costa del Sol and 12°C on the Costa Brava. In summer, along the Costa Blanca it can rise to 20°C. Winds from the south and east tend to raise the temperature and those from the west and north to lower them.

Radio and weather forecasts

Details of coast radio stations, weather forecasts, weatherfax (radio facsimile) Navtex and Inmarsat-C coverage follow. See individual harbour details for port and marina radio information. All times quoted are in UT (universal time) unless otherwise specified. France Inter on LW, 163kHz, France Info on MW and Monaco 3AC on 4363kHz all use local time. Details of frequencies, channel and times are to be found in ALRS Vol 3 (1), RYA Booklet G5 and on the internet.

Coast radio stations

VHF/MF

Coast radio stations are controlled from Málaga or Valencia – see diagram page 15. Full details will be found in the Admiralty *List of Radio Signals Vol 1 Part 1 (NP281/1)*.

On receipt of traffic, Spanish coast radio stations will call vessels once on Ch 16; after that the vessel's call sign will be included in scheduled MF traffic lists.

Weather forecasts

Marine VHF and MF

Inshore waters and sea area forecasts are broadcast in Spanish and English on marine VHF all round Mediterranean Spain and the Balearic Islands. There are also broadcasts of inshore waters forecasts and actual weather in Spanish only. For local area FM broadcast near Gibraltar *see page 27* for details of BFBS and Gibraltar BC.

Sea area and inshore waters forecasts are broadcast in Spanish as follows

MRCC Málaga	*VHF Ch*	*Times UT*
Cádiz	26	
Tarifa	81	0833, 1133, 2003
Málaga	26	
Cabo Gata	27	
MRCC Valencia	*VHF Ch*	*Times UT*
Cartagena	4	
Alicante	85	
Cabo La Nao	2	
Castellón	25	
Tarragona	23	0910, 1410, 2110
Barcelona	60	
Bagur	23	
Menorca	85	
Palma	20	
Ibiza	3	

Inshore waters forecasts and reports of actual weather are broadcast in English and Spanish as follows.

MRCC	*VHF Ch*	*Time UT*
CZCS Tarifa	10, 67, 73	H2+15
CLCS Algeciras	74	0315, 0515, 0715, 1115, 1515, 1915, 2315
CRCS Almería	10, 67, 73	H1+15
CRCS Barcelona	10	0600, 0900, 1500, 2000
CRCS Valencia	10, 67	H2+15
CLCS Tarragona	13	0533, 0933, 1533, 2033
CRCS Palma	10	0735, 1035, 1535, 2035

H1 = odd hours. H2 = even hours

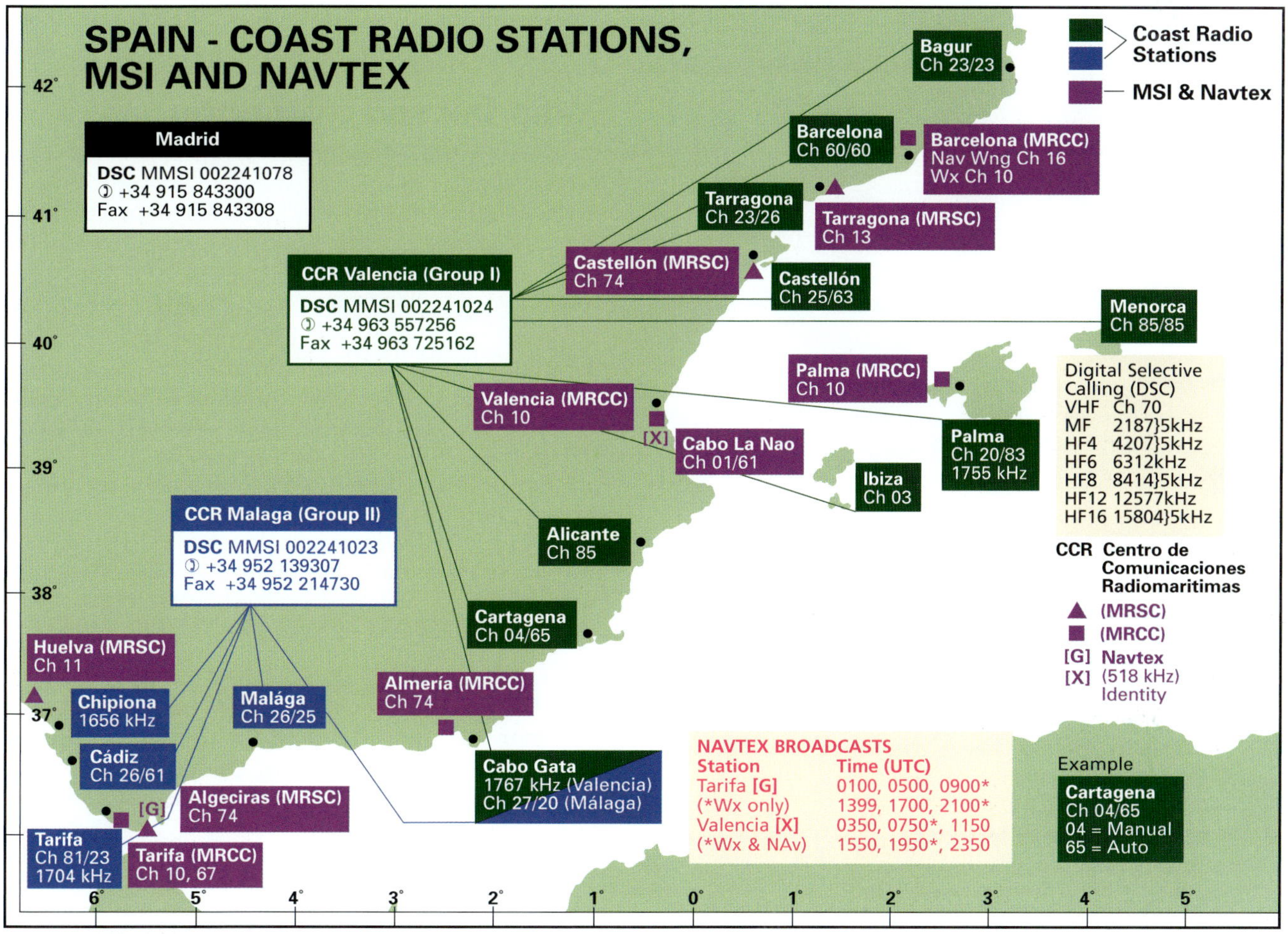

Sea area forecasts are broadcast in English and Spanish as follows

Station	*kHz*	*Time UT*
Chipiona	1656kHz	0733, 1233, 1933
Tarifa	1704kHz	0733, 1233, 1933
Cabo de Gata	1767kHz	0750, 1303, 1950
Palma	1755kHz	0750, 1303, 1950

Sea area forecasts can also be heard in English and Spanish on MF radio.

Non-radio weather forecasts

A recorded marine forecast in Spanish is available by ✆+34 906 36 53 71. The 'High Seas' bulletin includes the Islas Baleares.

Spanish television shows a useful synoptic chart with its land weather forecast every evening after the news at approximately 2120 weekdays, 1520 Saturday and 2020 Sunday. Most national and local newspapers also carry some form of forecast.

Nearly all marinas and yacht harbours display a synoptic chart and forecast, generally updated daily (though often posted rather too late to be of use).

Internet forecasts

There is now an enormous wealth of weather information available via the internet. Internet forecasts are, in layman's terms, either purely computer modelled, or they are interpreted by specialists who include local factors within the predictions. It is not always easy to know which forecasts are which, so it is a good idea to monitor several weather websites. During stable weather patterns the various sites will tend to give similar predictions. In less stable conditions the sites may vary widely in what they predict. This alone can be a very useful indicator. Crucially important to comfortable cruising, websites also provide expected swell and wave heights and directions.

GRIB coded forecasts

This service enables arrow diagram forecasts for up to five days ahead, and other information to be obtained in email form (or by marine HF and HAM radio). The data is highly compressed so that a great deal of information can be acquired quickly, even using a mobile phone connected to a laptop. See websites below. There is no charge for this service.

GRIB files do not incorporate any interpretation for coastal areas, but up to seven days of weather charts for your selected region are quick and easy to access using free downloads from www.grib.us

Other useful websites

Spanish websites are more likely to incorporate local knowledge within their weather predictions and may be more accurate for coastal sailing: www.aemet.es/en/eltiempo/prediccion/maritima or www.eltiempo.es/

The Spanish and French use a common set of sea areas and use the same names although spelling and pronunciation differ at times. The French names for the Mediterranean Sea areas are Alborán, Palos, Alger, Cabrera, Baléares, Minorque, Lion, Provence, Ligure, Corse, Sardaigne, and Annaba. In the approaches to the Mediterranean the French names are identical to the Spanish.

French sites are also a very useful reference:
http://marine.meteofrance.com/ or
http://marine.meteoconsult.fr/
Other useful sites may include:
www.passageweather.com/

Internet access

Increasingly ubiquitous smartphones and other mobile devices are making internet access on board quicker and easier than ever before. Data roaming charges can be excessive, depending on your contract. The use of a local SIM card for both data and voice may be a more affordable option. If you don't have a smartphone or tablet it is possible to use a laptop linked to a 'dongle', sometimes with an extension lead to allow the dongle to be suspended under the boom to gain better reception. Many marinas, harbours and anchorages now have Wi-Fi available. A booster may improve Wi-Fi reception on board. Internet access is also possible, with the appropriate modem, via Marine SSB or HF radio.

Rescue and emergency services

In addition to VHF Ch 16 (MAYDAY or PAN PAN as appropriate) the marine emergency services can be contacted by telephone at all times on ✆ 900 202 202.

The National Centre for Sea Rescue is based in Madrid but has a string of communications towers. On the spot responsibility for co-ordinating rescues lies with the Capitanías Marítimas with support from the Spanish Navy, customs, guardia civil etc. Lifeboats are stationed at some of the larger harbours but the majority do not appear to be all-weather boats.

The other emergency services can be contacted by dialling 112 for the operator and asking for policía (police), bomberos (fire service) or Cruz Roja (Red Cross). Alternatively the police can be contacted direct on 092 or *Guardia Civil* on 062.

Radio fax and teleprinter

Northwood (RN) broadcasts a full set of UK Met Office charts out to five days ahead on 2618·5, 4610, 8040 and 11086·5kHz. (Schedule at 0236, surface analysis at three hourly intervals from 0300 to 2100 and 2300.) Deutscher Wetterdienst broadcasts German weather charts on 3855, 7880 and 13882·5kHz. (Schedule at 1111, surface analysis at 0430, 1050, 1600, 2200.)

DWD broadcasts forecasts using RTTY on 4583, 7646 and 10001.8kHz (in English at 0415 and 1610), 11039 and 14467·3kHz (in German at 0535). Note that the 4583 and 14467·3kHz may not be useable in the Mediterranean. The most useful products are forecasts up to five days ahead at 12 hourly intervals and up to two days ahead at six hour intervals. Alternatively, a dedicated receiver 'Weatherman' will record automatically: see www.nasamarine.com.

UK Marine Mobile Net

The Net covering the Eastern Atlantic and the Mediterranean, can be heard daily on 14303kHz USB at 0800 and 1800 UT. On Saturday morning the broadcast sometimes contains a longer period outlook. Forecasts will be a rehash of what the Net leader has gleaned from various sources. No licence is required if a receive-only HF radio is used.

Monaco 3AC

Monaco 3AC broadcasts on 8728 and 8806kHz USB at 0715 and 1830 in French and English. The texts are those broadcast by INMARSAT-C for the western part of METAREA III. Monaco also broadcasts on 4363kHz at 0903 and 1915 LT in French and English and at 1403 in French only. Texts are as the latest Toulon NAVTEX broadcast.

NAVTEX and INMARSAT-C

NAVTEX and INMARSAT-C are the primary GMDSS modes for transmission of all Marine Safety Information. Broadcast times for weather are as follows

Transmitter	*Times (UTC)*
Tarifa – G (518kHz)	0900 and 2100
Cabo la Nao – X (Valencia) (518kHz)	0750 and 1950
La Garde – W (Toulon) (518kHz)	1140 and 2340
La Garde – S (Toulon) (490kHz)	0700 and 1900
INMARSAT-C METAREA III	1000 and 2200

I. ENTRANCE TO THE MEDITERRANEAN

Alcaidesa Marina: a mile N of Gibraltar *Agencia Pública de Puertos de Andalucía*

Strait of Gibraltar

PORTS

Introduction

This chapter covers the Strait of Gibraltar, Algeciras Bay and Gibraltar.

Other RCC Pilotage Foundation titles covering approaches to Gibraltar are:

From the Atlantic
Atlantic Crossing Guide
Atlantic Islands

From the north
Atlantic Spain and Portugal

From the south
North Africa

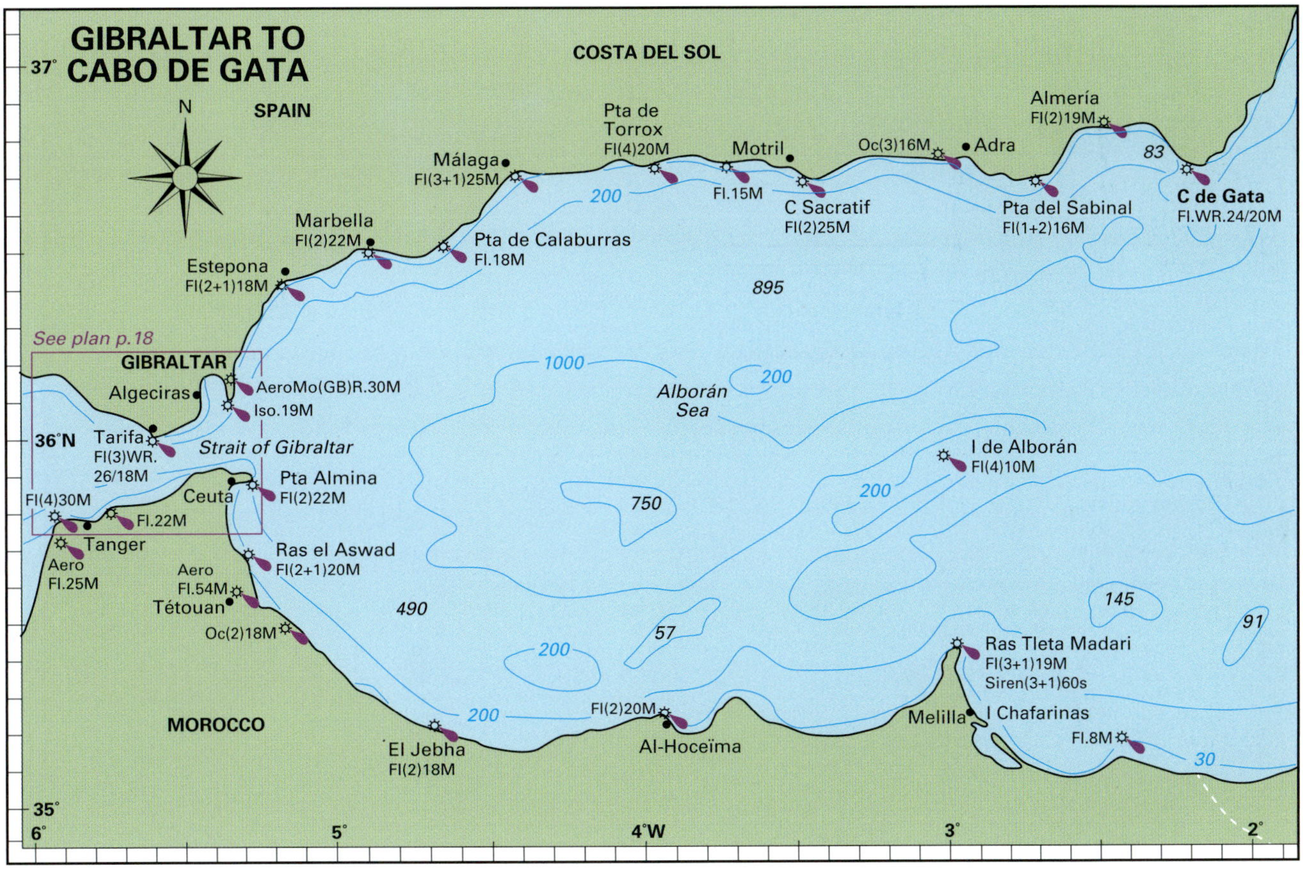

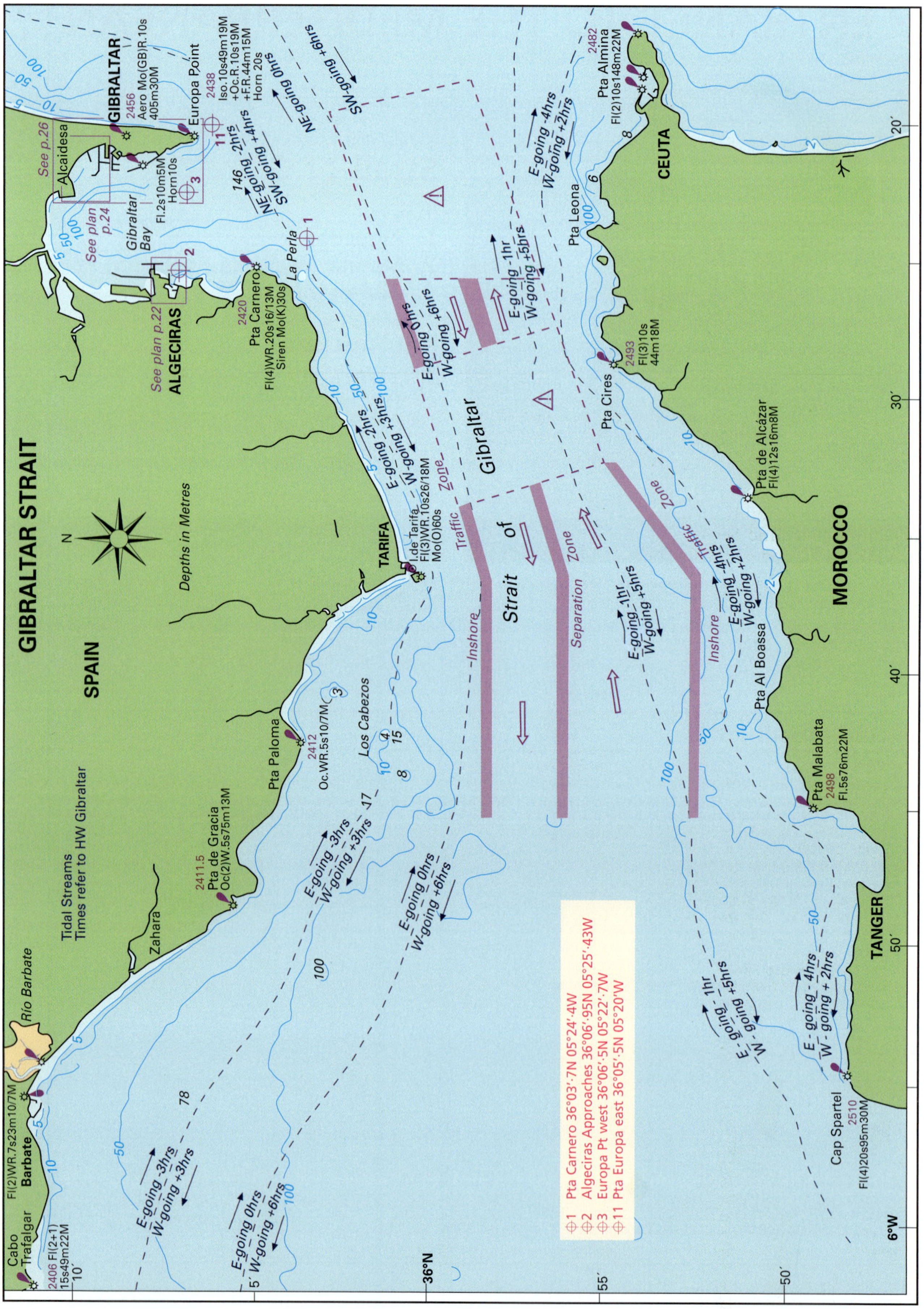
GIBRALTAR STRAIT
Tidal Streams
Times refer to HW Gibraltar
Depths in Metres
N
SPAIN
MOROCCO
GIBRALTAR
2456
Aero Mo(GB)R.10s
405m30M
Europa Point
2438
Iso.10s49m19M
+Oc.R.10s19M
+F.R.44m15M
Horn 20s
Alcaidesa
See p.26
See plan p.24
Gibraltar Bay
Fl.2s10m5M
Horn10s
See plan p.22
ALGECIRAS
2420
Pta Carnero
Fl(4)WR.20s16/13M
Siren Mo(K)30s
La Perla
TARIFA
I. de Tarifa
Fl(3)WR.10s26/18M
Mo(O)60s
2412
Pta Paloma
Oc.WR.5s10/7M
Los Cabezos
2411.5
Pta de Gracia
Oc(2)W.5s75m13M
Zahara
Rio Barbate
Barbate
Fl(2)WR.7s23m10/7M
Cabo Trafalgar
2406 Fl(2+1)
15s49m22M
CEUTA
2482
Pta Almina
Fl(2)10s148m22M
Pta Leona
2493
Pta Cires
Fl(3)10s
44m18M
Pta de Alcázar
Fl(4)12s16m8M
Pta Al Boassa
Pta Malabata
2498
Fl.5s76m22M
TANGER
Cap Spartel
2510
Fl(4)20s95m30M
Strait of Gibraltar
Inshore Traffic Zone
Traffic Separation Zone
NE-going 0hrs
SW-going +6hrs
146 NE-going -2hrs
SW-going +4hrs
E-going -4hrs
W-going +2hrs
E-going 1hr
W-going +5hrs
E-going 0hrs
W-going +6hrs
E-going -2hrs
W-going +3hrs
E-going -3hrs
W-going +3hrs
36°N
6°W
⊕1 Pta Carnero 36°03'·7N 05°24'·4W
⊕2 Algeciras Approaches 36°06'·95N 05°25'·43W
⊕3 Europa Pt west 36°06'·5N 05°22'·7W
⊕11 Pta Europa east 36°05'·5N 05°20'W

Around Gibraltar, weather usually conforms to the local area forecast, (unlike further E where local forecasting is notoriously difficult). There is almost always some wind in the Strait and can be expected to be either E (*levante*) or W (*poniente*). The E winds bring a large cloud which hangs over the W side of the rock, often for several days, producing high humidity and miserable conditions. On rare occasions, as low pressure and associated fronts move N from the Canaries in winter, strong SW winds bring rain and squally conditions. These winds often mean the airport is closed. The general summer wind pattern is light overnight, rising to Force 3 or 4 during the afternoon and going down at sunset.

Traffic Separation Zone

There is a Traffic Separation Zone in the Strait of Gibraltar between 5°25′·5W and 5°45′W – see plan on page 18. The Inshore Traffic Zone to the north is nowhere less than 1·7M wide (off the Isla de Tarifa) and generally more than 2M. Tarifa Traffic monitors VHF Ch 16 and 10 and vessels are advised to maintain a listening watch whilst in the area. Weather and visibility information for an area including the Traffic Separation Zone is broadcast on VHF Ch 10 and 67.

PRINCIPAL LIGHTS

Europe
2406 **Cabo Trafalgar** Fl(2+1)15s49m22M
White conical tower and building 34m
2411.5 **Punta de Gracia (Punta Camarinal)**
Oc(2)5s75m13M Masonry tower 20m
2412 **Punta Paloma** Oc.WR.5s44m10/7M
010°-W-340°-R-010° (over Bajo de Los Cabezos)
White 4-sided tower 5m
2414 **Tarifa** Fl(3)WR.10s41m26/18M
089°-R-113°-W-089° (over Bajo de Los Cabezos)
Racon Mo 'C'(–···)20M White tower 33m
Masonry structure 10m
2420 **Punta Carnero** Fl(4)WR.20s42m16/13M
018°-W-325°-R-018° (Red sector covers La Perla and Las Bajas shoals) Round masonry tower and white building 19m
2438 **Europa Point, Gibraltar**
Iso.10s49m19M 197°-vis-042°, 067°-vis-125°
Oc.R.10s19M and F.R.15M 042°-vis-067°
(Red sector covers La Perla and Las Bajas shoals)
Horn 20s White tower, red band 19m

Africa
2510 **Cabo Espartel** Fl(4)20s95m30M
Yellow square stone tower 24m
2498 **Pta Malabata** Fl.5s76m22M
White square tower on white dwelling 18m
2496 **Ksar es Srhir** Fl(4)12s16m8M
Column on metal framework tower 11m
2493 **Pta Cires** Fl(3)10s44m18M Brown truncated conical tower 8m
2482 **Pta Almina** Fl(2)10s148m22M
White tower and building 16m

Transiting the Strait of Gibraltar

Many yachts use Gibraltar as their departure point for trips to the east, west or south. Many elements combine to produce a complex system of tides and current in the Strait, an appreciation of which will greatly help yachtsman, especially when heading west as it is possible to spend many fruitless hours trying to make a passage through the Strait. The paragraphs below are included to assist the yachtsman transiting the Strait.

Eight miles separate Europe from Africa at its narrowest point in the Strait. The water at the western end of the 30 mile stretch is some 2–3m higher than at the eastern end, thus causing a constant surface flow into the Mediterranean. This is partially due to evaporation in the Mediterranean, which is three times faster than the rate at which the combined waters from rivers flow into it; and the fact that the Atlantic is tidal with a predominantly westerly swell, whereas the land-locked Mediterranean, is virtually non tidal. This produces a standing E-going surface current of between one and two knots.

Differences in salinity between the Atlantic and the Mediterranean force the heavier water down, causing a sub surface current in the opposite direction.

Wind also creates a surface current, depending whether it is E (*levante*) or W (*poniente*), which confuses the equation still further.

Then there are the tides, which are well documented in Admiralty tide tables. At the eastern end of the Strait the range is only half a metre and negligible once a few miles into the Mediterranean, whereas at Tanger, Morocco, the spring range is 3m. Barometric pressure differences also affect the height of water.

On the N side of the Western Strait is Tarifa. Winds in excess of 30 knots are said to blow there for 300 days of the year, whereas at the same time, winds at the eastern end may be negligible, resulting in conditions at one end of the Strait being very different from those at the other.

Currents also vary in different parts of the Strait, and even run in opposite directions at the same time, as shown on the tidal charts. From these conflicting and confusing parameters some guidelines can be extracted.

Waypoints
⊕1 Punta Carnero 36°03′·7N 05°24′·4W
⊕2 Algeciras Approach 36°06′·95N 05°25′·43W
⊕3 Europa Pt W. 36°06′·5N 05°22′·7W
⊕4 Gibraltar South Mole 36°08′N 05°22′·3W
⊕5 Gibraltar North Mole 36°09′N 05°22′·35W
⊕6 La Linea Approach 36°09′·5N 05°22′·2W
⊕11 Europa Pt E 36°05′·5N 05°20′W

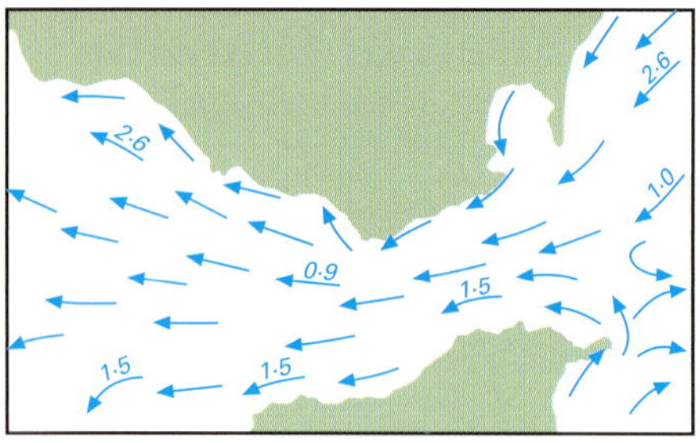

5 HOURS BEFORE HW GIBRALTAR

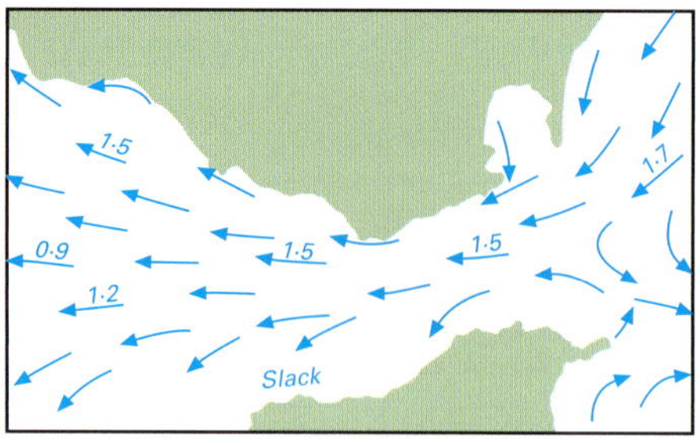

4 HOURS BEFORE HW GIBRALTAR

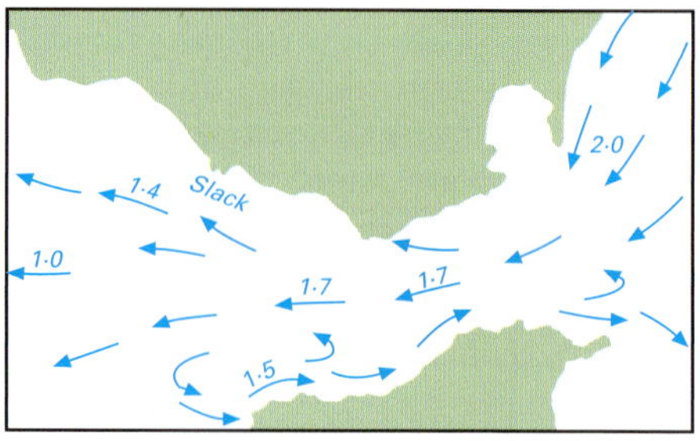

3 HOURS BEFORE HW GIBRALTAR

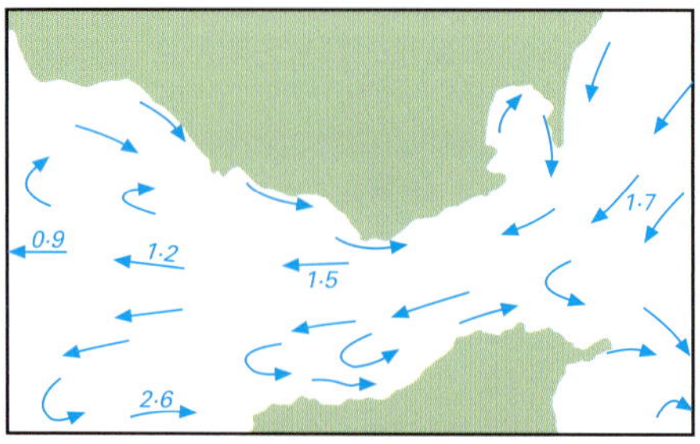

2 HOURS BEFORE HW GIBRALTAR

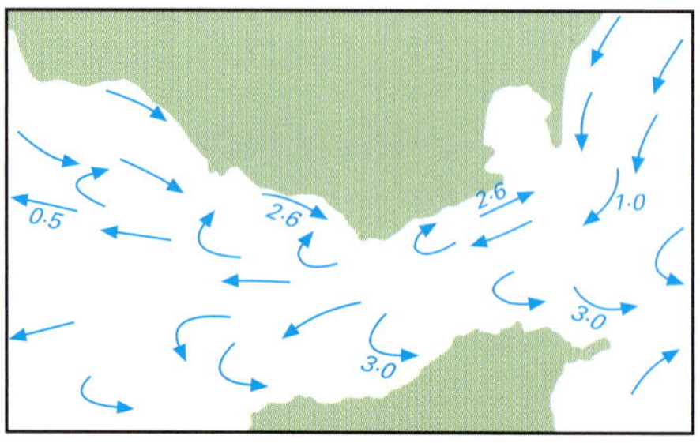

1 HOUR BEFORE HW GIBRALTAR

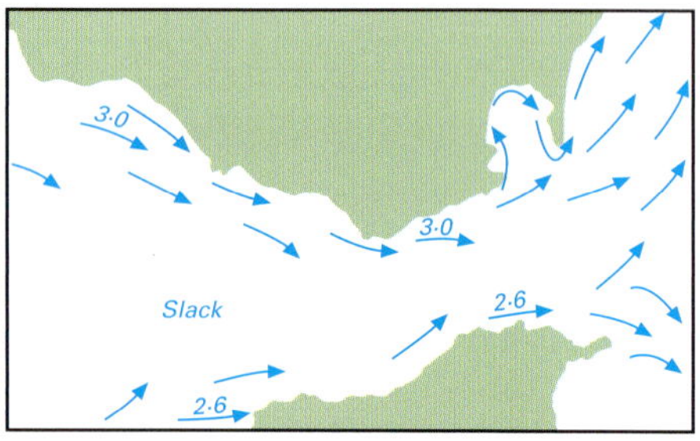

HW GIBRALTAR

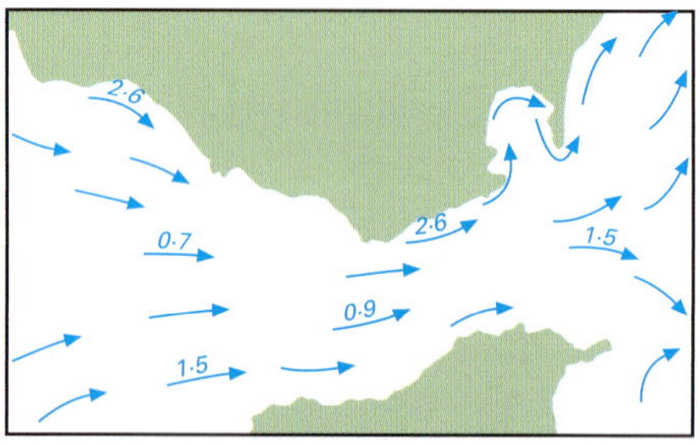

1 HOUR AFTER HW GIBRALTAR

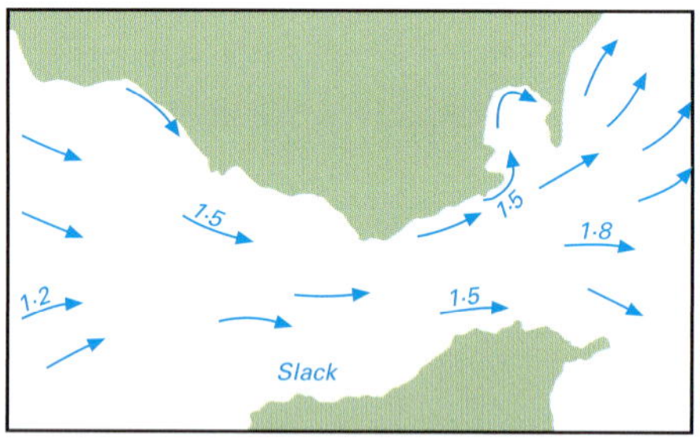

2 HOURS AFTER HW GIBRALTAR

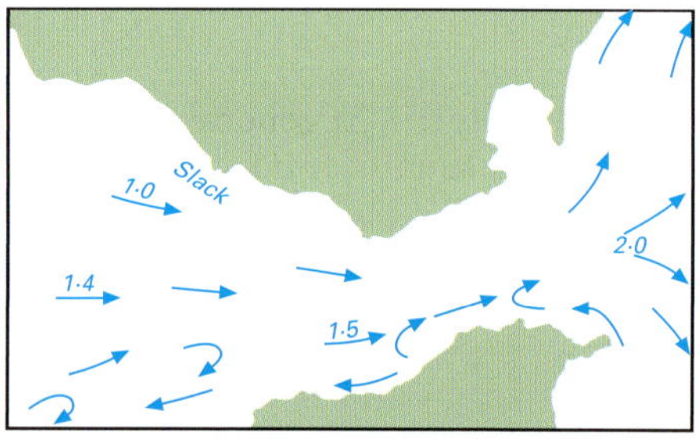

3 HOURS AFTER HW GIBRALTAR

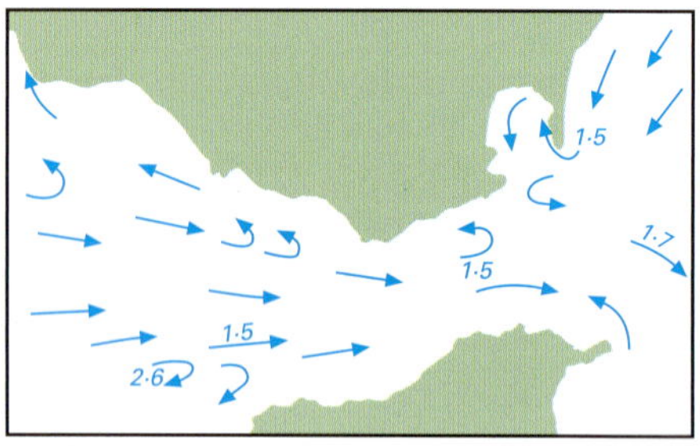

4 HOURS AFTER HW GIBRALTAR

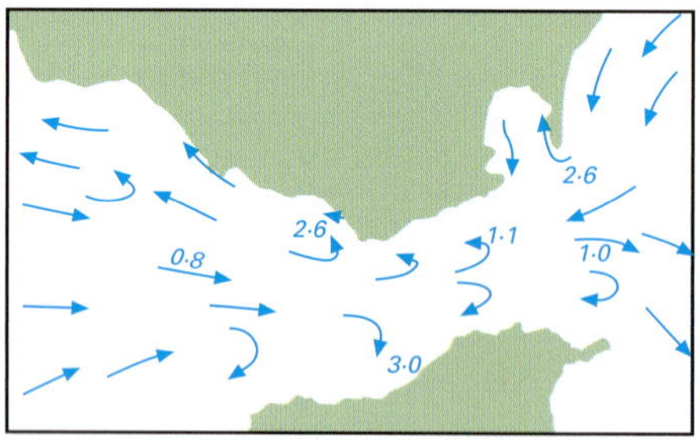

5 HOURS AFTER HW GIBRALTAR

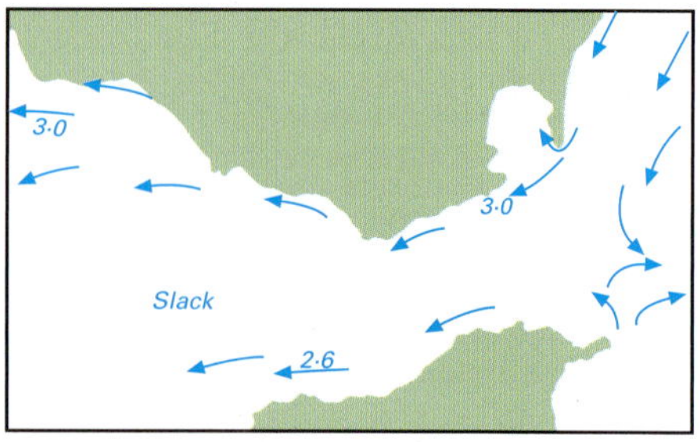

6 HOURS AFTER HW GIBRALTAR

These diagrams are published with the kind permission of Dr M Sloma, editor of *Yacht Scene*. Under no circumstances will *Yacht Scene* or the Pilotage Foundation be liable for any accident or injury, which may occur to vessels or persons whilst using the above current predictions

Eastbound vessels

For yachts entering the straits from the W there is no real problem going eastwards, unless there is a strong easterly wind, in which case the passage will be rough, especially around Tarifa, where winds often reach 40 knots. If strong winds are forecast, stay in Tanger or Barbate until it drops, or anchor in the lee of Tarifa if strong E winds are encountered once on passage.

During periods of light easterly winds, sea mist or fog may be persistent in the Strait, especially during the morning.

The best time to depart for the trip east is soon after LW. From Tanger, keeping close inshore, the light and increasing E-going current off Punta Malabata will be useful. If going to Gibraltar, most vessels cross to Tarifa from Punta Malabata, or from Punta Ciris, 12 miles further E.

Westbound vessels

In strong westerlies it is almost impossible to make headway W, due to the combined E-going current that can, with unfavourable tide, reach six knots or more, with heavy steep swell and overfalls off Ceuta Point, Tarifa and Punta Malabata.

In good conditions, to make use of the favourable current, set off from Gibraltar two hours after HW. Keeping close inshore, a foul current of around a knot will be experienced off Punta Carnero.

A favourable W-going current four hours after HW will assist passage during springs, although this is weak and E-going at neaps.

Crossing from Tarifa to Tanger it is usually wise to use the engine to make a fast passage, to combat the increasing E-going current, or anchor in the sheltered W side of Tarifa and wait for the next favourable tide, around LW, to make the crossing. It is possible, using the engine, to make a fast passage from Gibraltar without encountering heavy adverse currents.

From Ceuta, the timing is similar: set off two hours after HW, keeping close inshore to make use of the counter current.

Gibraltar to Ceuta

Crossing from N to S and vice versa can normally be undertaken at any state of tide, since winds through the Strait are predominantly E or W, although it is important to leave enough sea room to counter the tide and currents.

Remember, in general, a combined current of 1–2 knots is usually E-going, in addition to tidal effects. Beware of rough over-falls and stronger currents around Europa Point and Ceuta Point. Entering Ceuta harbour, this is particularly noticeable one mile NE, off the entrance.

The above information is based on several articles regarding tides, current and wind effects in the Strait of Gibraltar, as well as many hours testing out the theories in over 50 journeys transiting them.

The currents in the Strait are still full of surprises and for sailing purists who do not want a motor-assisted transit, this can be very challenging.

1. Algeciras

36°07'·05N 5°25'·64W Approach to Ensenada del Saladillo

Tides

Standard port Gibraltar
Mean time differences
HW –0010; LW –0010
Heights in metres

MHWS	MHWN	MLWN	MLWS
1·1	0·9	0·4	0·2

Or refer to *EasyTide* at www.ukho.gov.uk

Charts	*Approach*	*Harbour*
Admiralty	91, 773, 142, 3578, 1448	1455
Imray	C19, C50	
Spanish	44C, 45A, 105, 445, 445A	4451

⊕1 36°03'·7N, 5°24'·4W Punta Carnero
⊕2 36°06'·95N 5°25'·43W Algeciras approaches

Lights

Commercial Harbour
2425 **NE breakwater** Fl.R.5s11m7M Red round tower 8m
Work is still going on re-filling SE of Isla Verde and there are now two breakwaters that have nearly joined just N of the yacht basin. There are lights at the ends of the breakwaters but yachts should keep well clear of the on-going work.

Dársena del Saladillo (yacht basin)
2423 **South breakwater** Fl(3)R.9s4m3M
Red ▪ on red round post 1m

Night entry
Not advised, since all three marinas in the Dársena del Saladillo are private and anchoring is forbidden.

Coast radio station
Algeciras *Digital Selective Calling*
MMSI 002241001 VHF Ch 16, 74
Weather bulletins and navigational warnings
Weather bulletins in Spanish and English: VHF Ch 74 at 0315, 0515, 0715, 1115, 1515, 1915, 2315 UT
Navigational warnings in Spanish and English: on request

Port communications

Port Authority ✆ +34 956 585400/585431
Email comercial@apba.es www.apba.es
VHF Ch 08, 13, 16, 68, 74 (call *Algeciras Tráfico*)
Real Club Náutico de Algeciras VHF Ch 09, 16

The Dársena del Saladillo at Algeciras, seen from east-southeast. Although the Real Club Náutico de Algeciras, the Club Náutico Saladillo and the Club Deportivo El Pargo all have pontoons in the harbour, none currently accept visitors

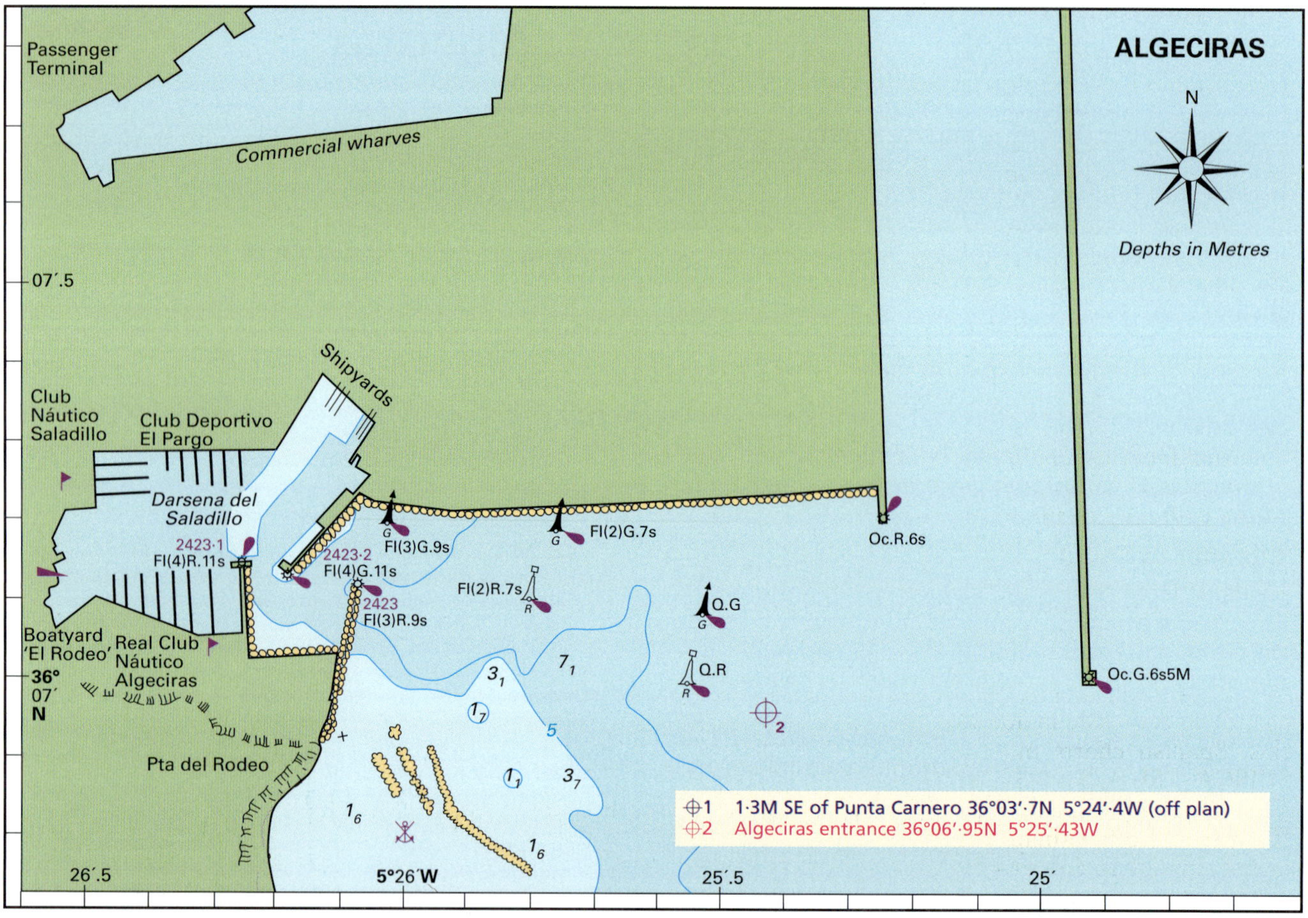

Major commercial harbour, with three private marinas in a separate basin

Algeciras is primarily an industrial and ferry port, through which pass many of the guest-workers returning to Africa with roof racks bending under their loads.

Yachts have their own basin – the Dársena del Saladillo – south of the main harbour, where three separate clubs run three separate marinas. Sadly none welcome visiting yachts (See *Berthing*). The following approach and entrance instructions are given for the Dársena del Saladillo in the hope that this situation may one day change.

Approach

The approaches to Algeciras are extremely busy with commercial traffic of all sizes. In particular, a sharp watch needs to be kept for the many high-speed ferries, including hydrofoils, which run between Algeciras and Morocco. These are notorious for maintaining their course and speed at all times, presumably adhering to the 'might is right' principle.

Coming from the west, there are dangers up to 1M offshore between Punta de Cala Arenas and Punta Carnero (⊕1). On rounding this headland the city and harbour will be seen some 3M to the north behind a mile-long breakwater terminating with a light. Various ledges run out from the headlands between Punta Carnero and the entrance to the Dársena del Saladillo (also lit).

If approaching from Gibraltar or other points east, the entrance to the Dársena del Saladillo should be easily seen south of the oil tanks on the commercial quay and it can be approached directly.

If approaching from the south, possibly from Ceuta or elsewhere in Morocco, ⊕1 lies in clear water southeast of Punta Carnero, a course of 346° for 3·4M leading to ⊕2 in the approaches to the Dársena del Saladillo, passing close to a spherical yellow ODAS buoy off Punta Calero en route.

Yachts can safely cut inside the east cardinal buoy placed nearly a mile offshore, though an offing of at least 0·5M should be maintained. Further ledges lie both north and south of the entrance, and the three buoys marking the approach should under no circumstances be ignored. Major infilling work is taking place to the north of the Saladillo entrance, outside of which a new breakwater is under construction, marked by additional east cardinal light buoys. Keep well clear.

Entrance

The dogleg entrance to the Dársena del Saladillo has been very well designed, such that when visited in a 30 knot easterly wind no swell at all found its way inside the entrance. As noted above, three buoys mark the final approach, after which the entrance itself is straightforward.

Berthing

As stated above none of the three marinas in the Dársena del Saladillo accept visitors. Taken clockwise on entry these are the Real Club Náutico de Algeciras, which previously had premises in the main harbour, the Club Náutico Saladillo and the Club Deportivo El Pargo. The first (southern) marina is also the largest by a considerable margin, and would undoubtedly be the best one to try in an emergency. It is also the club where some English is most likely to be spoken, and visitors are welcome to dine in the Real Club Náutico's restaurant.

Facilities

The Real Club Náutico marina is provided with all the usual facilities, including a fuel berth on the end of the breakwater which forms its eastern limit.

The west side of the basin is home to Astilleros y Varaderos 'El Rodeo', ✆ +34 956 600511, a shipyard primarily engaged with work on steel fishing vessels and other commercial craft, although a steel yacht ashore has been seen there. Almost opposite, across the busy harbourside road, will be found Náutica Iberia, where a limited range of chandlery is on sale in addition to smallcraft and jet-skis. Spanish charts may be obtained either from SUISCA SL ✆ +34 902 220007, *Email* admiraltycharts@suiscasl.com or in the Centro Blas Infante; or from Valnáutica SL ✆ +34 956 570677 at Avenida 28 de Febrero 33.

All the usual shops, banks, restaurants and hotels are to be found in the city, but at some distance, together with a post office, telephones, car hire and taxis. Trains run to many destinations including Madrid, and buses to La Línea, from which it is a short walk to the international airport at Gibraltar.

Alcaidesa Marina from NW with Gibraltar in the background. The marina is new and currently has a lot of space
Graham Hutt

2. Marina Alcaidesa (La Línea)

Charts

Admiralty	1455
Imray	C19, C50
Spanish	4451

⊕ 6 36°09'·5N 05°22'·2W Marina Alcaidesa entrance

Lights

2436.8 **Dique de Abrigo head** Fl.G.5s8m5M Green ▲ on green post concrete base 3m
2436.81 **Puerto Chico Jetty Muelle de San Felipe south head** Fl.R.5s Red ■ on red round column 3m
2437.05 **Puerto Deportivo de La Alcaidesa N Pier N head** Fl(4)G.11s5m1M Green round column 3m
S head Fl(2)R.7s5m1M Red tower 3m
2437.075 **Central Pier head** Fl(3)G.9s5m1M Green tower 2m
2437.08 Dique de Capitania, Head Fl(2)G.7s5m3M green post 3m
Note Three starboard hand buoys form an approach channel for the RoRo ferries.

Port communications

Puerto Deportivo Alcaidesa ✆ +34 956 021 660, *Email* rcorrales@alcaidesa.com www.puertodeportivoalcaidesa.es
Club Maritimo Linense ✆ +34 956 176 506,
Alcaidesa Group ✆ +34 956 791 000 www.alcaidesa.com

New marina in Gibraltar Bay

Marina Alcaidesa, in the NE corner of the Bay of Gibraltar, close to the Gibraltar airport runway, was officially opened in 2010. It has 625 moorings for vessels 8–50m. The marina is fully functional, although the supporting cafés, restaurants and shops have not yet been built, as of late summer 2013. The Club Nautico which has 11 pontoons at the N end of the marina, has no room for visitors. The club house and restaurant, however, are open to all (but expensive).

Prices for moorings and boatyard facilities are low and offer excellent facilities including a 75-ton travel hoist. Wintering afloat is good here, and dry-stack facilities for boats up to 8m are available.

Facilities

Alcaidesa Marina boatyard wasted no time in setting up substantial facilities for haul out and repairs. The following services are:

Berthing The Marina is equipped with service turrets providing water and electricity supply for all berths. There is a Wi-Fi internet service as well as TV and telephone services. Access to the jetties is through automatic gates. For yachts of less than 30m in length, the jetties are floating jetties, with fingers. For larger yachts the jetties are fixed concrete jetties with vehicular access.

Shipyard Equipped with a crane, 75-ton travel-lift system, pressure jet cleaning, dry marina and showers.

Dry Dock Storage for boats from 6–8m on a rental basis for winter usage.

Repairs The Alcaidesa Yacht Marina has earmarked an area of more than 17,000m² for the repair of every conceivable kind of vessel; a unique facility because of

I. ENTRANCE TO THE MEDITERRANEAN

⊕6 La Línea Approach 36°09'.5N 05°22'.2W

Marina Alcaidesa looking NW *Pública de Puertos de Andalucía*

its size and services. The Marina will also have a specialised workshop for any kind of task, including, of course, carpentry, painting and decorating, communications and other services.

Chandlers The Marina includes an area for premises specialising in nautical supplies, both for spare parts and any other necessary sailing requirements, covering a total surface area of almost 8,000m^2.

Parking facilities A total of more than 1,000 parking bays are distributed both in the area reserved for Marina clients, for whom access is available through a security checkpoint, and in the commercial area also serving the recreational and leisure areas.

Security Closed circuit television system and security surveillance and control.

Toilets, showers and laundry are good but currently only open at one end of the marina.

Fuel Refuelling Station.

Shops/Provisioning There is good shopping, including a large supermarket and an excellent produce market in the town. Gibraltar is well within walking distance but note it is necessary to show one's passport to cross the border.

3. Gibraltar

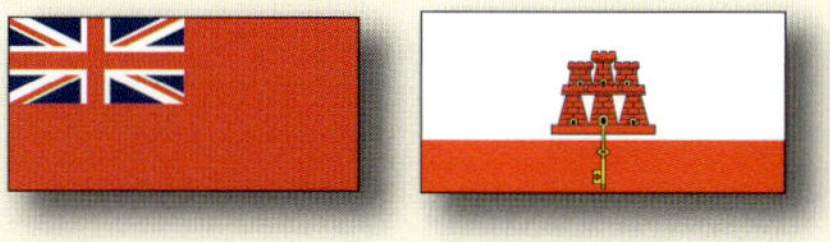

Tides

Gibraltar is a standard port.
Heights in metres

MHWS	MHWN	MLWN	MLWS
1·0	0·7	0·3	0·1

Charts	*Approach*	*Harbour*
British Admiralty	*91, 142*	*145*
	773, 3578	*144*
Spanish	*445, 445A*	*4452*
French	*7042*	*7026*
Imray	*M11, C19*	*M11*
	C50	*C50*

⊕3 36°06′·5N 05°22′·7W Europa Pt W.
⊕4 36°08′N 05°22′·3W Gibraltar South Mole
⊕5 36°09′N 05°22′·35 Gibraltar North Mole

Lights

Approach

2414 **Tarifa** 36°00′·1N 05°36′·6W Fl(3)WR.10s41m26/18M White tower 33m 113°-W-089°-R-113°

2420 **Punta Carnero** 36°04′·6N 05°25′·6W Fl(4)WR.20s42m16/13M 018°-W-325°-R-018° Round tower and white building 19m

2456 **Gibraltar Aeromarine** 36°08′·6N 05°20′·6W AeroMo(GB)R.I0s405m30M Obscured on westerly bearings within 2M

2438 **Europa Point** 36°06′·6N 05°20′·7W Iso.10s49m19M Oc.R.10s19M and F.R.15M 042°-vis-067° Horn 20s White round tower, red band 19m

Harbour

2442 **South breakwater, north end (A head)** Fl.2s10m5M Horn 10s White tower 7m

2445 **Detached breakwater, south end (B head)** Q.R.9m5M Metal structure on concrete building 11m

2446 **Detached breakwater, north end (C head)** Q.G.10m5M Metal structure on concrete building 11m

2448 **North breakwater, southwest arm (D head)** Q.R.18m5M Black 8-sided tower 17m

Port communications

Radio

Gibraltar Port Control VHF Ch 16, 6, 12, 13, 14 (24 hours)
Lloyds radio VHF Ch 8, 12, 14, 16 (24 hours)
Queens Harbourmaster VHF Ch 8 (0800–1600 Monday to Friday) All marinas VHF Ch 71 (0830–2030, later in summer)
GIBRALTAR MARINAS USE VHF 71 CALLING WORKING VHF 68 or 69.

Telephone and email

Port Captain ✆ +350 200 77254
Port Operations Room ✆ +350 200 78134/ 200 77004
Queensway Quay ✆ +350 200 44700,
Email qqmarina@gibnet.gi
Marina Bay Office ✆ +350 200 73300,
Email pieroffice@marinabay.gi
www.marinabay.gi
Ocean Village ✆ +350 200 40048
Email info@oceanvillage.gi
www.oceanvillage.gi
Sheppards Marina Repair facilities
✆ +350 200 76895, Chandlery ✆ +350 200 77183

Gibraltar: Rounding Europa point. Note the mosque behind the light *Graham Hutt*

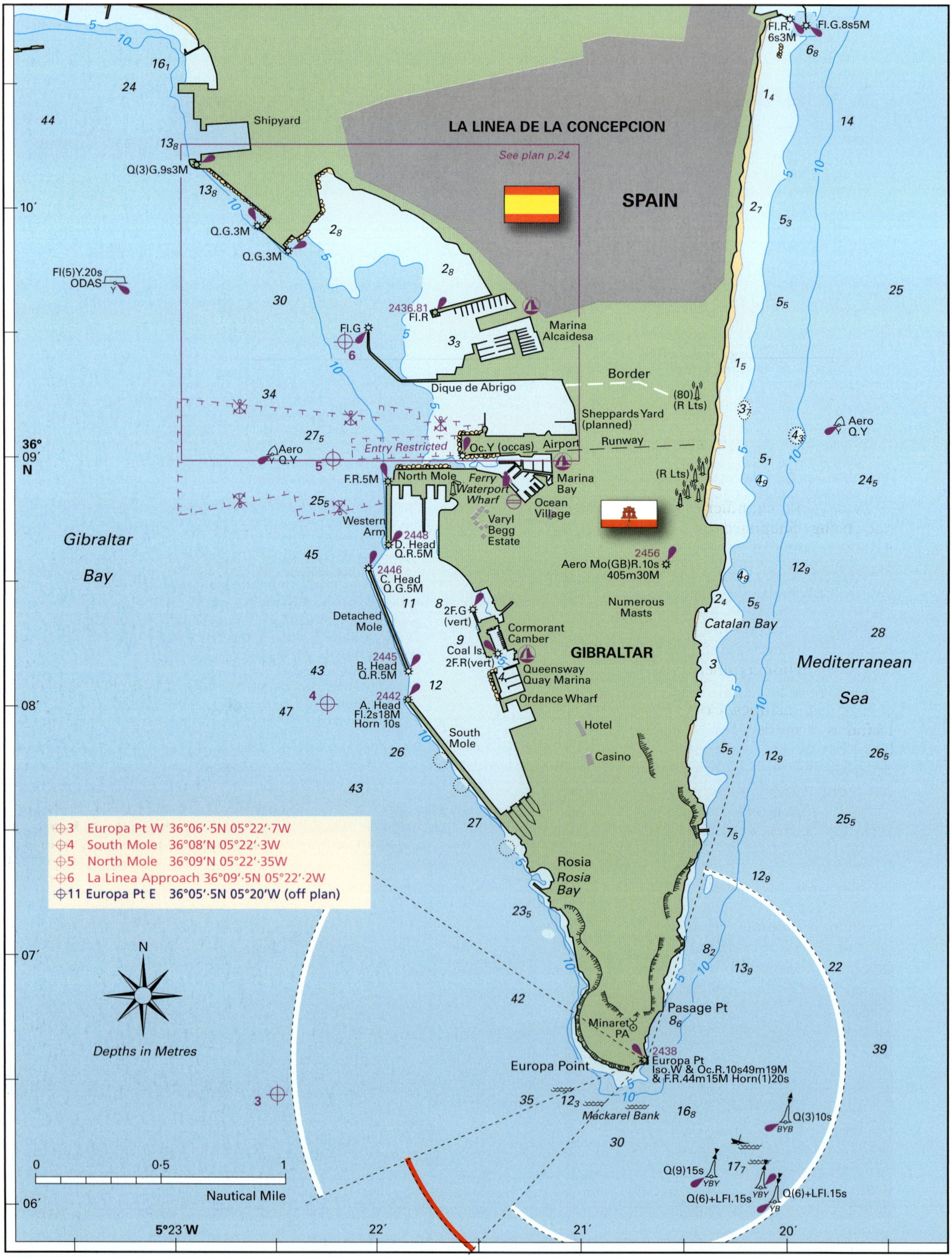

LA LINEA DE LA CONCEPCION
See plan p.24
SPAIN
Shipyard
Q(3)G.9s3M
Q.G.3M
Q.G.3M
Fl(5)Y.20s
ODAS
2436.81
Fl.R
Fl.G
Marina Alcaidesa
Dique de Abrigo
Border
(80)
(R Lts)
Sheppards Yard (planned)
Runway
Airport
Aero Q.Y
Entry Restricted
Oc.Y (occas)
F.R.5M
North Mole
Ferry
Waterport Wharf
Marina Bay
Ocean Village
(R Lts)
Varyl Begg Estate
Western Arm
2448
D. Head
Q.R.5M
2446
C. Head
Q.G.5M
2456
Aero Mo(GB)R.10s
405m30M
Numerous Masts
Gibraltar Bay
Detached Mole
2F.G (vert)
Coal Is
2F.R(vert)
Cormorant Camber
Queensway Quay Marina
Ordance Wharf
GIBRALTAR
Catalan Bay
Mediterranean Sea
2445
B. Head
Q.R.5M
2442
A. Head
Fl.2s18M
Horn 10s
Hotel
Casino
South Mole
Fl.R.
6s3M
Fl.G.8s5M
⊕3 Europa Pt W 36°06′·5N 05°22′·7W
⊕4 South Mole 36°08′N 05°22′·3W
⊕5 North Mole 36°09′N 05°22′·35W
⊕6 La Linea Approach 36°09′·5N 05°22′·2W
⊕11 Europa Pt E 36°05′·5N 05°20′W (off plan)
Rosia
Rosia Bay
Passage Pt
Minaret PA
2438
Europa Pt
Iso.W & Oc.R.10s49m19M
& F.R.44m15M Horn(1)20s
Europa Point
Mackarel Bank
Q(3)10s
BYB
Q(9)15s
YBY
Q(6)+LFl.15s
YBY
Q(6)+LFl.15s
YB
N
Depths in Metres
0
0·5
1
Nautical Mile
10′
36°
09′
N
08′
07′
06′
5°23′W
22′
21′
20′

GIBRALTAR

INTRODUCTION

The Gateway to the Mediterranean

Gibraltar: a tiny self-ruled British Colony and Sovereign territory of 30,000 nationals with its own government. Different pressures are being applied which affect the border crossing between the two states producing long delays for those wishing to cross. Gibraltar has a substantial port with dry docking facilities and two marinas. Currently it is probably the only economy in Europe that can boast growth – GDP at around 5%.

Its location at the tip of the Iberian peninsula and its predominantly English speaking population, make it invaluable to British yachtsmen. It has an airport with daily flights to different destinations in the UK, duty free fuel and extensive repair facilities. Since Sheppards relocated, there is no longer a travel hoist available, but a 75-ton hoist is located in the nearby Alcaidesa Marina less than a mile from Gibraltar.

There are several large supermarkets, including Morrisons, Coviran and Eroski making it an ideal stop for supplies.

Two yacht chandleries are operating: the main one being Sheppards – close to Ocean Village. Another operates from the Hire-U-Shop at Watergardens, nearby. If an item is not in stock, it can easily be ordered and, if the yacht is in transit, there is no duty to be paid.

There are two marinas, both on the W side of the Rock, with others planned for the future.

Truly a major commercial port with good facilities.

There are other harbours apart from the commercial facilities. Cormorant Camber on Coaling Island is a marina for local vessels, and a military base lies S of Queensway Quay. These are not accessible to visiting vessels. Sheppards has light haul out and engineering facilities on Coaling Island.

Note There are currently considerable delays crossing the border with Spain (December 2013).

Approach

By day Gibraltar Rock, rising to 426m, is clearly visible except in fog, which is rare, though more frequent in summer. It is safe to enter the Bay of Gibraltar (Algeciras Bay) in almost any conditions but beware of squalls near the Rock once in the bay, particularly during strong easterlies, when strong downdraughts occur off the Rock. From the south and east, Europa Point is prominent, with its lighthouse at the end. A short distance further up the point, the minaret of a new mosque will be observed. Strong currents and overfalls occur around the tip of the point when wind is against tide. From the west, Pta Carnero (⊕1 36°03'·7N 05°24'·4W) light lies at the southwest entrance to the bay, near an old whaling station. The coast is fringed with wrecks from all eras, many popular as dive sites – any vessel flying International Code Flag A (white with a blue swallowtail) should be given a generous clearance. Yachts must also give way to naval and commercial vessels at all times.

Gibraltar weather forecasts

Radio Gibraltar (GBC) and British Forces Radio (BFBS) broadcast local weather forecasts (see table below). The marinas post weather faxes on their notice boards daily. See also www.bbc.co.uk/weather/coast/pressure/ and http://meteonet.nl/aktueel/brackall.htm for five day forecasts. Sites www.sto-p.com/atol and www.accuweather.com give complete hour-by-hour predictions over 16 hours and general forecasts up to 15 days.

Tarifa Radio broadcasts area weather on Channel 16 at regular intervals, in Spanish and English.

Gibraltar weather forecasts

LT	BFBS 1			BFBS2	Gibraltar BC		
	Mon-Fri	Sat	Sun	Mon-Fri	Mon-Fri	Sat	Sun
0530					X	X	
0630					X	X	X
0730					X	X	X
0745	X						
0845	X	X	X				
0945		X	X				
1005	X						
1030					X		
1200				X			
1202		X	X				
1230					X	X	X
1602			X				
1605	X						
Also storm warnings on receipt					1438 AM		
	93·5 FM			89·4 FM	91·3 FM		
	97·8 FM			99·5 FM	92·6 FM		
Includes high and low water times					100·5 FM		

By night The west side of the Rock is well illuminated by the town; and to the east by the bright red lights marking the radio antennas on the north face; which is itself illuminated by spotlights. This can be confusing even in good visibility and makes lights difficult to identify. The most conspicuous are likely to be those on the south mole's A head and north mole's D head. To the south is the lighthouse on Europa point, easily seen from north-northeast clockwise to north-northwest, with a small red sector indicating the dangerous rocky shoreline to the west between Pta del Acebuche and Pta Carnero, which must be given a wide berth. If

Gibraltar: Monkey keeps watch over the detached mole and Queensway Quay *Graham Hutt*

approaching in poor visibility beware the amount of traffic in the vicinity.

Entry formalities

Whereas in the past all yachts calling at Gibraltar first proceeded to the customs and immigration offices opposite Marina Bay, this no longer applies. Proceed to any marina where paper formalities are part of the check-in process carried out by marina staff. See note below.

Gibraltar, like the UK, is not party to the Shengen agreement, which has different visa requirements to Spain. Check for latest information from the Gibraltar government website www.gibraltar.gov.gi or contact the immigration department ✆ +350 200 46411, *Email* rgpimm@gibynex.gi.

Crew intending to remain ashore, or obtain work in Gibraltar should inform Immigration Authorities of their intention and supply an address.

Note: The Gibraltar authorities request all vessels to notify them in advance of arrival and to fill out the online entry form. This saves time and paperwork on arrival and gives advance notice if non EU nationals requiring a passport stamp are on board. This can be done before departing for Gibraltar from last port of call.
www.hmcustoms.gov.gi/index.jsf
Go to 'vessel pre-arrival notifications' under electronic pre-declarations.

Anchoring in the Bay

Once a very convenient and safe anchorage for vessels accessing both Spain and Gibraltar, anchoring in the N end of the Bay is now prohibited.

The area to the N of the runway is a Gibraltar airport security zone, whilst vessels attempting to anchor in the area along the Alcaiseda Marina *dique* and to the west, will be moved on by the Spanish authorities.

One of Gibraltar's important assets is the colony of Barbary Macaques seen here at their base half way up the west side of the Rock. In the background is Jebel Moussa in Morocco, on the other side of the Strait where similar colonies of monkeys live *Graham Hutt*

Queensway Quay Marina

Location 36°08'·1N 05°21'·3W

The Marina

Closest to Europa Point, Queensway Quay has the advantage of being furthest from the airport with its noise and dust. Over the past few years the marina has undergone several major changes to overcome problems with the original design of 2005. The entrance is now at the NW end of the marina and many steps have been implemented to overcome the surging which formally damaged many yachts during storms. This has now been overcome and it is a safe and comfortable marina in all conditions experienced to date.

This is a small pleasant marina, very well run with luxury apartments surrounding it and several good restaurants and bars on the quay. Morrisons supermarket is within walking distance and is also served by bus routes 1 and 3. *Marineros* are on hand to assist with mooring.

Entry formalities

Both marina and entry formalitles are now completed at the marina office.

Approach

The marina is approached through the main harbour via either of the two entrances, continuing towards the gap between Coaling Island and the new island which forms the W side of Queensway Quay. On passing through this gap the entrance lies immediately to starboard (⊕4 36°08'N 05°22'·3W). The buildings overlooking the marina are floodlit.

Berthing

Visitors' berths are few and it is imperative that you call on VHF 71 in advance of entry. Moorings are stern or bows-to on long floating pontoons with lines tailed. A limited number of deep moorings in 3–7m are available on the S wall of the marina. Pontoons are very low.

Note 1 a boom is drawn across the marina entrance at night from 2000 in summer and 2100 in winter. Reopening at 0830. This is to prevent oil from the bay entering as well as acting as a security device. The marina office is located at the NW end of the jetty overlooking the seaward entrance.

Note 2 During strong Levante conditions (E winds), very strong katabatic gusts blow from the Rock down into the marina and the S mole area. These often reach over 40 knots, but only last a few minutes.

Charges

High season April–October: Day £15. Low season November–April: Day £10.65. Multihulls: +50%. Plus metered electricity and water. Full information available on the web or by contacting the marina on email at the address given on page 25.

Queensway Quay (centre) with Coaling Island (right) and the military base (left) *Graham Hutt*

Facilities

Every berth has a service module with water and electricity (metered).

Other facilities are sat TV, Wi-Fi and phone lines, available for a monthly fee.

Pontoon access is via a locked gate with coded key pad. Security is excellent.

Car and bike parking is available within the marina complex.

Toilets and showers are sited near the marina entrance and car park. These are closed at night, but a smaller facility is available out of hours using the same lock code as the pontoons.

Laundry (plus self service) and dry-cleaners are available in the marina near the car park.

Restaurants Several excellent restaurants located along the main quay.

Marina office is at the NW end of the marina, overlooking the entrance.

Repairs None in the marina, but mechanics can be brought to the vessel. See under 'General Facilities' on page 30.

Ocean Village / Marina Bay

Location 36°08'·9N 05°21'·4W

Ocean Village and Marina Bay are under the same administration and management and are situated on either side of the main jetty running West to the marina office. Ocean Village took over the space vacated by Sheppards Marina on the S side of Marina Bay and is linked to the casino and recreational centre. It offers floating pontoons rather than lines tailed to the quay, and is closer to the shore facilities – bars and restaurants. There are around 300 berths available with a small number of places for super-yachts and mega yachts up to 150m.

Plans for the marina have changed several times over the past five years and another change took place in February 2014 when the 150m floating hotel *Sunborn* arrived. With 200 luxury cabins, the ship is now permanently grounded alongside the main jetty. It will be used as a permanent luxury accommodation vessel, conference and events centre, with a second casino. There are also plans (in early 2014) to re-orientate the floating pontoons to facilitate easier mooring with the prevailing winds on the Ocean Village side.

From the west, Marina Bay (left) and Ocean Village. The arrival of a large luxury cruise ship (*The Sunborn*), not pictured but now permanently berthed on the north side of the casino, reduces the number of yacht moorings available

Gibraltar: Ocean Village Marina. The arrival of the 150m Sunborn floating luxury hotel in February 2014, casting its long shadow in Marina Bay and Ocean Village Marina, has created some waves in Gibraltar and is a permanent fixture. Moored alongside the main jetty, it has reduced the number of yacht berths available and dwarfs the casino and luxury apartments behind *Graham Hutt*

Approach

The marina is 0·5M E of the N mole (⊕5 36°09'N 05°22'·35W) and is approached by rounding the N Mole's E head. At night a row of red lights at the end of the airport runway mark the N side of the channel. Note that yachts **may not move in the vicinity** while the runway lights are flashing, There is also a height restriction of 23m.

Berthing

Call the marina office on Ch 71 for berth allocation. Note: Depths in the marina are around 2·5m but some areas are less. Make sure the berthing master knows your draft to ensure the correct location in the marina. If staff are not around, berth alongside the office, towards the outer end of the main pier or find an empty mooring. Office open 24 hours. Berthing is Mediterranean-style – bow or stern-to with a buoy and lazy-line provided to the pontoon.

Gibraltar: The northern anchorage and entrance to Marina Bay

Charges for a 12m Yacht

Mooring charges in Gibraltar are cheaper than in Spain: check the relevant websites for up-to-date information.

Facilities at Ocean Village / Marina Bay

Every berth has a service module with water and electricity (metered).
Other facilities Wi-Fi (accessible throughout the marina) sat TV, and phone lines, available in Ocean Village.
Pontoon access is open.
Car and bike parking is available close to the marina complex.
Toilets and showers are sited near the marina office. Open 24 hours.
Laundry and dry-cleaners are available in the marina near the car park.
Several excellent restaurants are located along the main quay of Marina Bay, extending to the S end of Ocean Village.
Shops/Provisioning Many shops available.
Repairs Marine Maintanance Ltd (Perkins & Yanmar agent) ✆ +350 200 78954 *Email* marine@MMgib.com www.MMgib.com

General facilities

Gas Available from New Harbours ✆ +350 200 7026. All bottled gas is imported from Spain by Rumagas and sold through outlets including the Shell office at the fuel berth and most filling stations.
Fuel Diesel (and water) is obtainable at the Shell or BP stations opposite Marina Bay. Shell ✆ +350 200 48232, BP ✆ +350 200 72261.
Provisions Morrisons supermarket is a short walk from Queensway Quay and not far from Marina Bay. It is on the No. 4 bus route, fresh fruit and vegetables are best obtained from La Linea market, just across the border in Spain, on Wednesday mornings, Duty-free stores are available via Albor Ltd ✆ /*Fax* +350 200 73283, at Marina Bay – which doubles as a newsagent, bookshop and cybercafé – where almost anything in almost any quantity for a yacht in transit can be purchased.
Charts Gibraltar Chart Agency Irish Town ✆ +350 200 78954, *Email* charts@mmgib.com
Chandlery Sheppards have the best range of chandlery currently and will order anything required. The shop is one the Ocean Village side a short walk from Marina Bay. ✆ +350 200 77183, www.sheppard.gi
Repair facilities Marine Maintanance Ltd. (Perkins and Yanmar agent) ✆ +350 200 78954, *Email* marine@MMgib.com, www.MMgib.com
Sheppards (engineering) agents for Volvo and Mercury ✆ +350 200 76895 Including: at Coaling Island: light engineering, a small 5-ton lift-out facility. 30 ton facility at North Mole. Welding, mechanical services and electronic repairs. (Raymarine agents).
Medmarine Ltd ✆ +350 200 48889 (Yamaha agents)
Electro-Med (Queensway Quay) ✆ +350 200 77077, www.electro-med.com
Tempco Marine Engineering ✆ +350 200 74657 (refrigeration and radio repairs)

Engineers Sheppard's can handle light engineering, welding, engine servicing and repairs to most makes and are Volvo Penta agents. Also-Marine Maintenance Ltd ✆ +350 200 78954, *Email* fred@gibnet.gi (Perkins and Yanmar) at Manna Bav, and Medmarine Ltd ✆ +350 200 48888 (Yamaha) at Queensway Quay, Tempco Marine Engineering ✆ +350 200 74657, specialise in refrigeration and radio repairs Sheppard's workshops (as above) or ElectroMed ✆ +350 200 77077, *Email* mail@electro-med.com www.eletro-med.com at Queensway Quay, who can supply and repair equipment from most major manufacturers.

Sailmaker/sail repairs Sail makers, ✆ +350 200 41469 in South Pavilion Road, who also handle general canvaswork and upholstery. Alternatively Magnusson Sails ✆ +34 952 791241, about 35 miles away in Estepona, who may be willing to deliver/collect. Canvas work and sprayhood (but not true sailmaking) is also undertaken by ME Balloqui & Sons ✆ +350 200 78105, at 3941 City Mill Lane.

Rigging Sheppard's workshops, as above.

Liferaft servicing GV Undery & Son ✆ +350 200 73107, *Email* compass@gibtelecom.net (who are also compass adjusters). Note: Currently with the old Sheppard's boatyard and repair facilities in a temporary location, facilities in Gibraltar are limited. A crane can lift yachts, which are then placed on the hard and moved by travel lift. The process is expensive and not suited to larger displacement yachts. The plan to move the boatyard and haul-out facility to the N side of the runway has been abandoned. The nearest boatyard and travel hoist is now Marina Alcaidesa (page 23). Other possibilities for larger vessels are the old Naval shipyards S of Queensway quay.

Money The UK Pound Sterling is legal tender, along with the Gibraltar pound and of equal value, but only in Gibraltar. Beware of trying to exchange excess Gibraltar currency in the UK, as it is worth very little there. Euros can also be used in most shops but not in the Post Office where only sterling is accepted. There are several Bureaux de Change agencies in Main Street. Visa, Switch, American Express, Mastercard etc, are accepted almost everywhere, though not the post office and some government offices. ATMs at Barclays Bank in Main Street and Morrisons supermarket.

Banks Gibraltar has well established banking services for both offshore and local customers with a full range of international banks, including several UK institutions, Banking hours are generally between 0900–1530 Monday to Friday.

Yacht brokerage & yacht registration Boat Shed Gibraltar, John and Lynda Alcantara. Excellent agency and service ✆ 00350 200 78885, *Mobile* 00350 5800999 / 0034 667 666753
Email boats@boatshedgibraltar.com

International travel Gibraltar airport is located close to the frontier for daily flights to the UK and onward connections ✆ +350 200 12345. Málaga airport is a little an over an hour's drive up the coast (A7 or AP7 *peaje* toll road) for more destinations. Taxis are expensive – about €100 or £75.
There is a very reasonably priced airport carpark opposite the airport, near the border which charges about 50p an hour short term and £4 for 24 hour parking.
La Línea bus station is just across the border.

Gibraltar's new airport serving the UK, with few daily flights *Maria Kanayama*

Locally

Gibraltar may be a tiny enclave, but it has many interesting sites to visit. The upper rock is home to monkeys – actually barbary macaques – made famous by the remark of Churchill that Gibraltar would cease to be British if the monkeys disappeared. Also at the upper rock is a spectacular cave network – St Michael's cave. Bones have been found here and in other close locations indicating civilisation has existed on the rock for many thousands of years. Views from the road running around the upper rock are really spectacular, taking in Morocco, Ceuta, Spain and on a good day, down to Tanger. A cable car is located near the Queens Hotel, close to the end of Main Street to transport visitors to the St Michael's cave area. Organised tours are available as well as taking a long walk to the different caves and artefacts. These are well preserved and presented. Information is available at the tourist office at the frontier with Spain and in Casemates Square. If you wish to do your own tour, just follow the signs to the 'Upper Rock.'

The upper rock is also home to the monkeys – who also forage down as far as Main Street.

There are reputed to be over 40 miles of tunnels inside the Rock of Gibraltar which have facilitated some great acts of military skill and determination over hundreds of years. Much of the tunnel and cave system is open to the public and well worth visiting. Tunnels which are usually closed can also be visited by arrangement with the Gibraltar Heritage Trust (John Mackintosh Square).

The 18th century was a key time in the history of Gibraltar, which finally saw a treaty between Spain and Great Britain, giving the Rock to the British for as long as the people wanted to be British. Spain wishes to abandon the 300 year old treaty (of Utrecht) with claims that Gibraltar should revert back to Spanish rule. Very long queues to enter and exit the frontier with Spain are the consequences of the dispute.

Main Street is worth a visit with its bustling shops and bazaars and very English pubs. Although Gibraltar is VAT free, there are other taxes which make local purchases similar to prices in Spain – apart from tobacco and alcohol.

II. COSTA DEL SOL

Introduction

GENERAL DESCRIPTION

The coastline between Gibraltar and 155M East to Cabo de Gata, is known as the Costa del Sol – The Sun Coast. An apt name in view of the average 300 days of sunshine per year. Not that it is hot all year round: although temperatures can occasionally reach over 40°C in August, ice can be found frequently on car windows in winter, even at sea level. The nearby Sierra Nevada mountain range is famous as a skiing resort in winter.

The three primary ports of the Costa del Sol are Gibraltar, Málaga and Almeria. A further 17 smaller harbours are covered. The Spanish coast from Cap de Nao further towards Barcelona and the French

Europa Point with mosque to left *Graham Hutt*

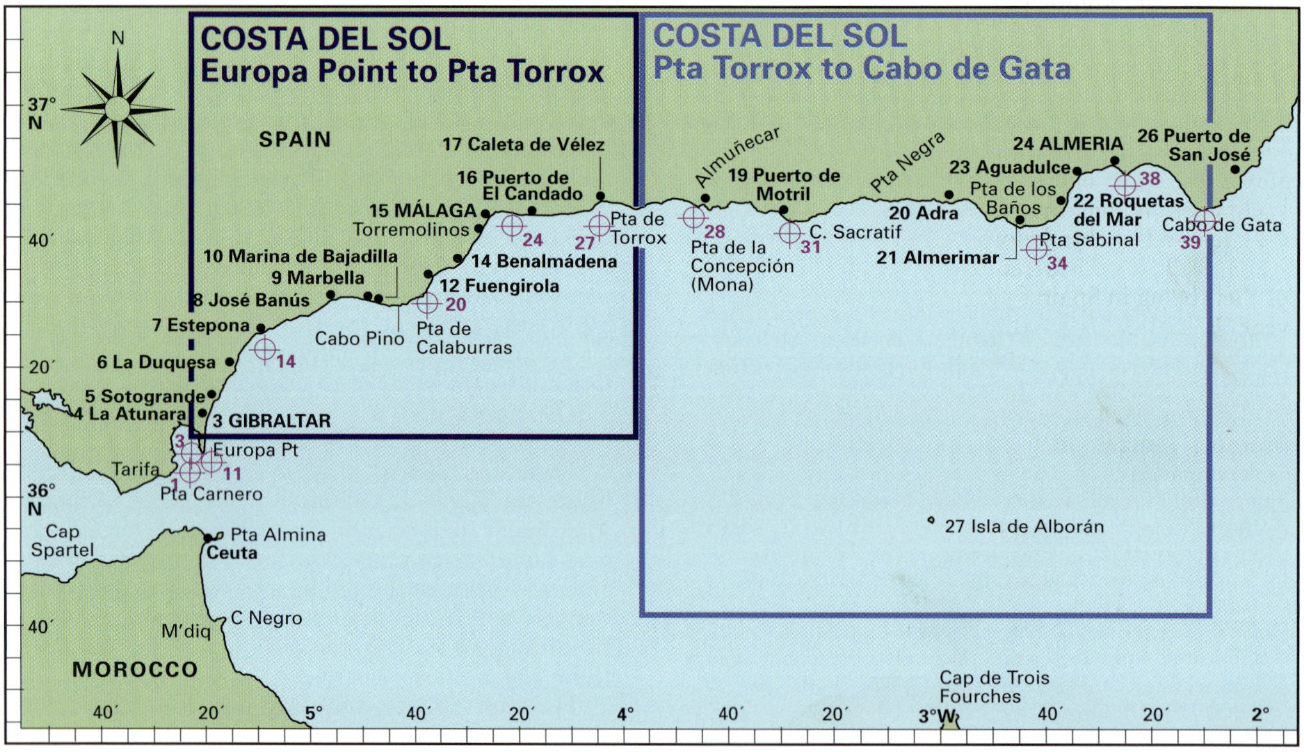

COASTAL WAYPOINT LIST

The waypoints listed form a series with which one is able to steer from off Gibraltar to Cabo de Gata. The waypoints are all at WGS 84 datum and although the track avoids the main fish farm areas these farms come and go, seemingly overnight sometimes, and a good lookout must be kept at all times. There are over 50 'official' farms along this section of coast, which are lit and reported in the light lists – however inshore and in various *calas* there are many more farms and these are usually unlit. It is therefore essential to keep a lookout at all times while making a coastal passage in this area.

⊕1	Pta. Carnero	36°03′·7N	05°24′·4W
⊕3	Pta Europa west	36°05′·5N	05°22′·7W
⊕11	Pta Europa east	36°05′·5N	05°20′W
⊕14	SE of Pta de la Doncella	36°22′·5N	05°08′W
⊕20	Pta de Calaburras	36°29′N	04°38′W
⊕24	Puerto de el Candado	36°41′N	04°20′·5W
⊕27	Pta Torrox	36°42′N	03°57′·4W
⊕28	Pta de la Concepción (Mona)	36°42′·5N	03°44′W
⊕31	Cabo Sacratif	36°41′N	03°28′W
⊕34	SSE of Pta de las Entinas	36°37′·5N	02°46′W
⊕38	S of Pta del Río	36°46′·5N	02°25′·5W
⊕39	Cabo de Gata	36°41′N	02°10′W

Pilotage and navigation

TIDES

The standard port is Gibraltar; secondary ports are Málaga and Almería. From Alicante to the north-east the tide is hardly appreciable. The figures are:

			Heights			Mean
		MHWS	*MHWN*	*MLWS*	*MLWN*	*Level*
Gibraltar		**1·0**	**0·7**	**0·3**	**0·1**	**0·50**
Differences						
HW	LW					
Málaga						
+0005	–0005	–0·3	–0·1	0·0	+0·1	0·45
Almería						
+0010	–0010	–0·5	–0·3	0·0	+0·2	0·40

CURRENTS

There is usually a standing E going current – around 2kns at La Línea (Mediterranean side) – decreasing to a knot or less towards Estepona. It is especially noticeable around headlands and is accounted for by evaporation of the Mediterranean sea. It is also very much influenced by the wind direction. Strong E winds, which sometimes blow for many days, will cancel and even reverse the surface current, often creating steep seas, whilst W winds will increase the flow E.

SOUNDINGS

In most harbours sand builds up at or near the entrance, particularly after a blow, and is periodically dredged. Reported depths are not necessarily accurate and care should be taken to sound whilst approaching and entering harbour.

MAGNETIC VARIATION

Costa del Sol (Málaga) 01°21′W (2013) decreasing 7′ annually.

RESTRICTED AREAS

Anchoring is not permitted in the following areas which should be avoided if possible:

- W and E of the Rock of Gibraltar
- The prolongation of the airstrip at Gibraltar
- An area 2M to E of Estepona
- An area 2M to SW of Málaga
- An area 1M to S of Málaga where passage is also forbidden.

TUNNY NETS

During the summer months, tunny nets may be set between February and October in the following localities:

- Off La Línea (Mediterranean side)
- Off the coast N of Fuerte de Santa Barbara
- Near Marbella
- Near Adra
- Off Punta del Sabinal
- To W of Cabo de Gata.

FISH HAVENS

There are many fish havens along the coast. Most are simply areas where fishing is prohibited.

Fish farms, however can take many forms and can be either totally submerged with exclusion zone extremities marked by cardinal buoys, or are floating rafts easily spotted. Fish havens can generally be sailed over, whereas fish farms usually present surface obstacles and need to be given clearance.

LANDINGS

Beaches are regularly patrolled by Guardia Civil officers who keep a good look out for drug smugglers and people-traffickers.

Note that many beaches along the coast have buoys stretched parallel to the shoreline in summer to protect bathers. It is illegal to anchor or sail inside these buoys with any vessel, including jet-skis. The buoys are spaced evenly and usually coloured yellow, extending around 50m from the beach, but further out if waters are shallow. Gaps in the buoyage enable jet-skiers and dinghies to transit in and out of the restricted zones.

PLASTIC SHEETS

Gales can rip off and blow the polyculture sheeting into the sea. These sheets can be up to 100m long, easily become entangled in the prop and stop an engine. This is a potential problem especially around Motril and the Bay of Almeria and has happened to me on two occasions.

Plastic sheets and tunnels cover vegetables and fruit over many miles of coastline. Some of these are over 100 metres long *Graham Hutt*

Across the Strait of Gibraltar to North Africa and the Spanish Enclaves

VISITS ACROSS THE STRAIT OF GIBRALTAR

Other possibilities for local visits outside of the area are across the Strait of Gibraltar and the Costa del Sol to Northern Morocco and the Spanish enclaves of Ceuta and Melilla.

For those wanting to explore further afield from a base on the Costa or from Gibraltar, most ports along the N coast of Morocco can be reached within 24 hours sailing time. Many motor vessels from the Costa are seen visiting Saidia and Marina Smir, where formalities are easy and fast. Ferries also run from some ports on the Costa to Melilla and, in summer, to Al Hociema.

The Spanish enclave of Ceuta lies a short distance across the Strait of Gibraltar, just 12 miles from Europa Point, giving access to Morocco and taking less than half an hour to cross the land frontier. The local towns are M'Diq and World Heritage city of Tetouan. Marina Smir is a popular destination from Gibraltar, Sotogrande and Estepona or Marbella, just 10 miles from Ceuta. Marina Smir is owned by Marina Marbella. Extensive repair, haul-out and wintering facilities are available in Marina Smir with excellent prices. Many RYA school yachts visit from Gibraltar on a weekly basis.

Further to the E from Ceuta are Al Hociema port and another Spanish enclave: Melilla. A new marina has just opened on the inland lake, Mar Chica, a few miles SE of Melilla and to the W of the huge new marina at Saidia.

Full details of the North Africa and Spanish enclave facilities are covered in the RCCPF *North Africa* pilot.

Melilla The ancient city, overlooking the lighthouse *Graham Hutt*

Cala Cangrejo near Jebha, North Morocco, a short distance from Costa del Sol *Terry Vadrouille*

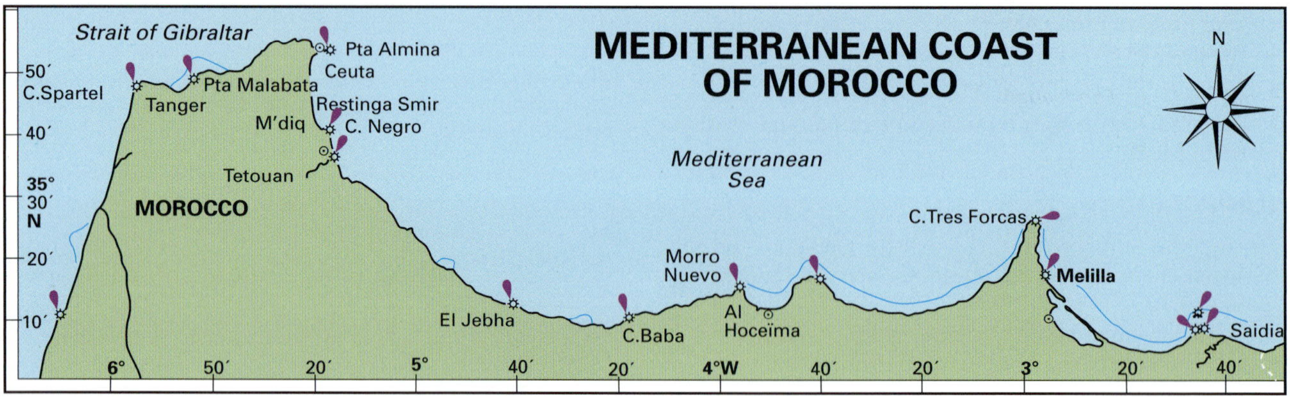

Europa Point to Pta del Torrox

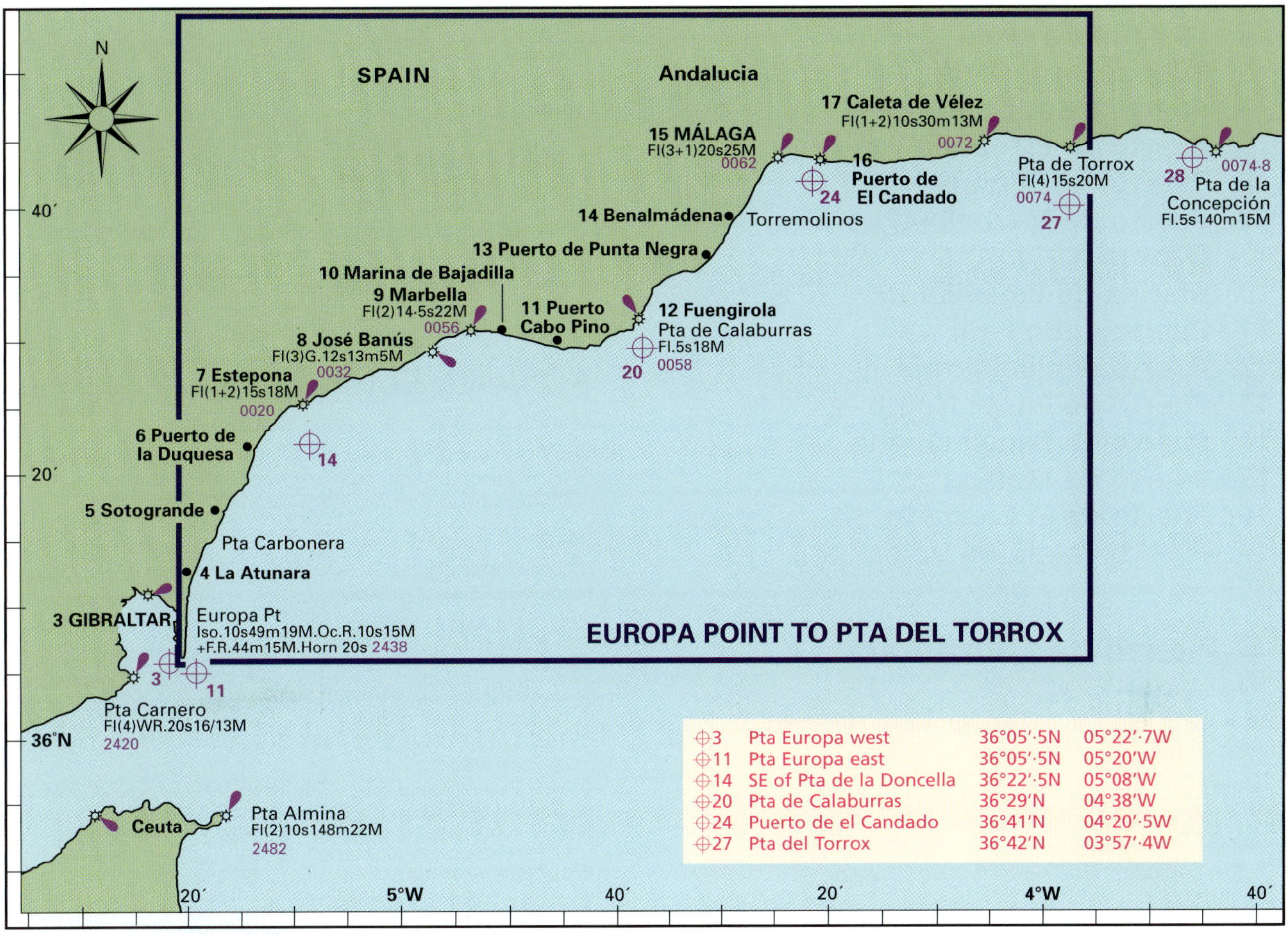

Costa del Sol planning guide and distances (See page 168 for full waypoint list)

⚓ Anchorage

Miles	Harbours, anchorages & headlands	
	3. Gibraltar *(page 25)*	Europa Point
8M	**4. La Atunara** *(page 38)*	
7M	⚓ *Río Guadiaro*	
	5. Puerto Sotogrande *(page 38)*	
5M	⚓ *Cala Sardina*	
	Punta de la Chullera,	
	Punta de la Salo de la Mora	
	6. Puerto de la Duquesa *(page 41)*	
5M	⚓ *Fondeadero de la Sabinilla*	
	7. Puerto de Estepona *(page 42)*	
11M		
	8. Puerto José Banús *(page 44)*	
4M	**9. Puerto de Marbella** *(page 46)*	
1M	**10. Marina de Bajadilla** *(page 48)*	
		Punta Calaburras
7M	**11. Puerto Cabo Pino** *(page 49)*	
9M	**12. Puerto de Fuengirola** *(page 50)*	
4M	**13. Puerto de Punta Negra** *(page 52)*	
12M	**14. Puerto de Benalmádena** *(page 53)*	
9M	**15. Puerto de Málaga** *(page 55)*	
4M	**16. Puerto de El Candado** *(page 57)*	
	⚓ *Fondeadero de Vélez-Málaga*	
14M	**17. Puerto Caleta de Vélez** *(page 58)*	
		Punta de Torrox
	⚓ *Fondadero de Nerja*	
	⚓ *Cala de la Miel*	
17M	⚓ *Cala de los Cañuelos*	
	⚓ *Ensenada de la Herradura*	
	18. Marina del Este *(page 62)*	

Miles	Harbours, anchorages & headlands	
		Punta de la Concepción
	⚓ *Ensenada de los Berengueles*	
	⚓ *Punta San Cristóbal and Almuñecar*	
	⚓ *Fondeadero de Almuñecar*	
	⚓ *Ensenada de Belilla*	
10M	⚓ *Ensenada de Robaina*	
	⚓ *Surgidero de Salobreña*	
	19. Puerto de Motril *(page 64)*	
	⚓ *Anchorage east of Cabo Sacratif*	
		Cabo Sacratif
	⚓ *Cala Honda*	
	⚓ *Anchorages to Castell de Ferro*	
26M	⚓ *Fondeadero de Castell de Ferro*	
	⚓ *Anchorages in La Rábita*	
		Punta Negra
	20. Puerto de Adra *(page 68)*	
	⚓ *Balerma*	
	⚓ *Punta de los Baños*	
		Punta de los Baños
12M	⚓ *Ensenada de las Entinas*	
	21. Puerto de Almerimar *(page 71)*	
14M	**22. Puerto de Roquetas del Mar** *(page 72)*	
4M	**23. Puerto de Aguadulce** *(page 74)*	
4M	**24. Puerto de Almería** *(page 75)*	
60M	⚓ *Cabo de Gata anchorages*	
		Punta del Río
		Cabo de Gata
	25. Isla de Alborán *(page 79)*	

PORTS

4. Puerto de La Atunara

36°10'·7N 05°19'·9W

A small shallow fishing harbour with no facilities whatsoever for yachts.

Lights

0008 **Dique de Abrigo head** Fl.G.8s11m5M Green tower
0008.5 **Contadique head** Fl.R.6s8m3M Red tower

www.eppa.es/en/fishing-harbour-la-atunara

Some five miles north of Europa Point there has recently been built the small fishing port of La Atunara, a Mediterranean outlet for La Línea. It is solely for the use of commercial fishermen.

Apart from a fuelling point (for fishing trawlers only) there are no other facilities at the port apart from the normal café. It is a long way from any shops and the port is only included here to inform passing craft of a possible refuge.

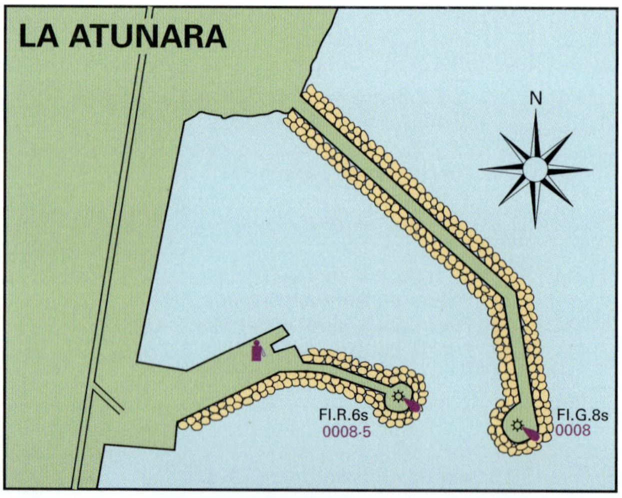

⚓ PUNTA CARBONERA

36°16'·9N 5°17'·9W

This insignificant point just south of Sotogrande is now lit with light 0012 Oc.4s39m14M from a 14m white tower.

⚓ RÍO GUADIARO

36°16'·9N 5°16'·6W

The river is permanently silted up and should not be approached as a sandbar extends some distance E and towards Sotogrande marina entrance.

5. Puerto Sotogrande

36°17'N 05°16'W

The first marina on entering the Mediterranean, 10 miles NNE of Europa Point, this large and safe marina has 1,380 moorings with facilities for yachts up to 70m.

Charts

British Admiralty *3578, 773.* Imray *M11*
French *7658.* Spanish *453*

⊕12 36°17'N 05°16'·2W

Lights

0016 **Dique Levante S head** Fl(2)G.10s8m5M Masonry tower, green top 3m
0016.2 **Dique Levante N head** Q(3)10s8m4M E card (with ◆ topmark)
0016.8 **External espigón** Fl(2)R.8s2m3M Red round pillar
0016.4 **Embarcadero Capitania** Fl(3)G.10s3m1M
0016.6 **Contradique head** Fl(3)R.15s4m1M Red post 2m

Port communications

VHF Ch 9. Port ✆ +34 956 79 00 00
Email informacion@puertosotogrande.com
www.puertosotogrande.com

Major marina village

A large marina complex easy to enter except in high winds and swell from the E. Surging problems within the marina have been resolved in recent years by the extension to the dique de Levante.

The marina has an excellent, though expensive, boatyard. This is one of the safest marinas on the coast, quiet and peaceful for most of the year. Like all other marinas, July and August are busy months with lots of sailing activities organised by the local yacht club. New facilities have now been built to house the yacht club and sailing school.

Approach

From the south Having rounded Europa Point follow the coast at 500m in a general NNE direction. Torre Nueva and Torre de Punta Carbonera may be identified. The mass of buildings at Puerto Sotogrande can be seen from afar.

From the NE Follow the coast at 500m in a general SSW direction. The harbour and breakwaters of José Banús, Estepona and La Duquesa may be seen but caution is needed as there are a number of rocky sand-retaining breakwaters which can be mistaken for harbours.

A mile N of the port are two high blocks of flats – the only ones around. Between these blocks and

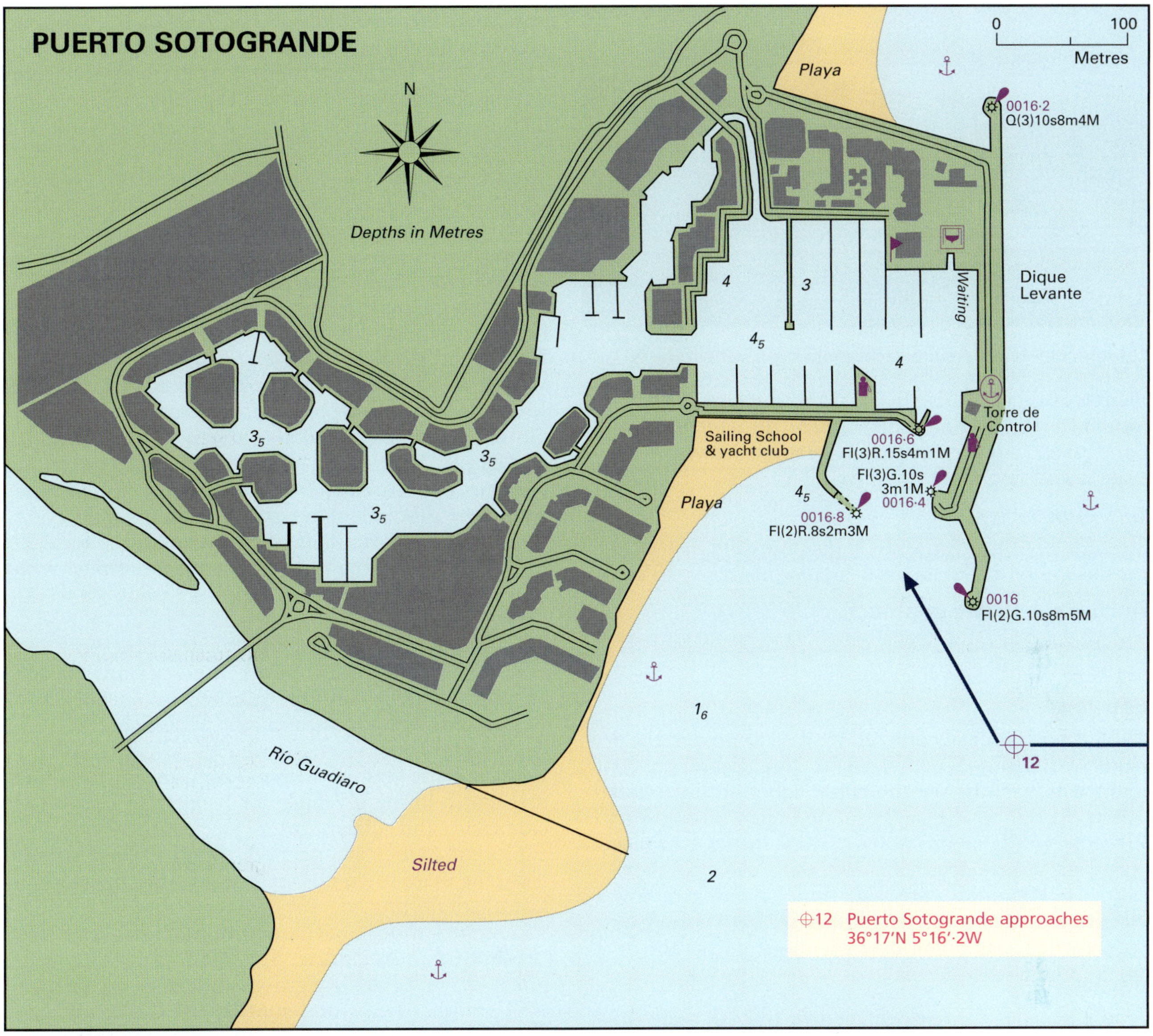

Puerto Sotogrande. A huge, well run and pleasant marina
Pública de Puertos de Andalucía

Sotogrande Marina – superyacht moorings *Graham Hutt*

Puerto Sotogrande is the bay and anchorage: Cala Sardina. The marina office *(torre de control)* is a handsome, square, castellated stone tower with cupola and flag-staff.

GPS approach

Steer for ⊕12 from an easterly quadrant and then steer for the end of the breakwater (approximately 0·12M).

Anchorage in the approach

Anchor in 3m sand 300m offshore to N or S of the harbour.

Entrance

The harbour is easily entered by day: approach the S head of the dique with around 30m clearance. At night it is hard to see the entry lights until around 100m off due to the background lights. Strong S to E sector winds create quite a swell in the entrance requiring a fast approach rounding close to the S dique to maintain steerage and avoid the tow beachward. Entry is dangerous in very strong E winds when seas break over the dique de Levante.

Berths

Secure beneath the *torre de control* and ask there for a berth which will be on one of the yacht harbour pontoons. Two bow lines may be needed.

Formalities

If entering from abroad (e.g. Gibraltar) the office in the *torre* will arrange for customs clearance, should that be required.

Facilities

Max length overall 70m, with alongside facility for up to 100m.
Water and electricity at every berth
Shower and toilet facilities with access key
Gymnasium
Chandlery
200 ton travel lift and full dockyard and storage facilities
Cover maker, manufacturer and trimmer (sail covers, spray hoods, biminis, etc).
Aqu Covers ✆ +34 637 47 33 22
Gasoleo A and petrol at the control tower.

Locally

Sotogrande marina is currently rather empty as a consequence of the deepening recession and the application of the matriculation tax. It is consequently spacious. Yacht berths are well separated and maintained. The marina is attractive and safe but lacks some basic amenities for visiting yachtsmen – like a supermarket or even a small store within the marina: all have closed in recent years. The nearest general store is a short walk to Torreguadiaro to the NE of the puerto.

Although there is no supermarket there is a post office (open 10–12a.m. Monday–Saturday), banks, excellent though generally expensive restaurants, boutiques, a gift shop and gym. All are grouped around attractive squares with orange trees and fountains. Good access to the beach. Staff are helpful and pleasant and most speak English. Poste Restante at the *torre de control*.

For more extensive shopping the well stocked Mercadona and Supercor supermercados are about 2km away opposite Pueblo Nuevo.

There is a bus stop on the main road near the marina for buses to Estepona, La Línea and Algeciras although these are infrequent, only every two hours. (Approximate times given in the local *El Periodico de Sotogrande* newspaper – along with other local information.) Taxi: ✆ +34 956 78 01 01 / 607 548550 (English spoken).

Sandy beaches extend either side of the port and are well used in summer and clean. Beach restaurants (*chironghitos*) are set up in July and August providing locally caught fresh fish.

Sotogrande is a safe marina in which to leave a yacht for any length of time. Gibraltar is close, and it is worth hiring a vehicle for local trips, or use the extensive and cheap inter-city coach service to explore the cities of Cadiz and Sevilla. These depart from the main town bus stations in Algeciras and La Línea connecting via the service mentioned under 'Communications'. Sevilla is a microcosm of all that is beautiful in Andalucia. Splendid countryside with miles and miles of olive groves and citrus orchards as well as other fruits and sunflowers. In the city are some of the most spectacular buildings in the world with the Moorish, Berber and Arab architecture, many of which are as fine today as in the 9th to 12th century when they were built.

Closer to home are the mountain top villages of Castellar and Jimena de la Frontera and Ronda, just a few miles inland. On the way is the ancient villa of the Moorish Mayor, Almoirama, which today has the original timber Mosque tower and is now a splendid hotel and conference centre. Local game is a speciality of the restaurant – partridge, pheasant, wild boar, etc.

⚓ CALA SARDINA

36°18'·5N 5°15'·3W

A pleasant anchorage 1·5M N of Sotogrande. Punta de la Chullera is a low sloping point with a conspicuous tower and a few houses amongst the trees. On the other side of the bay a square fort-like building, Casa Cuartel, is easily seen. Anchor in 3m sand and pebbles about 75m off. There is foul ground 100m off Punta de la Chullera which is sometimes called Punta Europa. The main coast road is behind the beach.

6. Puerto de la Duquesa

36°21'·3N 05°13'·7W

A small busy marina between Sotogrande and Estepona with berthing for 328 vessels up to 20m.

Charts

British Admiralty *3578, 773.* Imray *M11*
French *7658.* Spanish *453*

⊕13 36°21'·1N 05°13'·6W

Lights

0018 **Dique de Levante S head** Fl.G.7s8m5M White truncated tower green lantern and base 4m
0018.3 **Dique de Levante N head** Q(3)10s7m5M Yellow truncated tower black band 4m
0018.4 **Contradique head** Fl(2)R.7s6m3M White tower red top 4m
0018.41 **External espigón head** Fl.R.5s7m3M Metal strucure, red top 5m

Port communications

VHF Ch 9. Port ✆ +34 952 89 01 00
Email duquesa@marinasmediterraneo.com
www.marinasmediterraneo.com/duquesa.htm

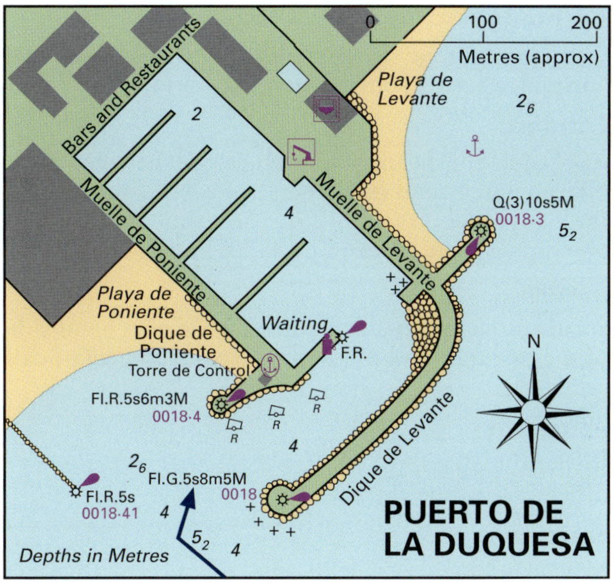

⊕13 Puerto de la Duquesa 36°21'·1N 5°13'·6W (off plan)

Small busy marina near Gibraltar

A marina surrounded by blocks of apartments and with good facilities. Approach and entrance are easy and good shelter is available inside. It is a useful first port of call after Gibraltar which is less than 20M away. Good beaches on either side of the harbour. With many restaurants in the marina, this used to be a good stop for lunch on the way to or from Gibraltar, but a charge is now made even for lunch stops.

This is a safe marina for long or short stays although subject to some surging with a W wind. The marina has a pleasant 'lived in' community feel to it.

Approach

From the south Punta de la Chullera, with a tower, has rocks extending up to 100m offshore. Castillo de la Duquesa just SSW of the harbour is conspicuous.

From the north Punta de Salto de la Mora with its old watch tower can be seen. Foul ground extends 200m off this point. The new buildings around the harbour and its breakwater are visible during the closer approach.

GPS approach

Steer for ⊕13 from an easterly quadrant and then steer for the end of the breakwater (approximately 0·13M).

Puerto de la Duquesa

Anchorage

Good anchorage is available to the NE of the harbour, about 150m offshore in 5m sand.

Entrance

Approach the head of the Dique de Levante on a NW course, round it and enter on a NE course. Give the breakwaters a 25m berth; underwater obstructions are marked by small buoys.

Berths

Secure alongside fuelling berth on the port hand side of the entrance and ask at the *torre de control* or call on Ch 9.

Formalities

If entering Spain, the *capitán de puerto* and *aduana's* offices are in the *torre de control.*

Facilities

Maximum length overall: 20–25m.
Limited workshops on E side of harbour.
75-tonne crane on NE side of harbour.
Water taps on pontoons and quays.
Showers at *torre de control.*
220V AC on pontoons and quays.
Ice on fuel quay.
Gasoleo A and petrol.
Clubhouse with pool.
Local supermarket. Other shops in Manilva village 1½M away and Las Sabinillas ½M away.
Washing machine in *torre de control.*

Communications

Bus service. Airfield at Gibraltar. ✆ Area code 952.
Taxi ✆ +34 952 80 29 00.

Duquesa looking SE *Pública de Puertos de Andalucía*

7. Puerto de Estepona

36°24'·8N 5°09'·4W

One of the oldest Spanish marinas and an ancient fishing port. There are 447 moorings up to 35m very welcoming to visitors.

Charts

British Admiralty *3578.* Imray *M11*
French *7658.* Spanish *453*

⊕15 36°24'.65N 05°09'.6W

Lights

Approach
0020 **Punta de la Doncella LtHo** Fl(1+2)15s32m18M Dark 8-sided tower, grey lantern, white house 25m
Harbour
0022 **Dique de Abrigo spike** Q(6)+LFl.15s9m5M Black tower, yellow top 6m
0022.2 **Dique de Abrigo head** 36°24'.8N 5°09'.4W Fl.G.5s9m5M Green pole 7m
0024 **Dique de Poniente** Fl(2)R.7s9m3M Truncated tower 4m
21010(S) **Buoy** 36°25'.2N 5°08'.4W Q(6)+LFl.15s6m2M ↧ card S

Port communication

VHF Ch 9. Capitanía de Marina ✆ +34 952 80 18 00
Email estepona@eppa.es
Club Náutico de Estepona ✆ */Fax* +34 952 80 09 54
Email cnestepona@teleline.es
www.marinasmediterraneo.com/workspaces/estepona

Harbour and tourist resort

A town of Roman origin developed from a fishing village into a close-packed tourist resort with restaurants, shops and a supermarket. There is an early morning fishmarket at the harbour. Local holidays are from 24–29 June.

This marina is part of the group 'Groupas Marinas Mediterraneo' which also own Duqesa, Benelmadena and Marina del Este.

A small number of berths are operated by the local Club Nautico. These are usually occupied.

Approach

The harbour is backed by four tower blocks of flats. The dark octagonal lighthouse 31m high capped by a grey lantern is to the NE of the harbour entrance. The outer breakwater (Dique de Abrigo) has been extended westwards leaving the old entrance tower in its original position.

GPS approach

Steer for ⊕15 from a SE quadrant and then make for the breakwater head (approximately 0·1M).

Anchorage in the approach

Anchor 200m to the NE of head Dique de Abrigo in 5·5m sand.

Entrance

Approach the head of Dique de Abrigo on a N course, round it at 20m and enter on a NE course.

In a SW gale the entrance could be dangerous. The breakwaters have underwater projections. Dredgers may be in operation as this harbour's mouth frequently silts up. Most harbours along this

Estepona from the south *Pública de Puertos de Andalucía*

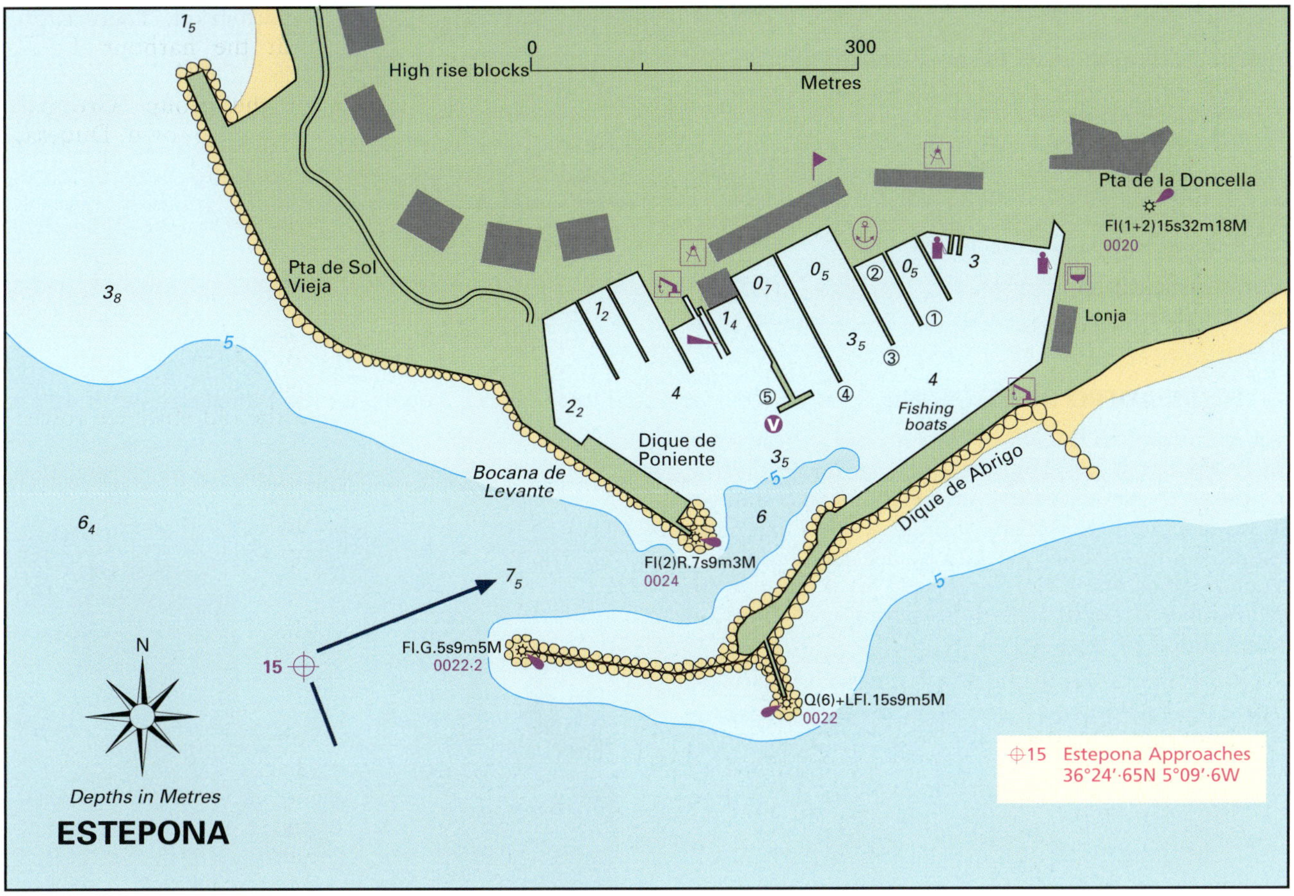

coast have reported severe reduction in entrance depths in spring due to winter storms.

Berths

Secure to the Muelle de Espera, which is at the end of Pantalan 5, and ask at the *capitanía* which is in a blue building, like a towered wedding cake with white icing, on the north side of the harbour. The *pantalanes* have lockable gates at their shore ends.

Harbour charges

Medium to high.

Facilities

Maximum length overall: 30m.
Repairs (most services) at a shipyard to NE of the harbour.
Sailmaker under the club nautico is Magnusson Sails (Antonio Rodriguez Carrasco) ✆ +34 952 79 12 41 (the only sailmaker on the west of Costa del Sol. Excellent work has been reported and English is spoken).
80-tonne travel-lift and 3·5-tonne mobile crane.
Yachts up to 25-tonnes may be hauled out on the slipway immediately SW of the *club náutico*.
Hardstandings.
Chandlery in harbour.
Life-raft servicing.
Water taps on quays and pontoons.
Butane: the Marina can arrange refills for 10lb Calor bottles.
220V AC on the Dique de Poniente and pontoons, 380V on berths 20–35m.
Ice from the fish auction building or waiting quay.
Gasoleo A and petrol.
Club Náutico de Estepona has showers, a restaurant and bar and is usually open to non-members.
Provisions from shops in the town about 1M away and from supermarket on N side of the harbour and one nearby, across the main road.
Laundry in port, launderettes in the town.
To the N of the marina Estepona has a huge 'Poligono Industrial' within which are units capable of undertaking almost any type of mechanical, carpentry or electrical repairs or manufacturing.

Communications

Bus services. ✆ Area code: 952 Taxi ✆ +34 952 80 29 00

⚓ FONDEADERO DE ESTEPONA

An anchorage to the NE of the harbour off the town of Estepona, 500m from the shore in 5m sand. To E of the harbour where five breakwaters were built is a submerged breakwater parallel to the coast and about 400m offshore marked by a S card buoy. The anchorage is somewhat protected by Punta de los Marmoles, a small cliffed headland with a tower surrounded by trees.

Note Further East, anchoring is forbidden between Torre del Padrón and Punta de Guadalmaza because of submarine cables.

8. Puerto José Banús

36°29'N 04°57'·2W

A truly excellent high class marina with facilities for over 900 yachts up to 50m. Absolutely humming in the summer evenings and catering for the rich and famous with their super-yachts. Very expensive!

Charts

British Admiralty *3578, 773.* Imray *M11*
French *7658.* Spanish *454*

⊕16 36°28'·9N 05°57'·4W

Lights

0031 **Dique de Benabolá W head** Fl(3)R.10s7m3M
Truncated masonry tower red lantern 4m
0031.1 **E Head** Q(4)R.10s1M Red post
0032 **Dique de Levante W head** 36°29'.1N 04°57'.2W
Fl(3)G.12s13m5M Truncated masonry tower green lantern 9m
0032.2 **E head** Q(6)+LFl.15s10m3M ⯆ on black post 6m

Port communications

VHF Ch 9. *Capitanía* ✆ +34 952 90 98 00
Email torrecontrol@puertobanus.com
www.puertojosebanus.es
Club de Mar José Banús ✆ +34 952 81 77 50
Email info@puertojosebanus.es
www.puertojosebanus.es/club/ing/presentacion.htm

Upmarket marina

An up-market marina handling large and very large yachts, motor and sail, and correspondingly pricey. The enclave also contains apartments, shops boutiques, restaurants, night clubs, casinos and so forth, patrolled by armed security guards and protected from the outside world by automated barriers allowing the passage of selected vehicles. It has good repair facilities.

There is a hotel beach and swimming pool to W of the harbour which is available to yachting visitors. Entrance tickets from third floor office of the tower. It is worth escaping to Ronda by taxi.

Approach

The lone rocky-peaked mountain Pico de la Concha in the Sierra Blanca, called Sierra de Marbella on British charts, can be seen from afar. Closer in, some yellow tower blocks 2M to W and the very large Hotel Nueva Andalucía, the bull ring close E and a

José Banús *Capitania* and light

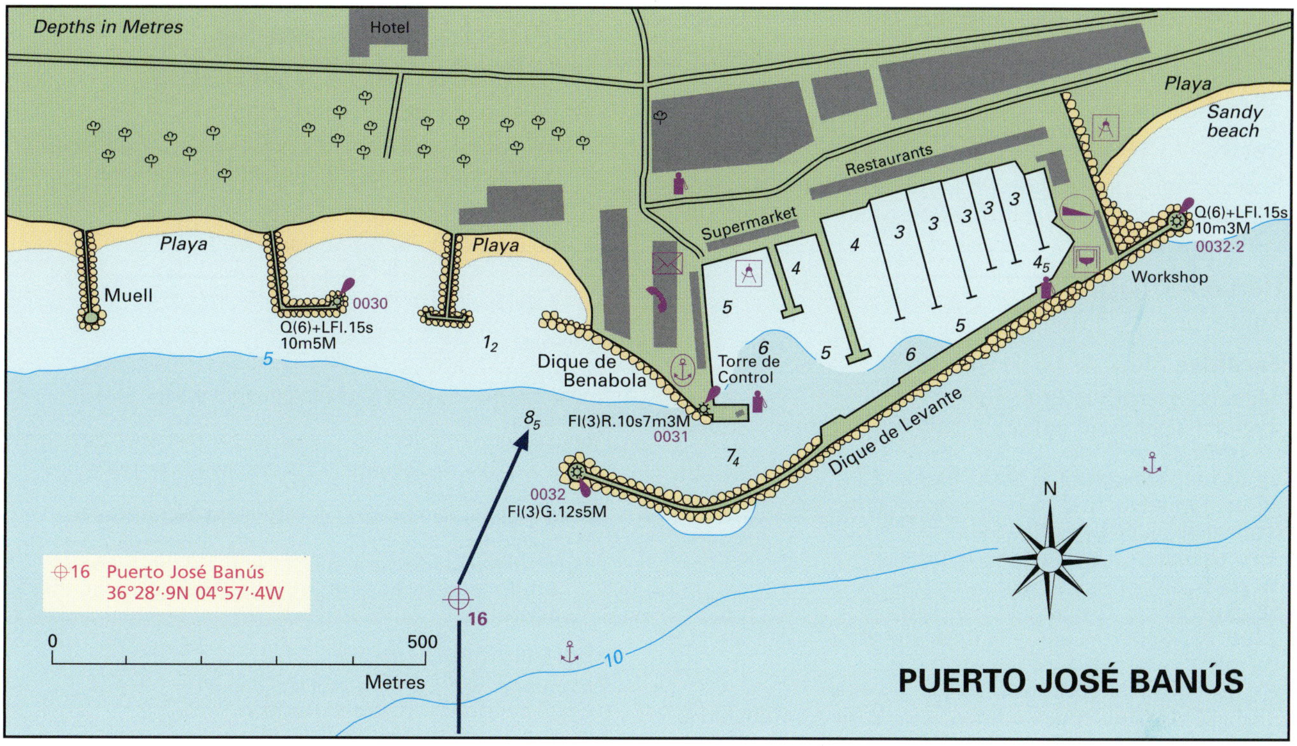

white flag-poled terrace are conspicuous. The old stone tower with a number of windows at the entrance and the mass of buildings around the harbour are also conspicuous.

GPS approach

Steer to ⊕16 from southerly quadrant and steer for breakwater end (approximately 0·08M).

Anchorage in the approach

200m S of S head of Dique de Levante in 8m sand.

Entrance

Approach the S head of Dique de Levante on a N course, leave it 50m to starboard and enter on an E course.

Puerto José Banús *Pública de Puertos de Andalucía*

In a SW gale, the entrance could be difficult except for powerful vessels as it involves turning sharply across the waves in a restricted area of disturbed water.

Berths

Secure alongside E side of Dique de Benabolá near the fuel station for the allocation of a berth from the control tower.

Harbour charges

High.

Facilities

Maximum length overall: 80m.
Two travel-lifts, 50 and 25 tonnes and a 5-tonne mobile crane.
Launching slipway at E of the harbour.
Most shipwright and electronic work possible.
Sailmaker on N side of harbour.
Two chandlers beside the harbour.
Water points on quays and pontoons.
Showers by the tower.
220V AC to berths and 380V AC to berths over 15m.
Petrol.
Ice from fuelling point or slipway.
Yacht Club: Club Náutico Internacional Nueva Andalucia.
Supermarket at the harbour but fresh food has to be obtained from Marbella, 15 minutes away by bus or taxi, or from San Pedro.
Laundry in port and launderette behind the house on Dique de Riberea.

Locally

This is an excellent night spot with bars, clubs and restaurants as well as a nearby supermarket.

As with Marbella, this is a good place from which to visit Ronda; a mountain village built by the Moors in the 10th century. It has one of the most spectacular bridges in Spain, connecting two sides of a ravine. The scenery on the journey is spectacular. A train also goes daily to Ronda from Algeciras, stopping also at the nearby Estacion San Roque. Worth the trip even just for the scenery *en route*.

Communications

Bus service. ✆ Area code 952. Taxi ✆ +34 952 78 38 39.

Ronda bridge over the ravine. Typical superb Arab architecture built to last. Standing and in use for over a millennium
Graham Hutt

9. Puerto de Marbella (Marbella Yacht Harbour)

36°30'·3N 04°53'·4W

A busy marina, especially in summer with 377 moorings up to 20m. Prone to silting but regularly dredged.

Charts

British Admiralty *3578, 773.* Imray *M11*
French *7658.* Spanish *454*

⊕17 36°30'·25N 04°53'·55W

Lights

Approach
0056 **Marbella LtHo** Fl(2)14·5s35m22M White round tower 29m
Marina
0056·2 **Dique de Levante** Fl(2)G.7m4M White tower, green top 4m
0056·6 **Dique de Poniente** Fl.R.4s6m2M Red pyramidal tower 4m
Note There may be several fish farms off this harbour which normally have four buoys, Fl.Y.5s marking their extent

Port communications

Capatania VHF Ch 9 ✆ +34 952 77 55 24
Email puertodeportivo@marbella.es
www.marbella.es/puertodeportivo

The marina

Opened 35 years ago, Marbella Yacht Harbour is another older facility. Approach and entry are easy although a swell builds in the entrance with SW winds, making entry dangerous in strong winds. Depths are not more than 3m in the marina.

Visitors are berthed on the N side of the dique after checking in at the fuel jetty / small boatyard.

The entrance is prone to silting and regularly dredged.

The harbour is noisy at night during the high season and during the day the long sandy beaches on either side of the harbour are often crowded.

The local holidays are 10–18 June, Ferias de San Bernabé. 18–24 August, Semana del Sol. 18 October, San Pedro de Alcantara.

Approach

The mass of skyscraper apartments and hotels along the seafront and the high Sierra Blanca mountain range behind make the whereabouts of the marina easy to locate. The marina itself is immediately S of Marbella light; in day time the lighthouse is difficult to spot as it is the middle of a group of high-rise buildings. Do not be confused by a number of rocky jetties between the marina and the fishing harbour, built as breakwaters to retain sand for bathing beaches, and look out for a fishing platform at 36°30'·0N 04°52'·4W, about half a mile off the fishing harbour. The marina breakwater has been heightened to give extra protection within.

GPS approach

Steer to ⊕17 from southerly quadrant and steer for breakwater end (approximately 0·04M).

Marbella Yacht harbour *Pública de Puertos de Andalucía*

Anchorage in the approach

Anchor in 5m sand anywhere 200m to SW of the entrance to the yacht harbour.

Entrance

Give the jetty heads a good berth as they are not vertical at the foot. Line of small red can buoys on the north side of the entrance and a wreck on the south side, leave to port and starboard respectively.

Berths

Secure to the fuelling station on the port side of the entrance and ask at the *capitanía*, behind the fuel station.

Facilities

Maximum length overall: 15–20m.

A fork-lift type hoist on a tractor, rated at 16 tonnes.

A small slipway in NE corner of the harbour and a slipway on the W side of the harbour.

Small hardstanding.

Chandlery shop in the town.

Water from *club marítimo* and on pontoons and quays.

125V, 220V AC on quayside and pontoons and 380V on berths of 20m.

Gasoleo A and petrol.

Ice from factory 100m NE of the *club marítimo*.

Club Marítimo de Marbella is really a high quality hotel and restaurant with showers and other services in the basement.

There is a market about 1M to N of the *club marítimo*. Buy food from shops in back streets, they have better quality provisions and are cheaper.

Several launderettes in town.

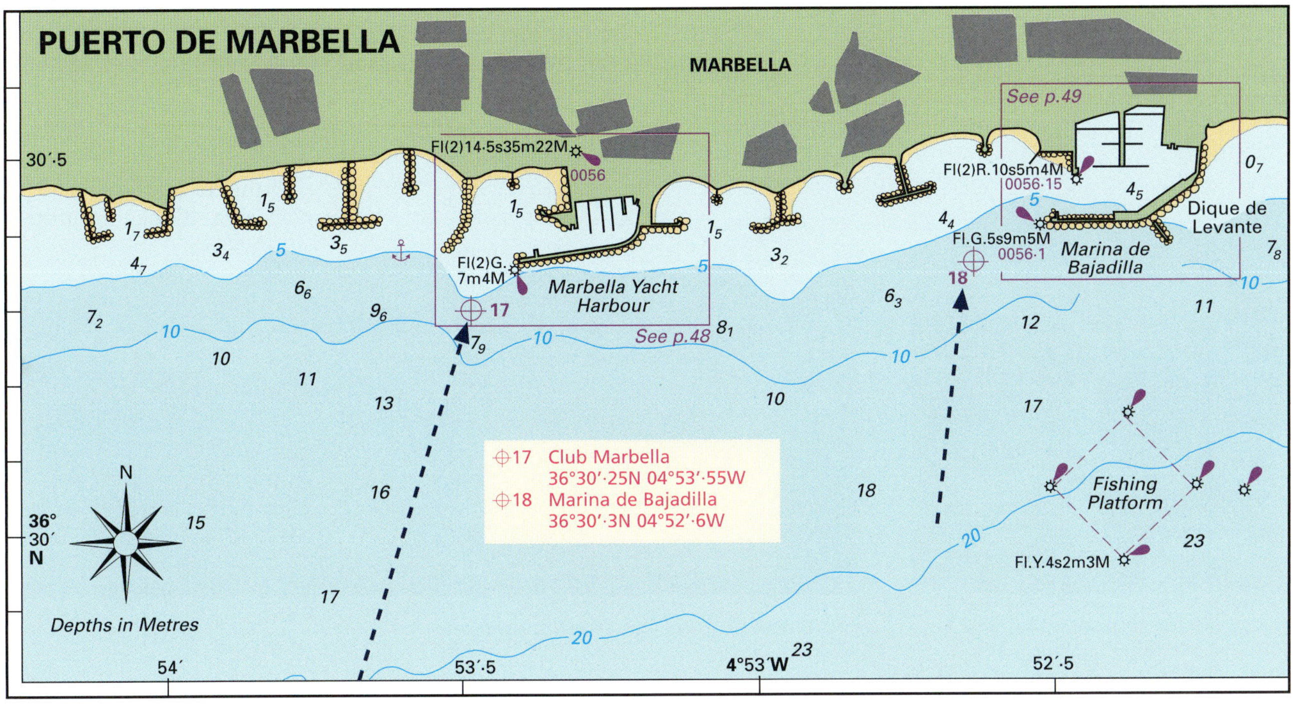

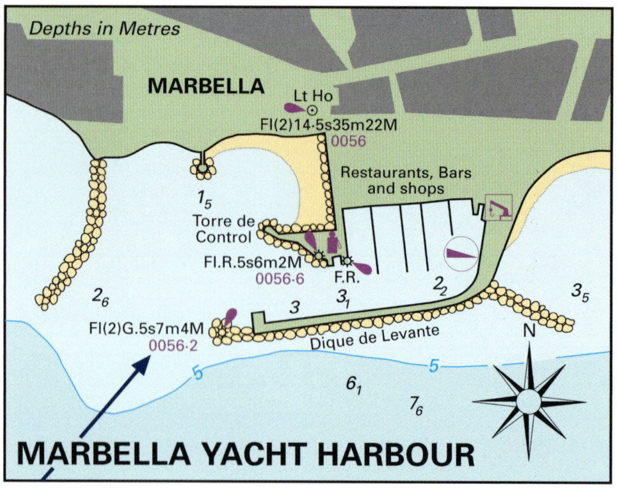

General

Despite the recession (late 2013) the town, which extends to the marina, is busy and bustling, frequented by celebrities from across the world. In summer, sounds of the marina surroundings – bars, restaurants and street entertainers – fill the air. It gives a good atmosphere for those loving the nightlife. However, the atmosphere disguises the fact that Marbella has suffered badly from the recession, being one of the first to be affected by the downturn in residential tourism as so many expatriates have returned to their home countries. The demise of Marbella is partly due to the scandals surrounding a former corrupt Mayor who spent millions of public money to boost the personal assets of his family and friends. Many of the town's businessmen, lawyers, bankers and politicians were involved and trials continue 10 years on. But the marina is one of the best and busiest on the *costa*, fun at night and inexpensive.

Communications

Bus service along the coast. ☏ Area code 952.
Taxi ☏ +34 952 77 44 88.

10. Marina de Bajadilla

36°30'·4N 04°52'·5W

Formerly a busy fishing harbour, this is now a quiet and friendly marina with 250 moorings up to 15m, very welcoming to visitors. Negotiations are ongoing for a massive extension funded by the ruling family of Qatar.

Lights

0056.1 **Dique de Levante head** 36°30'·4N 04°52'·5W Fl.G.5s9m5M White tower, green top 4m
0056.15 **Dique de Poniente head** Fl(2)R.10s5m4M Grey tower, red top 3m

⊕18 36°30'·3N 4°52'·6W

Port Communications

VHF Ch 9. *Capitanía* ☏ +34 952 867266
Email marbellad@eppa.es
www.eppa.es/en/marina-la-bajadilla

Fishing harbour turned marina

This used to be the fishing harbour where yachts were definitely not welcome but recently it has been developed into a 260-berth marina with all the usual facilities. The entrance is quite straightforward but the harbour is subjected to swell from W and SW.

GPS approach

Steer to ⊕18 from southerly quadrant and steer for breakwater end (approximately 0·07M).

Approach

Marbella with its line of high-rise buildings can be seen from afar but the tall (35m) Marbella lighthouse is difficult to spot amongst them. Close the coast aiming at the east end of the high-rise buildings until the breakwater and/or the lighthouse can be identified. The marina is just over half a mile east of the lighthouse. 50m E of the marina is a large blue glass tinted building which is more easily seen than the Marbella lighthouse.

Note: Fishing nets and hundreds of buoys are in place just outside and running parallel to the S dique at a distance of around 80m running almost the full

Marbella lighthouse: Insignificant among the taller buildings and many lights at night *Graham Hutt*

Marbella entrance. Note the lighthouse far left *Graham Hutt*

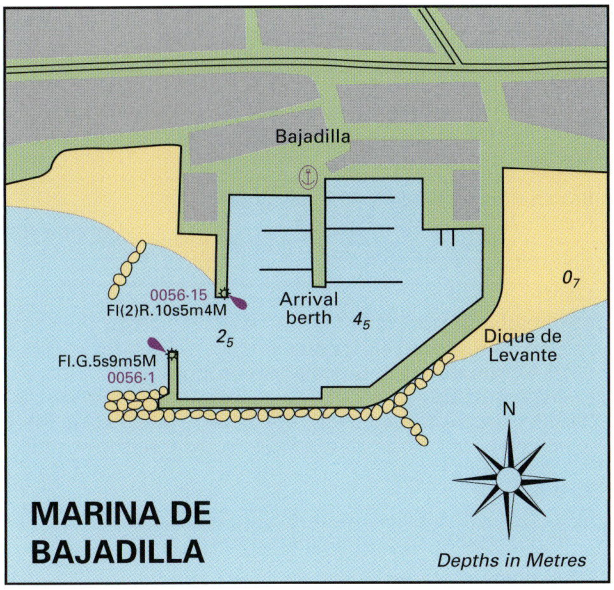

length of the dique. Entry from the E can be between the dique and the nets, though depths are unknown. The nets are clear of the entry at the W end of the marina.

Berths

Moor to the end of the main pontoon, where a sign reads '*Muelle de espera*' (waiting quay), not at the fuel berth. If you have called in on VHF Ch 9, a *marinero* will be waiting. The *capitania* is at the end of the quay in the NW corner of the harbour.

Facilities

Maximum LOA 15m.
Crane, travel-lift, hardstanding, etc.
Water and electricity on pontoons.
Showers etc at base of main pier.
Restaurant in marina.
Shops in town.

A new marina is planned for Marbella Bajadilla funded by a Qatari Sheikh Il Thani. This will become a major port, marina and ferry terminal in the coming years if it goes ahead.

Marina de Bajadilla. Note the tinted blue building behind marina *Pública de Puertos de Andalucía*

11. Puerto Cabo Pino

36°29'N 04°44'·4W

A small harbour closed for some years due to silting. Only shallow draft motor boats can enter.

Charts

British Admiralty *3578, 773.* Imray *M11*
French *7658.* Spanish *454*

⊕19 36°28'·8N 04°44'·5W

Lights

Note 3F.R vertical means port closed.
To the east
0058 **Punta de Calaburras** Fl.5s46m18M Truncated conical tower 25m

Port communications

VHF Ch 9. Port manager ✆ +34 952 83 19 75
Email marinacabopino@terra.es

Small private harbour (Closed)

This harbour has been closed for some years because of an inability to prevent frequent silting in the entrance. It remained closed in summer 2013 and is not expected to open any time soon. Only small local motor boats have access. Three vertical lights at night and shapes by day indicate that the port is closed. However, I have come across a cruiser with a lifting keel, *Southerly*, who called ahead by phone and was allowed in. His comments were that the staff are very friendly and welcoming. He confirmed the lack of depth.

An attractive small private harbour with houses built in the local style; it is one of the less oppressive in terms of not being surrounded by high rise buildings and boutiques. The approach and entrance may be problematic – see below – but there is good protection once inside. Facilities are good and there are beaches on either side of the harbour.

Approach and entrance

Do not approach the marina – for information only

Cabo Pino lies 8M to the E of Marbella and 4M to WSW of Punta Calaburras lighthouse, both of which are easily recognised. The high white apartment blocks and harbour breakwater can be seen from afar. The partly ruined square, Torre de Cala Honda, located just to W of the harbour will be seen closer in.

The approach and entrance silt. Enter on the flood, sounding, and pass the Dique de Levante at about one third the distance between it and the Espigón Antiarena; sand builds up off the head of the Dique de Levante. Care is particularly necessary in strong SW–W winds or swell which may effectively reduce depths. If in doubt, call the marina and inquire about depths.

GPS approach

Steer to ⊕19 from southerly quadrant and steer for breakwater end (approximately 0·14M).

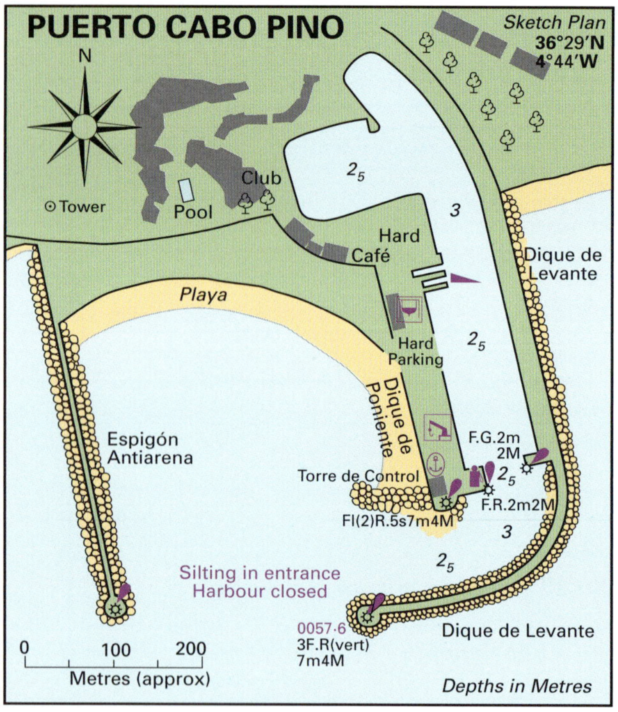

⊕19 Puerto Cabo Pino approaches
36°28′·8N 04°44′·5W (off plan)

Anchorages

The sea floor near the harbour is mainly stony with poor holding, particularly on the E side, though some sandy patches may be found.

In the approach

Cala Moral 36°29′·8N 04°40′·7W 2M to ENE has a sandy bottom. Anchor between Torre Pesetas on Punta de la Torre Nueva and Torre de Cala Moral 200m from the shore in 3m sand.

Berths

Secure to the fuel berth which is just inside the harbour to port and near the F.R light and ask at the *torre de control* for berthing instructions.

Harbour charges

High.

Facilities

Maximum length overall: 16m (Four berths only).
Small yard which can pressure clean and apply anti foul.
8-tonne crane and 26-tonne travel-lift.
Slipway on W side of the harbour.
Engine mechanics.
Water points on all quays.
Showers at *torre de control.*
220V AC points on all quays. Some at 380V by the larger berths.
Gasoleo A and petrol.
Ice from the bars or from fuel quay.
Supermarket behind the harbour.
Launderettes near harbour.

Communications

Bus along the coast. ✆ Area code 952.
Taxi ✆ +34 952 77 44 88.

12. Puerto de Fuengirola

36°32′·5N 04°36′·9W

A small friendly harbour with close access to shops, bars and restaurants, with 226 moorings up to 20m.

Charts

British Admiralty *3578, 773.* Imray *M11*
French *7658.* Spanish *455, 454*

⊕21 36°32′.6N 04 36°65′W

Lights

0059 **Dique de Abrigo** 36°32′·6N 04°36′·8W Fl(3)R.10m5M Red metal pyramidal tower 4m
0059.4 **Contradique** Fl.G.6m3M Green truncated pyramidal tower 4m
0058.5 **Espigón S head** 36°32′·8N 04°36′·7W Fl(3)G.5m3M Green tower 4m (on submerged groyne to the north of entrance)
To the west
0058 **Punta de Calaburras** 36°30′·5N 04°38′·3W Fl.5s46m18M Truncated conical tower 25m

Port communications

VHF Ch 9. Port ✆ +34 952 46 80 00
Email puertofuengirola@gmail.com
www.marinasdeandalucia.com

Harbour with good shelter and facilities

Planned as a harbour in two parts, only the western side has been built. It has good shelter and facilities. All necessary provisions may be bought from large modern tourist town nearby. Usually the approach and entrance are easy but could be difficult with strong NE–E winds and/or swell. In these conditions parts of the harbour are uncomfortable.

The town is very busy and noisy in the season. There are good beaches each side of the port but they are crowded in summer. Local holidays: three days in August and 7–10 October for their Patron Saint.

Approach

From the SW The low headland of Punta Calaburras with its conspicuous lighthouse and a mast 6·2M to N, is about 2M SW of Fuengirola. An old castle on a small hill lies halfway between this point and the harbour. The town of Fuengirola with its high-rise hotels and apartments is easily seen.

Punta de Calaburras

From the NE The massive high-rise tourist development around Torremolinos continues with minor interruptions along the coast as far as Fuengirola after which it peters out.

The four minarets in the marina are no longer conspicuous, having lost the tinted roof cappings. Only the framework remains.

With strong E and NE winds it is advisable to enter close to HW, rounding the dique with speed enough to maintain steerage to counter the surging currents towards the beach near the entrance. Once inside, there are no problems. The extra half metre of depth at HW seems to make quite a difference in this marina when entering in adverse conditions.

GPS approach

Steer to ⊕21 from easterly quadrant and steer for breakwater end (approximately 0·13M).

Anchorage in the approach

Anchor 200m to N of the head of the breakwater in 3m sand. An alternative deeper anchorage lies 500m to SE of the harbour in 15m sand.

Entrance

Approach the head of the Dique de Abrigo on a NW course and round it. A shallow area has developed on the starboard side of the entrance; keep in mid-channel.

Berths

Pick up a mooring line and go bows- or stern-to one of the new concrete pontoons and check with the office near SW corner of the port.

Facilities

Maximum length overall: 20m.
Repairs – limited; there is a small yard to the SW of the harbour.
35-tonne travel-lift and 6-tonne crane.
Chandlery.
Water taps on quay and pontoons.
220V AC on pontoons and quays.

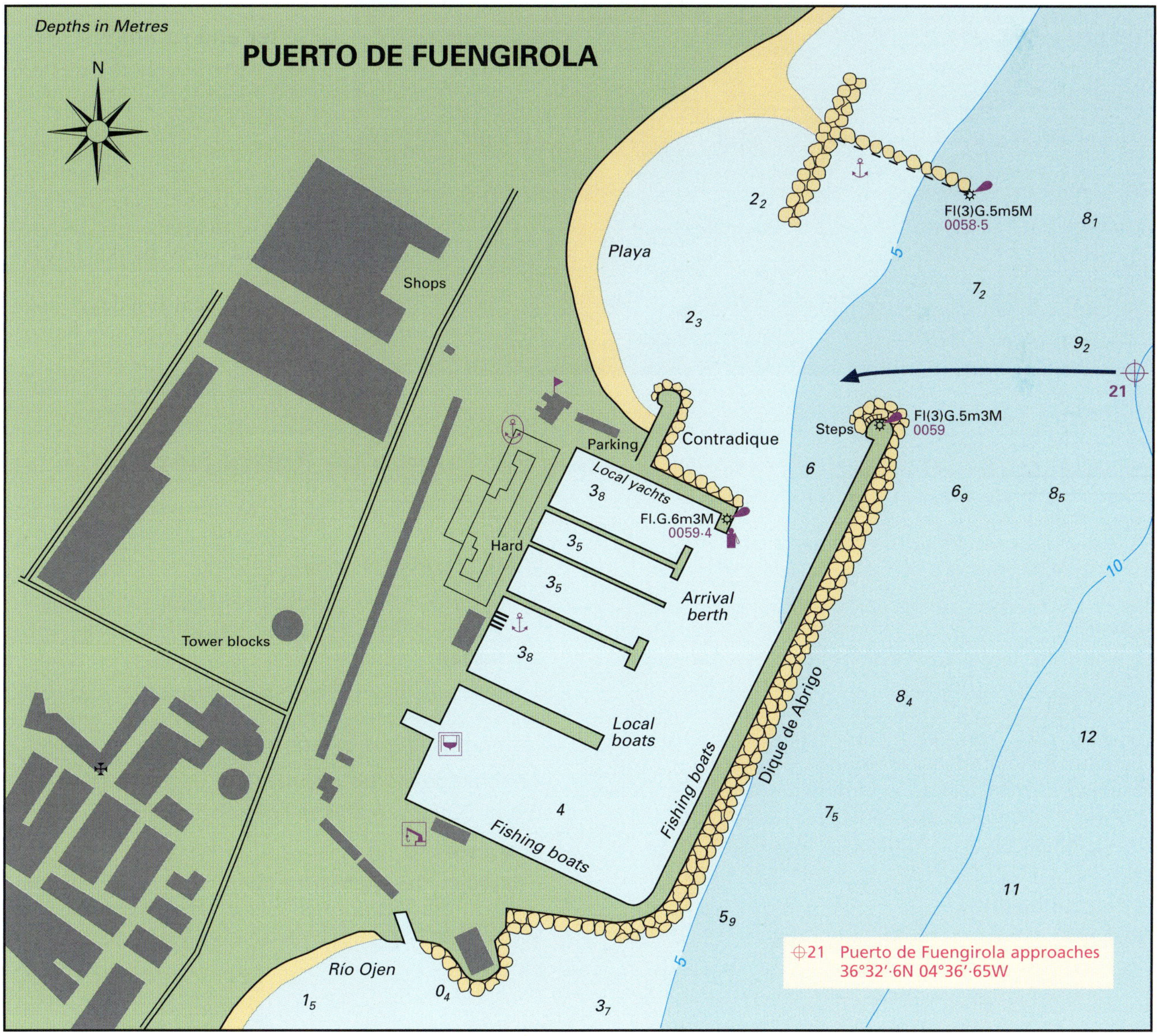

Fuengirola looking east

Fuengirola
Pública de Puertos de Andalucía

Gasoleo A and petrol.
Ice at the SW end of the harbour.
Club náutico – inquire about using its facilities.
Shop in the town for provisions.
A market near the centre of town and an open market on Tuesdays.
Launderettes in the town.

Locally

Fuengirola has many cheap touristy restaurants. Finer ones are around, but harder to find. It is a busy town and marina with many bars and restaurants within the harbour. The marina is close to Benalmádena and Torremolinos and not far from Málaga airport. There is only Benalmádena marina between Fuengirola and Málaga, so it is a good place from which to visit Málaga or Ronda. A local rail and bus service ply from the town centre to Málaga.

Communications

Rail and bus service. Airport at Málaga.
✆ Area code 952. Taxi ✆ +34 952 47 10 00.

13. Puerto de Punta Negra

36°34'·7N 04°32'·43W

Small private harbour

This very small private harbour for small yachts and runabouts is part of the casino complex.

Approach

The harbour lies 4M to NE of Fuengirola and 0·5M to SW of Puerto Principe at Torremolinos. The casino building is conspicuous.

Anchorage in the approach

Anchor 200m to S of the entrance in 7m sand.

Entrance

Approach the casino building heading NNW and identify the entrance in the centre of the harbour breakwater. Go in to either basin. Depths believed to be 2m or less

14. Puerto de Benalmádena

36°35′·7N 04°30′·7W

One of the largest marinas along the coast with a very safe – if noisy – inner complex. Over 1,100 berths available up to 30m.

Charts

British Admiralty *773*. Imray *M11*
French *7658*. Spanish *455, 455A*

⌖22 36°35′·5N 04°30′·5W

Lights

0060·3 **Laja de Bermeja** Q(3)10s7m5M ♦ E card post 7m
0060.4 **Dique Sur SW head** Fl(2)G.5s9m5M Conical masonry tower with green band 5m
0060.5 **Dique Sur NE corner** Q(3)10s9m3M ♦ Truncated conical masonry tower 5m
0060.7 **Dique Sur inner head** Fl(3)G.9s4m4M Conical tower, green band 3m
0060.6 **Dique del Oeste head** Fl(2)R.5s4m3M Truncated conical masonry, red band 3m

Port communications

VHF Ch 9. *Capitanía* ✆ +34 952 57 70 22
Email puertodeportivo@benalmadena.com
www.puertobenalmadena.es
Club Nautico Maritimo ✆ +34 952 44 42 34
Email info@cnmbenalmadena.com
www.cnmbenalmadena.com

Huge yacht harbour

This is a huge artificial yacht harbour enclosing 150,000 square metres of water located at the SW end of Torremolinos. The area near the harbour is a mass of soulless high-rise buildings but as it is very difficult to find a berth in Málaga, Benalmádena is a good alternative. Good beaches on each side of the harbour and a considerable range of tourist bars and restaurants. As in most harbours, there is also a '*Club Nautico*.' This is a private members club and more expensive than the main *Puerto Deportivo*. Plans are at an advanced stage to increase the size and capacity of this marina.

Approach

The approach requires care to avoid the shoal, Laja de Bermeja (see plan) which breaks in heavy weather. The entrance is easy and good protection is offered once inside though there is some swell in outer harbour with W gale.

From the west The prominent walls of Benalmádena can be seen when passing the large casino building and small harbour of Punta Negra. Keep over ½M off the coast to pass south of the Laja de Bermeja and make for a position where the S end of the harbour is due W.

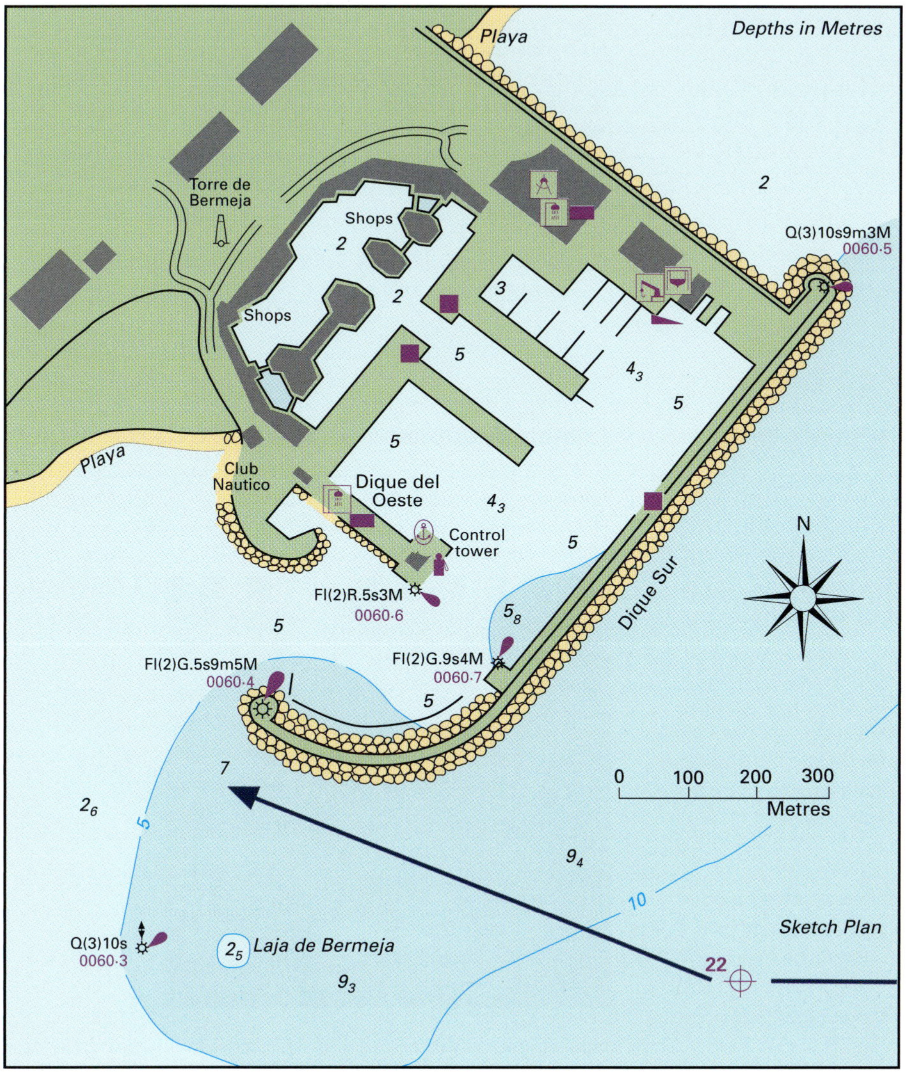

⌖22 Puerto de Benalmádena approaches
36°35′·5N 04°30′·5W

II. COSTA DEL SOL: EUROPA POINT TO PTA DEL TORROX

Benalmádena *Pública de Puertos de Andalucía*

From the east Passage is forbidden through the area of an oil terminal located 1M to S of Puerto de Málaga. This area is about ½M square and lies ¾M off the coast. From Puerto de Málaga keep ½M off coast and pass inside prohibited area. Pay attention to an exposed wreck in the area. The mass of high rise blocks of flats at Torremolinos ends shortly before Benalmádena. Keep well to the east of Laja de Bermeja.

GPS approach

Steer to ⊕22 from easterly quadrant and steer for breakwater end, leaving the Laja de Bermeja post well to port (approximately 0·3M).

Anchorage in the approach

Anchor 200m to the NE of the E end of the Dique Sur in 5m sand.

Entrance

The Laja de Bermeja (2·5m), lying some 250m S of Dique Sur head light, is the easterly outlier of a large rock strewn and shallow area to the west of the actual rock. The E cardinal post marks this large shallow area (although to the west of the actual Laja de Bermeja!)

From a position ½M out and where the S end of the harbour is due W, approach on this course leaving the Laja de Bermeja post well to port. Follow the Dique Sur to its head then round it, keeping at least 30m clear and enter on an east-northeasterly course.

Berths

Go to the fuelling point and ask at the control tower for a berth. (There may be significant swell on outer wall). It seems to be usual practice here always to be told there is no space available, and then to be offered a berth very much longer than your vessel – at a correspondingly higher price.

Facilities

Maximum length overall: 30m.
Most yacht maintenance services including sailmaker.
Slipway in the E corner of the harbour.
50-tonne travel-hoist and 5-tonne crane.
Chandleries inside and outside the port.
Water taps on all quays.
Showers.
220V AC and 380V AC on berths between 18–30m.
Gasoleo A and petrol pumps by the control tower.
Ice on fuel quay.
Supermarket in port.
Shops and supermarkets in Benalmádena Costa and Torremolinos, 1M away. Good shops and market (Friday) at Arroya del Miel 1½M inland.
Laundry collected within the port and launderettes in the town.
Diving school.

Communications

Bus and rail services to most parts of Spain, bus stop on main road near the marina. Airport at Málaga.
✆ Area code 952. Taxi ✆ +34 952 44 15 45.

Hams (*jamons*) are a speciality of Spain. Quality and price can vary from a few euros/kg to €4,000. Generally, the older and more disgusting they look, the better they taste. The more expensive ones are cured over several years *Jane Russell*

15. Puerto de Málaga

36°43'N 04°25'W

This huge commercial fishing and passenger port has a small yacht club for members but does not welcome visitors.

Tides

Time differences based on Gibraltar / *Height difference* / *Mean level*

HW	LW	MHWS	MHWN	MLWS	MLWN	Mean level
+0005	–0005	–0·3	–0·1	0·0	+0·1	0·45

⊕23 36°41'.7N 04°25'.0W

Currents

Offshore these are normally E-going but a counter-current sometimes runs off the entrance. The tidal streams up to 0·5 knots run NE and SW in the entrance.

Charts

British Admiralty *1850, 1851.* Imray *M11*
French *7658, 7294.* Spanish *455, 455A, 4551*

Lights

Approach
0062 **Málaga LtHo**
Fl(3+1)20s38m25M 243°-vis-047° White truncated conical tower on white two-storey building 37m
Harbour
0064 **Dique del Este head** Fl(2)G.7s13m3M 000°-vis-200° Conical masonry tower 4m
0064.5 **New Dique de Levante NE head** QR.1s12m3M Black tower, yellow band 2m
0065 **New Dique de Levante S head** Fl.G.5s7m5M Green tower 4m
0065.3 **Submerged breakwater head** Q(6)+LFl.15s3M ⯯ cardinal post 4m
0065.7 **Contradique E head** Fl.R.5s5M Red pyramid 5m.
0066 **Dique del Oeste head** Fl(2)R.7s13m4M 374°-vis-231° Conical masonry tower 8m
0067 **Puerto Pesquero Espigón Sur** Q.R.4m2M Conical stone tower 3m
0067.5 **Puerto Pesquero Espigón Norte** Q.G.5m2M Conical stone tower 4m
0068 **Dique Transversal del Este head** Fl(2)G.7s6m2M Conical masonry tower 5m
0070 **Muelle Transversal del Oeste head** Fl(2+1)R.12s7m2M Tower with red top 4m
0070.2 **Muelle de Romero Robledo** Fl(4)R.11s7m2M Tower with red top 5m
0069 **Small craft basin. Dique Norte** Fl(3)R.9s6m2M Red post 4m
0069.2 **Small craft basin. Dique Sur head** Fl(3)G.8s6m2M Green post 4m
0069.4 **Muelle Canovas del Castillo head** Fl(2+1)G.12s6m2M Tower with green top 4m

Port communications

Port VHF Ch 9, 11, 12, 13, 14, 16
✆ +34 952 22 85 28
www.puertomalaga.com
✆ +34 952 125000
Email sac@puertomalaga.com
Real Club Mediterraneo VHF Ch 9
✆ +34 952 226300
Email cbotes@realclubmediterraneo.com
www.realclubmediterraneo.com

Storm signals

Storm signals may be displayed at the signal station.

Málaga Port

Yachts are turned away from Málaga by the harbour authorities and sent to Benalmádena. It has been reported that this applies even in difficult conditions, as there is now, effectively, no room for pleasure craft in Málaga.

This is a port to be avoided unless prior arrangements have been made for a berth, especially now with the extensive works going on in the harbour. It is the major commercial and fishing port of the Costa del Sol, without special provision for yachts. There is very limited room at the Real Club Mediterráneo de Málaga, which is an exclusive club.

Approach by day

From the west The line of high-rise apartments and hotels at Torremolinos and Puerto de Benalmádena are conspicuous, as are the round storage tanks and the power station with two very tall chimneys 1·5M to SW of the port. Keep within ½M of the shore or more than 1½M off-shore to avoid the Passage Prohibited Area. Pay attention to the exposed wreck in the area.

From the east A grey cement factory about four miles to E of the port is identifiable and the wide flat valley between high ranges of mountains where the port and city are located can be seen from afar. Avoid the prohibited area.

GPS approach

Steer to ⊕23 from a south easterly quadrant and steer for breakwater end (approximately 0·2M).

Prohibited area

There are a number of mooring buoys and yellow lit buoys 1½M S of the port, opposite the oil terminal, about 1M offshore and surrounding an oil pipeline terminal. Passage is forbidden through these buoys. Pass inside within ½M of the shore or more than 1½M offshore.

Anchorage in the approach

Anchor to E of port with lighthouse about 300m to NW in 6m sand. Open to the S and W with swell due to large ships entering.

Entrance

Enter on a NE course between breakwater heads. Then on a N course between the inner two quays, the port hand quay being very low.

Berths

The Real Club Mediterráneo de Málaga is on the E side of Darséna de Heredia.

Larger yachts are sometimes allowed alongside the N side of the Dique Transversal del Oeste while on other occasions yachts have been directed to the NE corner of the Dársena del Guadiaro where the quay wall is high.

As stated: this is no place for visiting yachts.

Real Club Mediterráneo, Málaga *Pública de Puertos de Andalucía*

Harbour charges

Very high.

Formalities

Check with the harbour authorities on VHF Ch 9.

Facilities

Geared towards large commercial vessels. There are points for electricity and water. Cranes (no travel hoist), a slipway, ice etc. all something of a hassle to organise.

Chandleries, shops, supermarkets in town but the harbour is enclosed and only the main gate (which has to be negotiated) is open at night.

Spanish chart agency at the Comandancia de Marina near the lighthouse.

Communications

Málaga airport is halfway between Málaga and Benalmádena and has year-round international services. Ship ferry service to Tanger, Barcelona, Canary Islands, Genoa and Marseille. Rail and bus services. Railway.
☎ Area code 952.
British Consulate Málaga
Edificio Eurocom, Calle Mauricio Moro Pareto, 2-2°, 29006 Málaga ☎ +34 952 35 23 00.

The coast between Málaga and Candado

There are several bathing beaches along this stretch of the coast which are protected by breakwaters. From the sea they may appear to be harbours. They are not.

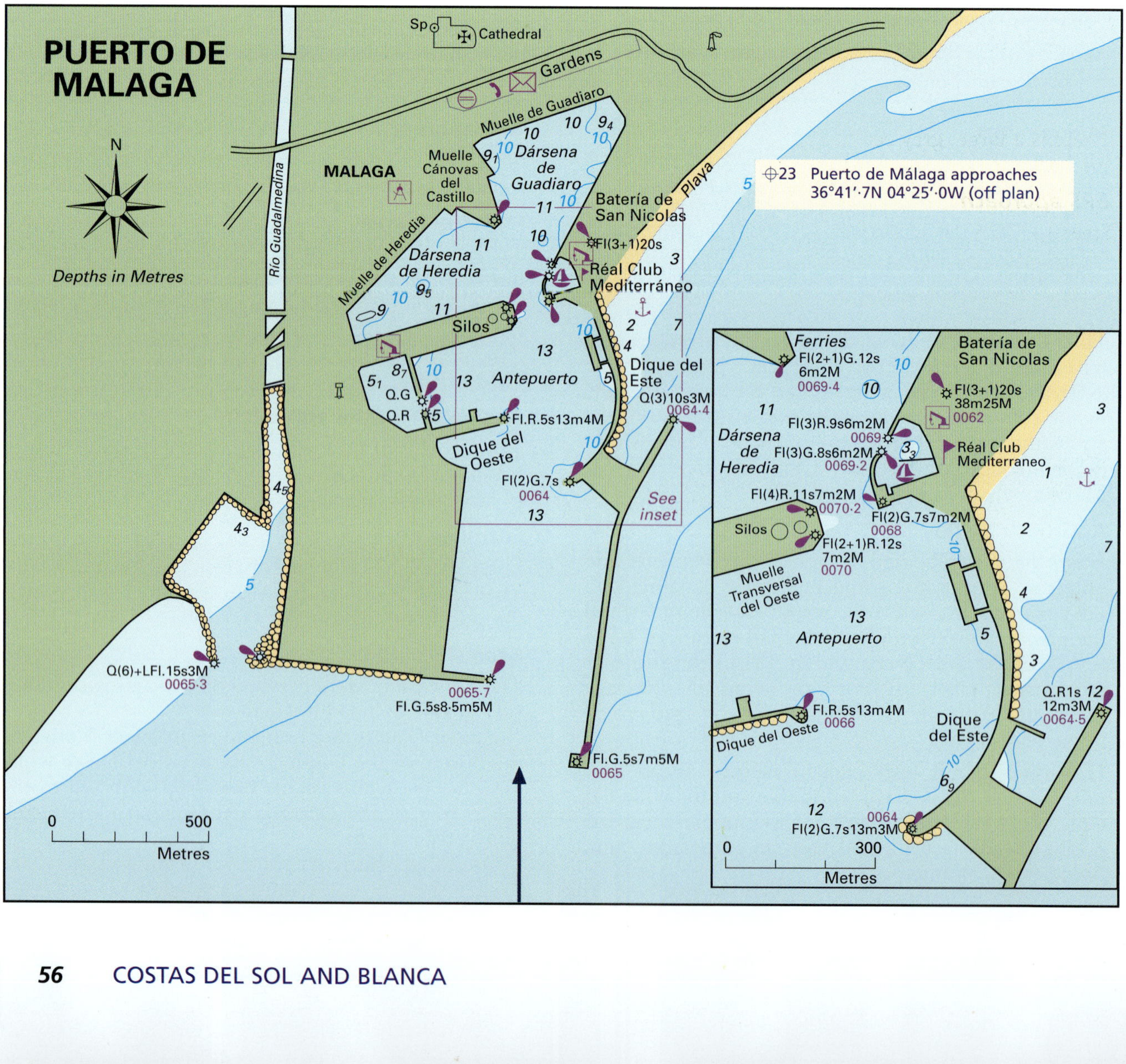

16. Puerto de El Candado

36°42'·8N 04°20'·8W

Small harbour with 280 berths up to 15m. Officially closed to visitors for some years with vertical red lights to indicate closure due to silting.

Charts

British Admiralty *773.* Imray *M11*
French *7658, 7294, 6569.* Spanish *455*

⊕25 36°42'.8N 04°20'.9W

Lights

0071 **Dique de Levante head** LFl.G.8s7m3M

Port communications

Club náutico VHF Ch 9 ☎ +34 952 296097
Email administracion@clubelcandado.com
www.clubelcandado.com

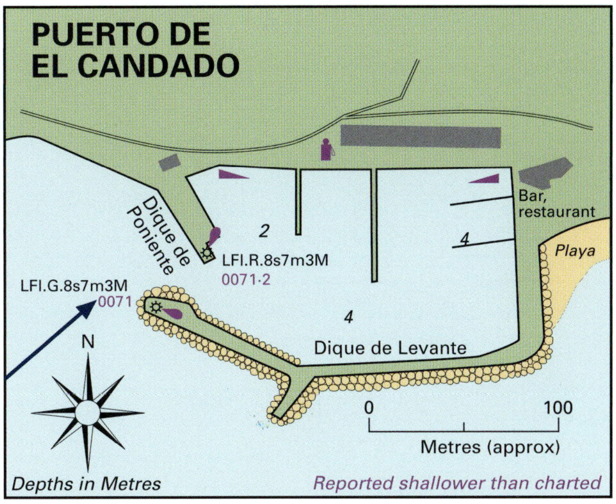

⊕24 36°41'N 04°20'·5W Puerto de el Candado (off plan)
⊕25 Puerto de el Candado approaches
36°42'·8N 04°20'·9W (off plan)

Small shallow harbour

A very small harbour, long silted up, 3·5M E of Málaga. All berths are privately owned and used by small motor boats only. Two fixed vertical lights by night and shapes by day indicate the harbour is closed.

The club appears to be thriving, however, and there are port and starboard buoys laid to lead the locals into the harbour. The depth in the entrance was stated to be 1·5m with a lot of hand-waving so it is probably less than that! This is another marina to bypass.

Approach

There is a large, grey cement factory just to the E of the harbour.

GPS approach

Steer to ⊕25 from a southerly quadrant and steer for breakwater end (approximately 0·08M).

Anchorage in the approach

Anchor 200m to SW of entrance in 10m sand.

Entrance

Approach a point 200m to NW of the entrance of the harbour, sounding continuously. Leave three small red buoys to port and four small green buoys to starboard. Leave the head of the Dique de Levante 10m to starboard.

Berths

Berth stern-to the quay or pontoon with anchor or mooring buoy from the bow.

Harbour charges

Low.

Facilities

Maximum length overall: 10m.
A hard in the corner of the harbour.
Water and Electricity (220V AC) on the pontoons and quays.
Chandlery to N of harbour.
Club náutico with bar, showers.

Communications

Bus service. ☎ Area code 952.

Puerto de El Candado
Pública de Puertos de Andalucía

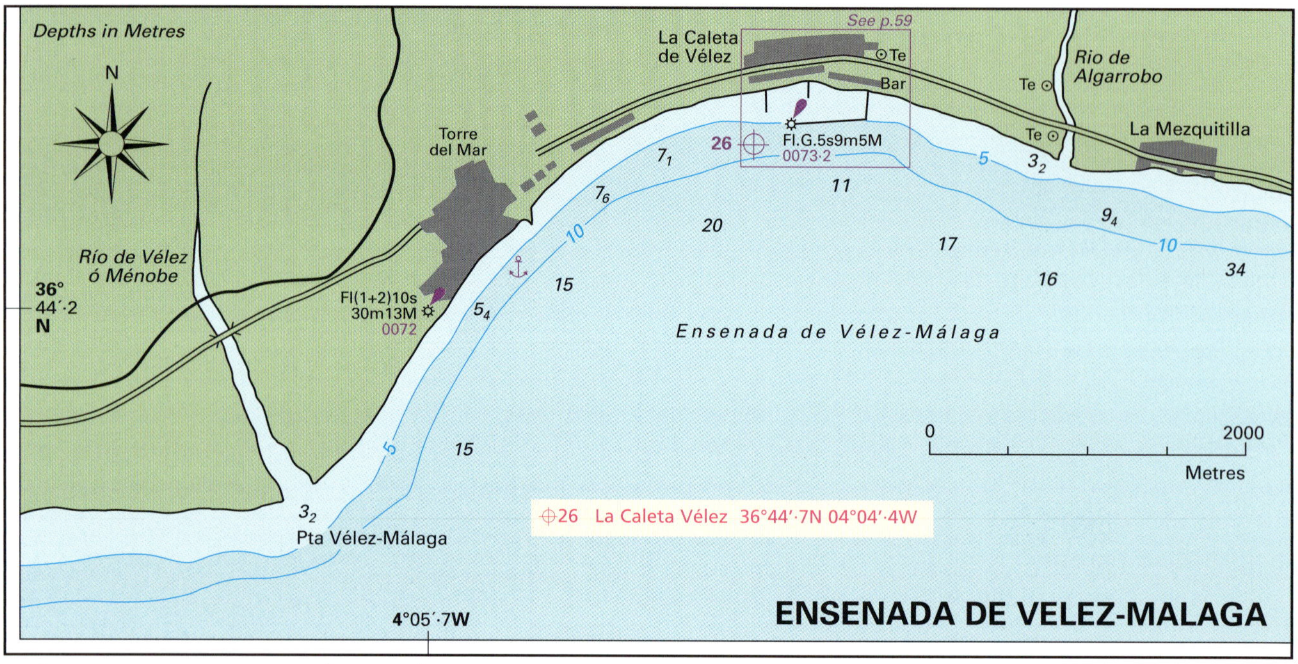

⚓ FONDEADERO DE VÉLEZ-MÁLAGA

36°44′·2N 4°05′·5W

An open anchorage off the town of Torre del Mar. Anchor in 6m sand 100m offshore, E of the lighthouse (0072 Fl(1+2)10s30m13M white tower 28m) or further NE. Everyday supplies from the town which has a *club náutico*. The new Puerto Caleta de Vélez lies 1½M to NE.

Puerto Caleta de Vélez looking NW across the marina *Graham Hutt*

Nerja caves: Of world renown, these caves are huge and truly spectacular *Graham Hutt*

17. Puerto Caleta de Vélez

36°44′·8N 04°04′W

A small quiet friendly fishing harbour run by Junta de Andalucia with 274 berths up to 20m.

Charts

British Admiralty *773*. Imray *M11*
French *6569*. Spanish *455*

⊕26 36°44′.7N 04°04′.4W

Lights

To the west

0072 **Torre del Mar (Torre de Vélez)** Fl(1+2)10s30m13M White round tower 28m

Harbour

0073.2 **Dique de Abrigo head** Fl.G.5s9m5M White and green truncated conical tower 4m

0073.3 **Breakwater Head** Fl.R.4s8m3M

0073.6 **Contradique** Fl(2)R.7s4m3M White post, red band 2m

To the east

0074 **Punta de Torrox** Fl(4)15s29m20M White tower and building 23m

Port communications

VHF Ch 9. *Capitanía* ✆ +34 951 509476 / +34 600 149214
Email caleta@eppa.es www.eppa.es
www.puertosdeandalucia.es/es/puerto-de-caleta-de-velez

Quiet fishing harbour

A quiet, in terms of it not being full of tourists, fishing harbour at the head of the Ensenada de Vélez Málaga. It is one of eleven yacht harbours run by the *Junta de Andalucía*. It is easy to approach and enter though care is necessary with heavy onshore wind and/or swell. Facilities for yachts are limited but it is a useful place to spend a day or two on passage between Málaga and Motril. Sand and pebble beaches either side of the harbour.

Approach

From the west The sandy coast from Málaga eastward is relatively featureless, lined with small

Puerto Caleta de Vélez *Pública de Puertos de Andalucía*

housing estates. Punta de Vélez Málaga, which is the delta of a river, is not prominent. Only after rounding it, will Torre del Mar light become plain among the houses and flats of the town. A factory chimney to its NE is conspicuous.

From the east Punta de Torrox is on a low, flat sandy delta which itself is not prominent. The lighthouse is conspicuous. The large block of flats at La Mezquitilla, 1M to the E of the harbour, and the road bridge over the Río del Algarrobo will also be seen. In the closer approach the harbour walls are conspicuous.

GPS approach

Steer to ⊕26 from a southerly quadrant and steer for breakwater end (approximately 0·1M).

Anchorage in the approach

Anchor 200m offshore in 5m sand either side of the harbour.

Entrance

Approach the W end of the Dique de Levante on a northerly course and round the dique noting the well marked espigon projecting a few metres N. Fishing boats exit the port at high speed and are obscured due to the high dique.

Berths

Secure stern to the quay or pontoon at the E end of the harbour. There are mooring buoys but they are private.

Harbour charges

Medium.

Facilities

Maximum length overall: 20m.
45-tonnes hoist. The whole E side of the harbour is hard.
Electricity and water on the quay.
Gasoleo A, petrol 0900–1230, 1600–2000hrs.
Supermarket 100m from the port, more in Torre del Mar and a hypermarket about 3km from the port towards Torre del Mar.

Locally

Vélez Málaga is an excellent place from which to visit Nerja and its nearby caves. The recently discovered cave complex with its huge towering stalactites and stalagmites rising several stories high became famous with evidence of occupation dating beyond neolithic times. Well worth a visit.

Communications

Bus service along the coast. ✆ Area code 951.

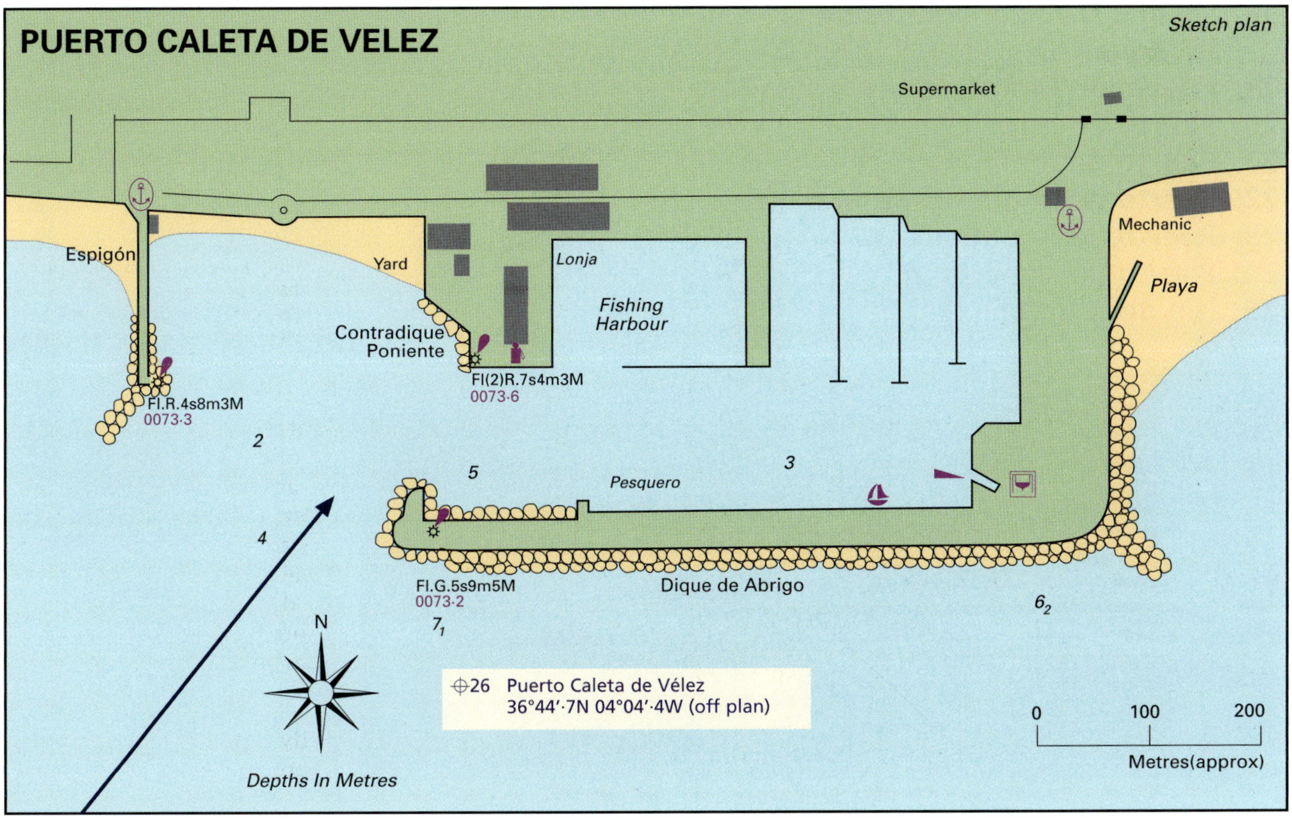

Pta del Torrox to Cabo de Gata and Isla del Alborán

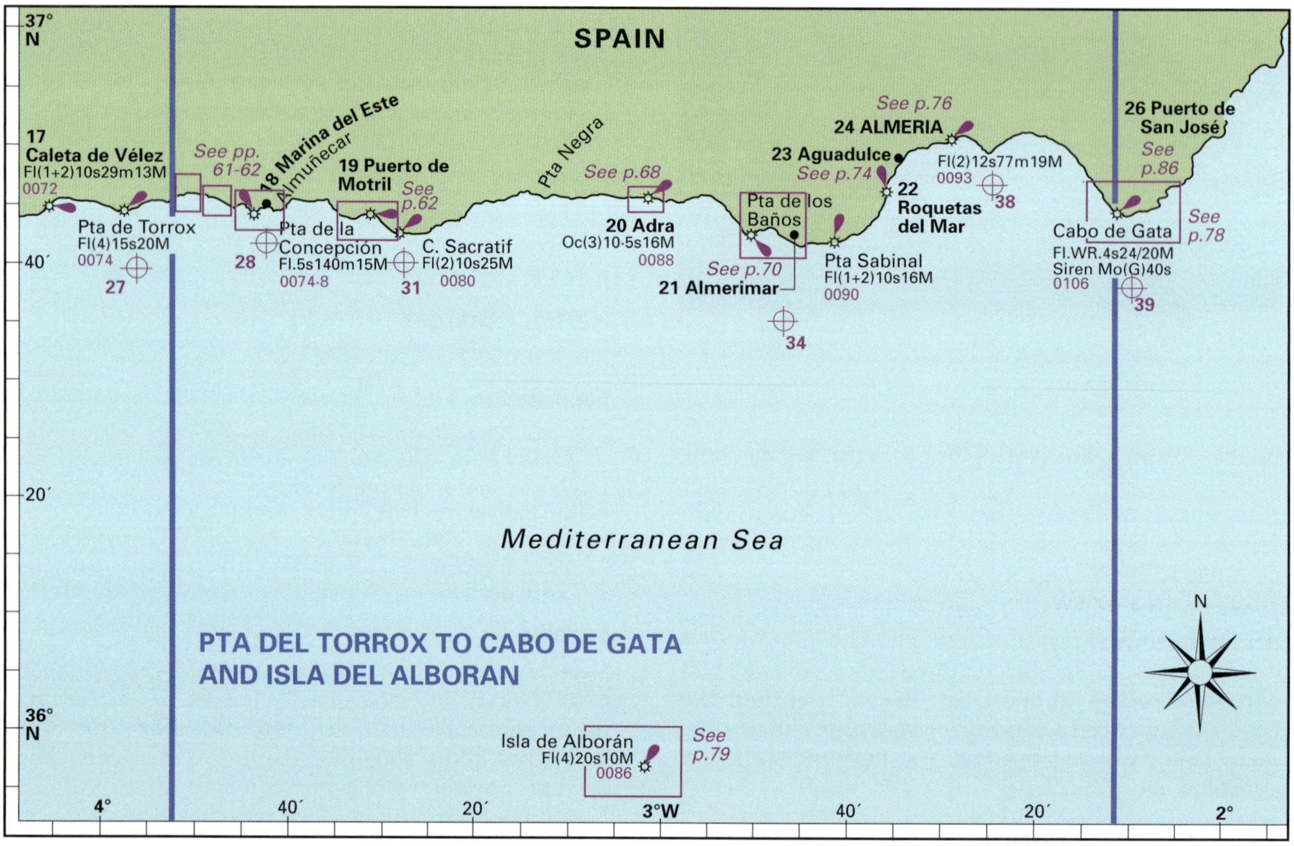

PORTS

COASTAL WAYPOINT LIST

The waypoints listed form a series with which one is able to steer from off Gibraltar to Cabo de Gata. It is essential to keep a lookout at all times while making a coastal passage in this area.

⊕27	Pta del Torrox	36°42'N	03°57'·4W
⊕28	Pta de la Concepción	36°42'·5N	03°44'W
⊕31	Cabo Sacratif	36°41'N	03°28'W
⊕34	SSE of Pta de las Entinas	36°37'·5N	02°46'W
⊕38	S of Pta del Río	36°46'·5N	02°25'·5W
⊕39	Cabo de Gata	36°41'N	02°10'W

Punta del Torrox

Anchorages between Pta del Torrox and Motril

⚓ FONDEADERO DE NERJA
35°45'N 3°51'·8W

A pleasant anchorage just E of Nerja where everyday supplies are available. Anchor 100m from the Playa de Barranja in 5m, sand, or 400m off in 18m, stones.

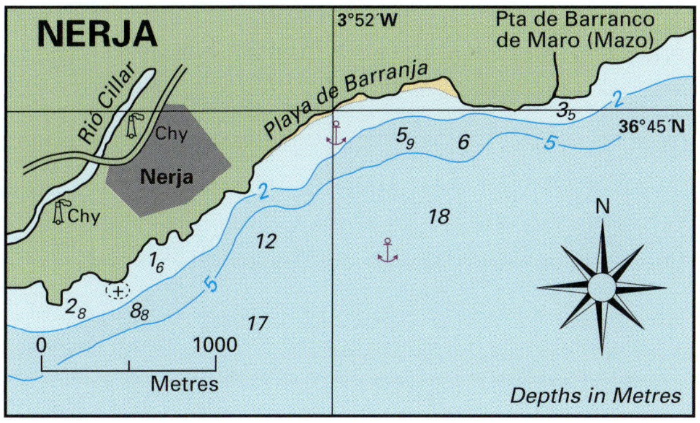

⚓ CALA DE LA MIEL
36°45'·1N 3°49'·5W

An interesting and attractive open anchorage with a stony beach and a track to the main road on the cliffs behind. Anchor in 5m sand and pebbles. Conspicuous ruined tower on cliff to W of bay with three small disused houses. There is a freshwater spring.

⚓ CALA DE LOS CAÑUELOS
36°44'·6N 3°47'·5W

Anchor in 5m sand and pebble off the centre of the shingle beach which has isolated rocks at either end of the beach. The track leads to the main road.

⚓ ENSENADA DE LA HERRADURA
36°44'N 3°44'·8W

A bay a mile wide between Puntas Cerro Gordo and de la Mona. Anchor in 5m sand 100m from the beach or 200m out in 11m mud. Additonal shelter at either end but beware rocks. Everyday supplies from the town.

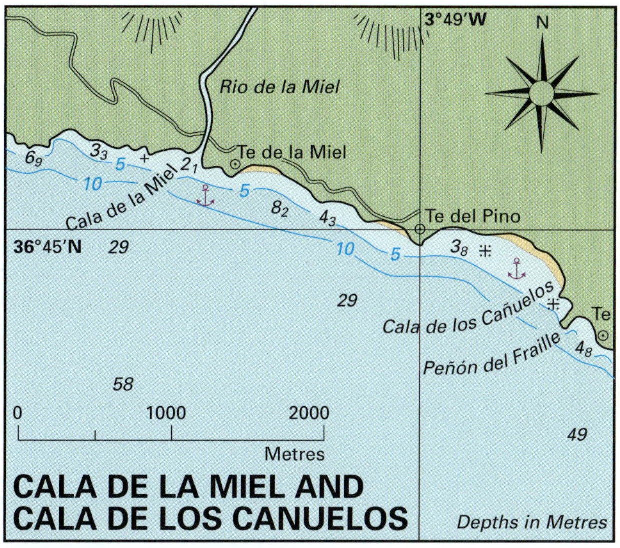

Above Cañuelos *Below* Herradura

Ensenada de la Herradura west

Ensenada de la Herradura east

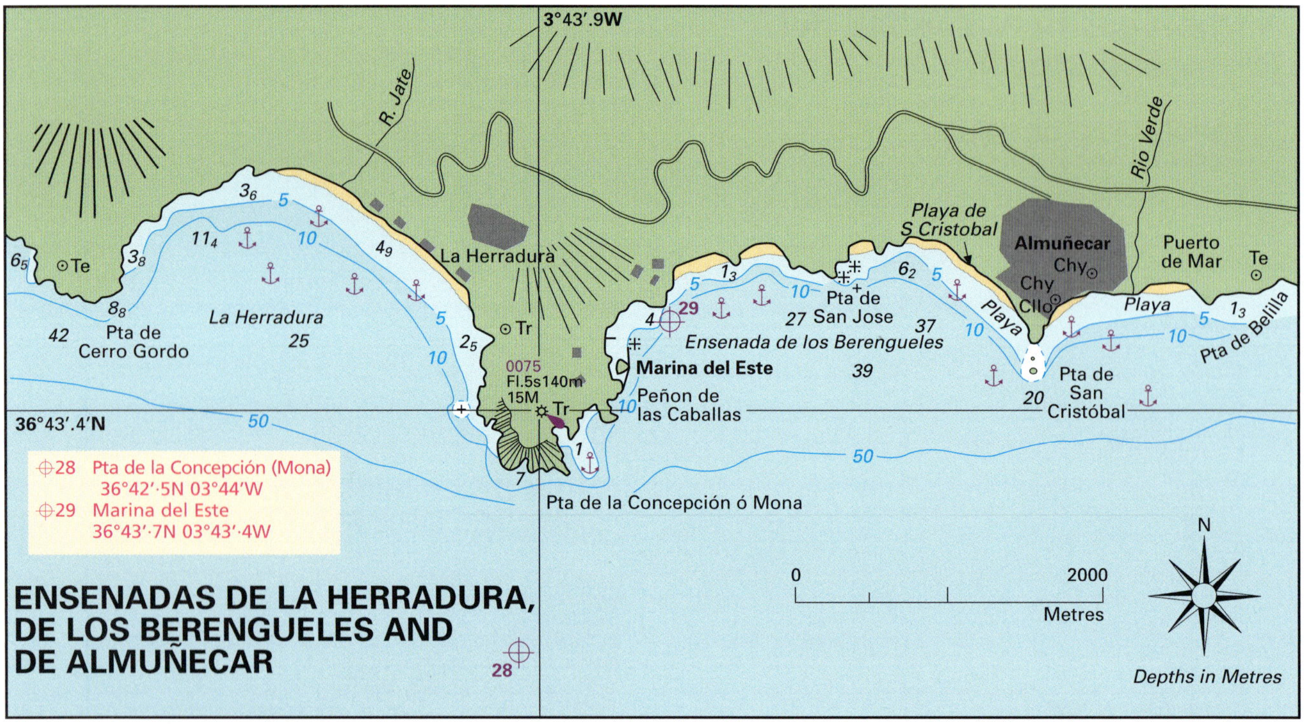

18. Marina del Este (Puerto de la Mona)

36°43'·7N 03°43'·5W

A small very pleasant harbour well sheltered from the W with 227 berths up to 30m.

Charts

British Admiralty *773*. Imray *M11*
French *6569*. Spanish *456*

⊕29 36°43'·7N 03°43'·4W

Lights

To the south
0074.8 **Punta de la Mona** Fl.5s140m15M Masonry tower 14m
Harbour
0075 **Dique de Abrigo** Fl(2)R.5s13m4M Red tower 5m
0075.2 **Contradique** Fl(2)G.6s5m3M Green tower 3m
To the east
0080 **Cabo Sacratif** Fl(2)10s98m25M White tower and building 17m

Port communications

Capitania VHF Ch 9. ✆ +34 958 640 801
Email marinaeste@marinasmediterraneo.com
www.marinasmediterraneo.com

Small harbour in beautiful area

A small artificial yacht harbour which forms part of a huge housing development in a beautiful area. Approach and entry are easy with generally good protection from the W sector. However, strong winds from the E and NE bring a very unpleasant swell and surging into the marina and make entry dangerous. It is particularly difficult for sailing yachts that often have to moor up against large motor vessels with high fixed protruding guardrails. Basic facilities are provided. This harbour, together with the Puerto Caleta de Vélez (Torre del Mar), form useful stopping places between Málaga and Motril, but prices are high. A small beach near the harbour, pool at yacht club.

Approach

From the west Nerja and the Punta de Cerro Gordo are easily recognised. The high prominent Punta de Concepción (Mona) is unmistakable; the harbour lies round the corner.

From the east After passing the delta of Río Guadalfeo the coast becomes hilly. Almuñecar with an old fort above it is conspicuous at the beginning of the Ensenada de los Berengueles. The harbour lies on the W side of this Ensenada, about half-way along the ridge leading to Punta de Concepción (Mona).

GPS approach

Steer to ⊕29 from a easterly quadrant and steer for breakwater end (approximately 0·06M).

Marina del Este *Pública de Puertos de Andalucía*

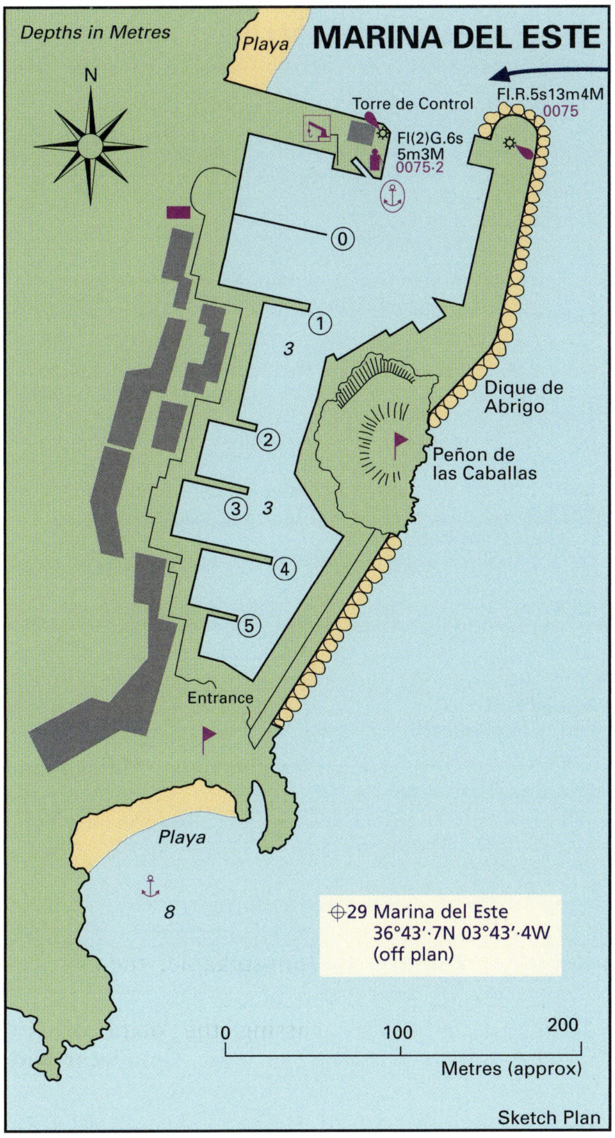

Anchorage in the approach

Anchor 100m off the beach in 5m sand in the NW corner of the Ensenada de Berengueles, or off the beach S of the marina.

Entrance

Approach the W side of the Ensenada de los Berengueles keeping 400m from the coast, due to off-lying rocks, until the N end of the harbour bears W then approach and round the head of the breakwater leaving it 25m to port and enter on a S course.

Berths

Secure to fuel berth on the starboard side on entering and ask at control tower.

Harbour charges

Low in low season (1 November to 1 March). Medium in summer.

Facilities

Maximum length overall: 30m.
30-tonnes travel-lift and a 3·3-tonne crane.
A large hard for laid-up yachts.

Marina del Este entrance and reporting berth
S. Terry SY Vadrouille

Limited repair facilities. The marine engineer and chandler can find specialists.
Water points on the quays and pontoons.
Showers at yacht club.
220V AC points on the quays and pontoons, 380V on large berths.
Gasoleo A and petrol.
Ice near the fuel quay.
Small supermarket and laundry in the marina. Other shops in Herradura 2M over the hill.

Locally

The prehistoric caves at Nerja, the old villages in the hills and the famous city of Granada can all be visited easily from here. The mountains of Sierra Nevada lying inland are very beautiful.

The nearby town of Almuñecar and the castle of San Miguel have some of the greatest historic treasures of Spain. The Alhambra palace of Granada is one of the most visited historical sites in the world and a World Heritage site.

Communications

Bus service on the main road 1M away – a long, steep climb. ✆ Area code 958. Taxi ✆ +34 958 63 00 17.

Marina del Este viewed from the north side of the rock towering above the port *Maria Kanayama*

⚓ ENSENADA DE LOS BERENGUELES

36°43'·9N 3°43'W

(See plan on page 62)

Another large anchorage on the E side of Punta de la Mona in attractive surroundings. There are several places where anchorage is possible – 100m off the Playa de San Cristóbal that lies to the W of Almuñecar in 5m sand or off the two beaches in the NW corner of the bay. All normal facilities from the town of Almuñecar and some repairs possible. Almuñecar fort is conspicuous.

⚓ PUNTA DE SAN CRISTÓBAL AND FONDEADERO DE ALMUÑECAR

36°43'N 3°42'·2W

(See plan on page 62)

Anchor 200m off the beach in 5m sand or 400m out in 20m stones. Punta de San Cristóbal gives protection from the west. Almuñecar has a conspicuous fort. Everyday supplies in the town.

⚓ ENSENADA DE BELILLA

36°43'·7N 3°41'·1W

(See plan on page 62)

An anchorage 150m off the Playa de Belilla in 5m clay and sand, or further out in 30m stones. Modern holiday development along the coast where everyday supplies may be found.

⚓ ENSENADA DE ROBAINA

36°44'·5N 03°39'·4W

A pleasant small anchorage 50m off a small pair of sand and pebble beaches in 5m sand. A conspicuous small fort is located on Punta de Jesus o del Tesorillo and a large block of flats behind the W beach.

⚓ SURGIDERO DE SALOBREÑA

36°44'·1N 03°35'·7W

Peñón and Surgidero de Salobreña: anchor either side of the conspicuous *peñon* (rock), 100m off the coast in 5m, sand and pebbles, or 400m out in 25m, mud. The Moorish castle above the town of Salobreña is easily seen.

Salobreña with conspicuous peñon at the left hand end of the shoreline

19. Puerto de Motril

36°43'·4N 3°30'·7W

A large commercial harbour with a small Club Nautico at the NW end with 193 berths – all usually occupied by club members.

Charts

British Admiralty *773, 774, 1854.* Imray *M11*
French *6569.* Spanish *4571, 457*

⊕30 36°42'.7N 03°30'.7W

Lights

To the west
0074.8 **Punta de la Mona** Fl.5s140m15M Masonry tower 14m
Harbour
0077 **Dique de Poniente head** Fl(2)R.6s11m10M Red truncated conical tower 5m
0077.5 **Dique del Este** Fl(2)G.7s9m5M Metal post 4m
0078 **Dique de Levante head** Fl(2+1)G.12s6m5M Green tower, red band 5m
0078.4 **Espigón head** Fl.R.5s6m2M Red truncated conical tower 5m
0079 **Nuevo Dique de Levante elbow** Fl(3)G.12s6m5M Green truncated conical tower 4m
0079.2 **Nuevo Dique de Levante head** Fl.G.5s6m2M Green truncated conical tower 5m
To the east
0080 **Cabo Sacratif** Fl(2)10s98m25M White tower and building 17m

Port communications

VHF Port Ch 12 (Tugs), 13. Marina Ch 9. ✆ +34 958 60 00 37
Email info@nauticomotril.com
www.realclubnauticomotril.com

Primarily a commercial harbour

A small fishing harbour that has developed into a commercial harbour which has recently been doubled in size. It has an easy approach and entrance but rather poor facilities for yachtsmen. The harbour is uncomfortable in strong easterly winds but some shelter can now be found behind the huge new *contradique.* The little village near the harbour can provide basic needs but there are many more shops in Motril itself, two miles away. Local holidays occur on 15 August and 15 October.

Reclamation work is continuing on the NE side of the harbour creating a major shipping terminal. Anchoring is no longer possible here.

Holding is in any case particularly poor in this harbour. Whilst sheltering here on three occasions in strong winds I have observed yachts laying their anchors over and over. On diving down, I discovered the bottom strewn with polythene sheeting blown in from the hydroponic farms, preventing anchors from digging in.

Approach

From the west The flat open plain of the delta of the Río Guadalfeo and the cranes, buildings and tall silos just to the W of Cabo Sacratif show the location of this harbour. Several large blocks of flats line the coast just to the W of this harbour. The town of Motril 2M inland shows in the closer approach.

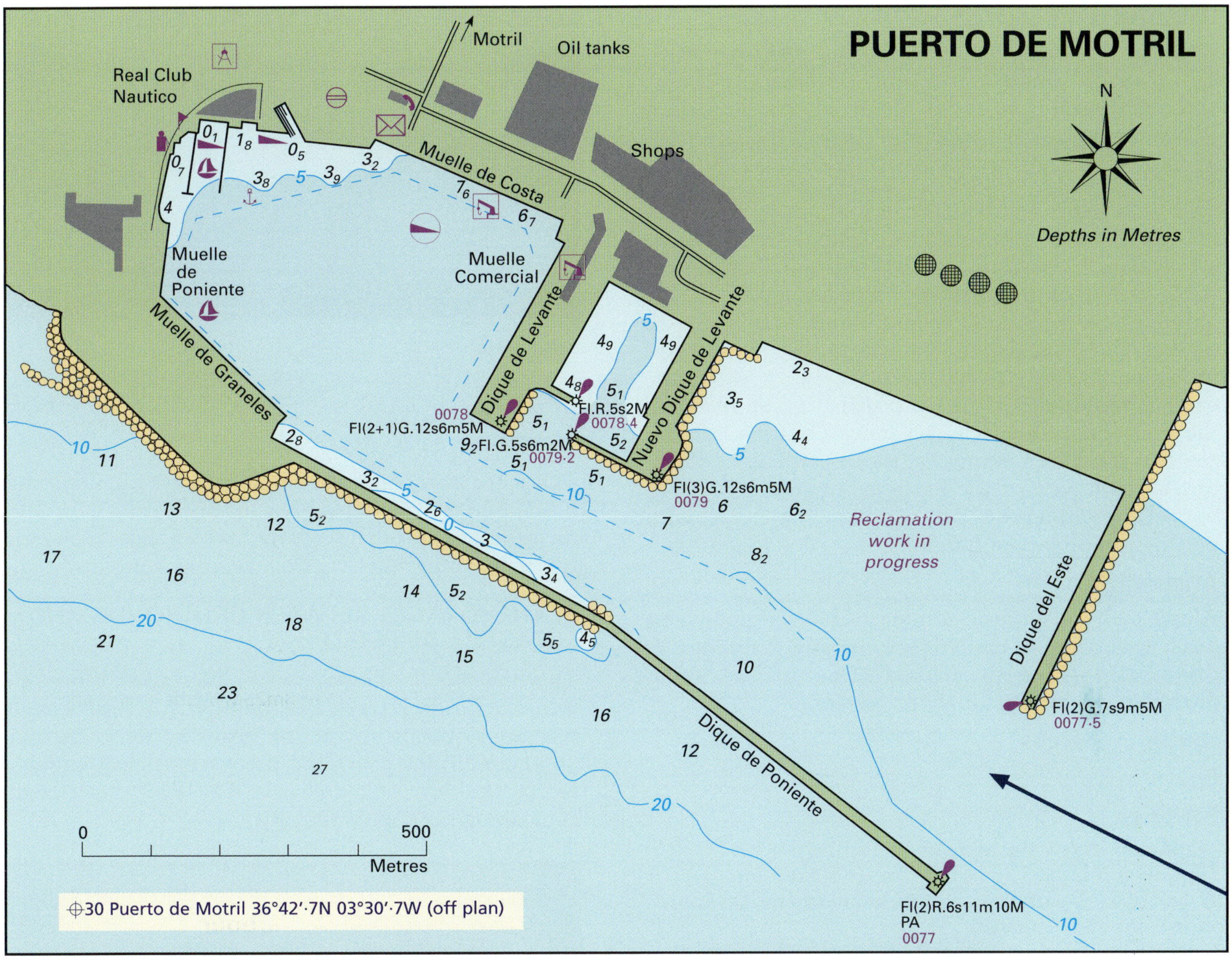

Puerto de Motril
Club Náutico
Pública de Puertos de Andalucía

From the east Cabo Sacratif, a distinctive headland with an isolated conspicuous lighthouse at its summit can easily be recognised from afar. There are two white radar domes on the mountain Sierra do Pelaos 4M to NE of this cape.

GPS approach

Steer to ⊕30 from a southerly quadrant and steer for breakwater end (approximately 0·27M).

Entrance

Approach the new head of the Dique de Poniente on a N course. Round it and enter between the heads, and steer parallel to the *dique* up the harbour on a WNW course.

Berths

The Real Club Nautico, located at the NW end of the port, is accommodating if it has a berth, but is ambivalent to visitors and always full, leaving no room to moor. Sometimes there is space on the hammerhead end of the W pontoon. It may be worth trying, particularly if the afternoon winds are impeding passage along the coast, as is often the case. Alternatively if there is space, go stern-to on the pontoons. Otherwise go stern-to either side but clear of the diesel pumps on the Muelle de Poniente on the west side of the harbour. In strong SE or E winds, lie alongside the Muelle Comercial with permission of the *capitanía*.

Anchorage

Along with most of the commercial harbours on this coast anchoring in the port is expressly forbidden. It may be possible to anchor close to the yacht moorings at the W end of the harbour.

Harbour charges

Low.

Facilities

Maximum length overall (*club náutico*): 20m.
Slipways at the yard in the NW corner of the main harbour and in the Puerto Pesquero can handle up to 100 tonnes.
Cranes up to 2·5 tonnes.
Engine and mechanical workshops outside the harbour.
A small chandlery shop in the village.
Water from points on quays and pontoons. For water hose, contact a harbour official if using water from quays.
220v AC points on quays and pontoons.
Gasoleo A on west side of harbour.
Ice from the ice factory in the village or from restaurant.
Club Náutico de Motril has bars, lounge, terrace and restaurants, also showers and a pool. Visiting yachtsmen are welcomed.
Supermarket just outside harbour area. Market and many more shops in Motril.

Communications

Frequent bus service to Motril. Buses to Granada and back (a long day's outing). ✆ Area code 958.
Taxi ✆ +34 958 60 18 54.

⚓ ANCHORAGE E OF CABO SACRATIF

36°41'·5N 03°28'W

An open coastal anchorage tucked under the E end of the rocky cliffed Cabo Sacratif. Anchor 100m offshore in 5m sand and pebbles. The main road runs a little way inland.

Calahonda

⚓ CALAHONDA

36°42'·1N 03°24'·7W

There are now yellow swimmers buoys all along the beach and the available area for anchoring is in 20+ metres of water. The village, which has a church tower like a lighthouse, has everyday supplies.

⚓ ANCHORAGES BETWEEN CALAHONDA AND CASTELL DE FERRO

This 3M stretch of high, rocky cliffed coast is broken into several deep bays. It is possible for experienced navigators to anchor at the heads of these bays in good conditions providing the water is clear enough to see the odd isolated rock. The busy coast road runs along the top of the cliff.

Fondeadero de Castell de Ferro

⚓ FONDEADERO DE CASTELL DE FERRO

36°43'·1N 03°21'·6W

Anchor in the corner of the bay near Punta del Melonar (at the left of the photograph), 100m from the shingle beach, 5m sand and mud or further out in 10m, mud. Good protection from the west. Everyday supplies in the village.

⚓ ANCHORAGES IN LA RÁBITA

36°44'·7N 03°10'·5W

A useful coastal anchorage at the W end of a gravel beach. Anchor 100m offshore in 5m sand and stones. The small village is readily recognised by the small blocks of flats 'hung' on a cliff face behind the village with a tower nearby. There is a small fort to the E of the tower. Everyday supplies from the village. Another possible anchorage is small bay to E of Punta Negra.

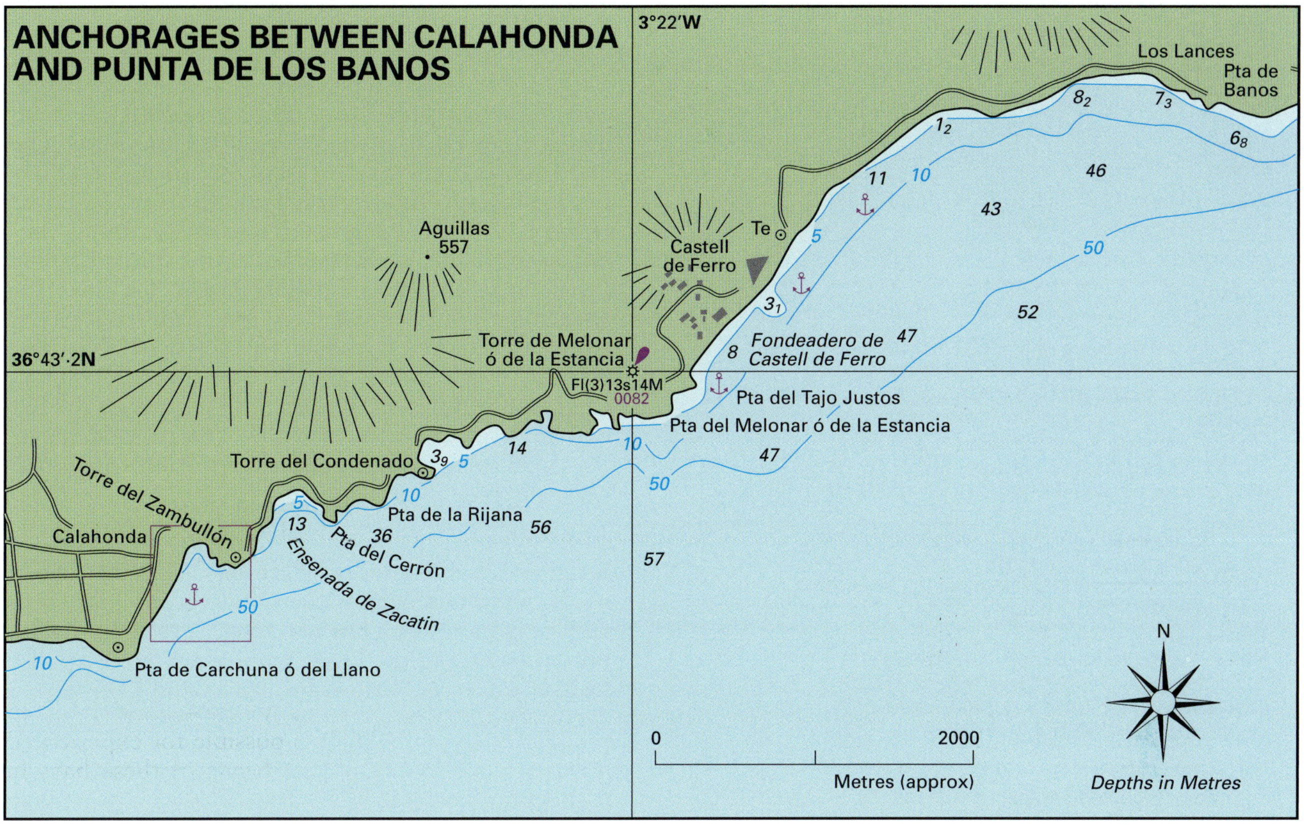

ANCHORAGES BETWEEN CALAHONDA AND PUNTA DE LOS BANOS

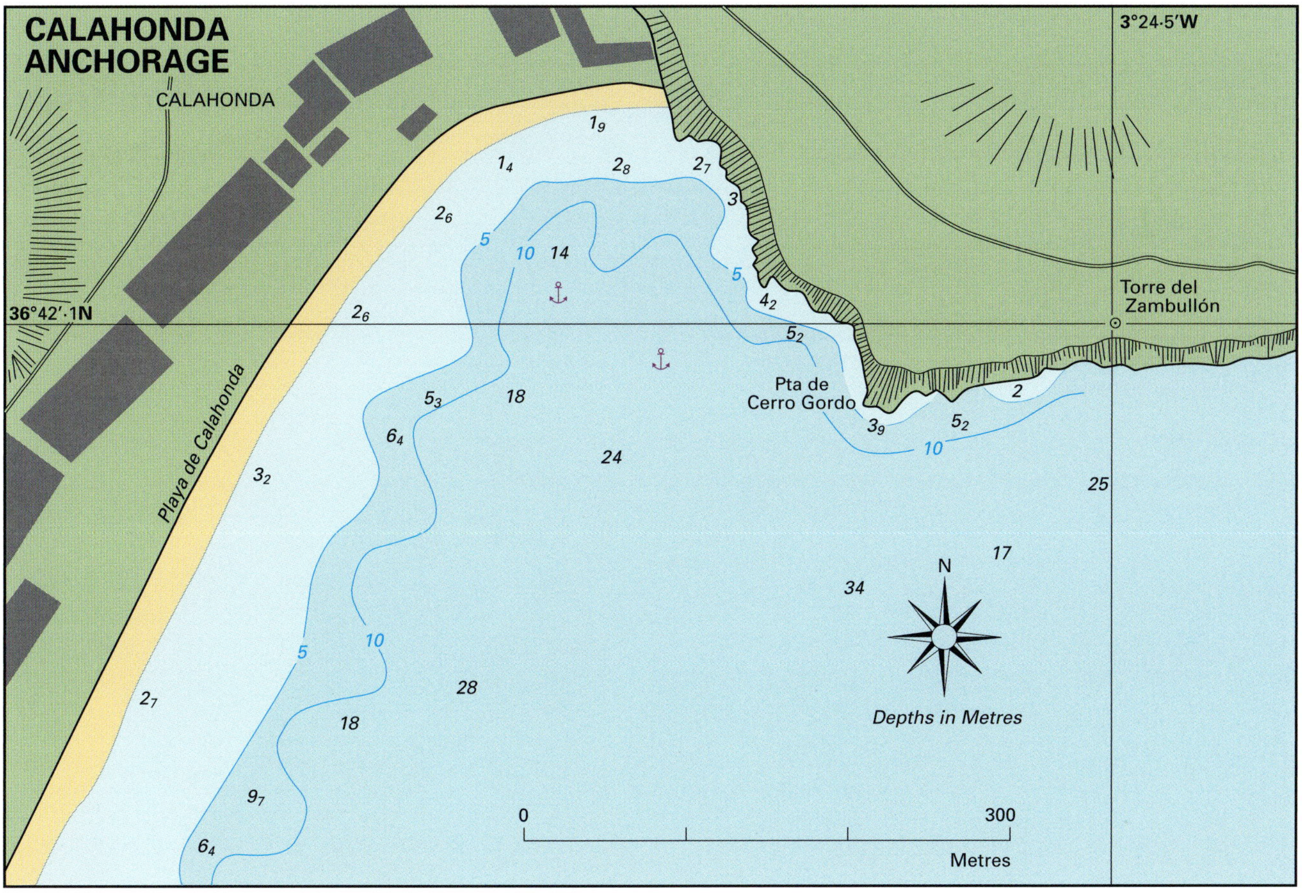

CALAHONDA ANCHORAGE

20. Puerto de Adra

36°44'·7N 03°01'·2W

A remote commercial harbour with few facilities for yachts but with 267 berths and plans to expand.

Charts

British Admiralty *773, 774, 1854.* Imray *M11*
French *6569.* Spanish *457, 458*

⊕32 36°44'·25N 03°01'W

Lights

To the west
0082 **Castell de Ferro** Fl(3)13s237m14M White tower 12m
0088 **Adra lighthouse** 36°44'·9N 03°01'·8W
Oc(3)10·5s49m16M White tower, red bands 26m
Harbour
0088.4 **Dique de Poniente head N end** 36°44'·6N 03°01'·1W
Fl(2)R.6s8m3M Red masonry tower 6m
0088.6 **Inner breakwater head** Fl(3)R.10s5m2M
Red post 3m
0089 **Dique de Levante head** Fl(2)G.10s8m3M
Green masonry tower 5m
0089.2 **Inner breakwater head** Fl(3)G.9s5m2M
Green post 3m
To the east
0089.5 **Punta de los Baños** Fl(4)11s22m11M
Rectangular white tower 21m
0090 **Punta Sabinal** Fl(1+2)10s34m16M
Tower above white houses 32m

Port communications

Capitanía ✆ +34 950 805061 / 600 149118,
www.eppa.es/en/marina-adra
Real Club Nautico de Adra ✆ +34 950 403487
Email rcna@realclubnauticodeadra.es
www.realclubnauticodeadra.es

A working harbour

A rather desolate commercial and fishing harbour, established by the Phoenicians, who called it Abdera, and in use ever since. It has accommodation for small motor boats but is less suitable for keeled yachts. The approach and entrance is easy in normal conditions but in strong winds, especially those from the E, the entrance can be dangerous and the harbour very uncomfortable. The harbour is also disturbed by the constant movement of fishing boats. Facilities for yachtsmen are poor but there are sandy beaches on either side of the harbour. The town is small and without much tourist development. Local holidays September 6 to 10 in honour of Our Lady of the Sea and St Nicholas of Tolentino.

A new marina is planned but no information is yet available.

Approach

From either direction the harbour can be identified by the lighthouse and by the very large and tall Torre de Perdigones which has windows. The upper half is brown brick and the lower painted white. A smaller similar tower is located further inland. There is a deep grey sandy beach along the SW side of Dique de Poniente which makes identification somewhat difficult from seaward as it merges into the shore line. However there is a sand elevator and other machinery and blocks of flats. A conspicuous factory with a pair of grey chimneys stands some 2M to W of the harbour.

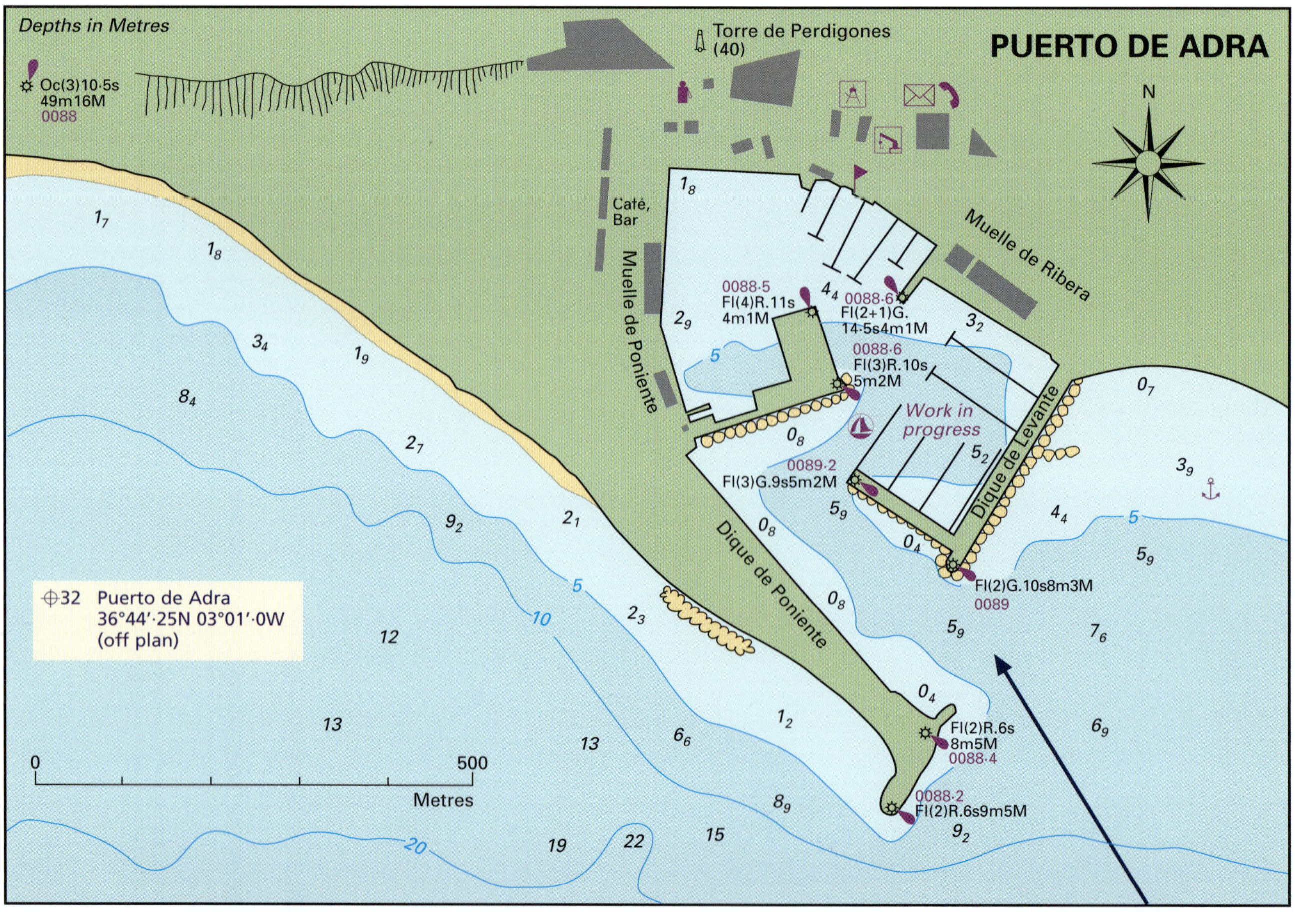

Puerto de Adra *Pública de Puertos de Andalucía*

GPS approach

Steer to ⊕32 from a southerly quadrant and steer for breakwater end (approximately 0·28M).

Anchorage in the approach

Anchor 200m to E of Dique de Levante in 5m sand and pebbles. Alternative anchorage in deep water S of the harbour.

Entrance

The head of the Dique de Poniente is T-shaped and the NE spur extends about 30m in that direction from the light. Give it a good berth and pass between the two inner moles. The depths in the entrance and harbour frequently change and are sometimes dredged; depths are approximate.

Berths

Alongside or stern-to the off-shore end of the Dique de Levante. The *club náutico* is crowded with small boats. It has four visitors berths but check to see if you will fit.

Harbour charges

High.

Anchorage

Anchor in 3m mud near centre of harbour using an anchor with a trip line. Anchor light and shape are necessary.

Facilities

Maximum length overall: 20m for berthing.
Shipyards geared towards fishing boats.
150-tonnes travel hoist and hardstanding in fishing harbour.
5-tonnes crane.
Several slipways which will take the largest yachts.
Chandlers shop in town.
Water from points on quay or from *club náutico*.
125V and 220V AC supply point near water point.
Ice factory on NE side of the harbour.
Club náutico with a bar and restaurant.
Supermarket and shops in the village.

Communications

Bus service along the coast. ✆ Area code 950.

General

Rumours have abounded for years that a new marina is going to be built here. From the port website indications are that plans for a recreational marina for 267 new berths giving a total of 458 berths up to 15m is being implemented. Many berths will be attributed to the local Club Náutico de Adra, so it is not known how many visitors berths will be allocated. It probably depends on local demand.

⚓ BALERMA
36°43'·6N 02°53'·7W

An open coastal anchorage some 100m off the beach in 5m sand and pebbles, opposite the low Torre de Balerma which has a few buildings around and a factory to NE. A somewhat unattractive flat coast with plastic-covered greenhouses stretching for miles.

Balerma: miles of plastic sheeting covering valuable crops for the markets of Europe. Strong winds can rip sheets off and carry them into the sea

⚓ PUNTA DE LOS BAÑOS
36°41'·6N 02°51'·2W

An extraordinary and rather exposed anchorage between the double spurs of a point. Anchor about 50m from the coast in 3m sand and stones. The very conspicuous Castillo de Guardias Viejas stands on a small hill just within the double point and Punta de Los Baños light is on the eastern side. There are a few buildings and shacks in the area but the nearest small village is about 2M away.

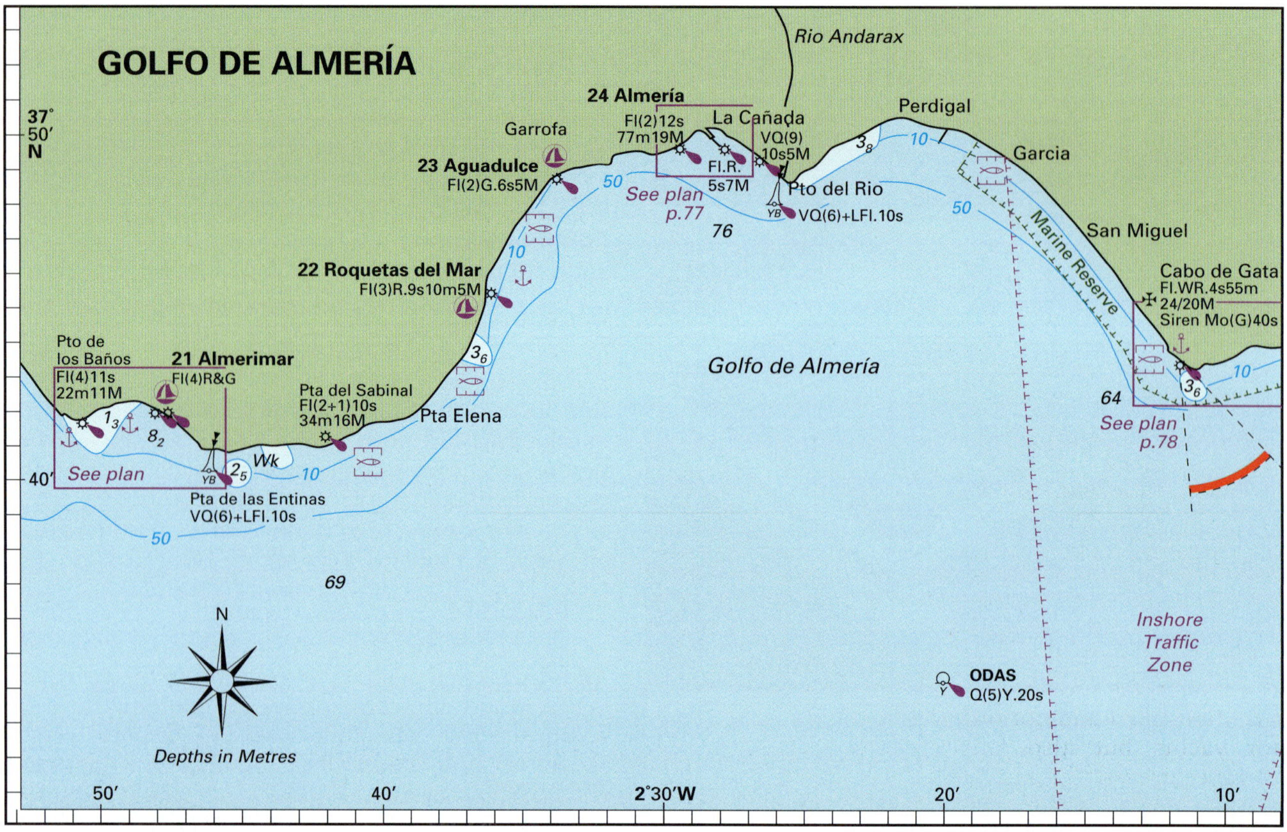

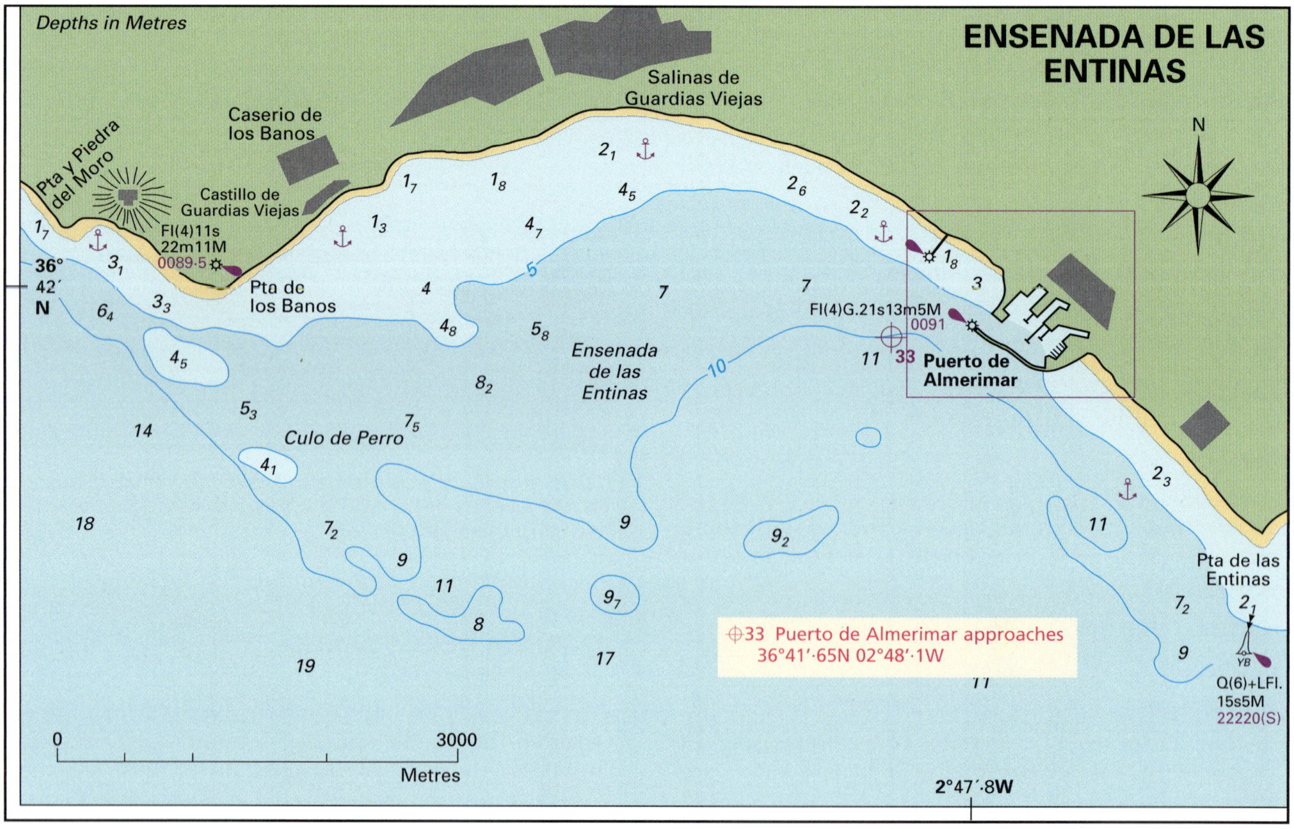

⚓ ENSENADA DE LAS ENTINAS

36°41′·8N 02°49′·0W

Spanish chart *3550*. A wide bay where anchorage is possible anywhere along the coast in three to 5m and 50 to 100m offshore. The shore is flat and the whole area covered with plastic greenhouses. The Castillo de Guardias Viejas on Punta de los Baños and the high-rise flats and buildings around the Puerto de Almerimar near Punta Entinas are both very conspicuous. Supplies from the Puerto de Almerimar.

21. Puerto de Almerimar

36°41′·7N 02°47′·6W

One of the best marinas along the coast. Cheap and safe in all conditions with a helpful staff, good facilities and berthing for almost 1,000 yachts up to 60m.

Charts

British Admiralty *774, 1589.* Imray *M11, M12*
French *6569.* Spanish *458*

⊕33 36°41′·65N 02°48′·1W

Lights

To the west
0089.5 **Punta de los Baños** Fl(4)11s22m11M Rectangular white tower 21m
Harbour
22187(S) **Red port hand buoy** Fl.R.7.5s2M
0091.6 **Espigón** Fl(4)R.11s5m3M Post on red turret 1m
0091 **Dique Sur head** Fl(4)G.21s13m5M Green tower 8m
0091.3 **Dique Sur Middle** LFl.G.9.5s4m2M Green turret 1m
0091.35 **Contradique head** Fl(2)R.9.5s2m2M Red tower 1m
0091.4 **Ldg Lts** *Front* Iso.10s3m2M White tower, winged top 2m
0091.41 *Rear* Oc.10s4m2M White tower, winged top 3m
To the east
22220(S) **Bajo Punta de las Entinas** Q(6)+LFl.15s5M ⧗ card buoy
0090 **Punta Sabinal** Fl(1+2)10s34m16M Tower on white buildings 32m
Buoys There may be five or six small yellow buoys marking the starboard and port hand of the entrance channel as the leading lines are sometimes difficult to make out.

Port communications

VHF Ch 9. Port Control ☎ +34 950 60 77 55 / 49 73 50
Email infomarina@almerimarpuerto.com
www.almerimarpuerto.com

Welcoming good yacht harbour

This artificial yacht harbour is very pleasant. Much of the hinterland is a sheet of plastic under which a major proportion of north Europe's winter vegetables are grown. The marina is built to an ambitious plan and not only provides good facilities for yachts but also for crews. Approach and entrance are easy except in strong SW winds which can build big seas at the entrance and sometimes send a swell into the harbour. Very secure with good shelter from easterly gales. Rates, which are on the low side, can be examined on the website.

Winter live aboard community.

Approach

From the west The coast from Adra is low and flat, Puerto de Adra and the Castillo de Guardias Viejas which is on a small hill near Punta de los Baños are easily recognised while the high blocks of flats to the E of Puerto Almerimar can be seen from afar.

From the east The conspicuous lighthouse on the low flat Punta del Sabinal will be seen and also the blocks of flats mentioned above.

GPS approach

Steer to ⊕33 from a southwesterly quadrant and steer for breakwater end (approximately 0·17M).

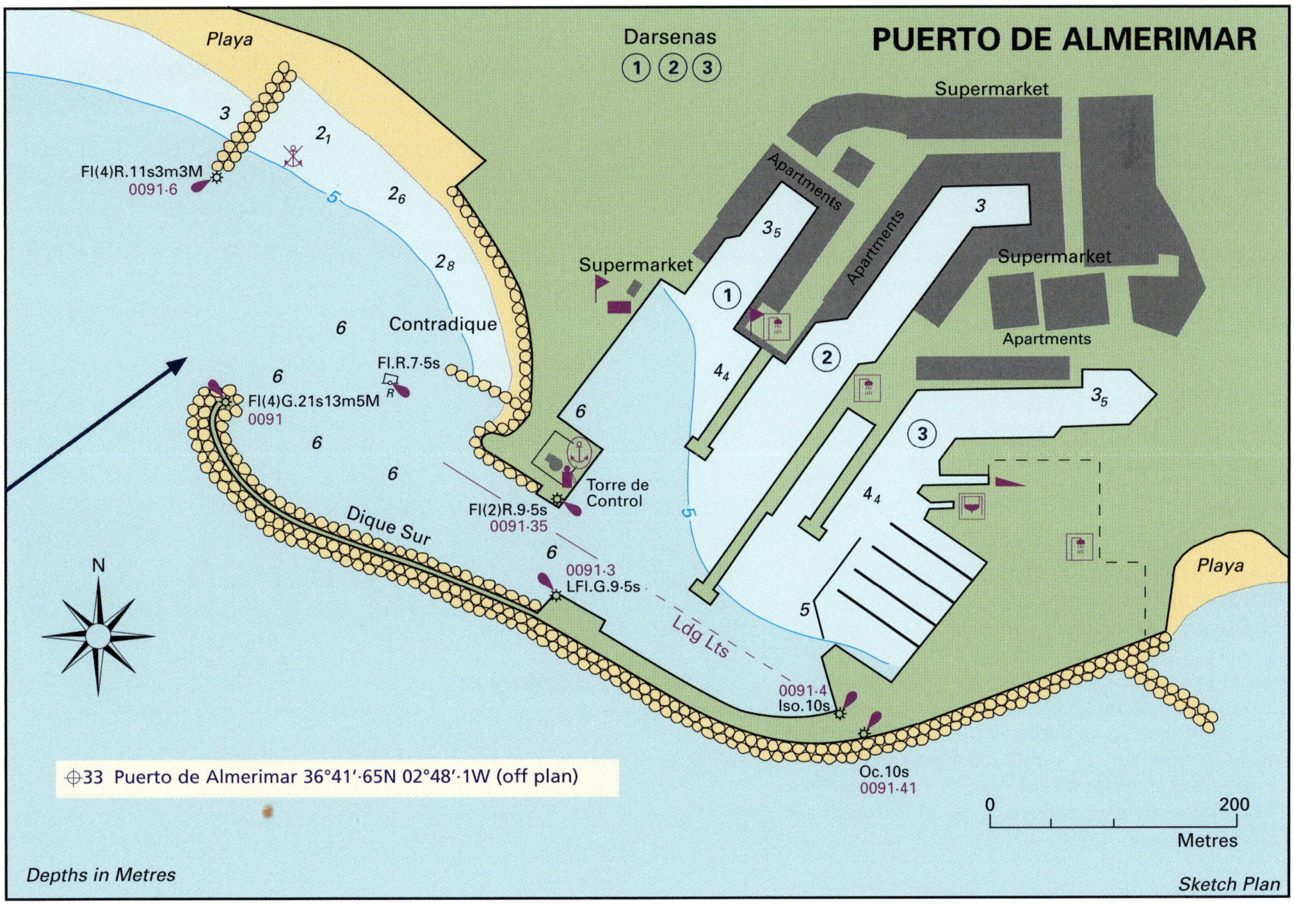

Puerto de Almerimar *Pública de Puertos de Andalucía*

Anchorage in the approach

It is possible to anchor either side of the harbour about 100–150m from the coast in 5m sand.

Entrance

The harbour entrance silts but is frequently dredged to 6m. In spite of frequent dredging it has been reported that there is a shallow patch running out along the breakwater. Exercise care and watch the echo-sounder on entry, giving the hooked end of the breakwater a reasonable berth (50m or so). Leave the red buoy to port and enter between two lines of small yellow buoys or pick up the leading lines at night.

Berths

Secure to fuel berth and ask at the control tower.
Note The four pontoons shown at the east of the harbour are for small craft only.

Harbour charges Medium.

Facilities

Maximum length overall: 60m.
Most repair and maintenance facilities.
Volvo dealer and servicing.
110 and 60-tonne travel-lift.
5-tonne crane.
Slipways on the E side of the harbour.
Large hardstanding.
Two chandlers in the port plus other useful shops.
Water points on all quays and pontoons – potable but taste before filling tanks.
Showers in the service block and in the port.
220V AC points on all quays and pontoons. 380V AC on the larger berths.
Gasoleo A and petrol.
Ice available from control tower and bars.
Club náutico.
A small supermarket at the west end of the harbour and a well-stocked one near the boatyard.
Launderettes.
An active Live-Aboard Club has a small club room near the boatyard.
A hypermarket is on the bus route to the town of El Ejido.
Yachtsmen are not allowed to work on their own vessels while in the yard.
Almerimar Marine Services has an excellent well stocked chandlery in the port and can undertake just about any marine repairs. Including rigging, electrical and electronic repairs and installation, refrigeration, marine engineering, etc. ✆ +34 619 99 25 20,
Email info@almerimarmarine.com
www.almerimarmarine.com

Note: Several electricity installations around the port are broken and in need of replacement. They use a non-standard connection socket and often need attention by the *marineros* before they work.

Locally

Almería and the Alcazaba are worth a visit. There are beaches on either side of the harbour. Fishing, wind surfing, diving, golf, tennis and horse-riding.

Communications

Regular bus service to El Ejido whence further buses.
Airport at Almería, year round services to Barcelona, Madrid and Melilla, summer charter flights from other European countries. ✆ Area code 950.
Taxi ✆ +34 950 57 06 11 / 48 00 63.

22. Puerto de Roquetas de Mar

36°45'·4N 02°36'·3W

A small, mostly shallow harbour with little to attract cruising yachtsmen.

Charts

British Admiralty *774.* Imray *M11, M12*
French *6569.* Spanish *459*

⊕35 36°45'·5N 02°36'·15W

Lights

To the west
0090 **Punta Sabinal** Fl(1+2)10s34m16M Tower on white buildings 32m
Harbour
0092 **Dique Sur head** Fl(3)R.9s10m5M Red round concrete tower 4m
0092.4 **Dique Norte head** Fl(3)G.9s5m3M Green round tower on square base 3m
To the east
0106 **Cabo de Gata** Fl.WR.4s55m24/20M 356°-W-316°-R-356° Siren Mo(G)40s White tower, grey lantern 19m

Port communications

Capitanía VHF Ch 9 ✆ +34 950 10 04 87 / 600 14 91 22
Email roquetas@eppa.es
www.eppa.es/en/marina-roquetas-de-mar
Club náutico ✆ +34 950 32 07 89
Email info@realclubnauticoroquetas.es
www.realclubnauticoroquetas.es

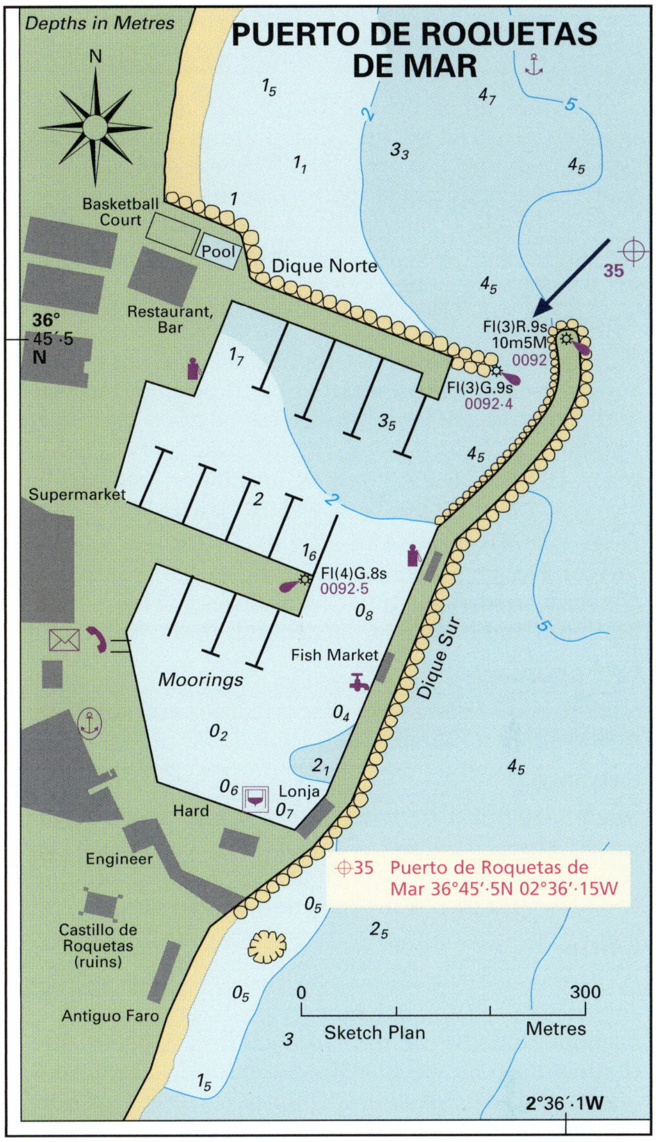

Primarily for fishing boats

A small harbour for sardine fishing boats and a few yachts. Easy to approach and enter but would be uncomfortable in heavy weather between SE and NE. Attractive in a simple way but tourist development is taking place around this area. There

Roquetas de Mar from NE *Pública de Puertos de Andalucía*

are a few facilities, some basic shops near the harbour and other, better shops in the village about two miles away.

The fuel point on the Dique Sur is for fishing vessels only. The yachts' fuel point is on the NW corner quay but it is very shallow there and fuel can only really be obtained with jerrycans.

Fine beaches each side of the harbour. Local holidays 7 and 8 October in honour of the Virgen del Rosario.

Approach

From the SW The low flat-topped headland of Punta Sabinal which has an isolated lighthouse and tower with radomes. A large tourist complex of high-rise buildings is located between this headland and the port. The old disused yellow lighthouse and small castle just S of the harbour are recognisable.

From the NE From Almería the cliffs reach within 4M of Roquetas which is at the edge of a plain covered with plastic greenhouses. There are buildings and blocks of flats behind the harbour.

GPS approach

Steer to ⌖35 from an easterly quadrant and steer for breakwater end (approximately 0·05M).

Entrance

Straight-forward between *dique* heads which have small stone towers. Give Dique Sur head a reasonable berth in case sand has built up off the end. The entrance is dredged and depths vary.

Berths

Bow or stern to pontoons on the north side of the entrance but make up wherever possible in the outer harbour and ask at the *club náutico*. Due to the shallow harbour, keel yachts should only attempt to berth at the easternmost pontoon. The harbour becomes crowded when the fishing fleet returns.

Anchorage

The area N of the harbour entrance is popular for local boats. In westerly winds the swell finds its way in. Tuck in as close to the N dique as possible outside of the swimming buoys.

Harbour charges

Low.

Facilities

Maximum length overall: 15m.
50-tonnes travel hoist and 8-tonnes crane.
220V and 380V AC points on quays.
Water on the quays.
Club náutico with restaurant and bar.
Several small shops and a supermarket in the village. A market and some other shops 2M away.

Communications

Bus service to Almería. ✆ Area code 950.

23. Puerto de Aguadulce

36°48'·9N 02°33'·7W

A good safe marina with 764 berths up to 25m. Many living aboard. Located 4M WSW from Almeriá.

Charts

British Admiralty *774*. Imray *M11, M12*
French *6569*. Spanish *459*

⌖36 36°48'.7N 02°33'.8W

Lights

To the west
0090 **Punta Sabinal** Fl(1+2)10s34m16M Tower on white buildings 32m
Harbour
0092.6 **Dique head** Fl(2)G.6s5m5M Green pyramid 4m
0092.8 **Contradique head** Fl(2)R.7s6m3M Red concrete tower 4m
To the east
0093 **San Telmo LtHo** Fl(2)12s77m19M White square tower oblong black stripes 7m
0106 **Cabo de Gata** Fl.WR.4s55m24/20M 356°-W-316°-R-356° Siren Mo(G)40s White tower, grey lantern yellow building 19m

Port communications

Capitanía/club náutico VHF Ch 9 ✆ +34 950 34 15 02
Email contacto@puertodeportivoaguadulce.es
www.puertodeportivoaguadulce.es

Popular harbour

Aguadulce provides a useful alternative to Puerto de Almería. Its harbour is easy to enter and provides good shelter except in strong ESE winds when some swell enters making it uncomfortable. Facilities are good. The Alcazaba at Almería should be visited. Long sandy beaches to SW. Popular for winter live aboards.

It is a very long walk around the marina to the town for visitors, who are usually berthed on the W site of the main Dique de Levante. The marina is somewhat run down with seemingly little maintenance over the years.

Local holidays: The 10 days before the last Sunday in August and the first two weeks in January.

Approach

From the SW Round the low headland of Punta del Sabinal with its conspicuous white, round lighthouse tower. Follow the low featureless coast dotted with various housing estates in a NE direction until Puerto de Roquetas del Mar which has a disused lighthouse, a small square fort and a breakwater, has been passed. Puerto de Aguadulce is located just beyond the point where a range of rocky hills reaches down to the coast. The rocky breakwaters, *torre de control* and low blocks of flats will be seen in the close approach.

From the east Round the unmistakable Cabo de Gata (⌖39 36°41'N 02°10'W) and cross the Golfo de Almería on a WNW course. The mass of buildings of Almería surmounted by the Alcazaba castle and fronted by the harbour breakwater are all conspicuous. The S cardinal light buoy, Q(6)+LFl, off Punta del Río may also be seen. This harbour is located near where the rocky range of coastal hills drops back and the low flat coast commences.

GPS approach

Steer to ⌖36 from a southeasterly quadrant and steer for breakwater end (approximately 0·09M).

Entrance

Approach the head of the *dique* on a course between SW and N, round it and then the head of the *contradique* to port.

Berths

Secure to the quay by the *torre de control* and report to the office for allocation of a berth.

Facilities

Maximum length overall: 25m.
Workshops at N end of harbour for mechanical, electrical and hull repairs; maintenance, painting etc. Work on own boat permitted.
50-tonnes travel-lift.
Slipway at N end of the harbour.
Hardstanding at N end of the harbour; additional space for 100 yachts under cover.
Sailmaking.
Water taps on quays and pontoons.
Showers.
220V AC on quays and pontoons.
Gasoleo A and petrol.
Ice at fuel quay.
Club náutico with good facilities.
Many shops and a large market at Almería about 5M away.
Swimming pool beside the harbour.

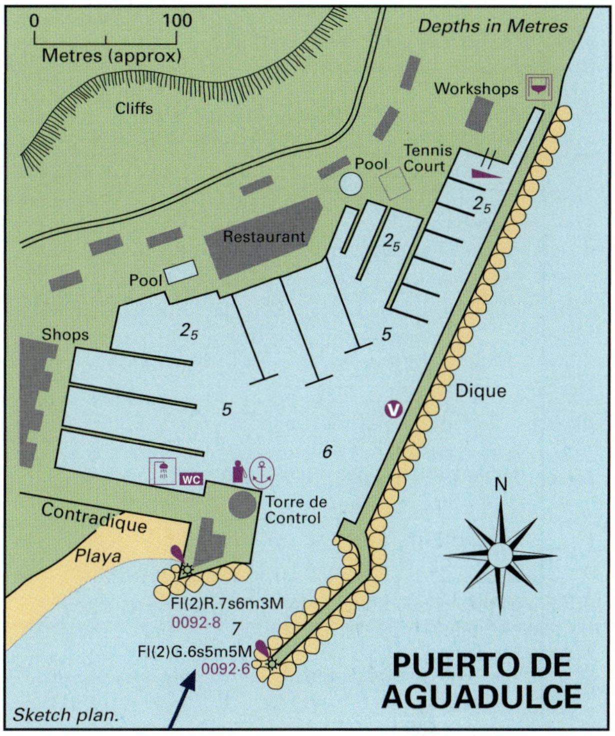

Sketch plan.

⌖36 Puerto de Aguadulce
36°48'·7N 02°33'·8W (off plan)

Locally

Almeria is well worth a visit, and especially the ancient Alcazaba. A local bus service runs frequently to the town.

Communications

Bus to Almería on road behind the harbour. Airport (11 miles) and rail (five miles) at Almería. ✆ Area code 950. Taxi ✆ +34 950 34 05 46.

Puerto de Aguadulce *Pública de Puertos de Andalucía*

24. Puerto de Almería

36°49'·8N 02°27'·9W

A large commercial and fishing harbour with a small yacht club just inside the entrance to accommodate 277 vessels: always full.

Tides

Time differences based on HW Gibraltar		*Height difference*				*Mean*
HW	LW	MHWS	MHWN	MLWS	MLWN	*level*
+0010	–0010	0·5	0·4	0·3	+0·3	0·40

Current

There is a constant E-going current across the mouth of the bay.

Charts

British Admiralty *774, 1589.* Imray *M11, M12*
French *7504, 6569.* Spanish *4591, 459*

⊕37 36°49 25N 02°27 75W

Lights

To the west
0093 **San Telmo LtHo** Fl(2)12s77m19M White square tower black band 7m
Puerto Pesquero
0094 **Dique del Oeste head** Fl(3)R.9s10m4M Red tower 5m
0095 **Dique Sur head** Fl(4)G.10·5s10m3M Green tower 5m
0095·5 **Interior mole head** Fl(4)R.11s5m1M Red tower 3m
Main harbour
0096 **Dique de Poniente head** Fl.R.5s19m7M White 8-sided tower, red top and base 12m
0102 **Cargadero No. 2 head** Fl.G.5s8m4M Green metal structure 3m
0101 **Cargadero No. 1 head** Fl.R.4s1M
0101.5 **Corner** Fl.Y.5s5m1M Yellow concrete tower
0101.4 **Club de Mar del Almería Dique de Abrigo** Fl(2)G.10s4m1M Green inclined concrete tower 3m
0101.6 **Club de Mar del Almería Contradique** Fl(2)R.10s4m1M Red 3-sided column 3m
0099 **Muelle de Poniente o Comercial E corner** Fl(2)R.7s5m1M Red 3-sided column 3m
0098 **Dique de Levante head** Fl(2+1)G.14·5s4m2M Green structure, red band 10m
0103 **Power station wharf head** VQ(9)10s11m5M ⧗ on yellow metal framework tower, black band 9m F.R on building 360m E
To the east
0106 **Cabo de Gata** Fl.WR.4s55m24/20M 356°-W-316°-R-356° Siren Mo(G)40s White tower, grey lantern 19m
Buoys
Black and yellow S card lightbuoy Q(6)+LFl ⧗ topmark off Punta del Río de Almería

Port communications

Port VHF Ch 12, 14 and 16. Club de Mar VHF Ch 9
✆ +34 950 23 60 33
Email almeria@apalmeria.com www.apalmeria.com

Useful commercial harbour

A commercial and fishing port with an old and interesting town and castle nearby. Approach and entrance can be made in almost any conditions and good shelter obtained but winds from the E cause an uncomfortable swell inside the harbour. The town, which is the capital of the province of the same name has good shops and markets. Yachts use the Club de Mar del Almería, outside the Dique de Levante; they are not welcome in the main harbour.

Reclamation and construction work has been going on in the harbour for some years making it a busy and dirty port. The yacht club is always full and visitors are directed to Aguadulce, 4M W. Another private yacht club at the NW end of the harbour is for members only. Anchoring is prohibited in the harbour.

Approach

From the SW Almería lies at the head of a wide bay at the foot of the mountains. The low flat headland of Punta del Sabinal with its isolated lighthouse is recognisable 10M to SW. The Alcazaba (castle) on a hill near the town is conspicuous at a distance but is dwarfed by tower blocks of flats to E. The town buildings and the long Dique de Poniente are seen in the closer approach.

From the east After Cabo de Gata, a rugged high promontory, the coast is low and flat. The town and harbour are visible from afar; there is a very tall port authority building on the end of the Dique de Levante which is prominent.

GPS approach

Steer to ⊕37 from a southerly quadrant and steer for breakwater end (approximately 0·35M).

Anchorage in the approach

Anchor close to SW side of Dique de Poniente. It is deep at 10–15m. Swell builds here in the afternoon breeze making it untenable in any S sector winds.

Anchoring within the harbour is prohibited.

Entrance

Straightforward but keep a lookout for commercial and fishing vessels leaving, sometimes at speed. Inside the harbour there are a number of unlit mooring buoys.

Berths

Visiting yachts are now sent four miles west to Puerto de Aguadulce. The Club de Mar moorings are reserved for members' yachts although occasionally, and with a great deal of persuasion space can be found for a visitor.

Almería Club de Mar, looking ENE *Pública de Puertos de Andalucía*

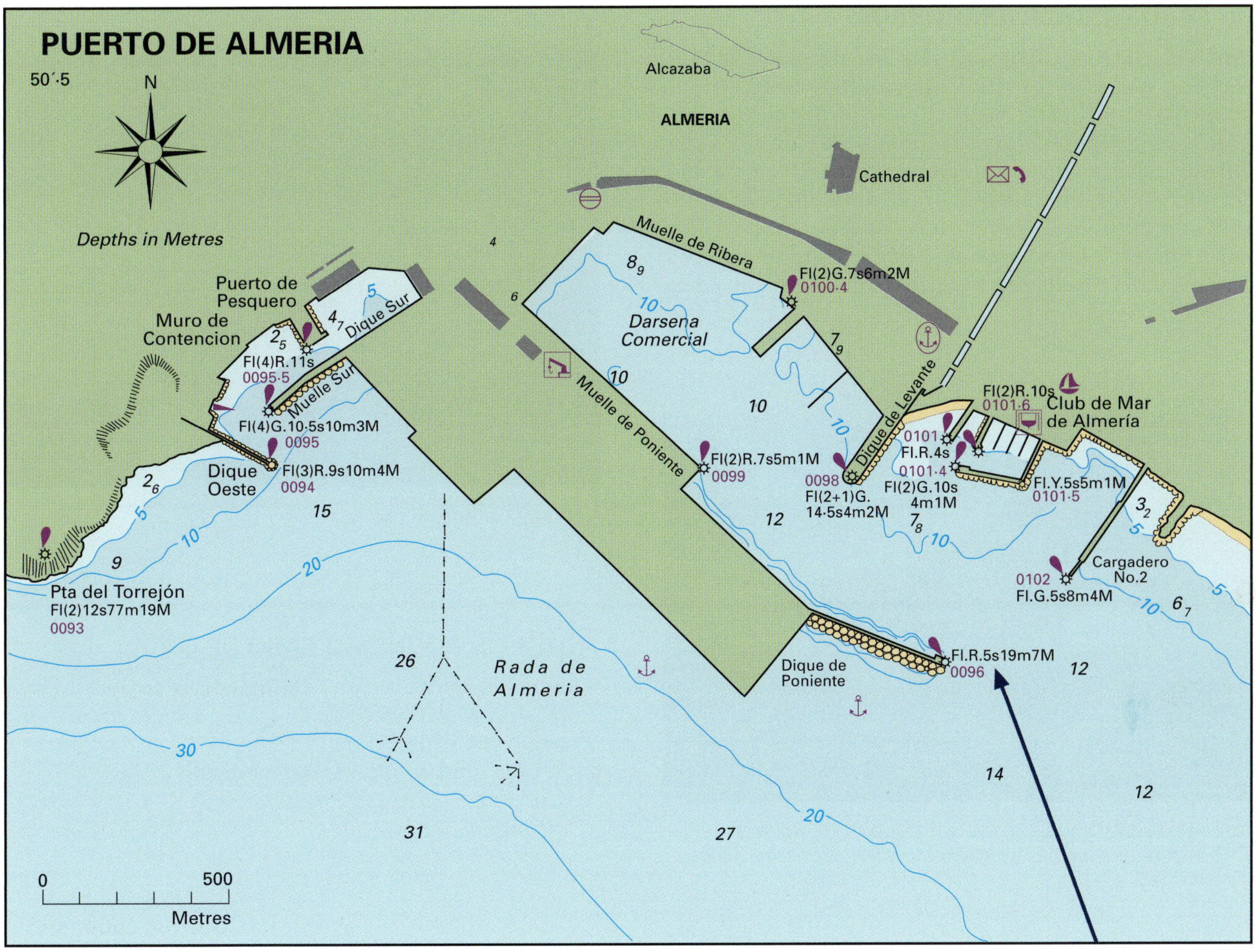

Anchorage

Anchor in 6m sand and mud 150m S or E of Club de Mar, clear of moorings. Depths vary 7–10m. Show anchor light and shape.

Harbour charges

High.

Facilities

The Club de Mar del Almería is a tennis and yachting club with a bar, restaurant, showers and terrace. Visitors should first contact the secretary for permission to use the facilities.

Maximum length overall: 15m in the Club de Mar.

Shipyards geared to fishing boats beside the slipway and also at the W end of Puerto Pesquero.

Slipways in both the main of the harbour and the Puerto Pesquero.

Cranes 4–12 tonnes in the harbour and a 4-tonne crane at the Club de Mar.

Several engineering workshops in town and one on the quay on Muelle Sur.

Chandlers and Engineers in the NW corner of the main harbour.

Water and 220V AC on all berths at Club de Mar.

Gasoleo A and petrol at Club de Mar.

Ice from ice factory between Puerto Pesquero and Dársena Comercial.

A number of small shops and a small market near the port. Many large and varied shops and a large market about 1M away in the town.

Several launderettes in the town.

Locally

The Moorish castle (Alcazaba) is very attractive and worth a visit. Several museums and ancient churches make a trip to the town worthwhile.

Local holidays are the 10 days before the last Sunday in August, and the first two weeks of January.

During the Summer festivities the locals re-enact the defeat of the Moors in their colourful costumes.

Communications

Airport with summer charter flights from Europe and year-round services to Madrid or Barcelona. Railway. Occasional service by boat to Marseille, Algeria, Canary Isles and South America. ✆ Area code 950.

Taxis ✆ +34 950 25 11 11.

Club de Mar del Almería

⚓ CABO DE GATA ANCHORAGES

Anchor off the village of San Miguel de Cabo de Gata to the NW of the Cabo and its conspicuous tower in 5m of sand some 200m off the coast. One can also anchor 100m off Playa de los Corrales further to the SE in sand, well sheltered from N and E. There is a sheltered anchorage 150m NW of Cabo de Gata light in 5m sand and stone, or about 400m offshore in 10m. There is a small settlement and conspicuous church by the saltworks on the road to San Miguel de Gata. Tunny nets are sometimes laid in this area.

Cabo de Gata from the east

Cabo de Gata: The distinctive white patch on the SW cliff face is a welcome sight when coming from the west
Jane Russell

NOTES ON ROUNDING CABO DE GATA

1. Stay close inshore or 1·0M offshore to avoid Laja de Cabo de Gata shoal (3m) which breaks in heavy weather
2. Winds tend to increase around this cape
3. Current is normally east-going and can be very strong.

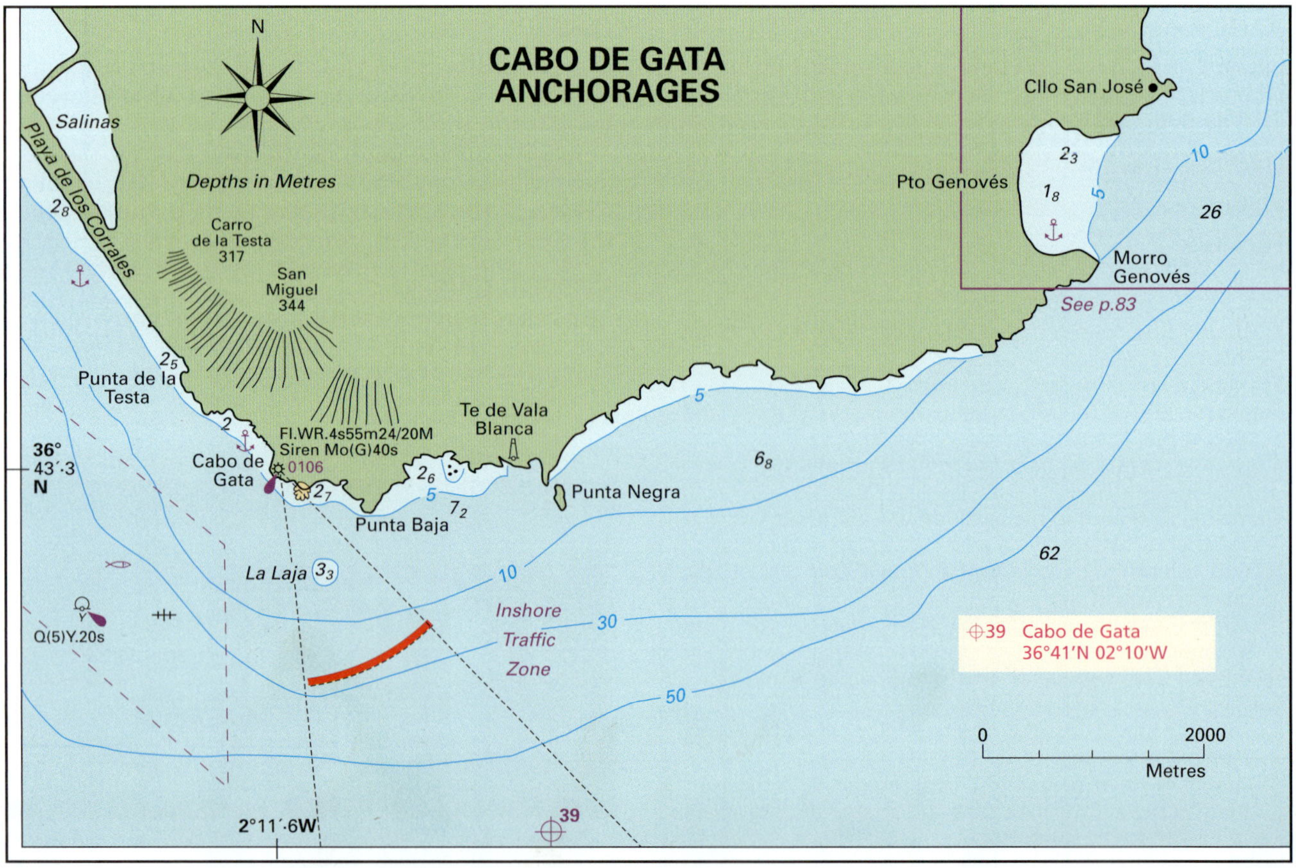

25. Isla de Alborán

35°56'·3N 03°02'·1W

A small island worth visiting but now with restrictions on anchoring imposed by the military.

Current

A permanent current of up to three knots runs past the island on an E and SE-going direction.

Charts

British Admiralty *774.* Imray *M11*
French *5864, 6569, 7672.* Spanish *4351, 435*

Lights

0086 **Alborán lighthouse** Fl(4)20s40m10M
Grey conical tower and house 20m
0087 **Puerto refugio E wharf head** Fl.R.3s4m3M
Red post 3m
0087.1 **Dique de Abrigo head** Fl.G.2s9m3M
Green square column 3m

Isolated island S of Puerto de Adra

This small island lies some 49M to S of Puerto de Adra and about 30M from the African coast. It is a bare, low, reddish-cliffed island 700m long and 300m wide with two small landing jetties and several anchorages. The sole inhabitants are the staff for the lighthouse and a military detachment.

Facilities are non-existent and, officially, in order to visit, permission must be obtained from the Naval Commander in Almería. If you arrive without permission you may or may not be allowed to stay for a short visit depending on the officer on duty.

Approach

The island can be approached from any direction but as it is low, it will not be seen until within 10M. There are a number of sunken rocks extending in places to 200m from the coast.

Entrance

Approach the E jetty on a W course with the jetty in line with the lighthouse. Keep a sharp lookout for submerged rocks during the last 200m of the approach.

Anchorages

There are several anchorages to suit the prevalent wind direction in about 6m sand and stone.

Formalities

Call on the military commander.

Facilities

In an emergency, water and food might be obtained from the garrison.

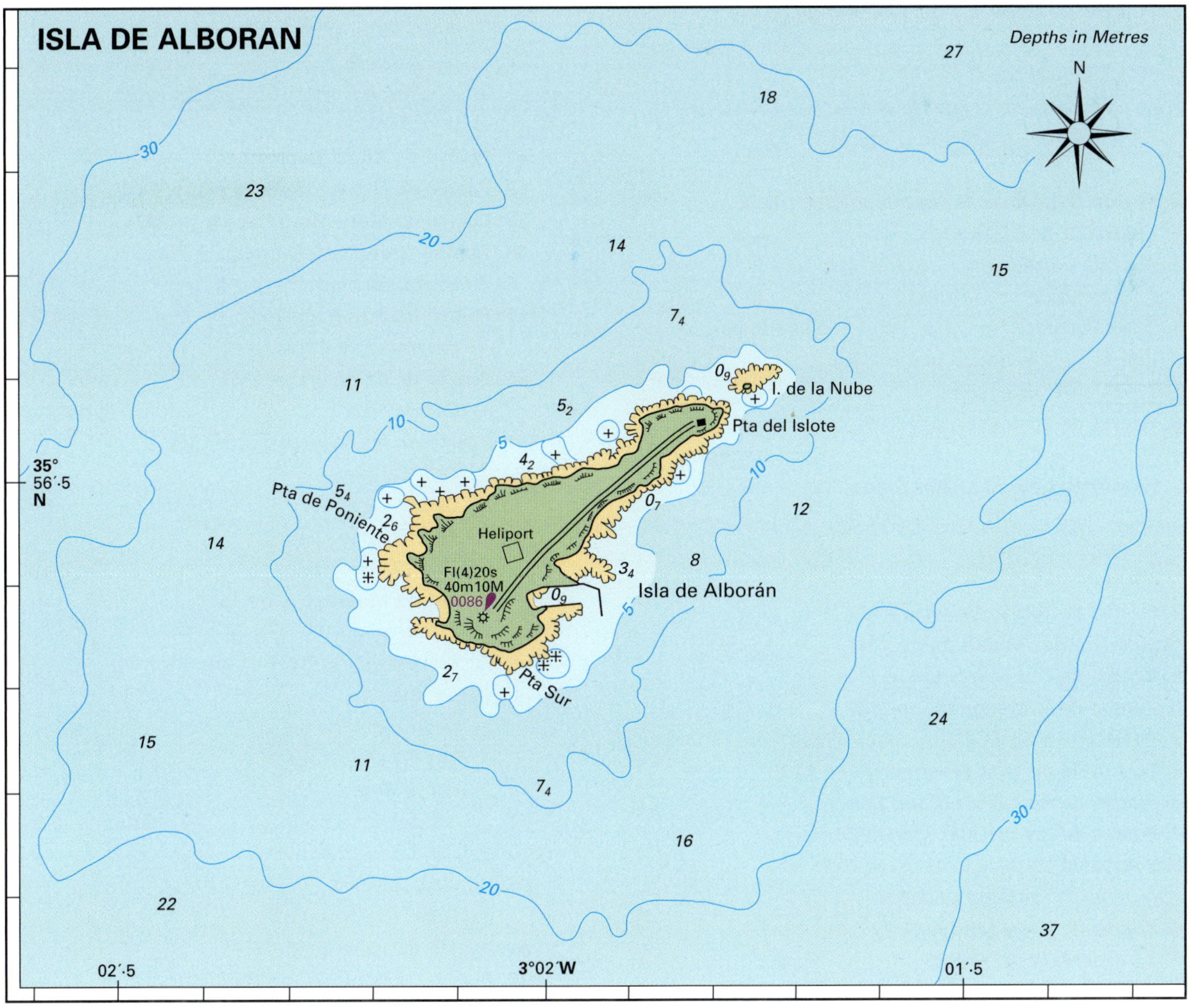

Costa Blanca planning guide and distances (See page 168 for full waypoint list)

⚓ Anchorage

Miles	*Harbours & Anchorages*	*Headlands*
21M	⚓ *Puerto Genovés*	Cabo de Gata
	⚓ *Ensenada de San José/Cala Higuera*	
	26. Puerto de San José *(page 86)*	
	⚓ *Ensenada de los Escullos*	
	⚓ *Ensenada de Rodalquilar*	
18M	⚓ *Las Negras*	
		Punta de la Polacra
	⚓ *Cala de San Pedro*	
	⚓ *Ensenada de Agua Amarga*	
	27. Puerto de Carboneras *(page 89)*	
	⚓ *2 commercial harbours – emergency only and Puerto Pescaro*	
14M	⚓ *Marina de las Torres*	
	⚓ *Punta de la Media Naranja*	
	28. Puerto de Garrucha *(page 91)*	
5M	⚓ *Palomares y Villaricos*	Río de Aguas
	29. Puerto de Villaricos *(page 93)*	Río Almanzora
0·3M	**30 .Puerto de Esperanza** *(page 93)*	
	⚓ *Anchorages 2M to N of Río Almanzora*	
14M	⚓ *Ensenada de Terreros*	
	⚓ *Punta Parda*	
	31. Puerto Juan Montiel de Aguilas *(page 96)*	
	32. Puertos de Aguilas y del Hornillo *(page 97)*	
		Punta Parda
19M	⚓ *Cala Bardina*	
	⚓ *Ensenada de la Fuente*	
	33. Club Regatas, Mazarrón *(page 101)*	
3M		Punta Negra
	34. Puerto Deportivo de Mazarrón *(page 102)*	
	⚓ *Ensenada de Mazarrón*	
	⚓ *Cala Cerrada*	
15M	⚓ *Rincón de la Salitrona*	
	⚓ *El Portús*	Cabo Tinoso
	35. Puerto de Cartagena *(page 104)*	
8M	⚓ *Cala del Gorguel*	
	36. Puerto de Portmán *(page 109)*	
9M		Cabo del Agua
	37 Puerto de Cabo de Palos *(page 111)*	
	⚓ *Cabo de Palos*	
8M	⚓ *Playa de Palos*	
	⚓ *Isla Grosa*	
	38. Puerto de Tomás Maestre and entrance to Mar Menor *(page 115)*	
	39. Puerto de Dos Mares *(page 118)*	
	40. Puerto de la Manga *(page 118)*	
	41. Puerto de Mar de Cristal *(page 118)*	
	42. Puerto de las Islas Menores *(page 120)*	
5M	**43. Puerto de los Nietos** *(page 121)*	
	44. Puerto de los Urrutias *(page 122)*	
	45. Puerto de los Alcázares *(page 123)*	
	⚓ *Puerto Santiago de Ribera*	
	46. Puerto de Lo Pagan *(page 124)*	
	⚓ *Ensenada del Esparto*	

Miles	*Harbours & Anchorages*	*Headlands*
	47. Puerto de San Pedro del Pinatar *(page 126)*	
3M	**48. Puerto de la Horadada** *(page 127)*	
3M	**49. Puerto de Campoamor** *(page 128)*	
2M	**50. Puerto de Cabo Roig** *(page 129)*	
5M	**51. Puerto de Torrevieja** *(page 131)*	
9M	**52. Marina de la Dunas (Puerto de Guardamar)** *(page 134)*	Cabo Cervera
6M	⚓ *Bahía de Santa Pola*	
	53. Puerto de Santa Pola *(page 135)*	
2M	**54. Puerto de Espato** *(page 137)*	
4M	**55. Puerto de Isla de Tabarca** *(page 137)*	
11M	**56. Puerto de Alicante** *(page 139)*	
3M	⚓ *Ensenada de la Albufereta*	
	57. Puerto de San Juan *(page 143)*	
7M	⚓ *Playa de la Huerta*	
	58. Puerto de Campello *(page 144)*	
9M		Cabo de las Huertas
	59. Puerto de Villajoyosa (Alcoco) *(page 145)*	
6M	**60. Puerto de Benidorm** *(page 147)*	
	⚓ *Ensenada de Benidorm*	
	⚓ *Cabezo del Tosal*	
7M	⚓ *Anchorage E of Punta de Canfali*	
	⚓ *Anchorage W of Punta de la Cueva del Barbero*	Punta de la Esalata
	⚓ *Anchorages NW of Punta del Albir*	
		Punta del Albir
2M	**61. Puerto de Altea** *(page 149)*	
1M	**62. Puerto de la Olla de Altea** *(page 151)*	
1M	**63. Puerto de Mary Montaña** *(page 152)*	
2M	**64. Marina Greenwich (Mascarat)** *(page 153)*	
	⚓ *Punta Mascarat*	
	65. Puerto Blanco *(page 155)*	Cabo Toix
2M	⚓ *Ensenada de Calpe*	
	66. Puerto de Calpe *(page 156)*	
3M	⚓ *Cala la Fosa*	Punta Ifach
	67. Puerto de las Basetas *(page 158)*	
	⚓ *Cala Canaret*	
3M	⚓ *Cala Blanco*	
	⚓ *Cabo Blanco*	
	⚓ *Cala del Dragon*	Cabo Blanco
	68. Puerto de Moraira *(page 160)*	
	⚓ *El Rinconet*	
	⚓ *Anchorages between Cabo Moraira and Jávea*	
	⚓ *La Grandadilla*	
11M	⚓ *Isla del Descubridor*	
	⚓ *Punta Negra*	
	⚓ *Isla del Portichol*	Cabo de la Nao
	⚓ *Cabo de San Martin*	
	⚓ *Cala Calce*	
	⚓ *Cala de la Fonta na*	
5M	**69. Puerto de Jávea** *(page 164)*	
	70. Puerto de Dénia *(page 166)*	Cabo de San Antonio

III. COSTA BLANCA

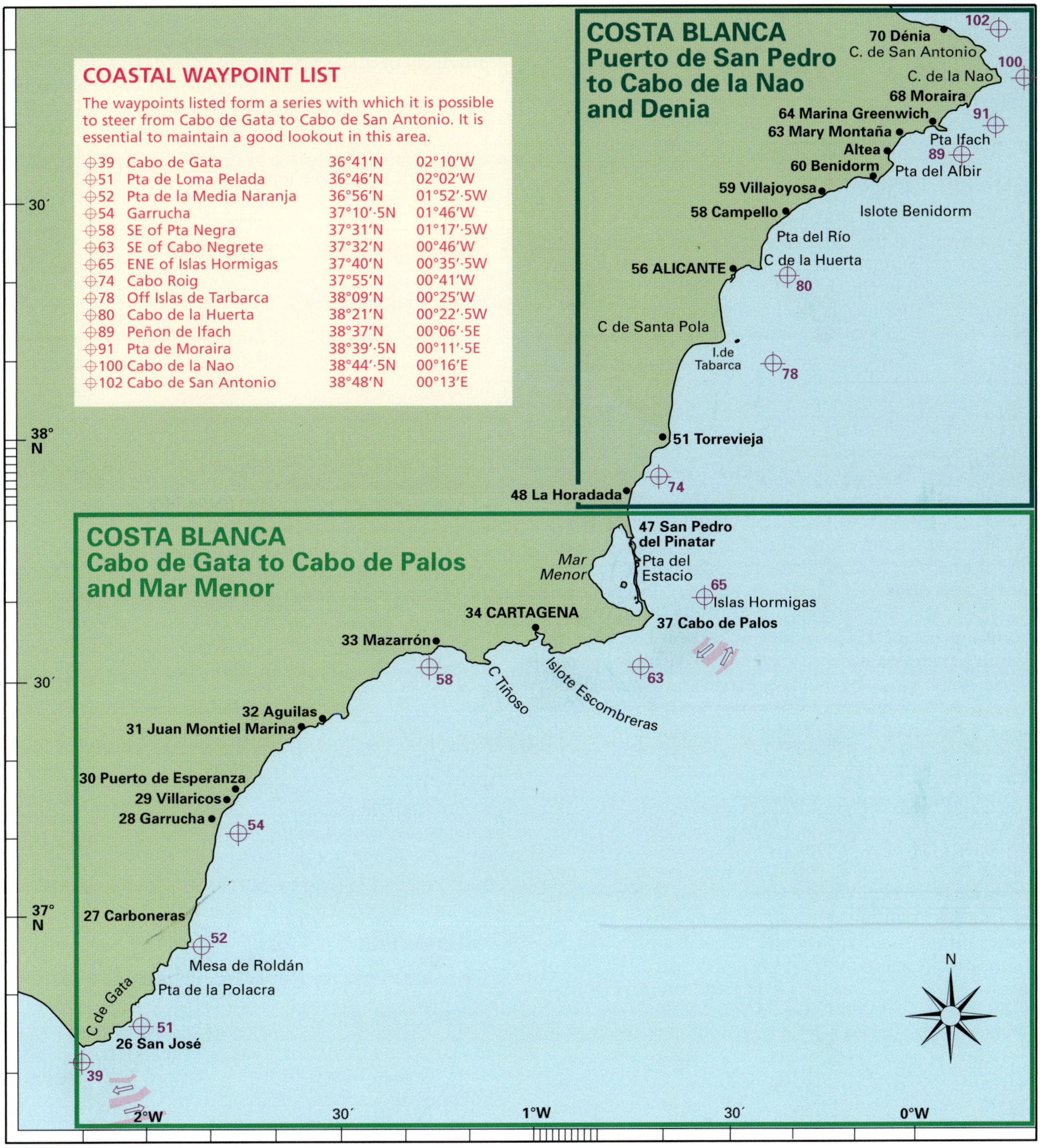

Introduction

CURRENTS

Along this coast the current is reasonably consistent and is not discussed under each port. Off Cabo de Gata the current is normally E-going and can be strong. It changes its direction to NE-going and becomes weaker along the coast, although it is stronger off Cabo de Palos. In the summer and autumn months this NE and ENE-going current is felt as far as Cabo de San Antonio but in the other months it is usually SW-going between Cabo de Palos and Cabo de San Antonio.

TIDES

Maximum spring range is less than 1m and its effects are small.

GALES – HARBOURS OF REFUGE

In the event of gales and heavy seas, Cartagena, Torrevieja and Alicante are the safest to enter. Shelter may sometimes be found where a small harbour is located behind a promontory which protects the entrance from the wind and swell.

GENERAL DESCRIPTION

This 195M stretch of coast between Cabo de Gata to just beyond Cabo de San Antonio is called Costa Blanca (the White Coast). Much of the coastal rock is a light grey which appears white in the bright sunlight. There has been much development in the past two decades. Communications and services have been much improved, many harbours have been built and old harbours adapted for yachts but the discovery of the Costa Blanca by the developers has resulted in many of the once deserted *calas* becoming surrounded by holiday homes and, in some cases, high-rise buildings for package tourists.

However, some sections remain comparatively deserted and with isolated anchorages. By no means all anchorages are noted here and the cruising yacht should be able to find unlisted spots where there is peace and quiet.

The section begins with the impressive promontory of Cabo de Gata which has several white patches of rock on its E side. The high coastal cliffs are broken by many valleys and small coves with good anchorages. The major promontories are high with steep cliffs; Punta de la Media Naranja (half an orange!), Cabo Cope and Cabo Tiñoso are examples.

Beyond Cartagena, which is one of the few natural harbours, lies the long, low sand bar that separates the Mar Menor from the sea, now looking more like a high-rise breakwater. From here to Alicante and beyond, the coast is made up of low rolling hills coming down to broken cliffs with long sandy beaches. Inland ranges of higher hills can be seen and these mountainous features reach the sea in places such as Cabo de La Huerta, Sierra Helada, Cabo de la Nao and Cabo de San Antonio.

Outlying dangers are the small islands: Isla de los Terreros near Aguilas, Isla Grosa and some smaller islets off the Mar Menor, Isla de Tabarca off Cabo de Santa Pola, Islote de Benidorm off Benidorm and the Isla de Portichol. In general, deep water can be carried quite close to the coast with the exception of some areas bordering the Mar Menor.

VISITS INLAND

Apart from places mentioned in the text, there are many interesting places to visit and things to see further inland which may be reached by taxi, bus or, in some cases, by rail. The narrow gauge FEVE runs from the north station of Alicante to Dénia and puts on the 'Lemon Express' for tourists during summer – an expedition which includes a bottle of 'champagne'. Suggestions for other expeditions can be obtained from the various information offices but the following are worth considering: Lorca, a very picturesque old town; Murcia, the capital city of the province of the same name, which has interesting churches, museums and art galleries; Orihuela, with an old church and valuable paintings; Jijona, where the nougat-like sweet turrón is made and with a ruined Moorish castle; and Alcoy, an old Visigoth town with many ancient remains.

Pilotage and navigation

TUNNY NETS

In spring, summer and autumn tunny nets may be laid at the places listed below (see the Introduction, page 5).

- Off San José
- Near Punta del Esparto
- Off Punta de la Polacra
- In Cala de San Pedro
- 2M to SW of Punta de la Media Naranja
- 1½M to N of Villaricos
- 3M to SW of Isla de los Terreros
- ½M to N of Isla de los Terreros
- 2M and 1M to SW and 1M to E of Aguilas
- In Cala Bardina
- S of Cabo Cope
- 1M to NE of Punta de Calnegre
- 5M, 3M and 1M to W of Punta Negra
- Off Punta de la Azohía
- Centre and E end of Ensenada de Mazarrón
- N of Cabo Tiñoso
- Off Puerto de Portmán
- Off Cap de Palos
- N of Cabo de las Huertas
- In the Ensenada de Benidorm
- W of the Peñón de Ifach
- Ensenada de Moraira

FISH HAVENS

There are extensive fish havens along this coast.

RESTRICTED AREAS

In Cartagena there are areas reserved for the Spanish navy which may not be entered by yachts. Submarines exercise in areas from Cabo de Gata to Cabo San Sebastian and there is a firing area S of Cartagena. Anchoring is prohibited in an area to the S of Puerto de Jávea where there are underwater cables.

MAGNETIC VARIATION

Costa Blanca (Cartagena) 01°25′W (2008) decreasing 7′ annually.

III. Cabo de Gata to Cabo de Palos and Mar Menor

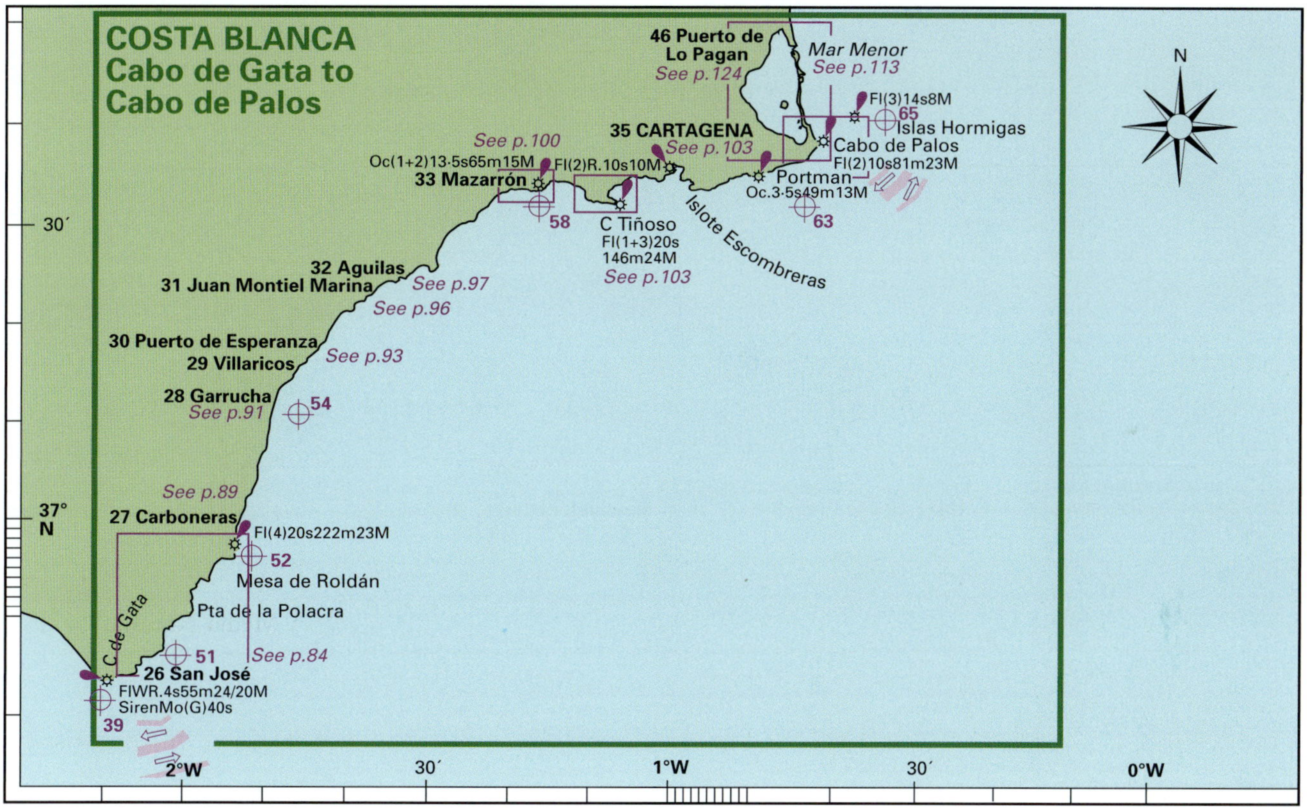

PORTS

COASTAL WAYPOINT LIST

The waypoints listed form a series with which it is possible to steer from Cabo de Gata to off Cabo de Palos. It is essential to maintain a good lookout in this area.

⌖39	Cabo de Gata	36°41′N	02°10′W
⌖51	Pta de Loma Pelada	36°46′N	02°02′W
⌖52	Pta de la Media Naranja	36°56′N	01°52′·5W
⌖54	Garrucha	37°10′·5N	01°46′W
⌖58	SE of Pta Negra	37°31′N	01°17′·5W
⌖63	SE of Cabo Negrete	37°32′N	00°46′W
⌖65	ENE of Islas Hormigas	37°40′N	00°35′·5W

THE PORTS OF MAR MENOR

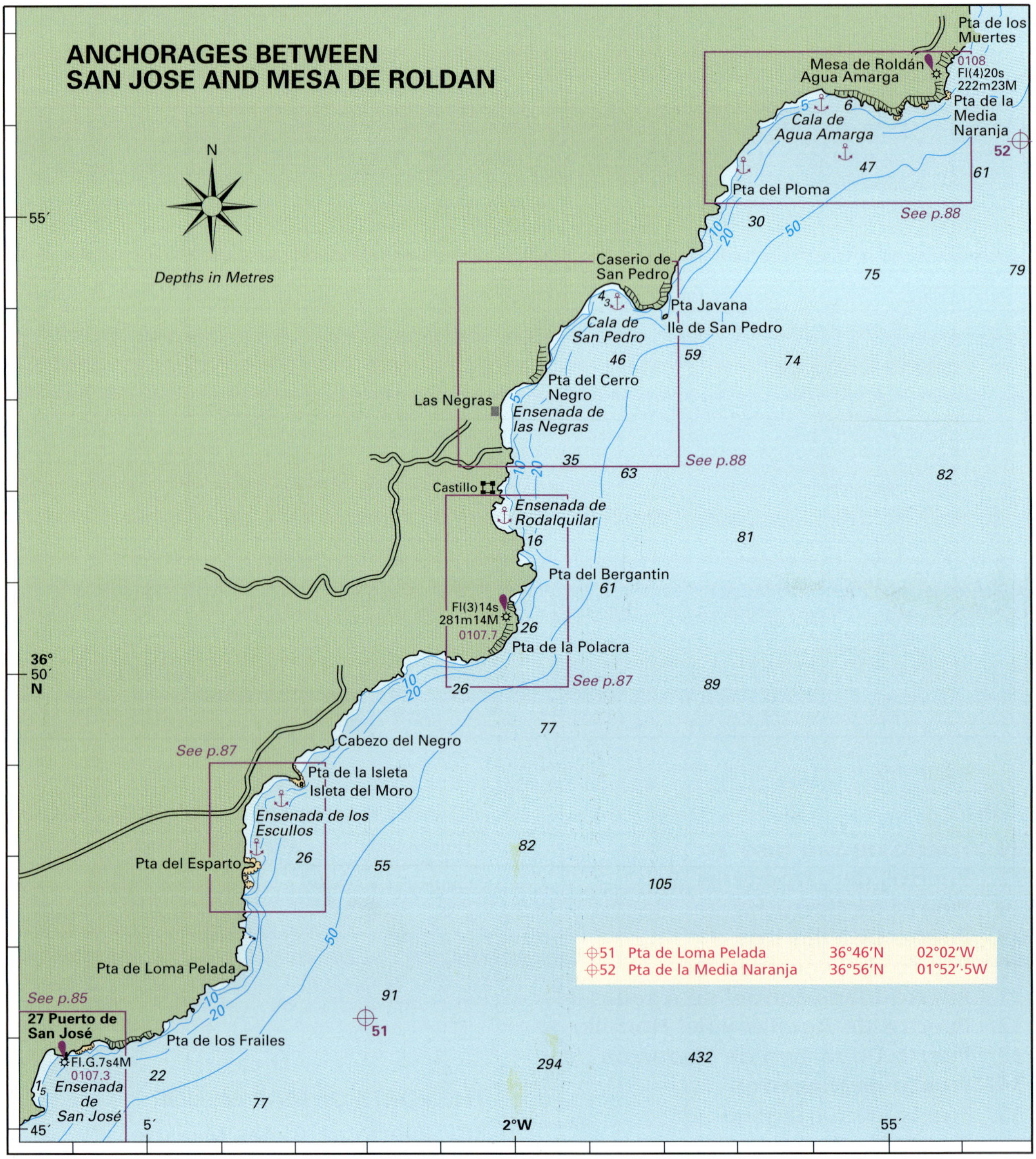

All the anchorages along this stretch of coast are susceptible to swell. With an E or NE wind, a surprisingly high and confused sea can develop due to the NE-going counter-current. Likewise with a W or SW wind, combined with the current going NE following the coast, the headlands concentrate the effect of a short sea, creating an unpleasant swell in the bays and, for those heading W, a slow passage.

During calm weather, there are many really beautiful bays to visit. Several Roman mine workings are clearly visible.

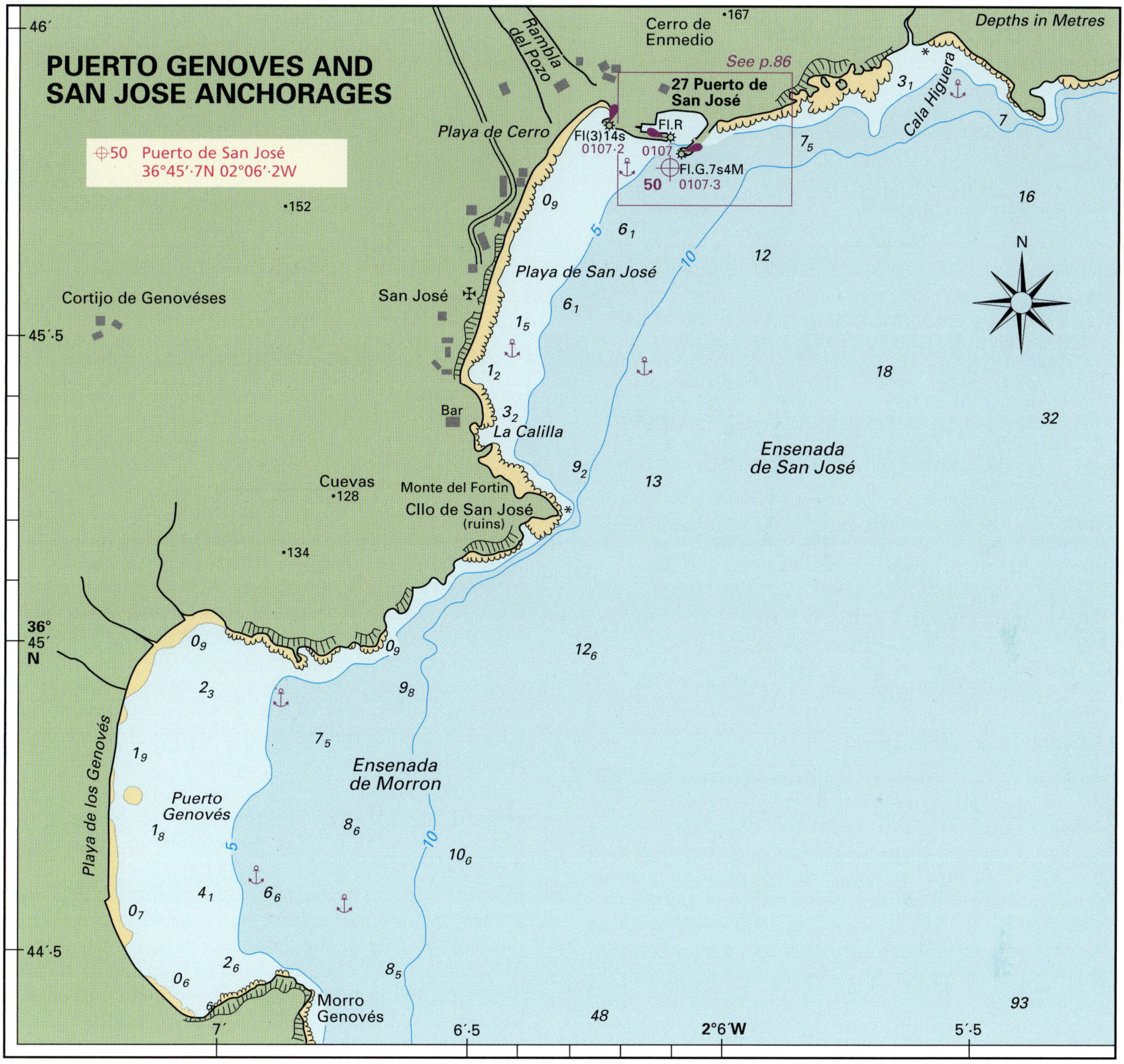

⚓ PUERTO GENOVÉS

36°44'·6N 2°07'W

A bay on the E side of Cabo de Gata with a gently sloping sandy bottom. Open between NE and SE with good protection from other winds especially close inshore at N and S sides of bay. Anchor to suit wind in 5m, sand and mud.

Note that there are rocks to the SE of Morro Genovese so do not pass too close to the cliffs on entering bay from the south.

⚓ ENSENADA DE SAN JOSÉ/CALA HIGUERA

36°45'·6N 2°06'·3W

Similar open bay to Puerto Genovés but with sandy and rocky beach with developments. A small village now exists with a road to Almería. Protection from N–NE winds at NE end of bay under cliffs.

In strong S to SW winds the swell curls round the headland into this *ensenada* but Porto Genovés is quieter and should be used in these conditions.

Puerto Genovés. The word 'Puerto' covers both an enclosed harbour and a bay with some shelter

26. Puerto de San José

36°46'N 02°06'W

A very small shallow yacht harbour with limited depths and 244 berths a short distance from Cabo de Gata. Usually full and not recommended for yachts over 12m.

Charts

British Admiralty *774.* Imray *M11, M12*
French *7671.* Spanish *461*

⊕50 30°45'·7N 02°06'·2W

Lights

To the southwest
0106 **Cabo de Gata** Fl.WR.4s55m24/20M 356°-W-316°-R-356° Siren Mo(G)40s White tower, grey lantern 19m
Harbour
0107.3 **Dique Este head** Fl.G.7s8m4M Green ▲ on truncated tower 3m
0107 **Dique Sur E head** Fl.R.6s7m3M Red ■ on truncated tower 3m
0107.2 **Dique Sur W head** Fl(3)14s4m2M White masonry tower 1m
To the northeast
0108 **Mesa de Roldán** Fl(4)20s222m23M White octagonal tower 18m
0107.7 **Punta de la Polacra** 36°50'·6N 02°00'·1W Fl(3)14s281m14M Tower 14m

Port communications

Capitanía VHF Ch 9. ✆ +34 950 38 00 41
Email correo@clubnauticodesanjose.com
www.clubnauticodesanjose.com

Attractive small harbour

A small yacht harbour in attractive surroundings which is a useful break in the 50M stretch of coast between Almería and Garrucha. The harbour is subject to swell from E–SE but is otherwise well protected. A small village nearby can supply basic requirements. There are walks in empty country, fine views from the hills, caves near top of Monte del Fortin and excellent sandy beaches. Unfortunately, there is rarely room for visitors and although the *capitan* and *marineros* are enthusiastic and welcoming, they have to turn visitors away – at least in summer.

Approach

From the south Round the prominent Cabo de Gata (⊕39 36°41'N 02°10'W) (344m), either close inshore or 1M offshore to avoid the Laja de Cabo de Gata shoal (3.3m) which breaks in heavy weather. It lies 1,300m SSE of Cabo de Gata light and in its red sector. 1M to E of the lighthouse there are some conspicuous white rock patches on the dark cliff face which, seen from afar, resemble sails. Keep ½M offshore rounding onto a NE course after the Morro Genovés which is conically shaped and lies at the S side of Puerto Genovés, a deep bay with a sandy beach. The Monte del Fortin, which has a ruined fort, separates Puerto Genovés from Ensenada de San José. This bay is lined with houses and the harbour lies in the N corner under a small white rock patch.

San José *Pública de Puertos de Andalucía*

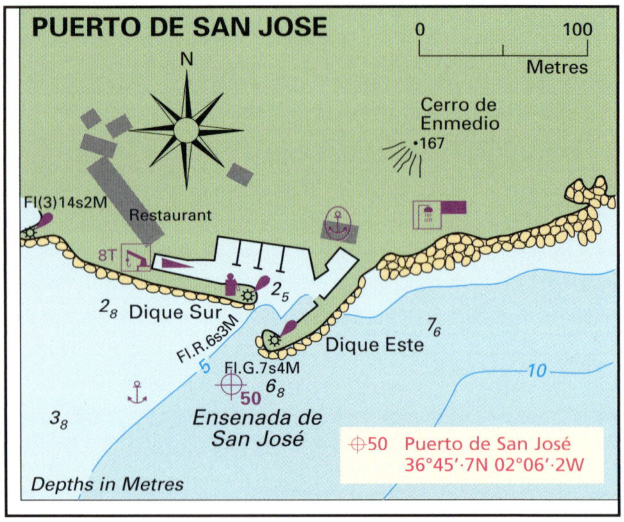

From the north The Mesa de Roldán is a high plateau (221m). The lighthouse is on Punta de la Media Naranja and can be seen from afar. Agua Amarga is just to the west of Media Naranja. These features can easily be identified. To the SW Punta Javana has a small island, Isla de San Pedro, off its point. Punta de la Polacra (263m) with a tower on its summit and Punta de Loma Pelada which has the high Cerro de los Frailes (489–444m) inland should be recognised. San José lies SW of this high ground. Keep over ¼M offshore.

GPS approach

Steer to ⊕50 from a southeasterly quadrant and steer for breakwater end.

Anchorage in the approach

The whole of the Ensenada de San José is suitable for anchorage – 200m to SW of the harbour entrance in 5m sand is recommended. If wind is strong from N an alternative is in a small bay off Playa de Cala Higuera, just under ½M E of the harbour.

Entrance

Approach the harbour heading N and give the head of Dique Sur 10m clearance.

Berths

Secure to starboard-hand quay or fuel berth to port and ask at the *capitanía* for a berth.

Charges

High.

Facilities

Maximum length overall: 14m.
Slipway.
8-tonne crane.
A few taps on pontoons but water may be salty.
220V AC.
Gasoleo A and petrol.
Shops in village.

Communications

Bus service to Almería. ✆ Area code 950.

⚓ ENSENADA DE LOS ESCULLOS

36°48′·2N 02°03′·2W

An open bay anchorage with sloping sandy bottom, some sandy beaches. Coast road, some development. The ruined castle, *guardia civil* barracks and a point with a white, skull-shaped rock, lie near the centre of the bay. The bay is wide open to E but some protection from NE in N corner of the bay is possible under Punta de la Isleta.

Punta de la Isleta

Los Escullos

⚓ ENSENADA DE RODALQUILAR

36°51′·6N 02°00′W

The holding is reportedly poor in places. Open between NE and SE.

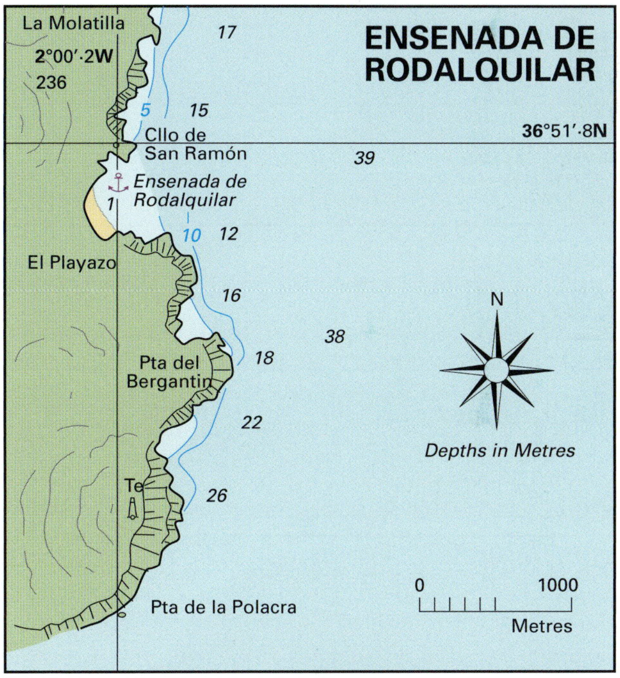

Rodalquilar

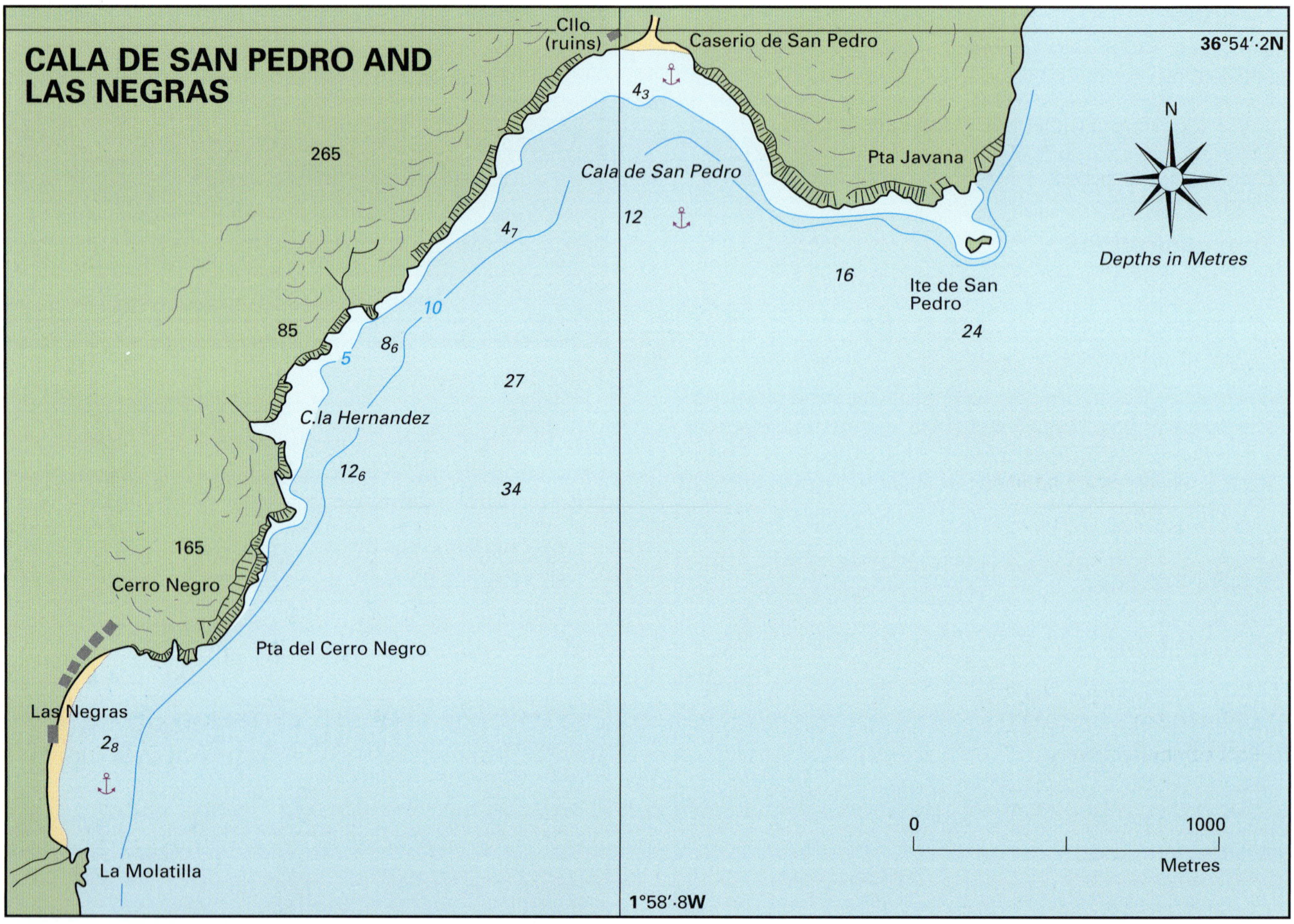

San Pedro

⚓ LAS NEGRAS 36°52′·6N 01°59′·9W

Anchor in 3m sand and weed off the village. Open between NE and SE. The beach is sand and rock. The village has some shops.

⚓ CALA DE SAN PEDRO 36°53′·9N 01°58′·7W

An imposing anchorage where fluky and strong gusts may be expected. Anchor to suit draught in sand and weed.

⚓ ENSENADA DE AGUA AMARGA (BITTER WATER BAY) 36°56′·0N 01°56′·0W

Anchor outside the small boat moorings in 6–8m of water. Excellent shelter from the NE winds but open between E and S. Alternative anchorages lie off the hamlet of El Ploma 2M to SW or off a small cove 1M to SW of Agua Amarga. Use these with care.

27. Puertos de Carboneras

36°59'·3N 01°53'·8W

Three busy commercial and fishing harbours in close proximity to each other. To be avoided unless in an emergency, but providing a useful anchorage protected from the SW swell from Cabo de Gata.

Charts

British Admiralty *1515, 774.* Imray *M12*
French *7671.* Spanish *4621, 462*

⊕53 36°59'·2N 01°53'·5W

Lights

South Harbour (Puerto de Hornos Ibéricos SA)
0109 **Dique Este head** Fl(2)G.10s12m5M Green round tower 3m
0109.2 **Dique Este elbow** Q(3)10s12m3M ♦ card BYB tower 3m
0109.3 **Dique Oeste head** Fl(2)R.10s7m3M Red round tower 3m
Middle harbour (PUCARSA – Puerto de Generar Electricidad)
0109.4 **Dique de Abrigo** 36°58'.5N 01°53'.6W Fl.G.10s14m5M Green metal post 4m
North harbour (Puerto Pescaro de Carboneras)
0109.6 **Dique Este** Fl(3)G.12s10m5M Green hexagonal tower 4m
0109.7 **Contradique** Fl(3)R.12s8m3M Red hexagonal tower 6m

Port communications

Puerto de Hornos Ibéricos VHF Ch 9, 12.
Puerto Departivo (northern harbour)
✆/*Fax* +34 950 13 07 39
Email Caroneras@eppa.es
www.eppa.es/en/fishing-harbour-carboneras

Commercial and fishing harbours

Three harbours, two commercial, large and forbidding, the Puerto de Hornos Ibéricos SA and the Puerto Generar del Electricidad and the third a working fishing harbour. However the first two offer good refuge from winds from all directions except SE though they should only be used in an emergency. Local facilities are about zero but provisions can be found in Carboneras village. The immediate area is dominated by the huge cement plant and electric generating station but the hinterland is wild and attractive. The fishing harbour is busy and has no special facilities for yachts. In poor weather it is likely to be crowded and a yacht would have to take its chance alongside a fishing boat.

Approach

From the south After Cabo de Gata the coast is broken by headlands enclosing sandy bays. Puerto Genovés is a wide sandy bay and the Ensenada de San José, which has a small harbour and village, can be identified. Further N, El Fraile (489m) is conspicuous as are the Isleta del Moro and Punta de la Polacra (263m) which has a tower. Cala de San Pedro which has a few houses and Agua Amarga may also be seen. The white lighthouse of Mesa de Roldán (221m) can be seen from afar. Once the points of La Media Naranja (⊕52 36°56'N 01°52'·5W) and Los Muertos have been rounded the large breakwaters and the industrial buildings belching smoke will be seen.

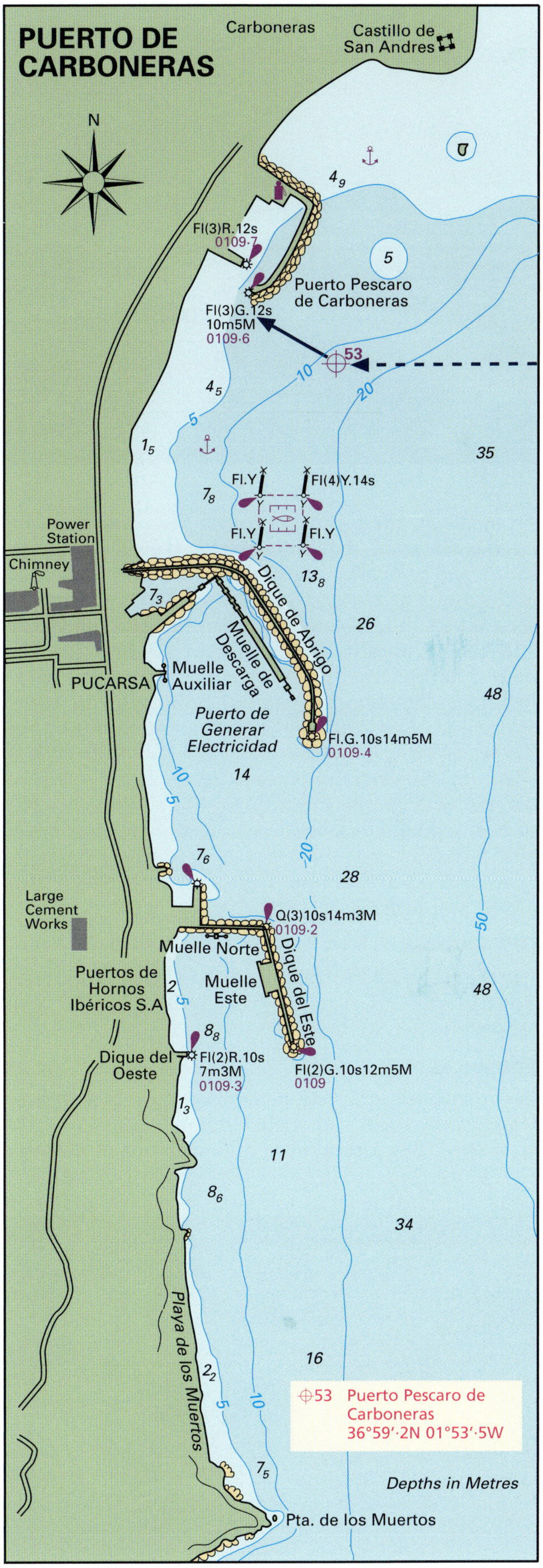

The two commercial harbours at Carboneras with Puerto Pescaro at top right

From the north From Puerto de Garrucha, backed by the town of the same name, the coast is flat, sandy and unbroken, with high ranges of hills inland and some low cliffs. The town of Mojacar may be seen on its hill, ¼M inland, then the buildings stop and the mountains begin, which last until shortly before Carboneras. The village of Carboneras stands behind a rather inconspicuous point with El Islote and Isla de San Andreas (14m) extending 600m off the point. Foul ground stretches nearly ½M from this point in a SE direction, otherwise the coast is free of dangers and can be followed at 400m. Once the Isla de San Andreas has been passed, the harbour walls and buildings may be seen. A 3·5m deep passage, running NE–SW, 150m wide, exists between this island and El Islote.

GPS approach

For the Puerto Pescaro steer to ⊕53 from an easterly quadrant and steer for breakwater end (approximately 0·3M).

Entrances

Both big harbours may be entered on a NW course leaving the head of either Dique Este 50m to starboard. Pay attention to and keep out of the way of any commercial vessel manoeuvring. The entrance to the Puerto Pescaro is straightforward but shoals and may be alive with traffic.

Berths

The two main commercial harbours are to be avoided and only used in an emergency. There are usually large commercial vessels in port, so even in an emergency it would not be easy to berth. There is a plan to extend the fishing port and a new breakwater is being constructed between the Puerto Pescaro and the dique protecting the north commercial harbour – NW of the fish farm.

Anchorages

Between Puerto de Carboneras and Puerto Pescaro there is a good anchorage inside the fish farm, off the beach, outside the swim buoys. This anchorage is well protected in strong W winds.

A temporary anchorage may be available in 5m sand and stone on the E side of the south and middle harbours, close inshore and clear of commercial works.

Outside, there are two possibilities: between Puerto de Carboneras and Puerto Pescaro and between Puerto Pescaro and El Islote. Both are open to the SE but the latter has better shelter from the NE. Sand, stone and weed.

Formalities

In the commercial harbours, contact the shore by radio for permission to stay. In the fishing harbour, inquire ashore.

Puerto Pescaro de Carboneras

⚓ MARINA DE LAS TORRES

37°09′·7N 01°49′W

An open coastal anchorage off the mouth of Río de Aguas in 5m sand, stone and weed. Exposed between NE and SE. The towns of Mojacar and Garrucha lie 2M and 1M away. There is a small landing jetty nearby. A road runs behind the beach and there is a conspicuous old factory chimney.

28. Puerto de Garrucha

37°11′N 01°49′·1W

A Commercial harbour with two marinas, one newly opened in 2013, to take 300 vessels up to 18m. Plenty of room for visitors.

Charts

British Admiralty *1515, 774.* Imray *M12*
French *7671.* Spanish *462*

⊕55 37°10′·5N 01°48′·8W Puerto de Garrucha approaches

Lights

0110 **Garrucha LtHo** Oc(4)13s19m13M White tower house 10m Reserve light 8M
0111·5 **Dique (unattached)** Q(3)10s4m3M ⬧ card BYB 3m
0111 **Dique de Levante head** head Fl(3)G.9s13m5M Green tower 11m
0112 **Dique de Poniente head** Fl(3)R.8s6m3M Red tower 3m

Port communications

Old marina ✆ +34 950 13 24 10
www.eppa.es/en/marina-garrucha
New marina ✆ +34 950 80 80 90 / 600 14 91 15
Call Ch 9 *New Marina Garrucha*

Busy commercial harbour with a small fishing fleet and new marina

A small town with an active fishing fleet, Garrucha is known for its seafood: *mariscos*.

The old marina with 250 berths up to 12m and fuel pump has always been accommodating, but overstretched, with little room for visitors. This is a convenient and inexpensive stopping place for yachts heading to Cabo de Gata and beyond, or to Cartagena and the Baleares. A well stocked supermarket is on the main road heading NE about 100m from the old marina.

In 2012 the port was extended to accommodate a new marina at the N end of the harbour. This is a substantial facility with over 300 berths up to 18m. Infrastructure was being completed in late summer 2013 with water and electricity available at all berths. The harbour is open to the S and SE, which causes some surging in strong E winds.

Approach

From the south The Sierra Cabrera, whose foothills are easily identified, lead to Garrucha; one of these hills is covered with tourist housing development. An isolated obelisk-like chimney on a small hill behind the town is conspicuous. The lighthouse shows at close range.

From the north The low plain and dry river mouths SSW of Sierra Almagrera lead to Garrucha which has an isolated chimney and cranes on the Dique de Levante.

Note: Fish farm indicated on charts 5M NE of Garrucha (centred 37°13′·4N 1°44′·9W) was not in place late Summer 2013.

GPS approach

Steer to ⊕55 from an easterly quadrant and steer for breakwater end (approximately 2·5M).

Anchorage in the approach

Anchor 200m S of elbow of Dique de Poniente in 5m sand.

Entrance

Straightforward, but commercial vessels have right of way. There is often a conspicuous large freighter moored on the inside S end of the Dique de Levante loading and unloading a cargo of gypsum. The ship is far more conspicuous than the dique, which can cause confusion until close.

Berths

The old Puerto Deportivo marina is still operating, along with the fuelling berth, though usually full with local vessels. It may be convenient to moor on the end of the T pontoon fuelling point if arriving at night, where there is room for two 12m yachts.

The new marina lies at the N end of the harbour, which has been extended and dredged. Few details or plans are published as of late summer 2013, but the marina is fully operational with yachts being berthed alongside rather than fore and aft, although lines are in place tailed to the quay in readiness for busier times.

Garrucha harbour with its north extension and the addition of its new marina in 2013
Pública de Puertos de Andalucía

Facilities

Maximum length overall: 18m in new marina
Simple wood hull repairs by yard on slipway or in workshop in terrace to W of port.
12-tonne crane on Dique de Levante.
Slipways.
Water on quays.
Showers in the office block (key from harbourmaster).
125V and 220V AC supply point on Dique de Poniente and on pontoons.
Gasoleo A and petrol.
Ice from factory on front near *capitán de puerto*'s office.
Club Cultural y Marítimo de Garrucha.
A number of shops and a small market in the village SW of the harbour.
Litter bins around the harbour.

Locally

This is an amazingly industrious area rich in minerals, including gypsum which is transported to the harbour daily and loaded onto freighters, creating a lot of dust. Many mines have been operating in the area since Roman times.

A few km NE of the harbour lies a huge holiday complex on the beach, mostly used by German and Scandinavian vacationers who come all year round. There are beaches either side of the port and many coves and isolated beaches all along the coast.

Communications

Bus service to Vera. Area code 950.

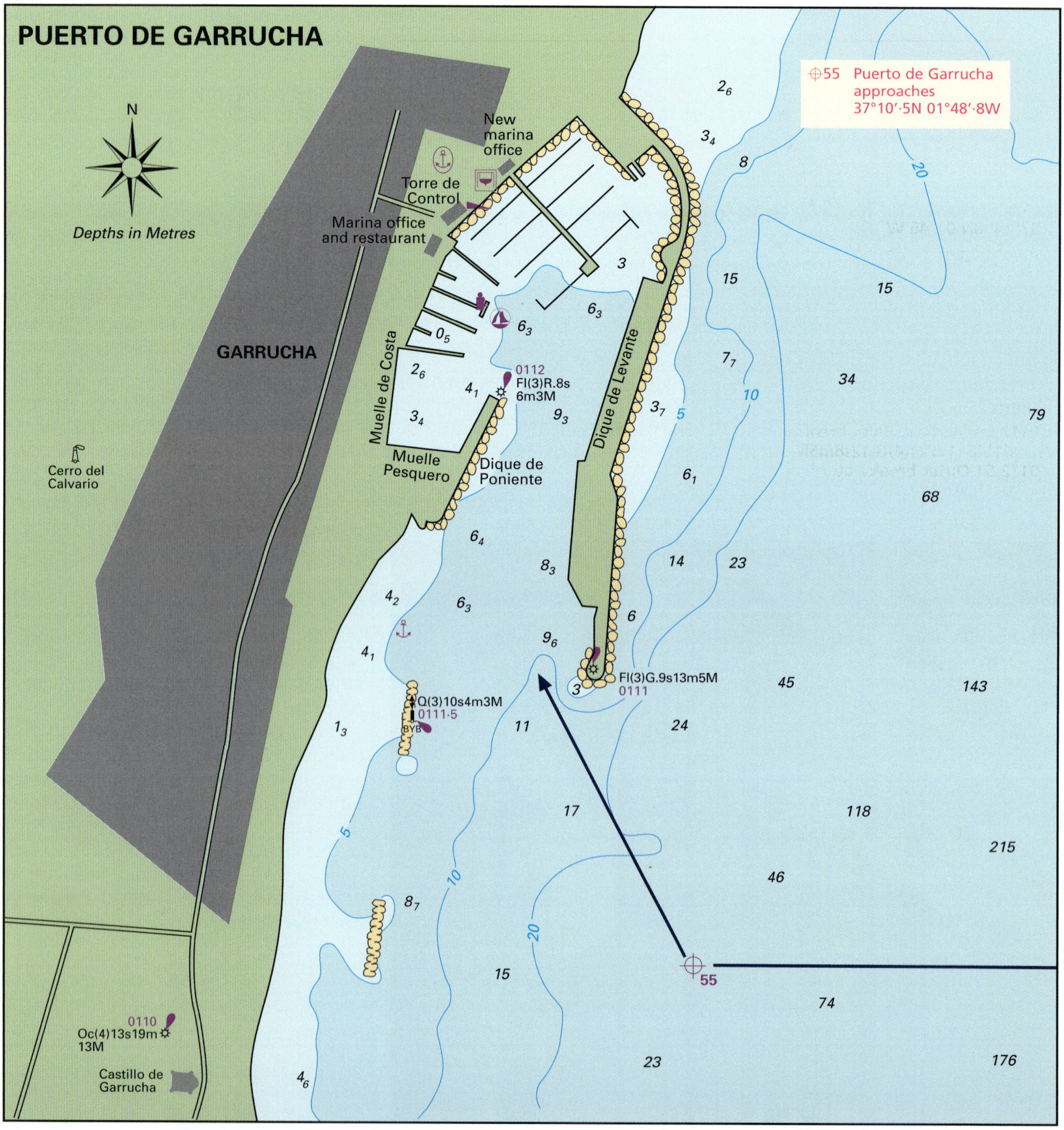

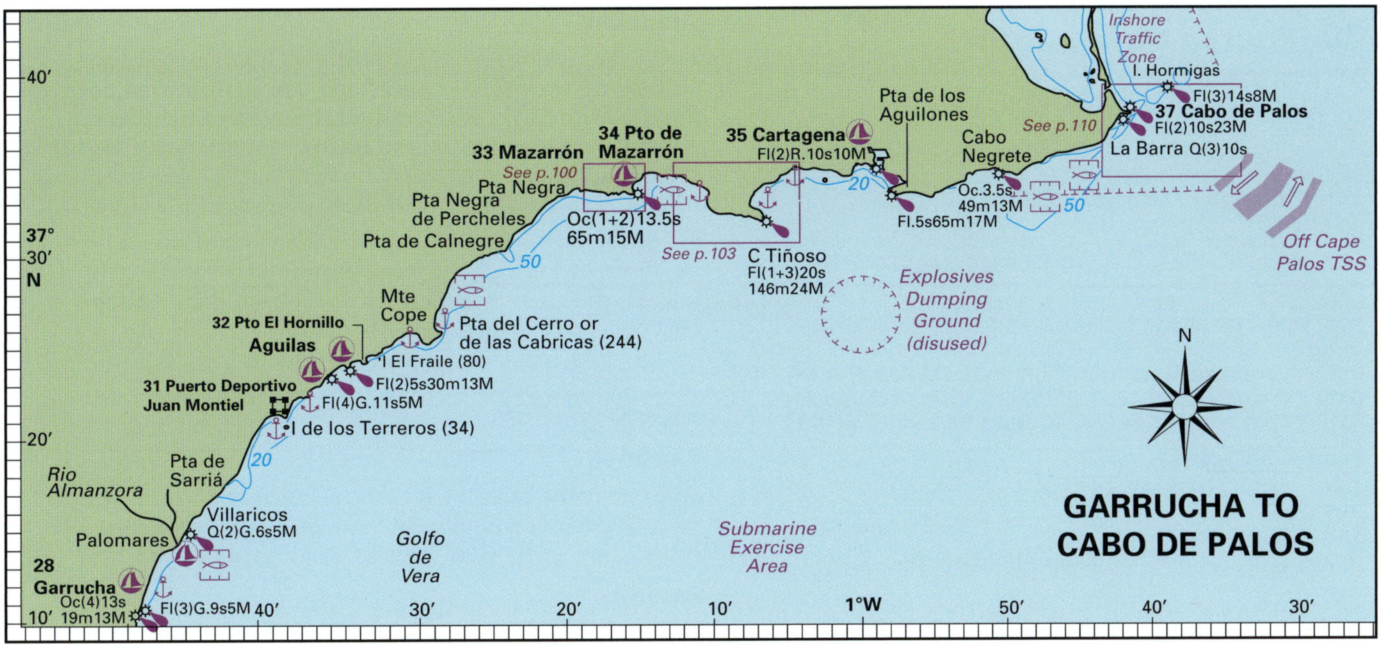

29. Puerto de Villaricos

37°14′·8N 01°46′W

A very small harbour just SW of Villaricos of 50 berths for local use with no room for visitors.

Charts

British Admiralty *774*. Imray *M12*
French *7671*. Spanish *462, 46*

⊕56 37°14′·9 01°45′·7 Puerto de Esperanza approaches

Lights

0112.5 **Villaricos. Balsa breakwater head** 37°14′.8N 01°46′.1W Fl(4)G.12s8m5M Green truncated tower 3m

0112.51 **Outer breakwater head** Fl(4)R.15s4m3M Red truncated tower 3m

Port communications

www.eppa.es/en/puerto-villaricos-la-balsa

No room for visitors

A pleasant but very small artificial harbour built for the town's pleasure craft (at last sighting there were only small motor boats). There is little or no room for visitors, no harbour facilities. Max length 5·6m.

⚓ PALOMARES Y VILLARICOS

Open anchorages either side of the mouth of the Río Almanzora. Note the shoals of the delta.

The village of Villaricos is right of centre in the photograph below.

Puerto de Villaricos *Pública de Puertos de Andalucía*

Puerto de Villaricos with Esperanza at the right of the photo

30. Puerto de Esperanza

37°15'N 01°46'W

A small fishing harbour just NE of Villaricos, with 80 moorings but no room for visitors.

Charts

British Admiralty *774.* Imray *M12*
French *7671.* Spanish *46, 462*

⊕56 37°14'·9 01°45'·7 Puerto de Esperanza approaches

Lights

0113 **Dique de Abrigo head** Q(2)G.6s8m5M Green tower 3m
0113·1 **Contradique (centre)** Fl(2)R.10s3m3M Red post 1m
0113·2 **Espigón** Fl(3)G.10s3m3M Green square column 2m
0113·4 **Contradique head** Fl(3)R.10s4m3M Red tower 3m

Port communications

Capitania✆*/Fax* +34 950 46 71 37
VHF Ch 9
Email villaricos@eppa.es
www.eppa.es/en/marina-villaricos-la-esperanza

Tiny fishing harbour

Villaricos' tiny fishing harbour is only suitable for small (<8m) craft for a short stay. It is an attractive setting but even one visiting craft may be too many. Depths are reported to be 2m in the approach and port but caution and careful sounding is advised during any approach.

Approach

From the south The coast north of Garrucha is flat and sandy with few features and can be followed at about 200m offshore except off the delta of the River Almanzora when 400m should be maintained. The village of Palomares may be seen south of the river mouth with the village of Villaricos north of the river.

From the north From the easily identified Ensenada de Terreros with its off-lying island (24m) and small village, the coast is cliffed with small sand and stone beaches in breaks of the cliffs. Inland the hills rise to 350m. The coast is steep-to; two off-lying shallows (6m) – Piedra del Celor and Losa del Payo – break in heavy seas.

Entrance

Approach the head of the Dique de Abrigo on a W to NW course, round it at 10m and pass fairly close to the quay extension with its small green tower.

Facilities

Slipway in SW corner
Shops in village 200m to SW.

⚓ ANCHORAGES 2M TO N OF RÍO ALMANZORA

At least 10 small anchorages in *calas*, some with piers and quays – use with care.

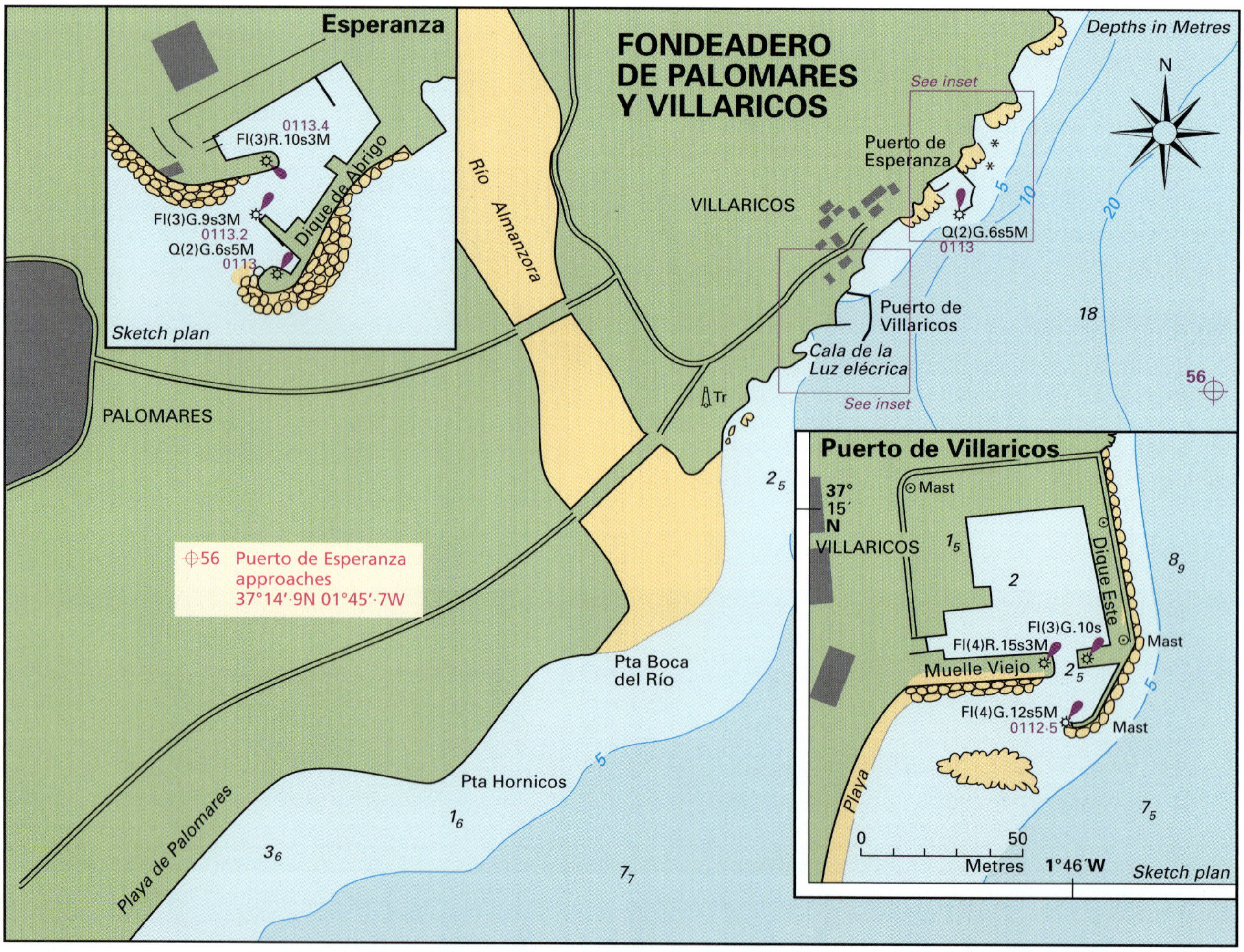

Anchorages to the SW of Aguilas

⚓ ENSENADA DE TERREROS
37°21'N 01°39'·7W

A well-protected anchorage but open to SE and subject to swell in all except N sector winds. The 600m passage between the Punta el Cañon and Isla de los Terreros (34m) is 6m deep. Anchor off San Juan de los Terreros in N part of bay. A few shops and the main road.

⚓ PUNTA PARDA
37°22'·5N 01°37'·5W

At the N end of Ensenada de los Tarais, which is open between E and S, there are two anchorages on the west side of Punta Parda, off Cala Reona and Cala Cerrada, and one on the east, Cama de los Novios (beware of the small island in the entrance to this bay). Anchor according to draught, sand and weed. Whether the name, Cama de los Novios, the bed of the newly-married, reflects turbulent or peaceful nights is anyone's guess.

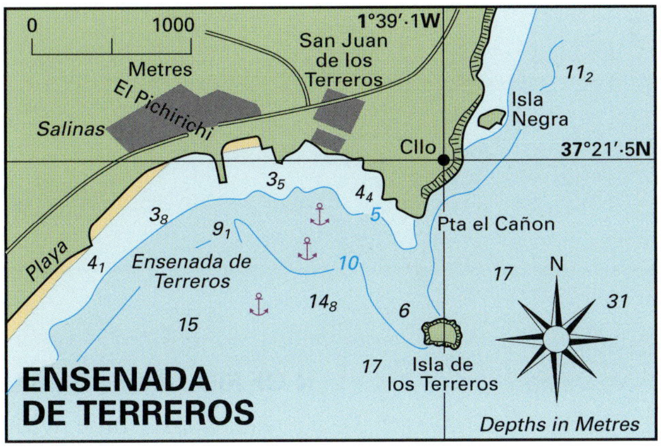

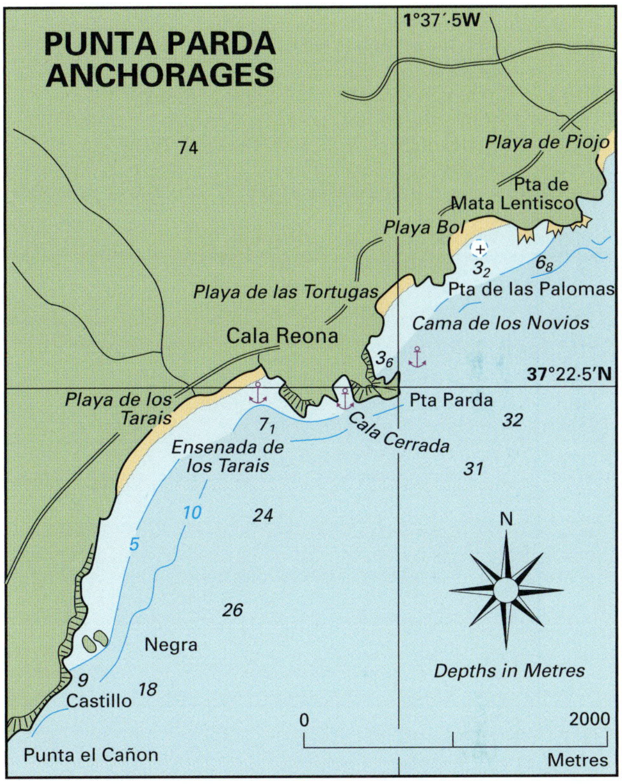

Looking N into Cala Cerrada with Punta Parda at right foreground; Cama de los Novios is just showing behind the point

31. Puerto Deportivo Juan Montiel de Aguilas

37°23'·69N 01°35'·93W

A new marina opened in 2012 with 355 berths up to 30m. Very welcoming to visitors. The marina is small but accommodating.

Charts

British Admiralty *1515, 774.* Imray *M12*
French *7671.* Spanish *463*

Lights

0113.42 **Juan Montiel (Casica Verde). Breakwater Head** 37°23'·63N 1°35'·97W Fl(4)G.11s5M Green truncated pyramidal tower
0113.44 **Jetty Head** 37°23'·70N 1°36'·40W Fl(4)R.11s3M Red round column 3m
0133.46 **Corner** 37°23'·70N 1°36'·00W Fl.R.3s1M Red round column 5m
0113.48 **Head** 37°23'·67N 1°35'·97W Fl(2)R.7s1M Red post 2m
0116.2 **Marina. S Breakwater. Head** 37°24'·39N 1°34'·40W Fl(2)G.7s6m3M White truncated tower, green top 5m
0116.4 **W Breakwater** 37°24'·42N 1°34'·41W Fl(2)R.7s5m1M White truncated conical tower, red top 4m

Port communications

☏ +34 968 41 49 68
Email info@puertodeportivojuanmontiel.com
www.puertodeportivojuanmontiel.es

New welcoming marina Puerto (Deportivo) Juan Montiel de Aguilas

A new small private marina owned by a hotel and holiday complex. Room for visitors alongside the Dique de Levante.

Entrance of Juan Montiel Marina: Reporting berth
Graham Hutt

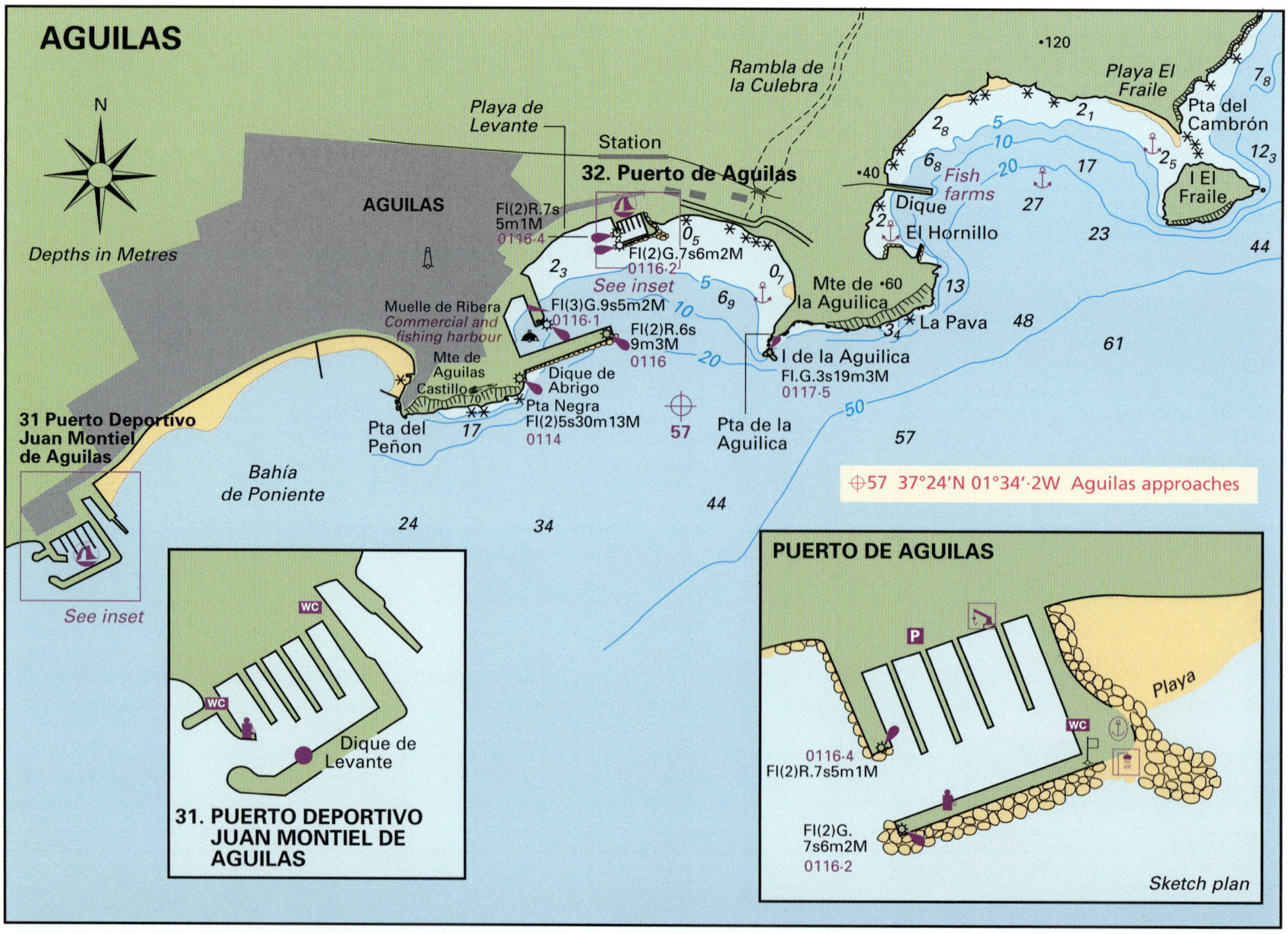

Puerto de Juan Montiel Aguilas. Approaching the new marina: easily identified by the chimney behind
Graham Hutt

32. Puertos de Aguilas y del Hornillo

37°24'·4N 01°34'·4W

A small club Nautico with 182 berths up to 12m. Nearby 1M to the W is a small fishing and commercial port with 150 berths to 10m with few spaces for visitors.

Currents

Currents inside these two bays tend to set in the direction of recent winds.

Charts

British Admiralty *1515, 774.* Imray *M12*
French *7671.* Spanish *463*

⊕57 37°24'N 01°34'·2W Aguilas approaches

Lights

Approach
0114 **Punta Negra** Fl(2)5s30m13M Black and white bands 23m
0117.5 **Islote de la Aguilica** Fl.G.3s19m3M Square white building
Commercial Harbour
0116 **Mole** head Fl(3)R.9s9m3M Red post 5m
0116·1 **Contradique head** Fl(3)G.9s5m2M Grey Post 3m
Yacht Harbour (Darsena Deportiva)
0116.2 **Dique Sur head** Fl(2)G.7s6m3M White truncated tower, green top 5m
0116·4 **Dique Oeste** Fl(2)R.7s5m1M White truncated tower, red top 4m

Port communications

Port VHF Ch 9 ✆/*Fax* +34 968 41 02 28
Club Náutico de Aguilas VHF Ch 9
✆/*Fax* +34 968 41 19 51
Marina *Mobile* 670445725 *Email* admon@cnaguilas.com
www.cnaguilas.com

Approach

A high chimney is conspicuous behind the marina.

Berths

Berth initially at reporting / fuelling berth port side of marina on entry. The office is just behind. Calling on Ch 9 will ensure a *marinero* is present to assist with lines. Visitors are berthed opposite side of the marina, alongside.

Useful anchorage harbour

Two bays, separated by a headland, Monte de la Aguilica, the western bay, Aguilas, has a small fishing port on its west shore and a small crowded yacht harbour on its N shore with room for 150 vessels of 10m max. To the east, the other side of the headland, is El Hornillo, an old anchorage with a project for a marina close to the north east. Both bays are open to the S and E sector and uncomfortable in a wind or swell from this direction but have attractive surroundings.

The fishing harbour at Puerto Aguilas and the yacht haven at upper right. Note that moorings take up much of the W side of the bay

Aguilas was an important Roman port which fell into disuse after repeated invasions by the Berbers. In 1765 the village and harbour were rebuilt and the castle restored by Count Aranda, a minister of Charles III. A climb to the castle of San Juan (18th century) on Montaña de Aguilas above the harbour is worthwhile for the view. Good beaches on either side of the harbour.

Note that there are two headlands with lights named Punta Negra in this area: Punta Negra de Aguilas, normally listed under Punta Negra and Punta Negra de Mazarrón, normally listed under Mazarrón.

Approach

From the SW Follow the coast, passing the conspicuous Isla de los Terreros. In the distance four high, steep-sided headlands will be seen (Mt de Aguilas, Mt de la Aguilica, Isla el Fraile and Mt Cope). Aguilas lies behind the first headland, which has a small castle on its summit. A tall lone chimney stands in the bay to the W of the first headland.

From the NE Having rounded the large promontory of Mt Cope, see plan on page 93, a group of tree high, steep-sided rocky headlands will be seen, the first actually on an island. The harbour lies between the second and third headland.

GPS approach

Steer to ⊕57 from a southeasterly quadrant and steer for breakwater end (approximately 0·2M).

Entrance

In Aguilas, give the head of mole a 50m berth; a buoyed channel leads to the yacht harbour. Fishing nets are sometimes laid near the entrance to both bays. In heavy weather the entrance to both harbours might be dangerous.

Berths

In Aguilas yacht harbour secure to any vacant berth or as directed by harbour staff. In the fishing harbour a possibility is to go alongside at the root of the mole, clear of commercial craft; alternatively secure stern-to a fishing quay with a bow anchor using an anchor trip-line. Before arriving, check with the harbourmaster that there is room (VHF Ch 09).

Anchorages

It is possible to anchor almost anywhere clear of quays and swim buoys. There may not be much protected space in Aguilas outside the moorings if a S/SW swell is running. In these conditions there may be more shelter at El Hornillo.

Note Suggested anchorages are shown on the plan on page 96.

Facilities

Aguilas Fishing Harbour
50-tonne travel-lift and hardstanding.
12-tonne crane.
Slipway at the SW corner.
Engine repair mechanics in the town.
Small repairs to woodwork and hulls can be carried out at workshop by slipway.
Chandlers shop near the fish quay, another near the yacht harbour.
Water on the commercial mole. Supply also available at lonja de pescadores.
Ice from a factory to W of the town or at the harbourmaster's office.
Darsena Deportiva
Maximum length overall: 12m.
Water and electricity on the quays.
Gasoleo A and petrol.
Club Náutico de Aguilas at yacht harbour.
A good selection of shops in the town and a small market.

Communications

Bus and rail services. ✆ Area code 968.

Anchorages between Aguilas and Mazarrón

(See plans opposite and on page 93)

⚓ CALA BARDINA
37°25'·6N 01°30'·5W

The first 50m offshore is cordoned off for swimmers and small boats. A channel for these boats is marked with a red and a green buoy – watch out for a submerged rock some 20m south of the green buoy! There is still plenty of room to anchor in six to eight metres outside the buoys. Well protected from the N and E by Mt Cope (244m) but open between SE and SW and with swell from E winds.

⚓ ENSENADA DE LA FUENTE
37°26'·1N 01°28'·7W

An anchorage open to NE but well protected by Mt Cope from other directions. Anchor in SW corner of the bay in 3m sand.

⚓ OTHER ANCHORAGES WEST OF PUERTO DE MAZARRÓN

A large number of small coastal anchorages exist on this stretch of coast, see plan. Use with care. Most are off small, sandy beaches and any obstructions can be seen in the clear water. Some anchorages have a stony bottom but most are sand or shingle.

CALA BARDINA AND ENSENADA DE LA FUENTE
N
Depths in Metres
Pta del Ciscar
33
Playa de los Hierros
6_1
26
44
Playa Llarga
Cala Blanca
8_1
Pta de la Galera
Chapa de la Galera
43
14
Playa Abejorro
42
50
28
Playa Elena
7_9
Playa Rafal
1
5
10
72
Pta del Charco
3_3
Pta del Sombrerico
93
Aguilas
73
Te
Cope
3_8
Ensenada de la Fuente
Cala
Bardina
Mt Cope 210
Pta del Cerro de la Cruz
o de las Cabricas
Cala
Bardina
3_6
5
10
244
37°25′·6N
26
Pta del Peñón de S. Maria
25
Pta del Caballo
38
33
50
0
1000
2000
3000
Metres
01°27′·4W

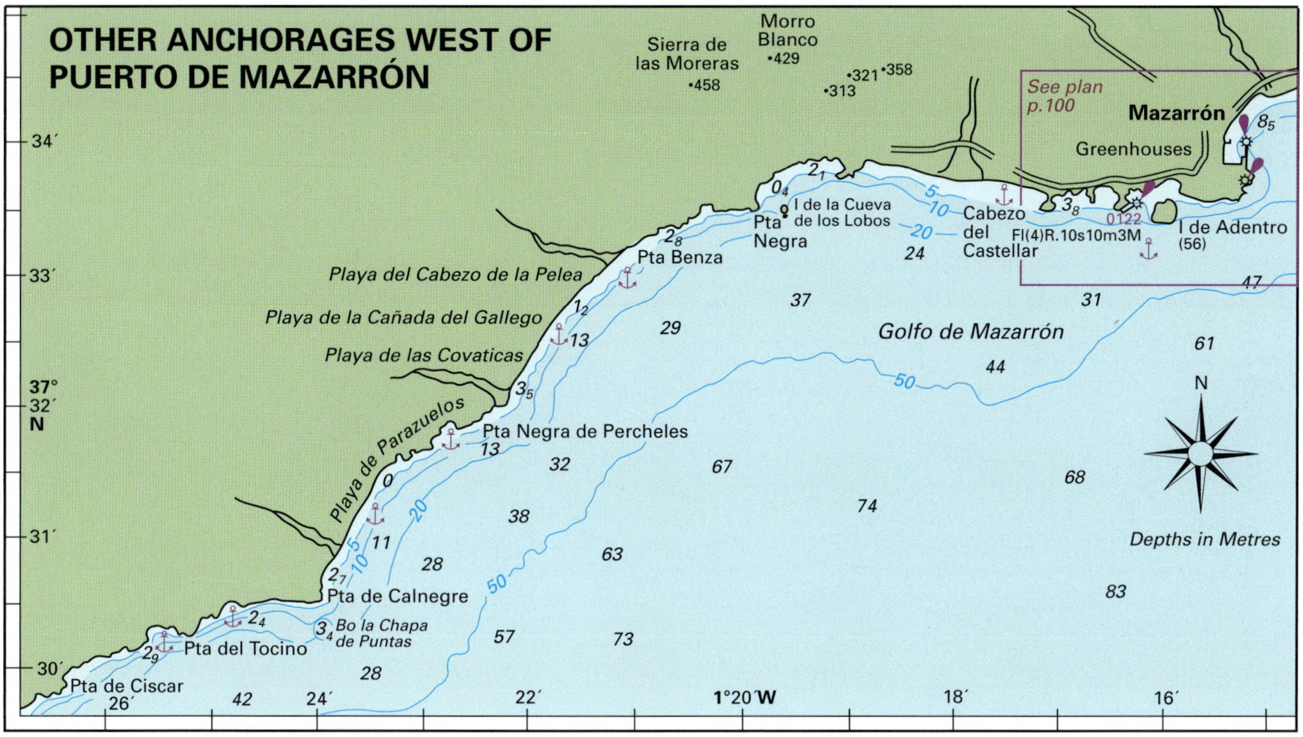
OTHER ANCHORAGES WEST OF PUERTO DE MAZARRÓN
Sierra de
las Moreras
•458
Morro
Blanco
•429
•321
•358
•313
See plan
p.100
Mazarrón
8_5
Greenhouses
34′
2_1
0_4
5
10
I de la Cueva
de los Lobos
Pta
Negra
Cabezo
del
Castellar
3_8
0122
Fl(4)R.10s10m3M
I de Adentro
(56)
20
24
33′
2_8
Pta Benza
Playa del Cabezo de la Pelea
37
31
47
1_2
Playa de la Cañada del Gallego
13
29
Golfo de Mazarrón
61
Playa de las Covaticas
44
50
37°
32′
N
3_5
N
Playa de Parazuelos
Pta Negra de Percheles
13
32
67
68
0
74
38
20
31′
11
Depths in Metres
5
10
28
63
2_7
50
Pta de Calnegre
83
2_4
3_4
Bo la Chapa
de Puntas
57
73
2_9
Pta del Tocino
28
30′
Pta de Ciscar
26′
42
24′
22′
1°20′W
18′
16′

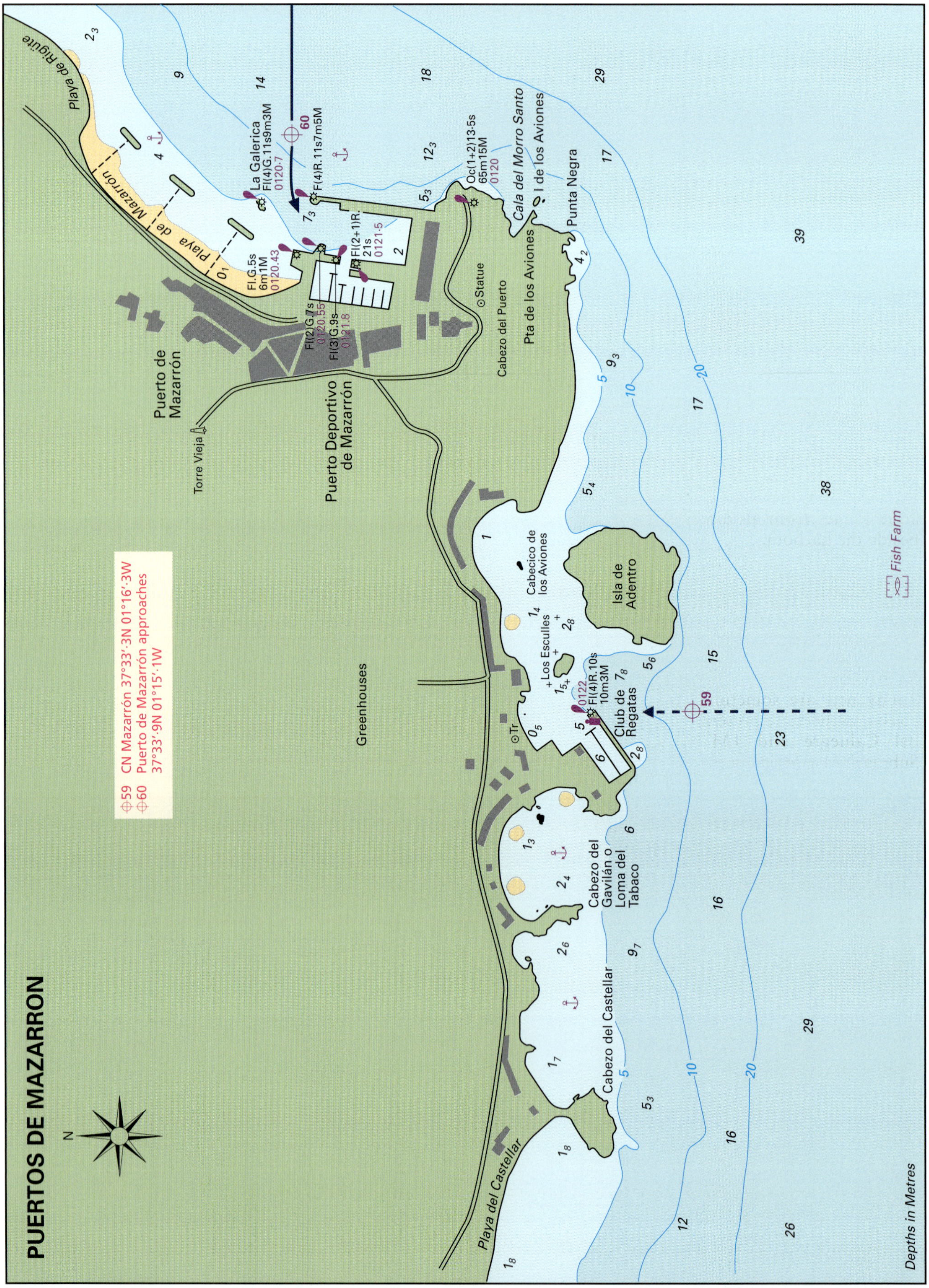
PUERTOS DE MAZARRON
⊕59 CN Mazarrón 37°33'·3N 01°16'·3W
⊕60 Puerto de Mazarrón approaches 37°33'·9N 01°15'·1W
Playa de Rigüite
Playa de Mazarrón
Puerto de Mazarrón
Torre Vieja
Puerto Deportivo de Mazarrón
La Galerica
Fl(4)G.11s9m3M
0120·7
Fl(4)R.11s7m5M
Fl.G.5s
6m1M
0120.43
Fl(2)G.7s
0120.55
Fl(3)G.9s
0121.8
Fl(2+1)R.
21s
0121·5
Oc(1+2)13·5s
65m15M
0120
Cala del Morro Santo
I de los Aviones
Punta Negra
Statue
Cabezo del Puerto
Pta de los Aviones
Cabecico de los Aviones
Isla de Adentro
Los Esculles
Fl(4)R.10s
10m3M
0122
Club de Regatas
Greenhouses
Tr
Cabezo del Gavilán o Loma del Tabaco
Cabezo del Castellar
Playa del Castellar
Fish Farm
Depths in Metres
N

33. Club de Regatas, Mazarrón

37°33'·4N 01°16'·3W

The westerly of two marinas in Mazarrón: a very clean and safe private marina with 200 berths, but not welcoming to visitors.

Charts

British Admiralty *774*. Imray *M12*
French *7671*. Spanish *4632, 463*

⊕59 37°33'·3N 01°16'·3W

Lights

0122 **Yacht club jetty head** Fl(4)R.10s10m3M Red metal tower, white band 4m
To the east
0120 **Mazarrón LtHo** Oc(1+2)13·5s65m15M White tower 11m

Port communications

VHF Ch 9. Yacht club ✆ +34 968 59 40 11
Email info@crmazarron.com
www.crmazarron.com

Pleasant harbour good shelter

Situated round the corner and about a mile west of the old fishing harbour of Mazarrón. It offers very good shelter from all directions. There are beaches beside the harbour.

Note that there are two headlands with lights named Punta Negra in this area: Punta Negra de Mazarrón, normally listed under Mazarrón, and Punta Negra de Aguilas, normally listed under Punta Negra.

Approach

Tunny nets are sometimes laid off this section of coast and there are presently fish farms 1M SE of Pta del Calnegre and 1M S of Isla de Adentro. Submarines exercise in the south of this area.

From the SW The Sierra de las Moreras, with two peaks (458 and 429m), and the Isla de Adentro (56m) are recognisable. Punta Negra de Mazarrón with its lighthouse and large statue of Jesus is unmistakable. The harbour lies to W of Isla de Adentro.

From the NE The 4M-wide Ensenada de Mazarrón is easy to identify as is Punta Negra, described above, which has the appearance of an island from this direction. When Punta Negra has been closed Isla de Adentro will be seen; the harbour lies to W of this island.

Club de Regatas, Mazarrón from the SW

GPS approach

Steer to ⊕59 from a southerly quadrant and steer for breakwater end (approximately 0·15M), leaving the Isla de Adentro well to starboard.

Anchorage in the approach

Depths to the NE of the harbour are shallow and the bottom is rocky so anchoring is not recommended but there is a very attractive sandy cove just west of the harbour with 3m in its centre.

Entrance

From the SW Approach Isla de Adentro on a NE course and, when 200m from it, turn onto a N course towards the harbour breakwater. Leave it 10m to port. Beware the rocky islet, Los Esculles, lying just to the north of the line between the north side of Isla de Adentro and the marina entrance.

From the NE Having identified the statue and Isla de Adentro round the Isla leaving it 200m to starboard (do not attempt to pass to the north of the Isla as the water is shallow with rocky outcrops) and proceed on a NNW course to close the breakwater end. Note the warning about Los Esculles in previous paragraph.

Berths

Secure to quay on port-hand side of entrance near fuel pumps and ask at the Club de Regatas office for a berth. Visitors berths are limited to three at the end of the 'T' pontoon. Visitors may be put elsewhere if there is room.

Facilities

Maximum length overall: 25m (four yachts only; more at lesser length).
Marine Engineer (Volvo agency).
Slipway at N side of harbour and for dinghies at E side.
8-tonne crane.
Hardstandings.
Water taps on pontoons and quays.
220V AC points on pontoons and quays.
Gasoleo A and petrol.
Ice at entrance.
Club de Regatas de Mazarrón has a bar, restaurant, showers etc.
Provisions from village of Mazarrón.

Communications

✆ Area code 968. Taxi ✆ +34 968 59 51 22.

34. Puerto Deportivo de Mazarrón

37°33'·9N 01°15'·W

A new marina with almost all 250 berths sold out to individuals. Visitors welcome, though space is limited.

Charts

British Admiralty *774.* Imray *M12*
Spanish *4632, 463*

⊕60 37°33'·9N 01°15'·1W

Lights

0120.5 **Dique de Abrigo head** Fl.R.3s7m3M Red post 3m
0120.6 **Dique de Abrigo corner** Fl(4)R.11s7m5M Red post 3m
0120.43 **Contradique N head** Fl.G.5s6m1M Green post 3m
0120.55 **Contradique Elbow** Fl(2)G.7s5m1M Green post 3m
0121.8 **Darsena N entrance** Fl(3)G.9s4m1M Green post 3m
0121·5 **Darsena S entrance** Fl(2+1)R.21s4m1M Red post, green band 3m

Port communications

Marina office VHF Ch 9. ✆ +34 609 36 02 60 / +34 968 15 40 65 *Email* boltursa@yahoo.es

Fishing and commercial harbour with a Puerto Deportivo for yachts

Due to be finished some years ago, the marina is only now in full operation. Several restaurants (some excellent) and bars on the quayside make it a busy and noisy place in summer. This fishing and commercial harbour at the W end of the Ensenada de Mazarrón is easy to enter and offers good protection from all directions except NE. Over the past five years there has been a vast injection of money and the rocky jetties of the 90s have been replaced with new quays and promenades with first class buildings and pontoons. The town of Mazarrón, about 3M inland, has good shops and may be reached by taxi or bus. A climb to the lighthouse is worthwhile for the view. Good beaches in the bay.

Puerto de Mazarrón

Puerto Deportivo de Mazarrón, green light atop reef near entrance 'La Galarita' *Graham Hutt*

Approach

Tunny nets are sometimes laid off this section of coast and there is a fish farm 1M south of Isla de Adentro. Submarines exercise in the south of the area.

From the SW The Sierra de las Moreras and a few islands close to the coast are recognisable. Punta Negra with its lighthouse and a large statue of Jesus is especially conspicuous.

From the NE Punta Negra resembles an island and, with its lighthouse and statue, is conspicuous across the wide Rada de Mazarrón.

GPS approach

Steer to ⊕60 from an easterly quadrant and steer for breakwater end (approximately 0·14M) leaving La Galerica well to starboard.

Entrance

Approach the head of the breakwater on a westerly course, keeping well clear of Isla de la Galerica and round the head at 25m.

Berths

This new marina is safe but with surging reported during NE and E winds. Most of the pontoon berths have been sold privately, leaving little room for visitors, who are berthed alongside the inner marina wall close to the bars and the office.

Anchorages

Anchor to E or N of the harbour entrance. Keep clear of La Galerica rock. In the E end of the bay anchor off village of La Subida (see plan on page 103) and N of Punta de la Azohía outside small-craft moorings.

Miscellaneous

The beacons on Punta de la Azohía mark a measured distance of 1857·47m on the N side of the bay, near the centre, on an axis of 104°.

Facilities

Two hards ashore with large travel-lift on centre quay.
Water from fish quay.
Ice from a small factory.
Shops and a supermarket and market in the village. Many more in the town itself some 3M inland.

Communications

Bus to Mazarrón town. ✆ Area code 968.

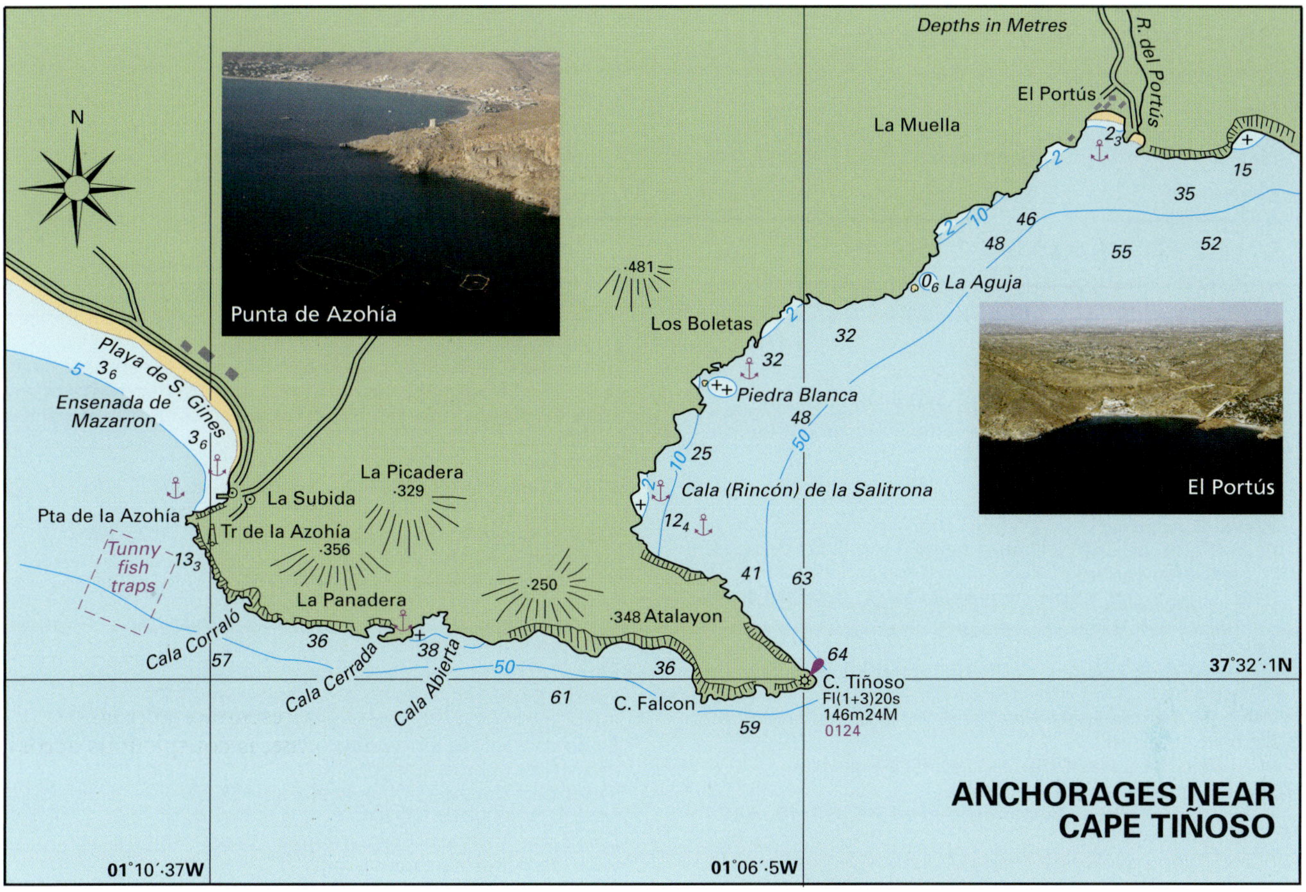

⚓ ENSENADA DE MAZARRÓN

37°33′·4N 01°10′·6W

It is possible to anchor almost anywhere around this bay in 5M sand and weed. The recommended places are to the sides of the three *ramblas* (dry river beds) or just NE of Punta de la Azohía off the small hamlet of La Subida, both open to S. Watch out for fishing boat moorings. A pair of beacons are situated NE and SW of the hamlet. A small supermarket is located in a housing estate ½M along the road to Mazarrón. In the centre of the bay a small private harbour has been developed alongside and behind the Isla Plana.

There is a fish farm off Punta de la Azohía, but one can go between the farm and the point.

Cala Cerrada

Rincón de la Salitrona

⚓ CALA CERRADA

37°32′·4N 01°09′·25W

Use with caution. Open to S. Anchor in the NE corner, in eight to 10 metres. The whole *cala* is very deep and is 8m even 20m from the beach.

⚓ RINCÓN DE LA SALITRONA

37°33′·2N 01°07′·5W

Anchor off the north beach, in 5m sand and weed, or the south beach which is more sheltered but deeper at eight to 10m. An alternative is off Los Boletas but pay attention to the rocks, Piedra Blanca. Freighters gain shelter N of C. Tiñoso in strong W and SW winds.

⚓ EL PORTÚS

37°34′·8N 01°04′·4W

Anchor off the sandy beach. Open between SE and SW. Small shops.

35. Puerto de Cartagena

37°35'·98N 00°59'·1W

One of the safest and most interesting ports in the Mediterranean with facilities for over 1,000 yachts in two marinas. Good safe wintering stop.

Charts

British Admiralty *774, 1700, 1189, 1194.* Imray *M12*
French *7642, 7671.* Spanish *4642, 464A, 464*

⊕61 37°33'.5N 01°00'W (outer)

⊕62 37°35'N 00°58'.9W (inner)

Lights

To the west
0124 **Cabo Tiñoso** Fl(1+3)20s146m24M White tower and building 10m. A magnetic anomaly 3M to S of Cabo Tiñoso has been reported.
Approaches
Plan below
Western Approach
0125 **Dique, Algameca Grande** Fl(4)R.11s10m7M White and yellow tower 5m
0125·3 **The Point, Algameca Grande** Fl(3)G.9s8m3M White and yellow tower 3m
Entrance
0128 **Dique de Navidad** Fl(2)R.10s15m10M White tower red top 11m
23430(S) **Bajo de Santa Ana** Fl(2)G.7s5M Green conical 5m
Eastern Approach
0127 **Bajo Las Losas** Q(6)+LFl.15s5m5M ⧗ card 5m
Escombreras
0126.2 **Dique Muelle Bastarreche head** Fl(2)G.7s10m5M White tower 7m
0126.1 **Dique de Abrigo head** Fl.G.3s10m10M Green and white tower 7m
0126 **Islote Escombreras** Fl.5s65m17M Tower with aluminium cupola on white building 8m

Harbour Plan page 106
0128 **Dique de Navidad** Fl(2)R.10s15m10M White tower red top 11m
0130 **Dique de la Curra** Fl(3)G.14s14m5M Cylindrical white tower green cupola 11m
0130.3 **Espalmador floating breakwater, Head** Q.R.1s1M Red column 4m
0130.5 **Muelle del Carbón head** Fl(2+1)R.14.5s8m3M Red post, green band 5m
0131.2 **Marina outer breakwater** Q.G.1s5m1M Green tower 4m
0131.5 **Muelle de Sta Lucia** Fl(4)G.12s5m1M Green post 3m
0132 **Muelle Santiago head** Fl(4)R.11s5m1M Red post 3m
0132.4 **Dolphin** Fl(2+1)G.16s5m1M Green column, red band 3m
Yacht basin
0131.3 **Darsena de Yates breakwater head** 37°35'.7N 00°58'.8W Fl(3)R.9s5m1M Red support 1m
0131.35 **Outer harbour elbow SW** Fl(2+1)G.12s3m1M Green column, red band
0131 **Club de Regatas mole SW corner** Q.G.3s5m1M Green post 5m

Port communications

Port VHF Ch 11, 12, 14. Marina VHF Ch 9.
Puerto Deportivo VHF Ch 9 ✆ +34 968 50 15 09
Real Club de Regatas Cartagena ✆ +34 968 50 15 07
Email contacto@clubregatascartagena.es
www.clubregatascartagena.es
Yacht Port Cartagena ✆ +34 968 12 12 13
Mobile ✆ +34 618 332101
Email marina@yachtportcartagena.com
www.yachtportcartagena.com

Storm signals

Flown from the signal station in Castillo de Galeras.

Major harbour with good facilities

A large naval, commercial and fishing port of great antiquity which is easy to approach and enter under almost any conditions. Cartagena is an attractive city with good shops, many restaurants and several museums.

There are two yacht clubs: RCRC – Real Club de Regatas Cartagena – and YPC – Yacht Port Cartagena. The RCRC is on the west side, adjacent to YPC.

The RCRC is pleasant and welcomes visitors if a berth is available but is primarily for members. It has a splendid club house and restaurant, which visitors in either marina are welcome to use. YPC is more geared for visitors with staff speaking English and responding quickly to VHF from land and rib to greet new arrivals. The marina was originally designated for super-yachts, but the failure to attract any resulted in a change of ownership and a re-organisation of the marina to accept any vessel from 6–25m but with a few places for 60m vessels near the office.

There are also a small number of moorings to the W of RCRC, along the old town quay belonging to the port authorities (Puerto Deportivo). These have always been occupied by tourist boats on my many visits to Cartagena.

Approach

From all directions the entrance to Rada de Cartagena is made obvious by the high steep reddish cliffs of Cabo Tiñoso to the W and Islote de Escombrera to the E. The large oil refinery near this island is visible from afar. A large chimney, with black top and white band is conspicuous between Castillo de San Juan and Punta de San Antonio. There is vast construction work going on to enlarge the port of Escombrera. The passage between the Islote and Punta del Borracho has been closed while an 800 metre breakwater now runs NW from the west point of the Islote.

From the west The course goes past Puerto de Algameca Grande, a naval port on the W side of the Rada de Cartagena which is prohibited to yachts. Large unlit mooring buoys are located opposite Algameca Grande and Chico. A firing range exists to the S of this port and submarines exercise in the area.

From the east From Cabo de Palos follow the land keeping a good watch out for fish farms, which proliferate in this area especially off Portman and Cala de Gorguel. Pass south of Cabo del Agua and Islote de Escombreras and steer parallel to the new breakwater until the entrance to Cartagena proper opens up. It is recommended to keep well clear of all the ongoing construction work at the port of

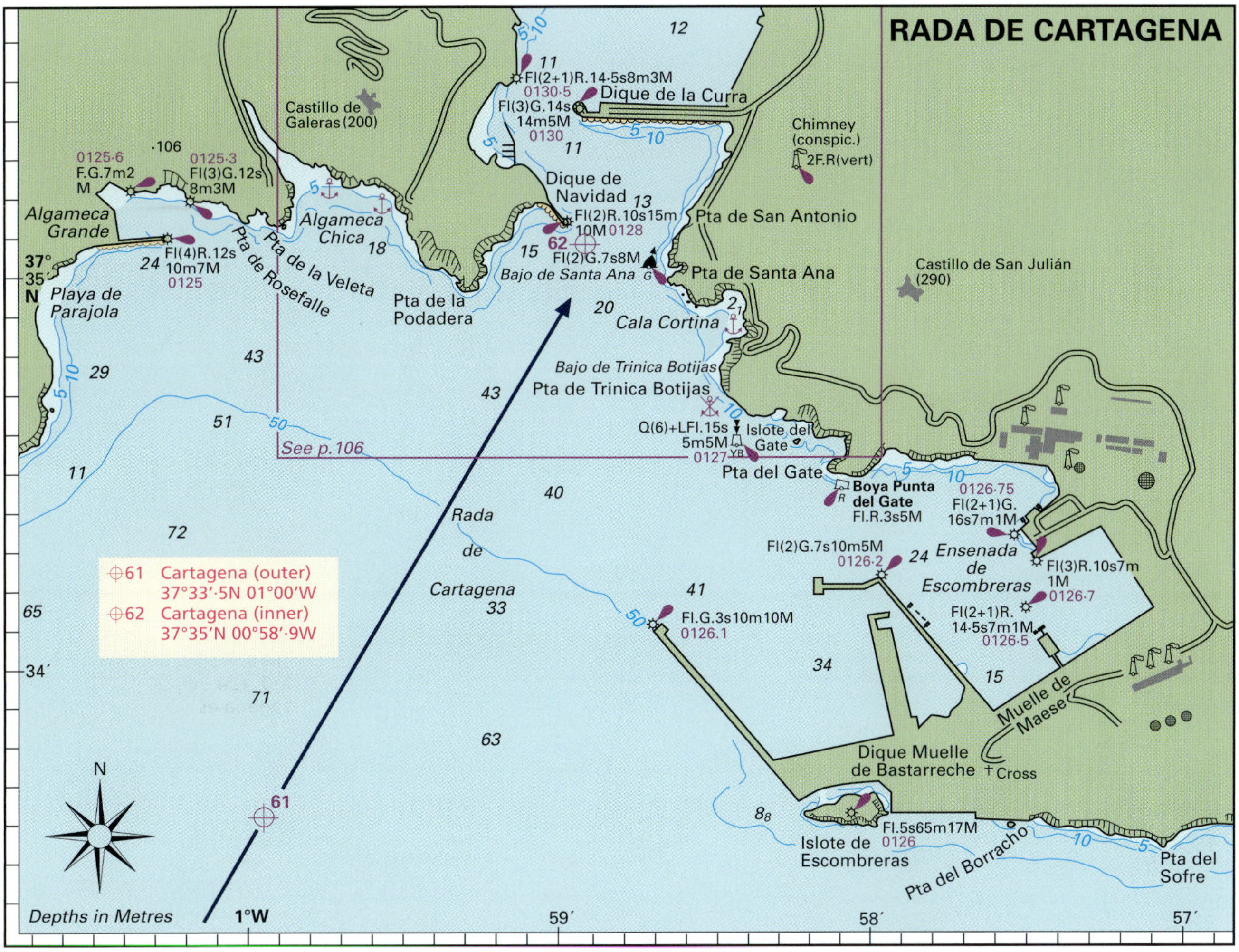

Cartagena from the S – four pontoons now exist in the new marina east of the YPC

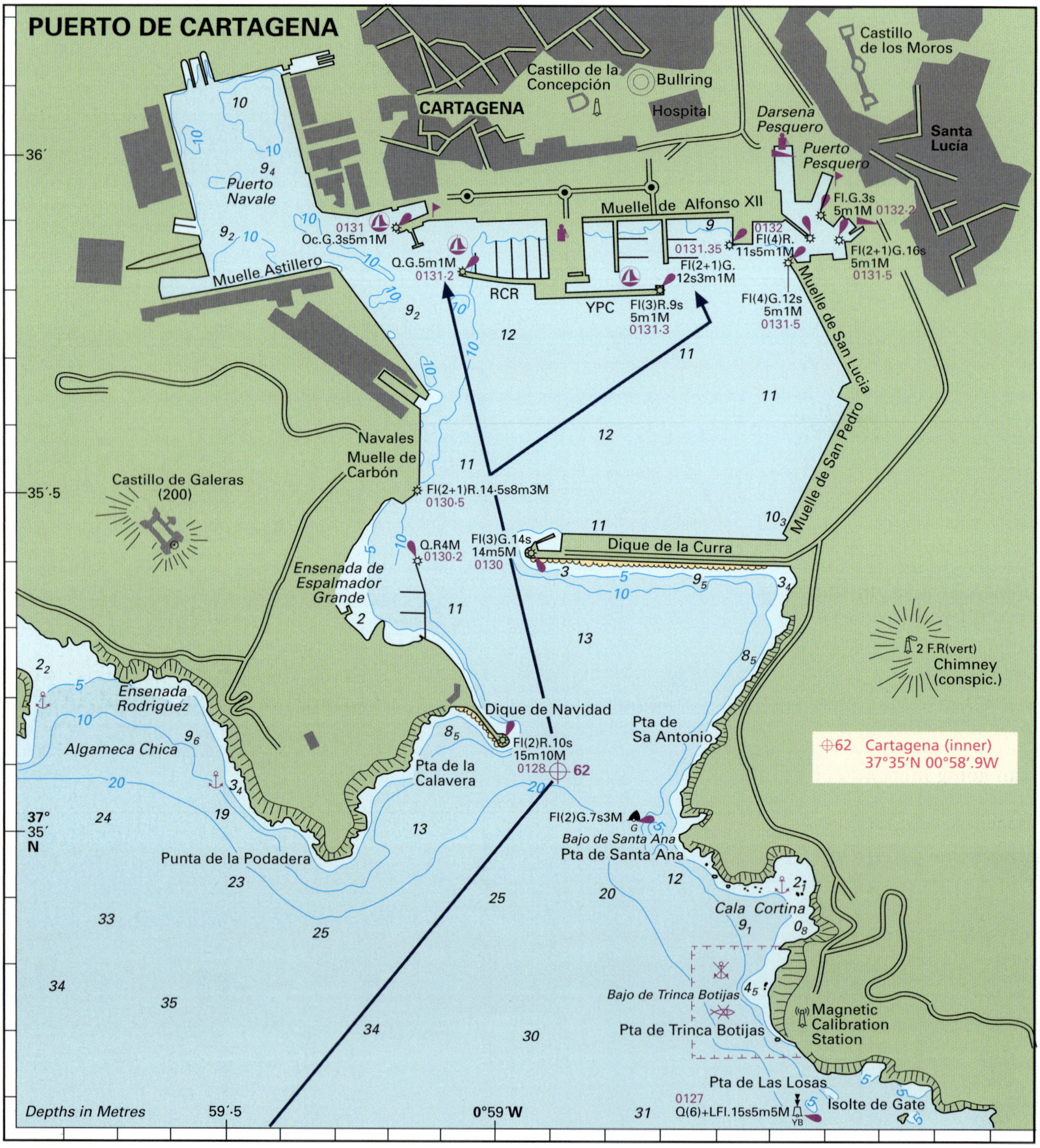

Escombrera. Although this port may be still used in dire emergency, one will normally be sent away to the marina in Cartagena.

Visiting yachts can go to either marina after confirming which one is on VHF. With fewer yachts arriving these days, there is healthy rivalry between the marinas and both listen out for arrivals and will respond to VHF Ch 9. This can be confusing as it is not always clear which one is responding, so do verify which marina is answering. YPC is almost entirely for visiting yachts and quick to respond on the VHF button!

GPS approach

Steer to ⊕61 from the southerly sector and make towards ⊕62. Leave Bajo de Sta. Anna to starboard and make for the end of the Dique de la Curra.

Entrance

Straightforward but check that there are no large vessels entering or leaving port. Seas build up in the entrance during strong onshore winds.

Anchorages

Anchoring is forbidden in the harbour or its immediate approaches. Anchoring is possible in Rincón de la Salitrona behind and to N of Cabo Tiñoso, El Portús 4M to W of the harbour, Algameca

YPC Cartagena Marina with Spanish Naval facility in background and the orange ocean going lifeboat

Chica and Cala Cortina (pay attention to rock on N side). Algameca Chica is smelly and may have fishing nets. Cala Cortina has a rocky bottom. Expect to be moved if you finish up in a defence or commercial area. In summer the entire bay can be closed off with swim buoys.

Berths

Calling on VHF will elicit a response with directions (for YPC) to pass Dique de la Curra and head on a course of 040° to the entrance, where a berth will be allocated over VHF. There is often a large orange ocean going lifeboat moored on the dique.

Cartagena: Cruise liners berth on S wall of Marina *dique*
Graham Hutt

For RCRC, head on a course of 350° from Dique de la Curra. The harbour and quays are sometimes oily and with a SE wind, smoke and fumes from the refinery at Escombrera can be unpleasant. Muelle de Alfonso Xll is often used by YPC for short stay visitors and can be unpleasant with a lot of rubbish being brought in on S sector winds. Ask for a different berth if this is the case. Staff are always helpful.

The YPC office (looking temporary, housed in two portacabins) and a small boatyard are on the E end of the Muelle de Alfonso XII, and quite a walk. There are as yet no club facilities at YPC, though there is a very contemporary building housing a museum and restaurant and bar just outside the marina fence.

Cartagena looking SSE. YPC: A spacious marina liable to some surging on the E side *YPC*

An amphitheatre right in the centre of town and beautifully restored in its original setting *Maria Kanayama*

A lovely clean elegant town, with so much to see! *Maria Kanayama*

Charges
Low.

Facilities
Maximum length overall: 25m.
All types of repairs, mostly by the naval workshops; contact the marina for advice.
Cranes up to 20 tonnes; contact *capitán de puerto*.
Marine radio shop next to the Scandinavian Consul's office in the Muralla del Mar.
Several chandlers, two near Dársena Pesquera.
Charts from Esqui Náuticas, Campos.
Water and 230/380V AC on marina pontoons.
Gasoleo A and petrol at the marina.
New shower and toilet facilities
Hypermarket 'Continente' about a kilometre away – ask for directions or take a taxi. Many varied provision shops and two markets in the town, none near.
Launderette in Plaza de San Francisco.

History of the port
A port well used by Phoenicians, it was developed by Hasdrubal about 243BC and became the centre of Carthaginian influence in Europe, helped by slaves working the gold and silver mines of the region. Hasdrubal's brother, Hannibal, used it as a base for his expedition across the Alps and it became the primary target of Scipio the elder ('Africanus' – Cathargo delenda est). The Romans duly destroyed Carthaginian influence. St James the Great is said to have landed here in AD 36 bringing Christianity to Spain from Palestine (a sea passage which according to legend took four days). It subsequently passed into the hands of the Barbarians and then the Moors. Philip II fortified the surrounding hills in the 16th century, Drake stole its guns in 1585 and took them to Jamaica, Charles III established the arsenal and naval base in the 18th century and the Republicans held out for months against Madrid during the Civil War in 1936. But the chief remnants of its troubled history lie in the minds of its inhabitants, not its artefacts.

Locally
There is a good view of the harbour from the Castillo de la Concepción and the old churches are worth visiting. A 10-day local holiday starts the Sunday before Trinity Sunday.

Do visit the tourist office close to the marinas and purchase the multi-museum ticket which covers all the museums and archaeological sites. It takes you on an amazing circuit of layers of the ancient city's beautifully preserved and inter-connected past, with amazing architecture. The modern town is hardly noticeable once you enter the labyrinth underground. A lift in the old castle wall ascends to the higher levels of the castle: again well worth a visit.

Communications
Murcia airport 30 minutes by taxi, international flights. Railway to Murcia from FEVE and Los Nietos from RENFE station and bus services. An occasional service by sea to the Canary Isles.
☏ Area code 968. Taxi rank at marina.

'Hotel Illegal'. Standing idle and never opened, this is one of thousands of properties along the Costa del Sol built in the past 15 years with illegally issued (or no) licences and now to be demolished after years of legal proceedings *Graham Hutt*

36. Puerto de Portmán

Lights

0134 **Punta de la Chapa** Oc.3.5s49m13M tower on white building 8m
0134.5 **Breakwater head** Fl(2)R.6s6m2M Red post 4m
0134.3 **Bajo de la Bola** Q(6)+LFl.10s5M ⧗ card buoy 4m

Silted up port with fish farms

Called Portus Magnus by the Romans, Portmán has been completely silted up by effluent from the lead and zinc mines inland. The scars in the hillside and the new wind farm on the top of the hill inland make recognition of Portmán relatively easy. There is a huge fish farm to the west of the bay which leaves little space to anchor. The small dinghy harbour, on the east side, has a breakwater running out from the beach with a red column at its end. The harbour is totally sheltered but only has about 0·5m depth at the entrance and is only for dinghies and RIBS. There is a *club náutico* on the west side of the beach but there are no facilities at all in the small village. Anchor between the two buoys in the bay in about 4m and land on the beach by dinghy – open between SE and SW.

Puerto de Portmán

Cala de Gorguel

⚓ CALA DEL GORGUEL

37°34′·4N 0°52′·5W

An unlit fish farm virtually blocks the entrance to this *cala*, approach with care from the east. The *cala* is full of floating gear and boats for the farm. Anchor (if there is room) in small rocky cove in 5m mud off the beach. There are off-lying rocks on W side of beach. Open between SE and S. There are also fish farms, mostly unlit, off-shore between La Manceba and Cabo Negrete.

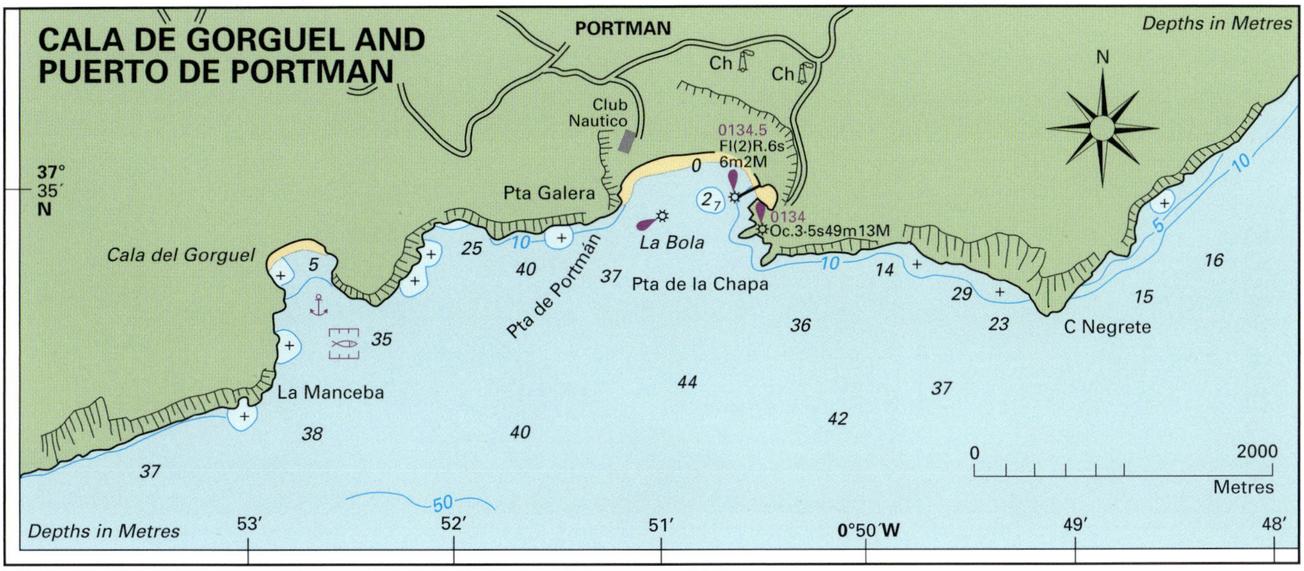

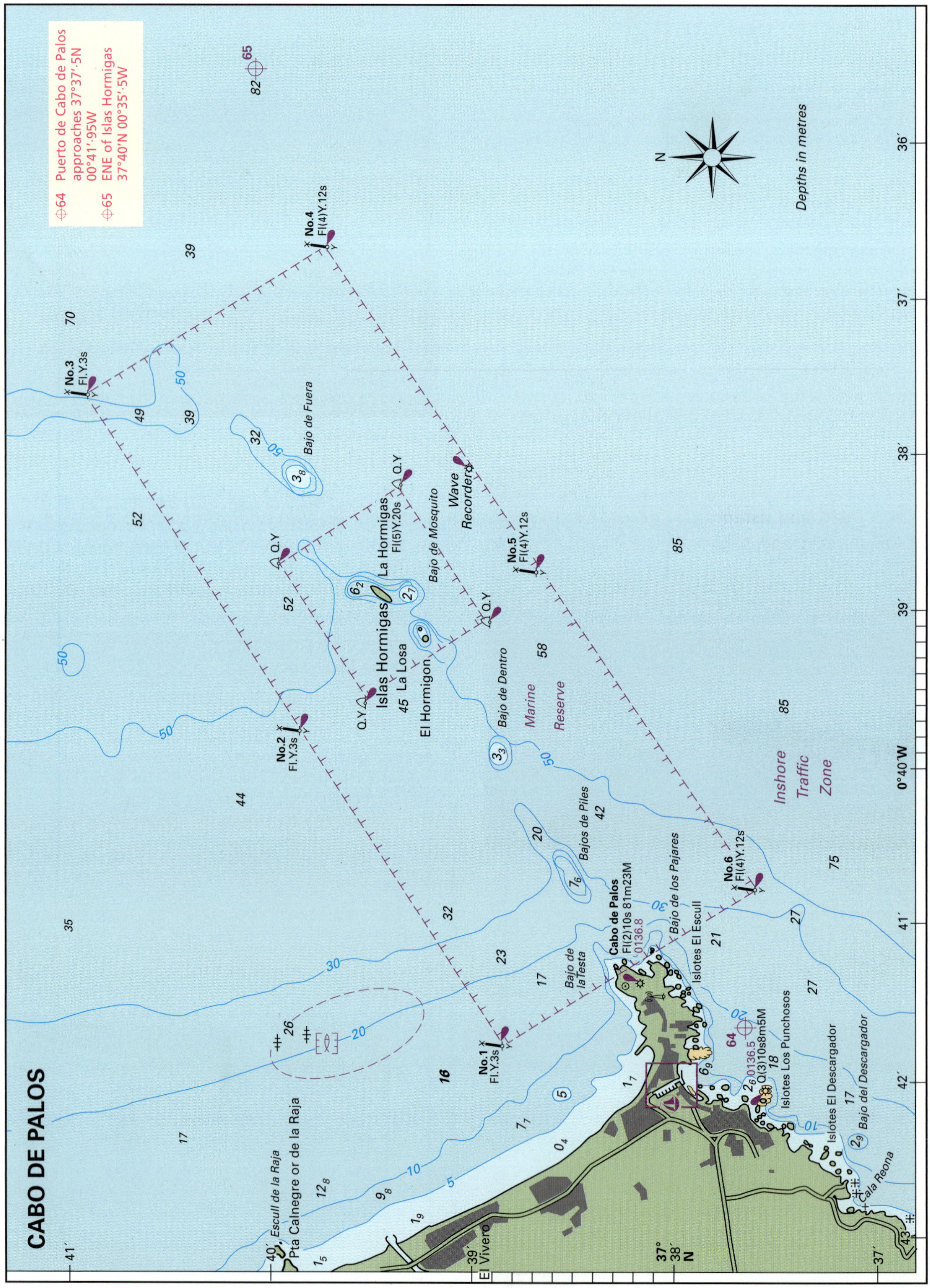

CABO DE PALOS
⊕64 Puerto de Cabo de Palos approaches 37°37'·5N 00°41'·95W
⊕65 ENE of Islas Hormigas 37°40'N 00°35'·5W
Depths in metres
No.3 Fl.Y.3s
No.4 Fl(4)Y.12s
No.2 Fl.Y.3s
No.5 Fl(4)Y.12s
No.1 Fl.Y.3s
No.6 Fl(4)Y.12s
Bajo de Fuera
Q.Y
La Hormigas Fl(5)Y.20s
Islas Hormigas
La Losa
El Hormigon
Bajo de Mosquito
Wave Recorder
Bajo de Dentro
Marine Reserve
Bajos de Piles
Inshore Traffic Zone
Cabo de Palos Fl(2)10s 81m23M
Bajo de los Pajares
Islotes El Escull
Bajo de la Testa
Q(3)10s8m5M
Islotes Los Punchosos
Islotes El Descargador
Bajo del Descargador
Cala Reona
Escull de la Raja
Pta Calnegre or de la Raja
El Vivero
37° 38' N
0°40'W

37. Puerto de Cabo de Palos (Cala Avellán)

37°37'·8N 00°42'·8W

A very small shallow harbour with 175 moorings prone to silting and with a tight 'dogleg' entry.

Charts

British Admiralty *774, 1700.* Imray *M12*
French *7670, 7671.* Spanish *464, 471*

⊕64 37°37'·5N 00°41'·8W

Lights

0137 **Espigón de la Sal** Fl(2)G.7s6m5M Green post 3m
0137.3 **Beacon** Fl(2)R.7s5m3M White post (4m), on red concrete base 1m
0136.9 **Escollo Las Melvas** VQ(6)+LFl.10s5m5M ⧗ card post YB 3m

To the northeast
0136.8 **Cabo de Palos** Fl(2)10s81m23M Round tower 51m

To the southwest
0136.5 **Los Punchosos** Q(3)10s8m5M Grey pole 5m

Port communications

VHF Ch 9. ✆ +34 968 56 35 15

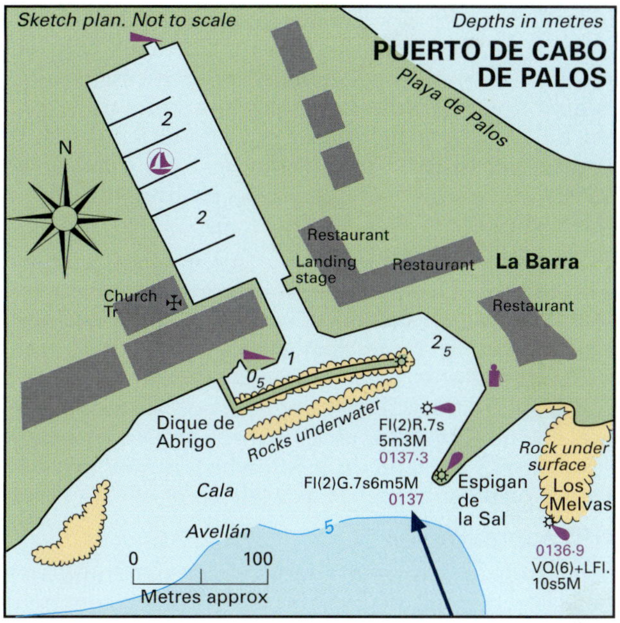

⊕ 64 37°37'·5N 00°41'·8W (off plan)

Small yacht and fishing harbour

A small yacht and fishing harbour located at the western edge of a prodigious tourist development running along the edge of the Mar Menor. It and its surroundings are crowded. A pleasant short walk out to the lighthouse. Excellent sandy beaches to N.

The zig-zag entrance requires care and is not really suitable for yachts over 12m.

Approach

From the south From Cartagena to Cabo de Palos the coast has steep rocky cliffs with a few sandy bays lying between points. The hinterland is rugged and

Puerto de Cabo de Palos – note underwater rock in the lower right-hand corner (now marked by beacon), looking N to Mar Menor on left and Isla Grosa on right

III. COSTA BLANCA

hilly. There are no dangers more than 200m off-shore and the coast is steep-to. Portmán may be recognised by the vast hillside of open-cast mining behind it with a wind farm with 8 turbines on top of the hill. The large lighthouse at Cabo de Palos (81m) is easily identified. The harbour lies ½M to the W of it. Pay attention to off-lying rocks in the approach to the harbour.

From the north Isla Grosa (95m) is unmistakable. The coast as far as the prominent Cabo de Palos, is low, flat, sandy and lined with high-rise buildings. No dangers lie more than 600m off-shore. Round Cabo de Palos at 200m paying attention to isolated rocks and islets in the western part of the bay inside this distance, in particular, the rock just under water southeast of Espigón de la Sal, which is now marked by a S cardinal beacon, Las Melvas.

GPS approach

Steer to ⊕64 from a southeasterly quadrant and head for the end of Espigón de Sal (approximately 0·33M).

Anchorage in the approach

The bottom to the S of Cabo de Palos peninsula is rocky out to the 20m contour. It is better to anchor in 5m sand to the N of this peninsula.

Entrance

Approach the harbour keeping the church, which has an unusual open-work, tripod tower with a bell on a cross bar and a cross on top, approximately NNW (between 325° and 345°), keeping the awash rock, Las Melvas, with its S cardinal pole, well to starboard. Turn to starboard around the end of the Espigón de la Sal (with its green post) keeping close to the quay, leaving the white pole on the 2m diameter red beacon well to port. Then turn to port round the end of the Dique de Abrigo and go alongside the quay parallel to the *dique*.

Cabo de Palos lighthouse *Graham Hutt*

Berths

Although there are pontoons inside the harbour these are for locals only and visitor berths are alongside the quay in the outer harbour.

Facilities

Maximum length overall: 10m.
A slipway at N end of the harbour and a small slipway in outer harbour to W of entrance to inner harbour.
Chandlery and diesel in the village.
Water taps and electricity on quays.
A few local shops.

Communications

Bus services to Cartagena, Murcia and La Manga where there is a large supermarket. ✆ Area code 968.

⚓ CABO DE PALOS
37°38'·1N 0°41'·55W

Anchorage in bay to NW of Cabo de Palos open to NE in 5m sand and stones. Shops in nearby Playa Honda and at La Barra. Note there is now a traffic separation scheme (TSS) some nine miles ESE of the lighthouse which should not seriously affect pleasure craft as they are generally closer to the point but one should be aware of its position.

MARINE RESERVE CABO DE PALOS

This low sandy point with its 51m-high grey lighthouse has a large marine reserve some 2M by 4M extending to the ENE. It is marked by six buoys, the three northern ones are Fl.Y.3s while the three southern ones are Fl(4)Y.12s. There is an inner reserve, around Islas Hormigas, marked with four buoys Q.Y some of which may be missing at times. There is also a yellow, spherical wave recorder buoy at 37°39'·3N 00°38'·2W with a light Q(5)Y.20s.

⚓ PLAYA DE PALOS
37°39'N 0°42'·7W

Coastal anchorage along a 6M stretch of sandy beach in 5m sand and weed. Wide open E and facing wall to wall high-rise buildings – access to the coast road is through private properties. A shallow patch, Banco El Tabal (1·7m), is near the centre of the beach.

⚓ ISLA GROSA
37°43'·5N 0°42'·6W

Anchorage in the W quarter of the island to suit draught in clay with weed. The island, 95m high, offers some protection from sea and wind. There are houses on the W side and a landing place. This area is occupied by the military and approach within 300m is discouraged.

Mar Menor

Depths in Metres
MAR MENOR
47 Puerto de San Pedro del Pinatar
Fl(4)G.12s13m5M
0141·5
46 Lo Pagán
Ciudad del Aire
San Javier
Santiago de la Ribera
Naval Pto de San Javier
Aero Fl.6s
Fl(4)G.11s1M
0141·1
Fl(4)R.11s1M
0141·2
Aeropuerto de San Javier
Pta de Casablanca
Playa de Pals
Los Punchosos
Pta de Algas
Escolletes de Fuera
Pta del Pudrimel
See p.116
Los Narejos
Pta Galera
Los Alcázares
45 Puerto de los Alcázares
Fl.G.5s5m5M 0141·3
0140·5 Fl.R.5s7m3M
68
0140·6 Fl.G.5s7m3M
38 Puerto de Tomás Maestre
Pta del Estacio
Fl(4)20s32m14M
0140
VQ(3)5s7m3M
0140·2
67
la Laja
El Farallón
Isla Grosa
(95)
Fl.3s97m5M
0139
Pta Seca
66
Entrance to Mar Menor
Mar Menor
Ite de la Galera
Airfield
Isla Perdiguera
Pta del Fraile
Isla Mayor (or del Barón)
Pta del Galán
44 Los Urrutias
Isla del Sujeto
See p.119
Isla Redondo
39 Pto de dos Mares
Escull de la Raja
Pta Calnegre o de la Raia
Isla del Ciervo
43 Puerto de los Nietos
42 Pto de las Islas Menores
41 Puerto de Mar de Cristal
40 Puerto de la Manga
Urmenor
Bajo del Piles
37 Cabo de Palos
Cabo de Palos
Fl(2)10s81m 23M 0136·8
0136·5
Q(3)10s8m5M
Islotes Los Punchoses
Islotes del Descargador
Bajo del Descargador
Pta de la Espada
Los Belones
49´
37° 45´ N
40´
50´
0°45´W
COASTAL WAYPOINT LIST
⊕66 S App Mar Menor Entrance 37 43´·2N 00°43´·0W
⊕67 N App Mar Menor Entrance 37°44´N 00°42´·8W
⊕68 W App to P Tomás Maestre 37°45´N 00°45´W

THE PORTS OF MAR MENOR

Mar Menor – An inland sea

An extraordinary inland sea some 12M long and 6M wide separated from the Mediterranean by a narrow band of sand, La Manga, from which a line of mini sky-scrapers rise. In addition to the intensive encouragement of tourists on land, yacht harbours are being built around the shores of the inland sea. The towns themselves are generally dull and the ports small and shallow but in terms of pottering around, anchoring off, small boating and so forth the Mar has its attractions.

Of the three entrances, one is deep and two very shallow. The major entrance is through Puerto de Tomás Maestre, which is the largest harbour of the Mar Menor and is supposedly dredged to 4m though 3m may be nearer the mark. Details of the approach and entrance are given later; the other two entrances are not described. The second largest harbour, San Javier in the NW, is a naval air force harbour and part of the air academy. It is not open to visitors. Seven small harbours are built around the Mar. A number of moorings have been laid but they are generally private.

The five islands are Isla Mayor or del Barón (102m), Perdiguera (45m), del Ciervo (46m) which is actually joined to La Manga by a causeway, Rondella or Redonda and del Sujeto. The first two are large and steep-to. The passage between Isla Mayor and La Manga has uncertain depths, generally less than 1m, and the passage between Isla del Sujeto and La Manga has even less water.

There are depths of 5–6m over the greater part of Mar Menor with gently shallowing sides and the bottom is sand or mud with weed. This makes anchoring possible almost anywhere, according to draught, but a strong wind can quickly kick up a nasty sea with marked currents. The north part is shallower than the south and though the Mar Menor is not tidal, the water level can vary by as much as 50cm or more over a period of weeks, driven by winds or changed by rain. In general terms, do not get on the shoreward side of any harbour entrance.

Beware floating nets; They may be set in a circle about 100m in diameter around a central buoy and supported by small floats which are difficult to see.

More on Mar Menor

Despite the extensive high-rise apartments, which surround much of the shoreline, the inner sea is a tranquil gem of a place. The water is clear, there is little fetch, as expected for an enclosed sea and there is opportunity to drop anchor almost anywhere, provided you are not too close to the shoreline, where depths reduce. It's particularly quiet and there is some 'entertainment' from passing wind-surfers, canoes, surf-paddlers, etc. The occasional jet-ski or little stinkpot don't present any problems either.

The seawater temperature is considerably higher than outside. Unfortunately there are lots of very large and small jellyfish, mostly *Rhizostoma pulmo*, and although not recognized as a vicious stinger, there are enough to put many off swimming amongst them.

As mentioned above, local fishermen deploy nets, which float near the surface, so keep well clear. The nets can occupy the area of around two or three tennis courts and are marked with small buoys. There may be a small fishing boat nearby or within the netted area. Nets are relocated regularly so be alert to the possibility of coming across one or two whilst underway.

In the S of the sea there is Puerto de la Manga. 200m W is an excellent quiet anchorage off a beach. Take a dinghy to the beach on the W side of the swimming area, which is close to a pleasure craft hire business on the shoreline. (Yellow buoys mark the swimming area which is about the size of three or four football pitches). Head directly off the beach and pass through some pedestrian gates (indicating private) into a caravan/mobile home-type holiday park. Follow the 20kmph roadway, keeping the tennis courts on the right hand side for about ¼M to the end of the road, which will bring you to the 'La Manga Spar' supermarket.

Note public refuse bins are by the tennis courts on this road.

Facilities

The better shops of the area are along La Manga and at Los Belones. Shopping elsewhere is basic. There are banks on La Manga (see Puerto de la Manga) Los Nietos and at La Union.

Communications

San Javier airfield, besides holding the Air Force Academy, handles charter flights during the summer. A light railway runs between Los Nietos, La Union and Cartagena (where the station is fairly close to the Continente hypermarket).

The ports of Mar Menor

38. Puerto de Tomás Maestre

Entrance into Mar Menor from the Mediterranean 37°44'·3N 00°43'·4W (between beacons of Los Escolletes).

Entrance from the Mar Menor 37°44'·5N 00°43'·8W

A large modern marina easily entered except during strong E or SE winds. Plenty of room for visitors.

Charts

British Admiralty *1700.* Imray *M12*
French *7670.* Spanish *4710, 471*

⊕66 32°43'·2N 00°43'·0W S approach
⊕67 37°44'N 00°42'·8W N approach
⊕68 37°45'N 00°45'W W approach

Lights

Entrance from seawards
To the south
0136.8 **Cabo de Palos** Fl(2)10s81m23M Round tower 51m
0139 **Isla Grosa** Fl.3s97m5M White round tower 2m
0138 **Islote La Hormiga** Fl(3)14s24m8M White tower 12m
0140 **Punta del Estacio** Fl(4)20s32m14M White tower, black bands 29m
0140.2 **Los Escolletes** VQ(3)5s7m3M ♦ on black column, yellow band 5m

Canal del Estacio
23954(S) **Buoy No.1** Fl.G.5s5M Green spar
23956(S) **Buoy No.1** Fl.R.5s5M Red spar
23956.1(S) **Buoy No.2** Fl(2)G.7s3M Green spar
23956.2(S) **Buoy No.2** Fl(2)R.7s3M Red spar
23956.3(S) **Buoy No.3** Fl(3)G.9s1M Green spar
23956.4(S) **Buoy No.3** Fl(3)R.9s1M Red spar
23956.5(S) **Buoy No.4** Fl(4)G.11s1M Green spar
23956.6(S) **Buoy No.4** Fl(4)R.11s1M Red spar
23956.7(S) **Buoy No.5** Fl.R.5s1M Red cylinder
23956.8(S) **Buoy No.6** Fl(2)R.7s1M Red cylinder

Mar Menor entrance
0140.5 **Dique N** Fl.R.5s7m3M Red tower 4m
0140.6 **Dique S** Fl.G.5s7m3M Green mast 3m.
Note that the entrance channel may be marked with small buoys in high season

Port communications

VHF Ch 9. *Capitanía* ☏ +34 968 14 08 16
Email puertomaestre@puertomaestre.com
www.puertomaestre.com

Tomás Maestre – canal, harbour, marinas

A modern marina has been built into the 1½M long canal which connects the sea with the Mar Menor. In normal conditions approach and entrance are easy but because the area is shallow, entry should not be attempted in strong E or SE winds which kick up heavy seas. Facilities are good except that provision shops are limited. It forms a useful base for the exploration of the Mar Menor and as a staging point between the port of Cartagena and the harbours further N. Golf course and swimming pool nearby.

The entrance is now marked with pillar buoys and the entrance to the Mar Menor may be marked from June to October with red and green light buoys joined with floating ropes.

Tomás Maestre marina from south

Approach from seaward

From the south Round the prominent and conspicuous Cabo de Palos at 200m off and follow the low-lying coast in a NNW direction at 1¼M. The narrow sand spit has wall-to-wall high-rise buildings along it with a small gap just before the approach to Tomas Maestre. The canal approach is 1M to NW of the off-shore Isla Grosa (95m).

From the north Cabo Roig is prominent and reddish in colour. It has a tower and some buildings above a small yacht harbour which lies on the S side of the cape. Two other small yacht harbours, which may be recognised, lie 1½M and 3M further S. Puerto de San Pedro del Pinatar is easily recognised by its high breakwater.

Follow the coast, which sprouts high rise buildings as Punta de Estacio is approached, in a SSE direction and at least ¼M offshore. Isla Grosa (95m) which is peaked should be easily recognised. Pass about half way between the island and Los Escolletes and then head N/NW for the entrance beacons. NE of Isla Grosa is the rock El Farallón and further out, a shoal of 1·3m – see charts. A shallow rocky spit sticks out a short distance south of Los Escolletes.

GPS approach

From the south steer to ⊕66 and from the north steer to ⊕67 and then steer to pass between the port and starboard buoys marking the canal entrance.

Anchorages in the approach

From the south Anchor to the west of Isla Grosa (see page 113).
From the north Anchor off Playa del Pudrimel (see page 113).
Outer harbour Anchorage (see note plan on page 116).

III. COSTA BLANCA

PUERTO DE TOMAS MAESTRE
AND ENTRANCE TO MAR MENOR
Until developed, the outer harbour makes a good anchorage. It is dredged to 4m except towards the north shore.
Pudrimel
Mar Menor
Boat yard
(hangers)
Fl.R.5s 7m3M
0140.5
0140·6
Fl.G.5s 7m3M
Lifting bridge
7·5m
Flats
Pta del Cocedor
Pta del Estacio
Fl(4)20s32m14M
0140
White pillar and ⊙ pole
Outer Harbour (to be developed)
Puerto de Tomás Maestre
Los Escolletes
VQ(3)5s7m3M
0140·2
Boya de Levante
Fl(2)G.5s3M
23954(s)
Boya de Poniente
Fl(2)R.5s3M
23956(s)
Low breakwater
Mar Menor
Mar Mediterrañeo
N
0
0·5
Nautical Mile (approx)
(off plan)
⊕66 Mar Menor approaches (S) 32°43′·2N 00°43′·0W
⊕67 Mar Menor approaches (N) 37°44′N 00°42′·8W
⊕68 Tomás Maestre approaches (W) 37°45′N 00°45′W
Depths in Metres

Tomás Maestre from the east

Canal Entrance

From seawards Having passed about halfway between Los Escolletes and Isla Grosa (coming from the north) or keeping Isla Grosa well to starboard (coming from the south) identify the two port and starboard buoys marking the entrance to the canal. Proceed on a west of north course to pass between the buoys and on through the outer harbour passing between a series of posts marking the narrow canal entrance. Passing the posts the channel bends round to a west-northwesterly course towards the swing bridge. Note that a falling barometer or an E sector winds can cause a two knot or more inflowing current; a rising barometer with W sector winds an outflowing current. The new lift bridge opens Monday to Friday at 1100 and 1700 and at 1100, 1400 and 1700 at weekends. The headroom is 7·5m when closed. Clients of the marina may call VHF Ch 9 or ✆ 968 14 07 25 at any time to have it opened. The canal continues for a further ½ mile past Tomás Maestre marina into the Mar Menor itself. In high season the channel into and out of the Mar Menor itself may be marked with two green and two red lightbuoys joined by floating ropes with small white floats attached.

Watch for stalled road traffic on either side of the bridge, to gauge when it is about to open.

Note Several yachts have reported depths no greater than 2·3m in the buoyed (posts) channel approaching either side of the lifting bridge.

From Mar Menor Straightforward between the pier heads but beware traffic.

Marina Entrance

The yacht harbour is on the south side of the canal, opposite the workshop area which has conspicuous working hangars.

Berths

Normal stern-to berths are available. Usually someone is around to tell you where to go. Otherwise, make up where you can and if nobody moves you, go to the *capitanía* under the entrance archway (a long way from most of the marina) to confirm your location.

Charges

High in Summer, medium in winter.

Facilities

Maximum length overall: 22m.
Facilities for most types of repairs (the boatyard is expensive).
100-tonnes slipway.
50 and 15-tonne travel-hoists.
5-tonnes crane.
Chandlers (also provide gas and one which repairs sails).
Water on quays and pontoons.
Shower block on pontoon.
220 and 380V AC on pontoons and quays.
Ice on fuel quay or from office.
Gasoleo A and petrol (the fuelling jetty is at the entrance and may be an awkward lie if there is a current running in the canal).

Communications

✆ Area code 968. Taxis ✆ +34 968 56 30 39. There may be an hourly bus to La Manga for shopping.

III. COSTA BLANCA

SHALLOW HARBOURS IN MAR MENOR

The following describes a number of mostly small, shallow, private harbours in Mar Menor, most with little room for visiting yachts, especially those over 12m with deep keels. These are built essentially for local motor vessels. Several have depths of less than 2m, which can be considerably reduced with high barometric pressure and with sustained strong offshore winds. Dredging takes place in most of these harbours as required, but there is no reliable information on when this was last done and marinas often carry out minimal work due to the cost. See plan on page 113.

39. Puerto de Dos Mares Club Nautico

37°40'N 00°44'·5W

A small private shallow harbour with 230 berths only suitable for small yachts.

Port communications

Club ✆ /*Fax* +34 968 14 01 17
www.clubnauticodosmares.com
Ch 9

Shopping stop off

May be useful for shopping along La Manga. Limiting factors are a depth of about 1·9m and maximum length overall length of about 12m. It may pay to investigate by dinghy before entering.

Approach

There is no channel between Isla Sujeto and La Manga. Enter between the red and green buoys on the north side of the entrance, with 1·9m in the channel.

Berth

Bows to floating pontoons.

40. Puerto de la Manga

37°38'·8N 00°43'·6W

Another small shallow harbour, only suitable for 180 smaller craft up to 9m.

Lights

0140.7 **Breakwater head** Fl(3)R.9s5m1M Red mast
0140.72 **Right bank** Fl(3)G.9s1M Green mast

Port communications

Club Náutico la Isleta ✆/*Fax* +34 968 14 53 39
Email admin@nauticolaisleta.net
www.clubnauticolaisleta.es
Ch 9

A private club

A private club where visitors are made welcome though not particularly encouraged. If in doubt about depths, a visit by dinghy would pay off.

The south and east sides of the harbour are beaches used for bathing.

Puerto de la Manga

Approach

The passage east of Isla Mayor should only be taken with local knowledge and there is no passage east of Isla del Sujeto. It is best to keep west of those two and of Redonda as well.

Entrance

Said to be 1·8m. Come in from the west. The harbour wall is marked 'Club Náutico La Isleta' and the entrance is at the southern end. Keep between the line of buoys, if placed (they are all likely to be small, red and spherical).

Berth

Bows-to piers.

Facilities

Maximum length overall: 12m.
Water and electricity at the berths.
The shops of La Manga: Bop's hypermarket, shops, banks at Plazas Cavanah and Bohemia.
Club Náutico La Isleta has a bar, showers and a part-time restaurant.
Do not pump ship in harbour.

41. Puerto de Mar de Cristal

37°38'·7N 00°45'·7W

A shallow private harbour with 160 berths up to 12m. Little room for visitors.

Lights

0140.8 **Breakwater head** F.R.3s5m5M
Red round tower 3m
0140.75 **Contradique** F.G.3s4m3M
White tower, green bands 3m

Port communications

VHF Ch 9. ✆ +34 968 13 34 28
Email mardecristal@convasa.com

Small shallow harbour

A small artificial harbour built as a part of a housing development and located on the SE corner of the Mar Menor. Easy to approach and enter. The facilities are limited. The name sums up the nature of the seas in this area: 'The sea of glass.'

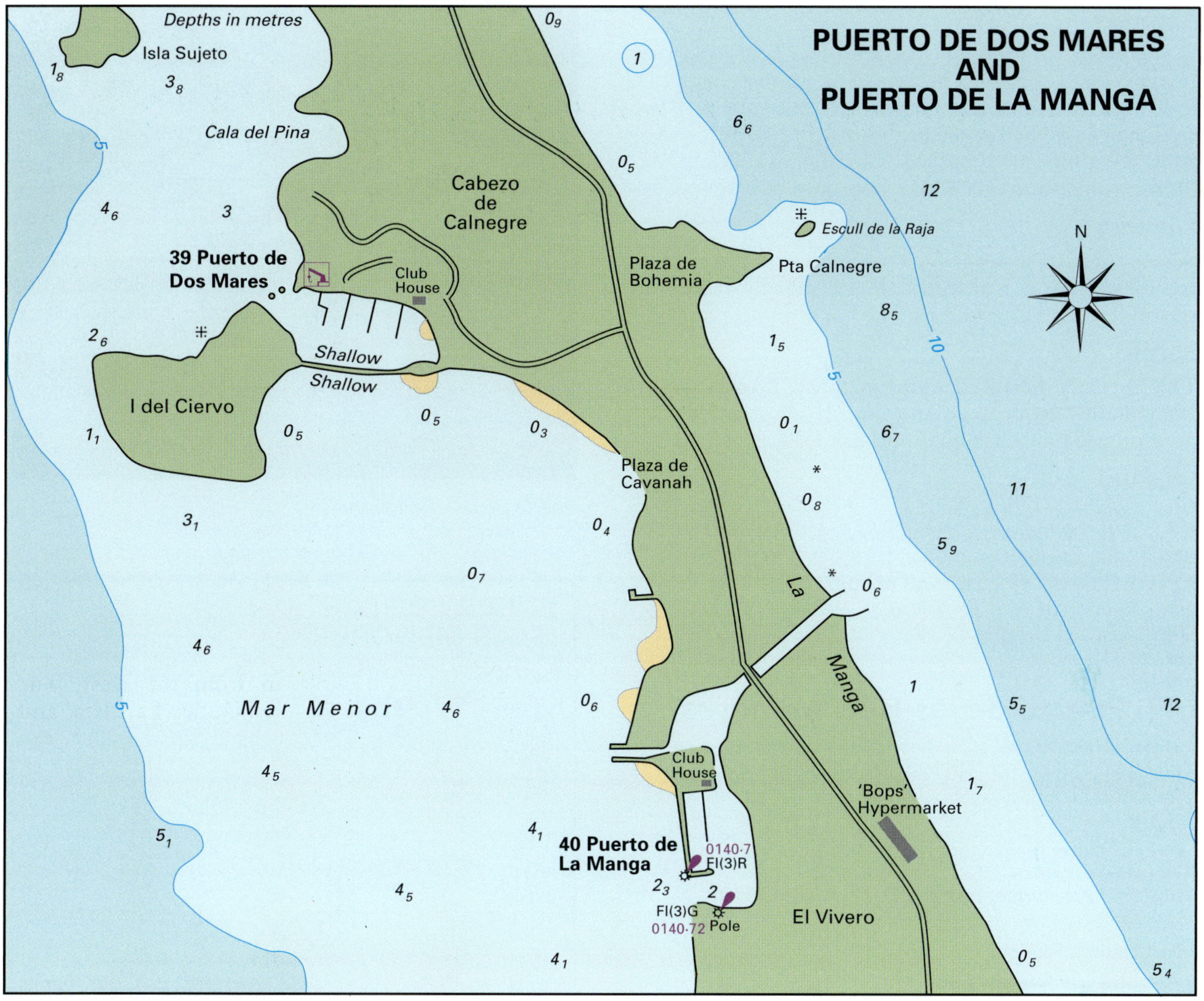

Puerto de Mar de Cristal

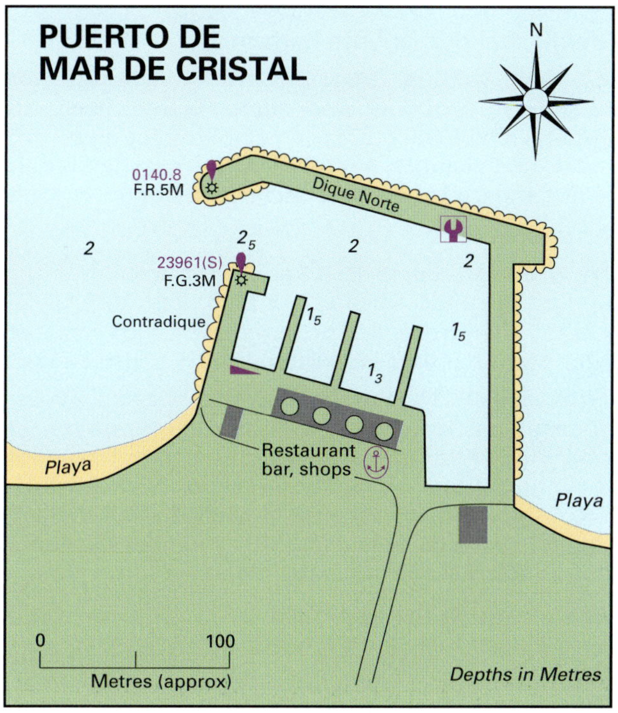

Approach

In the NW, from the hill El Carmoli (112m) and the tower of Los Urrutias the coast is almost straight, low and flat, and most is under cultivation. The village of Los Nietos, the harbours of Los Nietos and Islas Menores may be seen. In the SE, Punta de Plomo is low and has a lone house on it.

Entrance

When entering keep as far off-shore as is consistant with entering as the water shoals sharply near the shore.

Berths

The arrivals berth is alongside the North Wall, immediately to port on entering. If no room there, go alongside another boat and ask ashore.

Facilities

Maximum length overall: 10m.
Slipway in SW corner of the harbour.
Water on quays and pontoons.
220V AC points on quays and pontoons.
Club Náutico de Mar de Cristal.
Some shops in housing development.

42. Puerto de las Islas Menores

37°38'·9N 00°46'·1W

A small private yacht club with 100 berths but no room for visiting cruising yachts.

Lights

0140.85 **Outer breakwater** Fl(4)G.11s3M Green round column
0140.851 **Breakwater head** Fl(4)R.11s3M Red round column

Port communications

Puerto ✆ +34 968 13 33 44
Email info@clubnauticoislasmenores.com
Ch 9

Small, shallow, private harbour

A small shallow private harbour suitable for dinghies, runabouts and small yachts. Easy to approach and enter. It has a palatial yacht club with associated facilities, but other facilities are limited. It is not a place for cruising yachts.

Approach

From the SE Punta de Plomo with a single large house can be identified as can the Puerto de Mar de Cristal ¾M further E. The harbour projects into the Mar Menor and its large clubhouse is conspicuous.

From the NW The low, flat and almost straight coast is relatively featureless with the exception of El Carmoli (112m) and the town of Los Urrutias, until the large yacht harbour Puerto de Los Nietos, which is conspicuous, is reached. ¾M beyond it lies the low Punta Lengua de Vaca and ½M beyond lies the Punta de Los Barrancones with the harbour on the point.

Anchorage in the approach

Anchor to suit draught to N of this harbour in sand and weed.

Puerto de las Islas Menores

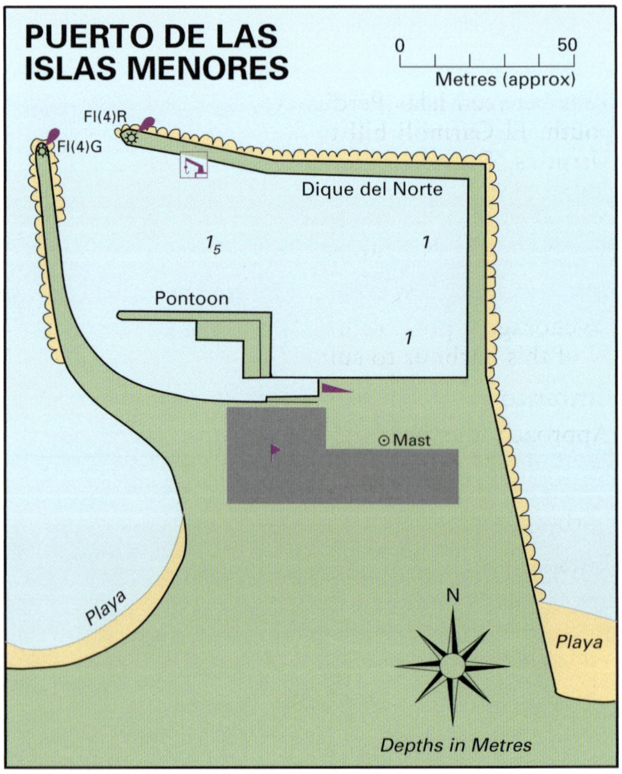

Entrance

Straightforward but harbour shoals to 1m.

Berths

Secure to the inside of Dique del Norte and ask at yacht club for allocation of a berth.

Facilities

Maximum length overall: 8m.
Slipway at yacht club.
Small davit-type crane at head of Dique del Norte.
Water from yacht club.
Small shops near harbour.
The Club Náutico des Islas Menores has bar, restaurant and showers.

43. Puerto de los Nietos

37°39'·2N 00°47'W

A large harbour with 440 berths constructed out from the shore on a spit across the shallows, connected by a causeway. Good wintering facilities. Most of the marina is less than 1·5m deep.

Lights

0140.9 **Muelle Norte NW head** Fl(3)R.9s3M Red round column 3m

0140.92 **Muelle Norte E corner** VQ0·5s1M ⧗ on black post yellow base 4m

0140.95 **Contradique head** Fl(3)G.9s5m1M Green tower 3m

Port communications

VHF Ch 4 or 9. *Capitanía* ☎ */Fax* +34 968 56 07 37
Club Náutico de Los Nietos ☎ +34 968 13 33 00
Email puerto@cnlosnietos.com / administracion@cnlosnietos.com
www.cnlosnietos.com

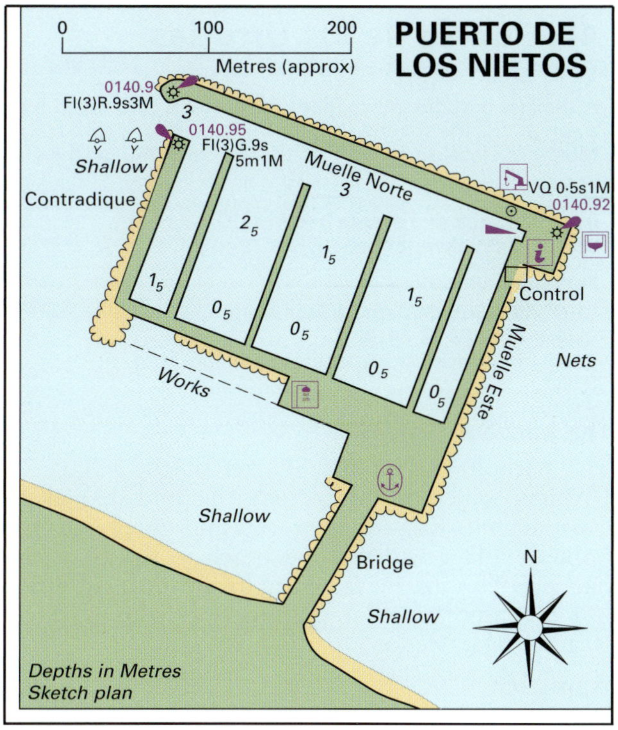

Large yacht harbour

A large artificial yacht harbour. Yachts can winter ashore or afloat.

Approach

Pass between Islas Perdiguera and Mayor and head south. El Carmoli hill to the west will identify Los Urrutias. To the south, there is a small, dark wood, just east of the Rambla del Beal. Los Nietos is just east of the wood. The breakwater and masts will be seen as the coast is approached.

Anchorage in the approach

Anchorage is possible in sand and weed anywhere to N of this harbour to suit draught.

Entrance

Approach the head of the Muelle Norte on a S heading. There may be a line of multi-coloured buoys to leave to starboard. Do not go inshore of the harbour entrance as the water shoals quickly.

Berths

Secure alongside the Muelle de Espera, immediately to port on entry (go alongside another if necessary) and ask at the office. Alternatively, call on Ch 9 or 4 before entering.

Charges

Low.

Facilities

Maximum length overall: 12m.
Slipway at the NE side of yacht club.
An 8-tonne crane at NE corner of the harbour.
A 28-tonne mobile crane.
Hardstanding for winter lay-ups.
Water taps on quays and pontoons (but tastes funny).
220V AC points on quays and pontoons.
Club Náutico de Los Nietos, ☎ +34 968 13 33 00, has a restaurant open at weekends, bar, showers and washing machine.
Supermarkets, ferreterías with gas, Post Office, butcher, baker, bank etc. at Los Belones, 2½km SE.
Bank without a cash point.

Communications

Light railway to Cartagena (where the station is close to the hypermarket Continente). ☎ Area code 968.

Puerto de los Nietos

44. Puerto de los Urrutias

37°40'·6N 00°49'·3W

A shallow harbour which, like Los Nietos, is connected by a spit across the shallows to the shore. Easy to approach. Mostly for local small craft up to 12m, with 250 berths.

Lights

0140.97 **Dique de Levante head** Fl(2)G.7s7m3M
0140.972 **Breakwater head** Fl(2)R.7s7m3M

Port communications

VHF Ch 9. Club de Regatas Mar Menor
☏ /*Fax* +34 968 13 44 38
Email informacion@clubregatasmarmenor.com

The harbour

The harbour lies at the SE end of the village of Urrutias which is underneath the odd-shaped El Carmoli hill. Easy to approach and enter. Spanish holiday village with a good beach to the N of the harbour. This marina is owned by the local authority but the concession for running it is with Club de Regatas Mar Menor.

Approach

From the north Past the airport and Los Alcázares. There is a conspicuous hangar-type building before the village and the yacht club is the last major building.

From the south Urrutias lies 2·5M NW of Puerto de los Nietos.

Anchorage

N or S of entrance to suit draught in sand and weed.

Berths

Secure to east wall and ask at the club secretary's office.

Charges

High.

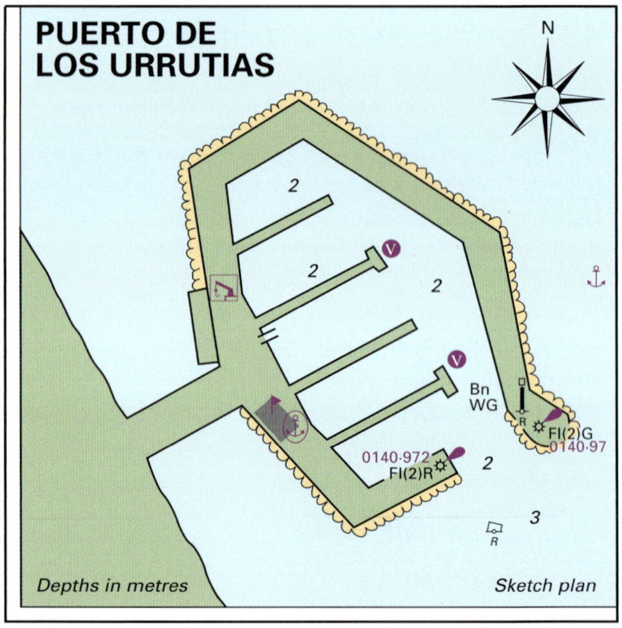

Facilities

Maximum length overall: 12m.
Slipway by crane.
10-tonne crane.
Water taps on pontoons and quays.
220V AC on pontoons and quays.
A few shops in the village, street-market every Thursday.
Club de Regatas Mar Menor has a restaurant, bar, showers and washroom.
Dinghy sailing school.

Communications

☏ Area code 968.

⚓ ISLA PERDIGUERA

Anchor to the SW in 4m sand and mud. Beach bars ashore at weekends.

Puerto de los Urrutias

45. Puerto de los Alcázares

37°44'N 00°50'·9W

Another shallow marina, with 280 berths up to 12m without much room for visitors or cruising yachts.

Lights

0141.3 **Dique Este head** Fl.G.5s5m5M Green tower
0141.4 **Dique Oeste** Fl.R.5s5m3M Red top tower

Port communications

Club Náutico los Alcazares VHF Ch 9 ✆ +34 968 57 51 29
Email cnautico@cnmarmenor.es www.cnmarmenor.es

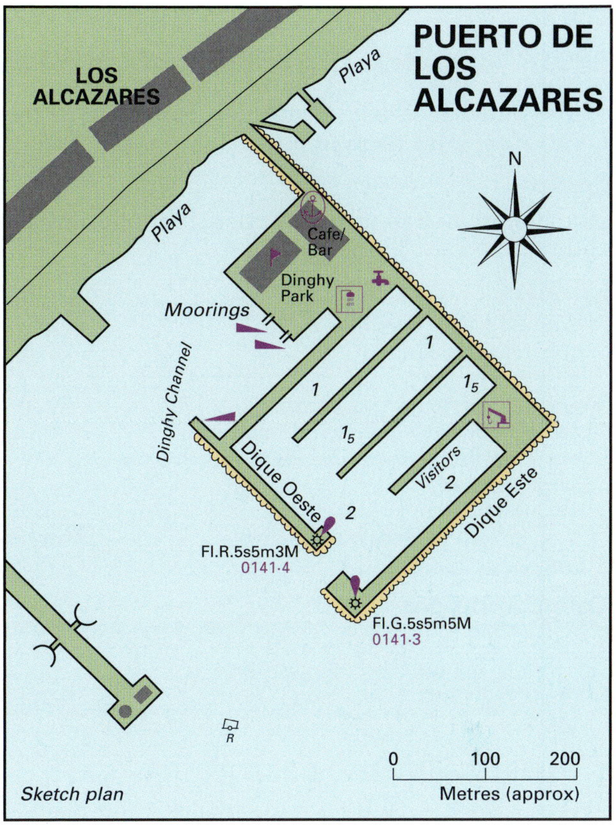

Shallow harbour

A shallow (2m or less), artificial yacht harbour alongside an attractive old Victorian-type seaside resort, least touched by mass tourism. Easy to approach and enter. The coast is lined with many piers and shelters of various sizes to enable the inhabitants to fish and bathe. The nearby Aeropuerto de San Javier, its associated harbour and a large amount of land around are part of the Spanish Naval Air Academy and should not be entered.

Approach

From the SE Follow the low flat coast in a NE–N direction. The town of Los Urrutias and El Carmoli (112m), a conical hill, will be recognised. Further E a light aircraft field and a camp site may be seen. Just S of this harbour is a long pier and some large old hangars. The houses of the town of Los Alcázares will be seen from afar.

From the NE The large town of Santiago de la Ribera and the Aeropuerto de San Javier, which has a large shallow harbour alongside (entrance forbidden), will be easily recognised. Punta Galera and Punta de las Olas are not easily identified. The town of Los Alcázares can be seen from afar.

Anchorage in the approach

Anchor off the harbour in suitable depth to suit draught in sand and weed.

Puerto de los Alcázares

Entrance

Approach the head of Dique Este on a course between W and NNW. A line of white buoys parallel to the military *espigón* marks the boundary of the no-go area; leave them to port.

Berths

Go alongside the pier immediately opposite the entrance and ask at the office.

Facilities

Maximum length overall: 12m.
Simple repairs possible.
Two slipways and a crane at E corner of the harbour.
Water taps on quays and pontoons.
220V AC points on quays and pontoons.
Many shops in the town including supermarket and a large market.
The Club Náutico de Mar Menor at N corner of harbour has limited facilities but they include open-air showers and a bar.

Communications

Excellent and regular buses to Alicante, Cartagena.
Coaches to Bilbao, Madrid, Barcelona.
✆ Area code 968.

⚓ PUERTO SANTIAGO DE LA RIBERA

An open anchorage off a large town serving the air base and the air port and with tourist interests. The *club náutico* has a pier for small boats.

Club Nautico Lo Pagan

46. Puerto de Lo Pagan

37°49'N 00°47'W

A shallow harbour with 350 berths up to 14m, with only a small number of visitors berths available.

Lights

24016.4(S) **Entrance buoy** Fl(2)G.7s Lateral starboard
24016.5(S) **Entrance buoy** Fl(2)R.7s Lateral port
0141.45 **Dique head** Fl(3)G.9s3m1M Green mast
0141.455 **Contradique head** Fl(3)9s3m1M Red post

Port Communications

Club náutico ✆ +34 968 18 69 69
Email info@clubnauticolopagan.es
www.clubnauticolopagan.es
VHF Ch 9

New marina but shallow

A new marina has been developed over the last few years off Lo Pagan at the north end of the Mar Menor. It has berths for about 350 craft and has reasonable shore side facilities of fuel, cranage and a slip. The water is very shallow at the north end of the Mar Menor and there are buoys to indicate the 'deep' entrance channel which is understood to be 1·8 metres, but great care should be exercised in the approach with constant attention paid to the echo-sounder.

Berths

It is essential to call ahead to enquire whether there is a berth available for your vessel, as there are only 20 berths allocated for visitors and these are mostly taken in the high season.

Facilities

All facilities are available for the yachtsman and there is reasonable shopping in the nearby town of Lo Pagan. Close by is the 'Parque Regional de las Salinas' which is an important wetlands area which is of great interest to birdwatchers. Note however, that if one does not wish to enter the Mar Menor, Puerto de San Pedro del Pinatar (see below) is but three kilometres to the east and is also close to this park.

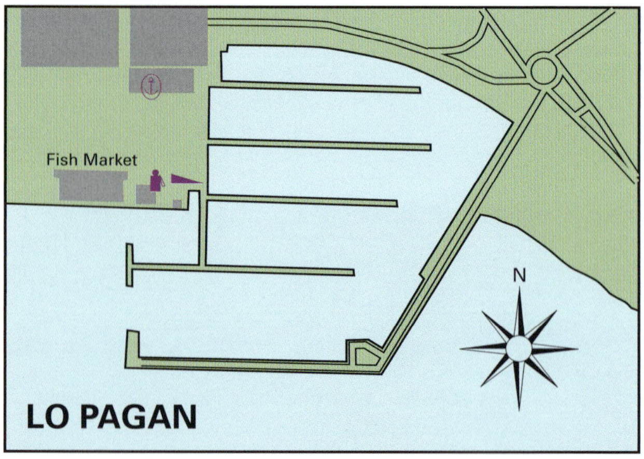

III. Puerto de San Pedro del Pinatar to Dénia

PORTS

47. Puerto de San Pedro del Pinatar

37°49′·2N 00°45′·3W

On the Mediterranean side of the northern limit of Mar Menor (see plan on page 113). Two private marinas with 600 berths between them up to 30m. Many moorings are privately owned. Room for visitors, though depths are said to be under 2m.

Charts

British Admiralty *1700*. Imray *M12*
French *7670*. Spanish *471, 4710*

⊕70 37°49′·2N 00°44′·9W

Lights

0141.5 **Dique Norte** Fl(4)G.12s13m4M Green post 3m
0141.6 **Dique Sur** Fl(4)R.12s6m3M Grey mast 3m
0141.8 **C.N. San Pedro Dique head** Fl.G.2s4m1M Green post 3m
0141.9 **C.N. San Pedro contradique** Fl.R.2s4m3M Red post 3m

Port communications

Club Nautico villa de San Pedro
✆ +34 630 42 21 26 / 968 18 28 80
Email administracion@marinadelassalinas.es
www.marinadelassalinas.es
Marina de las Salinas ✆ +34 619 27 49 32 / +34 676 38 87 90 VHF Ch 9

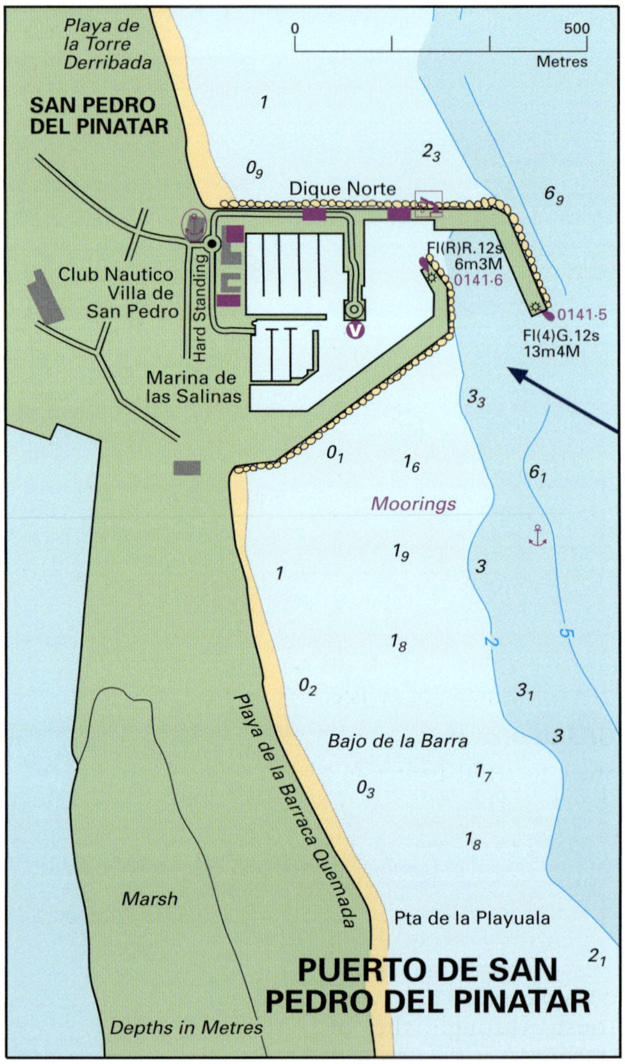

Two modern marinas

Two marinas built just to the N of the ever popular Mar Menor, but with limited depths.

At the NW of the harbour is Club NauticoVilla de San Pedro, with 400 berths up to 15m.

The S marina is relatively new: Marina de las Salinas, with 200 berths up to 30m, with most berths sold off to private yacht owners; a trend

San Pedro del Pinatar looking W and note there is a new marina constructed in the SW darsena - Marina de las Salinas

throughout Spain, as marinas are trying not to sink in the recession. There is a yacht club and stores around the port, but not all open in winter. Depths are not more than 2m and often around 1·5m.

To the S of the harbour is the smaller new Marina de las Salinas.

Note that this marina should not be confused with the Marina Salinas in Torreviejo some nine miles up the coast!

Approach

The high breakwater of Puerto de San Pedro del Pinatar can be seen from afar (and is a useful coastal mark).

From the south Follow the coast up from Punta del Estacio. (See plan on page 113.) Development along the sand strip bordering the Mar Menor dies away before the harbour is reached.

From the north Pass Punta de la Torre de la Horadada which has a tower on the point with buildings at its base and yacht harbour on its S side. There is a rocky reef off this head; keep at least 200m off. From there on, keep half a mile off-shore to avoid small rocky islets.

GPS approach

Steer to ⊕70 from the eastern sector and steer for the end of the breakwater (approximately 0·13M).

Entrance

Approach the end of the Dique Norte on a westerly heading rounding the head at 30m, keeping a close watch for fishing vessels leaving the harbour. Steer west of north and round the head of the Dique Sur keeping reasonably close to the Dique Norte. Steer south through the outer harbour, turning to starboard at the end of the internal quay.

Berths

Having entered the harbour moor to the end of the internal quay and enquire at the fuel berth or at the *capitanía* in the NW corner of the marina for berth availability. It is not possible to say anything about the berthing in the new Marina de las Salinas at the time of going to press but updates will be issued as soon as details become clearer.

Facilities

Maximum length 15m.
30-ton travel-hoist and crane.
Electricity and water at all berths.
Fuel.
Showers, WC and rubbish bins.
Club náutico
Bar and small shops for essentials.

48. Puerto de la Horadada

37°52'N 00°45'·5W

A large yacht harbour with over 500 berths up to 12m but with shallows in the approaches and a restriction to 12m.

Charts

British Admiralty *1700.* Imray *M12*
French *7670.* Spanish *471*

⊕71 37°51'·8N 00°45'·3W

Lights

0142 **Dique de Levante head** Q(3)10s8m3M
♦ on black tower yellow band 6m
0143 **Inner spur head** Fl(3)G.10s9m5M
Green and white column 6m
0143.5 **Contradique head** Fl(2)R.7s9m4M
Red and white column 6m
24090(S) **Channel outer buoy** Fl.G.2s1M
Green conical buoy
24091(S) **Channel outer buoy** Fl.R.2s1M
Red cylindrical buoy

Port communications

Club Nautico Torre Horadada ✆ +34 966 76 90 87
Email info@cnth.es
www.cnth.es

Shallow approaches to yacht harbour

A yacht harbour established in an old fishing anchorage to S of Punta de la Horadada. It is well-protected from all directions except S. Swell between W and S can make the approach dangerous as the water is shallow but otherwise it is easy to approach and enter. Facilities are limited.

Approach

The approach to this harbour is shallow and strangers should sound their way in.

From the south The long, low 10M-long sand strip that separates the Mar Menor from the sea is unmistakable as is Isla Grosa (95m) and the

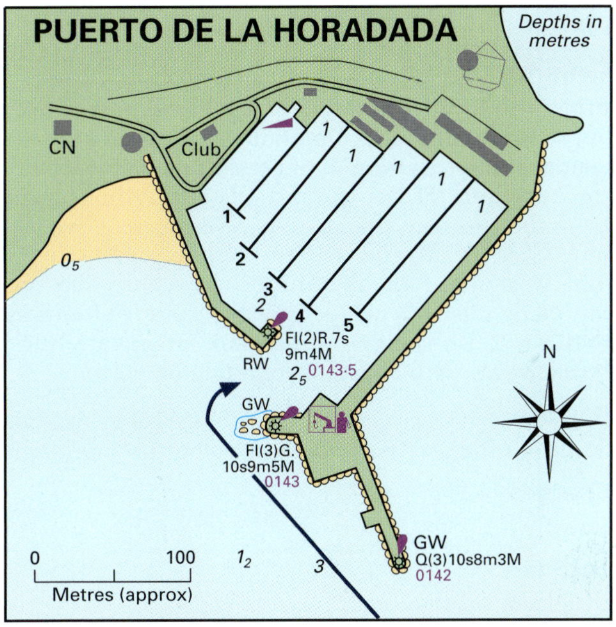

⊕71 Puerto de la Horadada 37°51'·85N 00°45'·3W (off plan)

III. COSTA BLANCA

Puerto de la Horadada

breakwater of the harbour of San Pedro del Pinatar. Between Pinatar and Horadada, 3M north, give the coast a ½M berth to avoid rocky islets. The Torre de la Horadada, on a low promontory, has buildings at its foot and is conspicuous. It has a rocky reef with exposed heads extending 150m off it. In the approach, the harbour walls will be seen.

From the north Between the large harbour of Torrevieja and Punta de la Horadada the coast is only moderately high with rocky cliffs in places. The small promontory of Punta Primo (or Delgada) lies between Torrevieja and Cabo Roig. Cabo Roig is of reddish sandstone and is prominent with a white tower and buildings on its summit. A small yacht harbour lies on the S side of Cabo Roig and another lies to the S of Punta El Cuervo which is to S of Cabo Roig. There are a number of small rocks and islets offshore along this section of coast and a berth of ½M is advised. The Torre de la Horadada is conspicuous from the north and has a reef extending some 150m to the NNE.

GPS approach

Steer to ⊕71 from the eastern sector and steer for the end of the breakwater (approximately 0·15M).

Entrance

From a position 200m to S of the harbour entrance, approach sounding continuously. Red and green channel buoys to the SW of the entrance now define the beginning of the entrance channel. About 50m from the entrance change to a NW course. Give the inner spur head at least 25m berth as rocks extend 10m west of it. Note the entrance frequently silts up, especially after SW winds and the depth is often less than the 2.5m shown on the plan. Great care must be exercised with constant sounding on entry.

Berths

Secure to the first pontoon and ask at the *capitanía*.

Charges

Low.

Facilities

Maximum length overall: 12m.
Small slipway in the NW corner of the harbour with 1m off it.
5-tonne crane to starboard side of the entrance and a large mobile crane.
Engine mechanics – Volvo agency.
Water taps on quays and pontoons.
Showers and WC.
220V AC points on quays and pontoons.
Some shops in the village.
Gasoleo A and petrol.

Communications

Coastal bus service on main road. ✆ Area code 966.

49. Puerto de Campoamor (Dehesa de Campoamor)

37°53′·9N 00°45′·9W

A private harbour with 350 berths primarily for motor vessels and with maximum depth of 2m.

Charts

British Admiralty *1700.* Imray *M12*
French *7670.* Spanish *471*

⊕72 37°53′·8N 00°44′·7W

Lights

0144 **Espigón Este** Iso.G.4s8m5M Green metal mast, white bands 6m
0144.2 **Contradique head** Iso.R.4s8m3M Red metal mast, white bands 6m

Buoys

Two small green conical buoys mark submerged rocks 200m off the root of the *contradique*

Port communications

VHF Ch 9. Club Náutico de Campoamor
✆ +34 965 32 03 86
Email cncampoamor@cncampoamor.com
www.cncampoamor.com

Harbour mainly for motor boats

A yacht harbour built primarily for motor boaters on the site of an old anchorage. It is organised as a residential club; there are a few berths for transit yachts but visitors who stay for any length of time may be expected to join the club, if found acceptable. Approach and entrance are not difficult but care must be taken as it is shallow. Facilities in the harbour and village cater for normal requests. Swell from S–SW tends to enter the harbour. Fine sandy beaches.

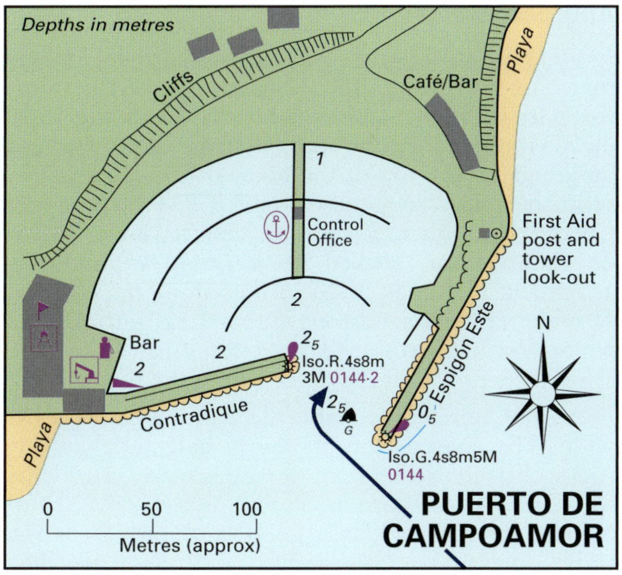

⊕72 Puerto de Campoamor 37°53'·8N 00°44'·7W (off plan)

Approach

From the south The high breakwater of Puerto de San Pedro del Pinatar is conspicuous. The low coast, which should be given a berth of ½M or more to avoid isolated patches of rocks and rocky islets, stretches as far as the Punta de la Horadada which has a *torre* with a building at its foot. The coast further N has low cliffs. Punta El Cuervo, which has a shoal 50m off its eastern edge, is inconspicuous unlike the high-rise apartment blocks behind Puerto de Campoamor.

From the north The large Puerto de Torrevieja is easily recognised. The coast to the S should be given a ½M berth due to off-lying dangers; this coastline has low rocky sandstone cliffs. Cabo Roig which is of a reddish colour has a tower on its summit and a small yacht harbour lies on its S side. Puerto de Campoamor lies just under 2M to S. There is a shallow river valley just to N of the harbour.

GPS approach

Steer to ⊕72 from the southeastern quadrant and steer for the end of the breakwater (approximately 0·15M).

Campoamor

Entrance

Keep well away from the harbour walls until the heads of the two *diques* are in line on approximately 320° and then approach, sounding. There is a shoal patch (0·3m) 500m SSE of the harbour, on an approach of approximately 337°. When 50m off the entrance, divert to port and then round the head of Dique de Levante.

Berths

Secure to the outer pontoon and ask at the control office in a hut on the centre pontoon or at the yacht club if no one is in the office.

Facilities

Maximum length overall: 14m.
Small hardstanding.
Slipway in the W corner of the harbour.
3-tonne crane also in the W corner of the harbour.
Water taps on the quays and pontoons.
220V AC points on quays and pontoons.
Gasoleo A and petrol.
Supermarket in the village.
Club Náutico de Campoamor on the W side of the harbour has a bar, showers etc.

Communications

Bus service on the main road. ✆ Area code 965.

50. Puerto de Cabo Roig

37°54'N 00°43'W

An attractive small harbour with 200 berths prone to silting in the entrance.

Charts

British Admiralty *1700*. Imray *M12*
French *7670*. Spanish *471*

⊕73 37°54'·6N 00°43'·7W

Lights

0145 **Dique de Levante head** Fl.G.3s9m5M Green and white pole 6m
0145.5 **Contradique head** Fl.R.3s4m4M Red and white pole
Inland to the North
0147 **Guardamar del Segura** 38°04'·4N 00°39'·7W, Aero, Oc.R.1.5s443m15M and 7F.R(vert).

Port communications

VHF Ch 9. *Capitanía* ✆ */Fax* +34 966 76 01 76
Email info@marinacaboroig.com
www.marinacaboroig.com

Pleasant small yacht harbour

A small, attractive yacht harbour at a well-established anchorage, only open to the SW. It is tucked away on the W side of Cabo Roig which is entirely given over to low-rise, detached buildings and gardens. The beach to the N is buoyed-off for swimmers. Inshore there is a small village at some distance which has everyday supplies. There is a castle nearby, sand and pebble beaches either side of the harbour and a golf course at Villamartin, 5M.

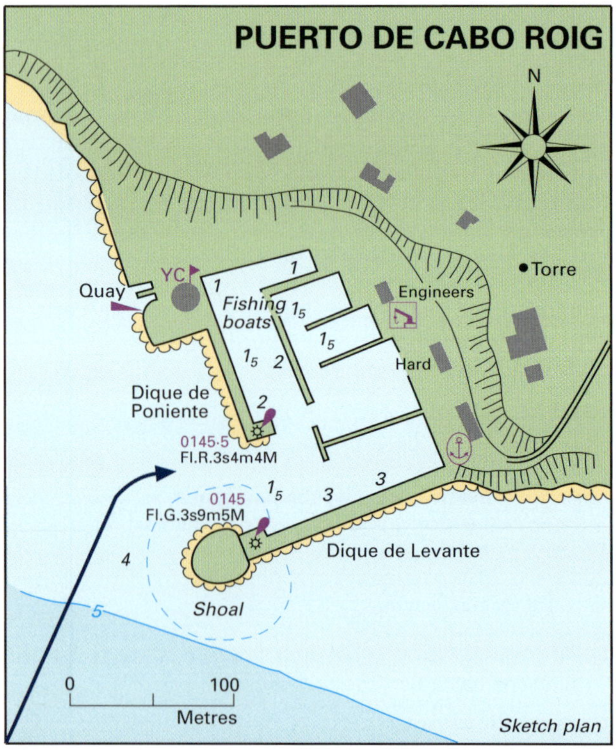

⊕73 Puerto de Cabo Roig
37°54'·6N 00°43'·7W (off plan)

Puerto de Cabo Roig during reconstruction

Approach

From the south From Puerto de San Pedro del Pinatar the coast northwards should be given a ½M berth as there are islets and submerged rocks. Puerto de Torre de la Horadada can be recognised by the tower and buildings on the top of the point of the same name. From here low rocky cliffs stretch 2M to Punta El Cuervo where there is another yacht harbour, Puerto de Campoamor, backed by a group of high-rise apartment buildings. 1½M further along the coast to N is the reddish sandstone Cabo Roig with a large white tower surrounded by trees and villas. The harbour is to SW of the point below the tower.

From the north The Bahía de Santa Pola is 14M wide. The coast is low in the N half and has low rocky cliffs in the S. Sierra de Callosa (547m), 11½M to WNW of Guardarmar, a town on the coast 5M to N of Cabo Cervera, is a good landmark as is the radio mast at Guardamar del Segura. The breakwaters of Puerto de Torrevieja and the town of the same name are conspicuous. 2M to S of this harbour is Punta Prima (or Delgada) which has rocky cliffs and 2M further on is the prominent Cabo Roig which has a white tower on its summit. The harbour lies SW of the tower.

GPS approach

Steer to ⊕73 from the southern sector and steer for the end of the breakwater, sounding carefully (approximately 0·1M).

Entrance

Sand often builds up off the head of the Dique de Levante and it is wise to give it a good 30m berth. There may be a small green buoy near the end of the dique, which signals the extent of the accumulated sand. Care must be exercised on entry with constant sounding recommended.

Berths

Secure to a pontoon T-piece and ask at the *capitanía* or the *club náutico*.

Facilities

Maximum length overall: 12m.
Slipway on NE side of the harbour – 1·5m of water off it.
1-tonne crane beside the slipway.
Water taps on quays and pontoons.
220V AC points on quays and pontoons.
Supermarket in village.
Club Náutico de Cabo Roig has all normal facilities.

Communications

Bus service on main road 1M inland to Torrevieja.
✆ Area code 966.

51. Puerto de Torrevieja

37°58'·3N 00°41'·2W

A very large and safe harbour with three marinas and over 2,000 berths: plenty of room and a good reception for visitors.

Charts

British Admiralty *1700*. Imray *M12*
French *7670*. Spanish *4710*

⊕75 37°57'·5N 00°41'·1W

Lights

0146 **Dique de Levante head** Fl.G.4s15m7M
Octagonal tower 10m
0146.2 **Muelle de la Sal** Fl(3)R.11·5s11m2M
Metal framework tower 6m
0146.3 **Pontoon head** F.R
0146.4 **Dársena Pesquera breakwater NW head**
Fl(2)G.7s4m2M Green structure 3m
0146.6 **Club Náutico jetty E head** Fl(4)R.11s4m2M
Red column 3m

To the north
0148 **Isla de Tabarca** Oc(2)10s29m15M
White tower 14m
Inland to the north
0147 **Guardamar del Segura**, Aero Oc.R.1·5s 443m15M and 7F.R(vert)
24170a(s) 37°58'·3N 0°41'·4W Buoy Fl.R.6s Red
(This buoy signals the construction work going on to build a new jetty for the fishing fleet)

Port communications

VHF Ch 06, 09, 11, 14.
Real Club Nautico de Torrevieja ✆ +34 965 71 01 12 / +34 679 183104 (night number)
Email info@rcnt.com www.rcnt.com
Marina Internacional de Torrevieja (Puerto Deportivo) ✆ +34 965 71 36 50
Email info@puertodeportivomarinainternacional.es
www.pertodeportivomarinainternacional.com
Marina Salinas ✆ */Fax* +34 965 709 701
Email info@marinasalinas.com www.marinasalinas.com

Useful major harbour

A nice clean harbour with some good yacht berths on pontoons, a good yacht club and an excellent anchorage west of the marina (rare along the coast), but where yachts have sometimes been banned by the harbourmaster. This has been challenged by the local yachtsmen but it seems to be a general feature all along this stretch of coast which comes under the jurisdiction of Valencia. The yacht harbour, Marina Internacional de Torrevieja SA is on the northwest side of the harbour. The commercial quay, Muelle de la Sal, handles large quantities of salt. The approach and entrance are simple and there is good shelter from winds except those from S to SW which make parts of the harbour uncomfortable. There is now a new marina, Marina Salinas, in the SE corner of the harbour. It has 700-odd berths and should be a great benefit to yachtsmen on this crowded coast.

The town is of no great interest but it has several restaurants and there are shops quite close to the harbour. A visit to the saltworks, the 'Salt Cellar of the World', is of interest. Good beaches on either side of the harbour.

Approach

From the south Isla Grosa (95m), off the breakwater of Puerto de Tomás Maestre and near the centre of the 10M building strip separating Mar Menor from the sea, is unmistakable as is the high breakwater of Puerto San Pedro del Pinatar. The following three promontories all have yacht harbours on their S sides: Punta de la Torre de la Horadada with a tower on the point and buildings around its base; Punta El Cuervo which has a group of high-rise buildings; and the reddish-coloured Cabo Roig which has a white tower. Keep at least ½M off the coast. From Punta Prima (or Delgada) the rocky cliffs fall away to a low, flat coast near Torrevieja. The breakwaters and town of Torrevieja are visible from afar though quite well inset from Cabo Cervera.

From the north Cross the wide Bahía de Santa Pola which has cliffs in its S part. The Sierra de Callosa (547m) 11½M to WNW of the town of Guardamar and the radio mast at Guardamar del Segura are useful marks. Cabo Cervera is prominent but low; to S of it are several smaller rocky points with coves between. The harbour breakwaters appear when these points have been rounded.

GPS approach

Steer to ⊕75 from the southeastern quadrant and steer for the end of the breakwater (approximately 0·4M).

Anchorage in the approach

Anchor just west of the Muelle Sal to suit draught but keeping out of the way of the harbour entrance.

Torrevieja: Ample space for super-yachts *Jane Russell*

III. COSTA BLANCA

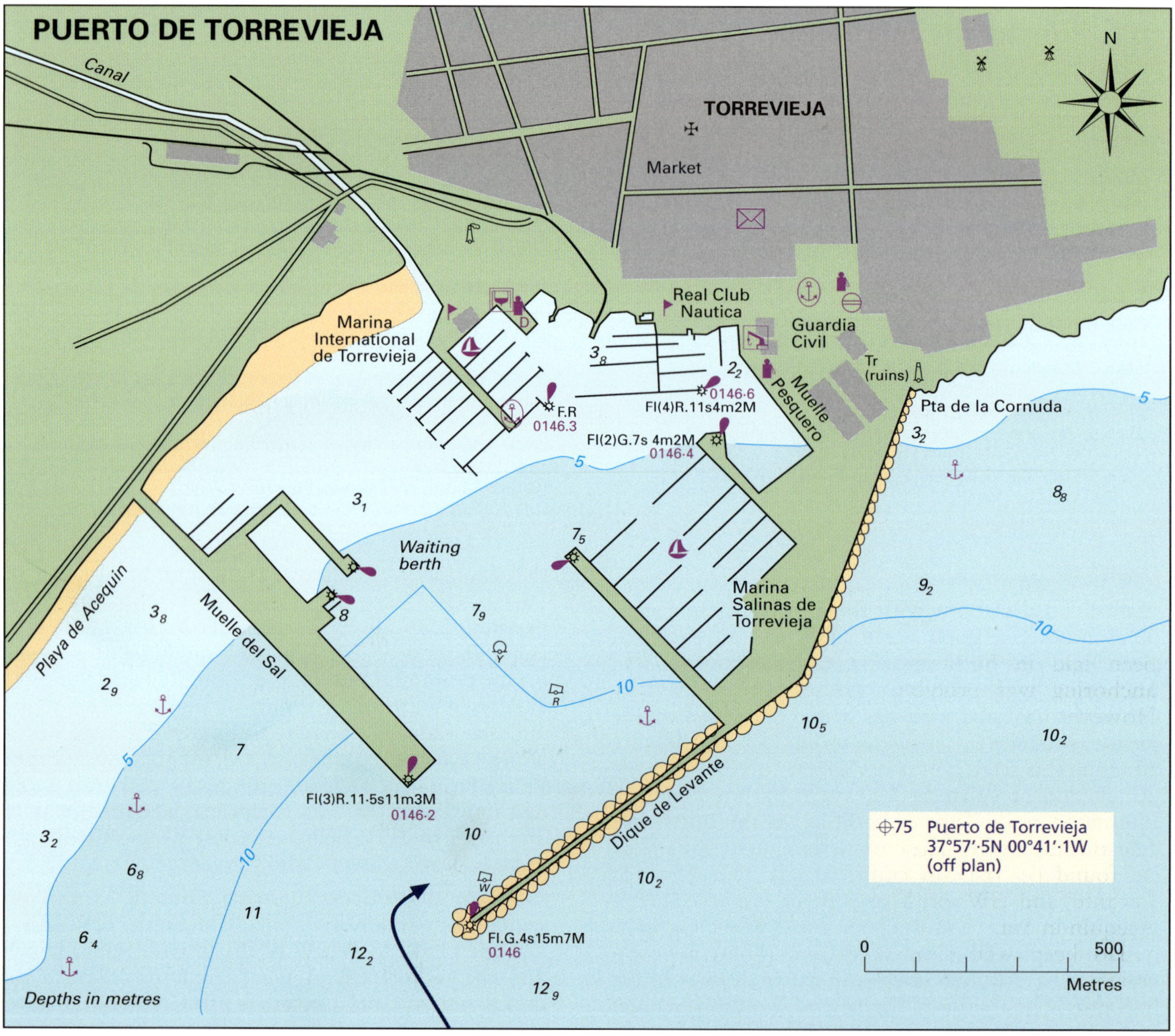

Entrance

Straightforward but fishing boats move at speed and, at night, often without lights. Their wash can make the outer berths at the marina uncomfortable.

Note Ships manoeuvring off the salt quay take hawsers out to a yellow buoy in the centre of the harbour. Beware of these cables, being just submerged. If in doubt, leave the buoy to port on entering the harbour.

Berths

There are several possibilities within the harbour. The original marina was the Real Club Nautíco. This welcomes visitors but is primarily for local members and long term cruising yachts. It has a superb club house, bar and restaurant which can be used by anyone. In the late '80s, what is now called Marina International de Torrevieja, was constructed in the NW of the harbour. This has served visiting and wintering vessels and crews for years and continues to do so. More recently Marina Salinas has opened due to a need for more moorings. All welcome visiting yachts for long and short stays. Pontoons in the extreme W of the harbour are without facilities, very shallow and for dinghies or small local motor vessels only.

The new Marina Salinas usually berths visitors on the pontoons at the W end of the marina: a very long walk to the office and town. It is worth asking for a berth more conveniently located if you intend to stay more than a day or two.

Note that the larger berths for both Marina International de Torrevieja and Real Club Nautico are on the outer S and SE jetties, which are rather exposed and experience surging with strong S and SW sector winds. I noticed in late summer 2013 that several larger yachts berthed on the outer jetties used their own ground tackle to supplement the local ground lines.

Anchoring

Excellent anchorages are to be found within the huge harbour SW of Marina Salinas and to the SW of Marina International de Torrevieja. Buoys have

Club Nautico (on right of photo) and Marina Torrevieja moorings

been laid in both areas (September 2013) and anchoring was prohibited as long ago as 2007. However, as elsewhere, this led to contention between local yachtsmen who demand to use these areas, and the port authorities. The situation seems to be that officially, anchoring is prohibited anywhere in the harbour, but is usually overlooked! Just outside of the harbour, good anchorages are to be found on the 5m contours NE of Muelle de Levante and SW of Muelle del Sal, near Playa Acequin in 5m.

Do keep well clear of Muelle de Sal, where freighters moor and load salt on either side of the muelle and take a wide turning circle.

Facilities

Maximum length overall: Club Nautico vessels up to (and over) over 50m.
Marina internacional up to 30m
Marina Salinas up to 35m.
Repairs and technical service area, contact yacht club for advice.

Maritime museum includes this Delfin class submarine. Well worth a visit *Jane Russell*

Slipway alongside the yacht club and a large one near root of Dique de Levante.
80-tonne travel-lift.
Cranes up to 12 tonnes.
Chandlery – Network Yacht & Rigging Services (run by an English couple) have a well stocked shop between the International Marina and the Club Nautico Marina. There is another chandler in the town and also one outside of town on the road to Cartagena.
Water taps on the pontoon and on the quay.
220V AC points on pontoons.
Gasoleo A and petrol.
Ice from factory near customs office or from club.
The Réal Club Náutico de Torrevieja has good facilities including bar, restaurants, lounges, terraces and showers. Visitors are made welcome.
Good shops and small market in the town.
Supermarket in street behind the garage on the N side of the main road in town.
Launderette in the marina or two streets back from the *club náutico*.

Locally

Torrevieja is a large tourist town with many Scandinavian, British and German visitors, thanks to budget price flights from Northern Europe. Within the harbour complex is a maritime museum which includes a Delfin class submarine. This is the first maritime museum to open on the Costa and well worth a visit. Fascinating for anyone who wondered how 30 crew members live for weeks submerged in a 'sewer pipe' (as we ex-RNs affectionately call these boats!).

The tourist office is now located next to the main entrance of Club Nautico: a good starting point for any trip into town in summer as they have great air conditioning and a helpful friendly staff.

Communications

Rail and bus services. ☎ Area code 965.
Taxi ☎ +34 965 71 22 77.

52. Marina de las Dunas (Puerto Guardamar)

38°06'·5N 00°38'·6W

A good private marina at the mouth of Rio Segura with 500 berths: 116 for use by visitors.

Charts

British Admiralty *1700.* Imray *M12*
French *7670.* Spanish *472, 4721*

⊕76 38°06'·7N 00°38'·0E

Lights

0147 **Guardamar del Segura** Oc.R.1·5s443m15M and 7F.R(vert). Antenna white and red bands 440m (light is 2·5M S and 0·5M inland of marina)
0147.5 **S Breakwater head** Fl(3)R.9s8m5M Red tower 5m
0147.2 **Interior elbow** Fl(4)R.11s4m1M Red column 3m
0147.51 **N Breakwater head** Fl(3)G.9s5m3M Green tower 5m
0147.52 **Middle breakwater head** Fl(4)G.11s5m1M Green tower on white base 3m
0147.53 **Centre** Fl.G.3s4m1M Green column 3m
0147.54 **W of Fish Wharf** QG.4m1M Green column 3m
0147.55 **Fish Wharf W head** QG.4m1M Green column 3m
0147.7 **Starboard hand entrance** Fl(2+1)G.15s6m1M Green tower, red band, white base 3m
0147.72 **Port hand entrance** Fl.R.3s6m1M Red tower on white base 3m
Buoys A number of small yellow and white buoys mark the 3m channel into the marina.

Port communications

VHF Ch 9. *Capitanía* ✆ +34 966 72 65 49
24 hour *Mobile* +34 639 68 71 57
Email administracion.madusa@telefonica.net
www.marinadunas.es

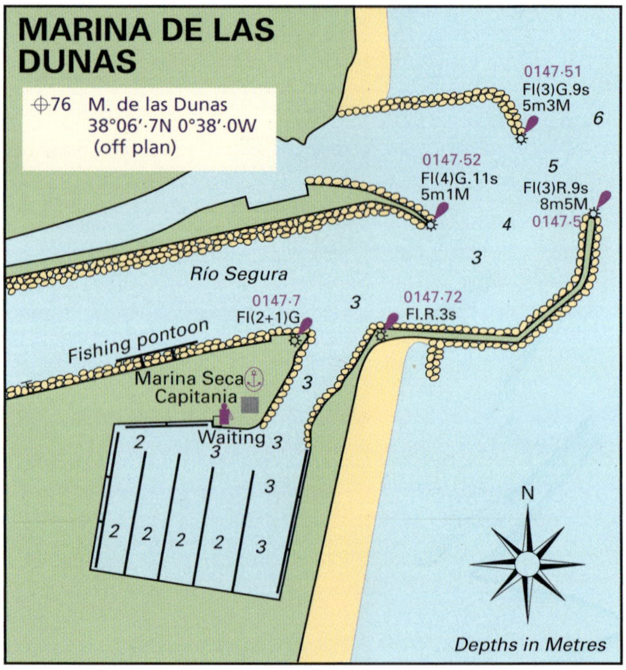

Quiet sheltered marina

The mouth of the Río Segura has been widened and a channel dug to the south of the old river mouth to give access to a 500-berth marina. The land approach is to the NW corner where a new road leads to the town of Guardamar – about 1km away.

The marina is fully operational with a café and some small shops.

Río Segura and Marina de las Dunas

Approach

From the south The large harbour and town of Torrevieja is easily recognised. To N of this harbour are a series of points with small *calas* between, the coast being rocky cliffs. The coast from Cabo Cervera to N is low and sandy. The town of Guardamar, which has a ruined castle, lies 1M to S of the mouth of the Río Segura which has rocky breakwaters. The radio mast Guardamar del Segura is 4½M to NNW of Cabo Cervera.

From the north Cross the Bahía de Santa Pola from Cabo de Santa Pola on a SW course leaving Isla de Tabarca to port and Puerto de Santa Pola to starboard, both of which are easily identified. 2½M to N of Río Segura is the Torre del Pinet off which at 2M ESE lies a fish farm. The coast is low and sandy.

GPS approach

Steer to ⊕76 from the eastern sector and steer for between the breakwaters (approximately 0·21M).

Entrance

Although the entrance has been dredged to 6m between the breakwaters it is liable to silting. Approach the mouth of the river, half way between the green and red towers at the ends of the breakwaters on a SW course, sounding carefully. Once inside the mouth keep between the lines of yellow buoys until abeam of the marina entrance, turn to port and enter the marina itself. The waiting berth is immediately to starboard on entering, in front of the *capitanía*.

Charges

Medium.

Facilities

Maximum length 15m.
Café and small shops in high season.
Electricity and water on pontoons.
Repair yard with crane and travel-hoist.
Hardstanding with covered hangers.
Fuel berth.
Showers and toilets.
Parking.
24-hour security.

⚓ BAHÍA DE SANTA POLA

38°11'.3N 0°34'.9W

Anchor to suit draught along the coast from Cabo Cervera to Santa Pola in sand, mud and stones with weed. Sandy beach with low cliffs, road inland and some development. Flamingos use the nearby *salinas*. See plan page 125.

53. Puerto de Santa Pola

38°11'·2N 00°33'·8W

Two very friendly yacht harbours and a fishing port dating from Roman times. No allocated visitors berths in the yacht club, but visitors berths available in Marina Miramar up to 60m.

Charts

British Admiralty *473, 1700.* Imray *M12*
French *7670.* Spanish *4721, 472*

⊕77 38°10'·7N 00°33'·9W

Lights

To the south
0147 **Guardamar del Segura** , Aero, Oc.R.1·5s 443m15M and 7F.R(vert)
Harbour
0154 **Dique de Levante head** Fl.G.5s9m5M Green and white tower 8m
0155 **Contradique head** Q(2)R.5.3s8m3M Red and white octagonal tower 5m
0154.3 **Espigón head** 38°11'.3N 00°33'.6W Fl(2)G.7s4m1M Green post 3m
To the east
24420(S) **Wave buoy** 38°15'.1N 00°24'.9W Q(5)Y.20s Yellow spherical
To the northeast
0152 **Cabo Santa Pola** Fl(2+1)20s152m16M Square white tower with metal superstructure 15m vis over 270° arc

Port communications

Club náutico VHF Ch 9. ✆ +34 965 41 24 03
Email admin@cnauticosantapola.com
www.cnauticosantapola.com
Marina Miramar VHF Ch 9, ✆ +34 650 56 98 69 (24 hours)
Email info@marinamiramar.com
www.marinamiramar.com

Busy fishing port with friendly club and new marina

An old Roman port and settlement, now a busy, small fishing port with a good harbour for visiting yachts and an unattractive tourist town. There are repair yards, adequate shops and a good market. In high season, the disco may be very noisy.

Approach

From the south The town of Guardamar and nearby Guardamar del Segura are easily identified, as is Cabo de Santa Pola which lies to NE of this harbour. There is a large yellow crane and building at the end of the Dique de Levante and a large blue boat shed at the end of the *contradique*.

From the north Cabo de Santa Pola and the Isla de Tabarca are easily recognised. There is a large yellow crane and building at the end of the Dique de Levante and a large blue boat shed at the end of the *contradique*.

GPS approach

Steer to ⊕77 from the southern quadrant and steer for the breakwater head (approximately 0·34M).

Anchorage in the approach

Anchor 200m to E of the Dique de Levante in four to five metres on mud and weed.

Entrance

Approach on a NE course and round head of Dique de Levante at 20m to starboard. Keep a watch for fishing boats leaving at speed.

Berths

There are two areas to berth, to the east the public pontoons have been removed and there is now a new marina, Marina Miramar, in their position. To the west are the yacht club pontoons. Normal 10m+ craft in the approach should call the YC or the new marina on VHF Ch 9 (or, preferably, phone) for berth availability – there are no actual visitor berths but the club and/or marina will do their best to find a berth for you but berths are very limited and virtually non-existent in high season.

Facilities

Maximum length overall: 15m.
Two major fishing boat repair and building yards located to the E of the harbour will undertake yacht repairs.
Hard at the shipyard and at N of harbour.
Two large slipways on the coast to E of the harbour.
Cranes at the shipyards and two on Dique de Levante. A special crane for yachts to S of pontoons.
Two small chandlers in the town near quays.
Water from taps on the quays and pontoons.
220/380V AC in shipyard.
Wi-Fi available in Marina Miramar.
Gasoleo A.
Ice available in the town and on fuel quay.
Club Náutico de Santa Pola with bar, restaurant and swimming pool.
A number of fairly good shops in town and a good market.

Locally

There is a 16th-century castle and for the energetic, excellent views of the coast from Cabo de Santa Pola. The *salinas* west of the town has flamingos, stilts, avocets and other birds in winter and spring. Beaches on both sides of the harbour.

Communications

Bus service on the main road. ✆ Area code 965.
Taxi ✆ +34 965 41 35 36.

⚓ PUNTA DE ESPATO

Anchorage in the approach

A good anchorage in 7m sand and weed lies 500m to S of Punta de Espato. This is a useful anchorage for yachts on passage up or down the coast and to and from the Balearics.

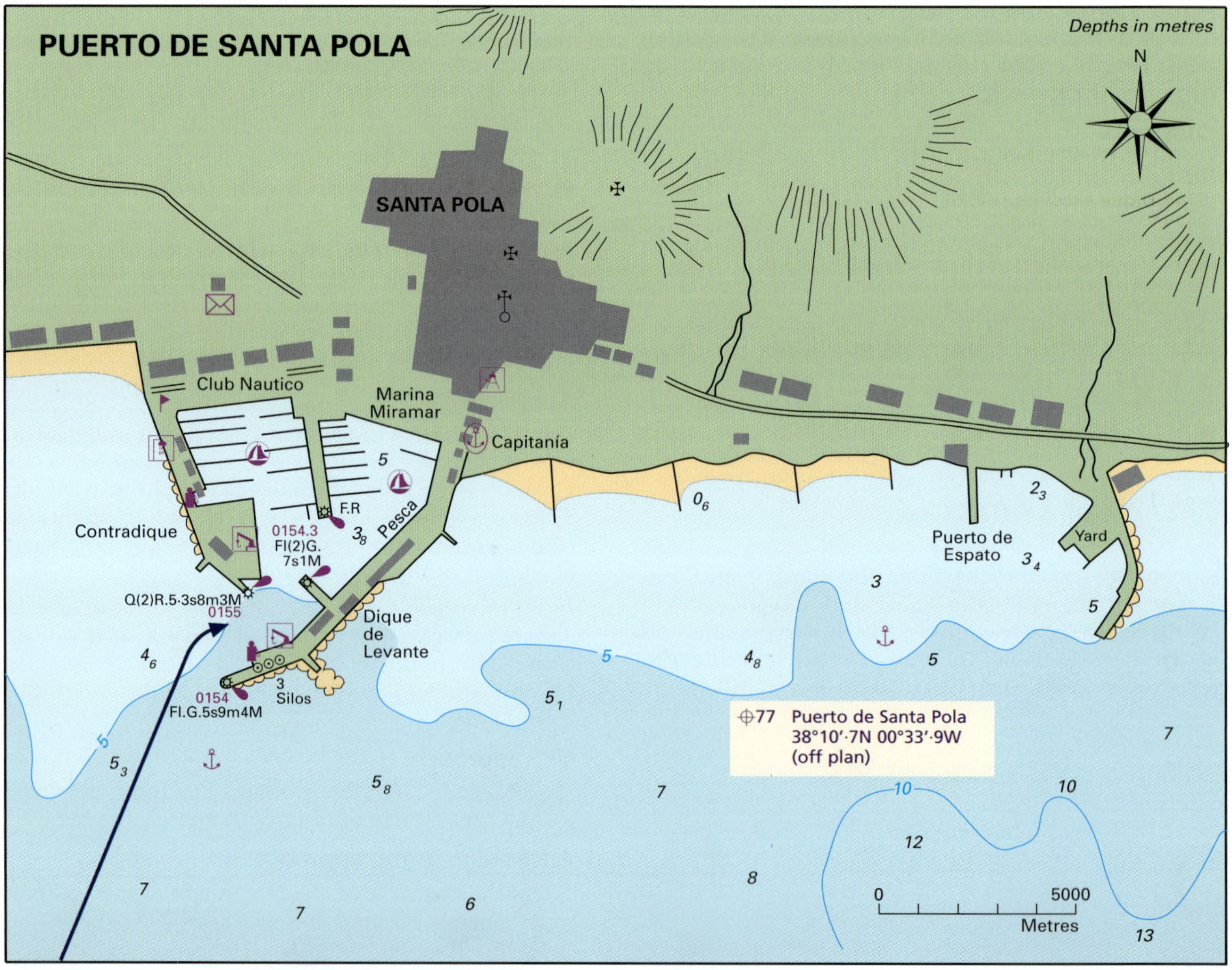

54. Puerto de Espato

38°11'·2N 00°38'W

Service station

This is more of a service station than a port, immediately to the north of Punta Espato. It has large slipways, hardstandings and a travel-lift.

Facilities

Some heavy engineering.
50-tonne travel-lift.
Hardstanding.

Puerto de Espato

55. Puerto de Isla de Tabarca (Isla Plana)

38°10'N 00°28'W

Not much of a harbour, but with space for 25 yachts up to 10m along the S side of the Escolera.

Charts

British Admiralty *473, 1700.* Imray *M12*
French *7670.* Spanish *472A, 472*

⊕78 38°09'N 00°25'W Off Islas de Tarbarca

Lights

0148 **Isla Tabarca** LFl.8s29m15M
White round tower 14m

Harbour

0149 **Dique-escolera** Fl(2)R.6s9m3M Metallic tower 4m
24290(S) **Bajo de la Nao** Q(3)10s5M ♦ card E buoy 4m

Port communications

Asociación de Empresarios de Turismo de Tabarca
✆ +34 965 96 12 72
Teléfono de Información Turística ✆ +34 902 10 09 10
VHF Ch 9

Island and marine reserve

A large area around this island is a reserve where fishing, diving and anchoring is forbidden (see chart page 138). The reserve is marked by six buoys, the northern three are Fl(4)Y.12s, while the southern three are Fl(5)15s, all with cross topmarks.

Approach

From the SW Make for the prominent Cabo de Santa Pola, passing about halfway between the extreme W of the island and the mainland. When the N coast of the island has opened up and the lighthouse bears 300°, approach with the lighthouse lined up with the head of the *dique*.

From the NE Aim at the centre of the island. In the closer approach the *dique* will be seen. Head for it on a southeasterly course.

Entrance

Go for the *dique* head between 300° and 315° and leave it 30m to port.

Berths

Secure to quay. In any swell, use an anchor to hold off. Leave space for ferries to the mainland and fishing boats near the head of the *dique*.

Anchorage

An area around the island is marked with buoys to define a 'protected' nature reserve. Anchoring and fishing is technically prohibited, but locals ignore these zones.

Facilities

Water from the village if you must – it is in short supply, stored in a cistern and issued each evening.
A few small shops in the village.

Locally

The island was once an old pirate base. They were eventually driven out and a small fortified village built to hold the island against further occupation and garrisoned by Spaniards who were exchanged prisoners of war. The inhabitants have, for generations, lived a very frugal, isolated life based on a small fishing fleet. There is an old fort from the reign of Charles III which is falling into disrepair and small beaches on the S and E side of the island.

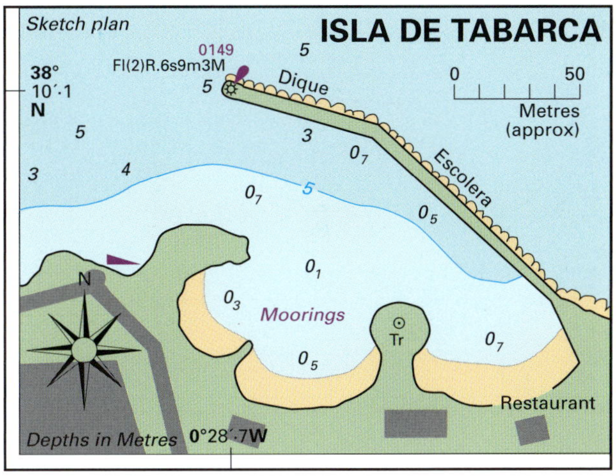

Isla Tabarca

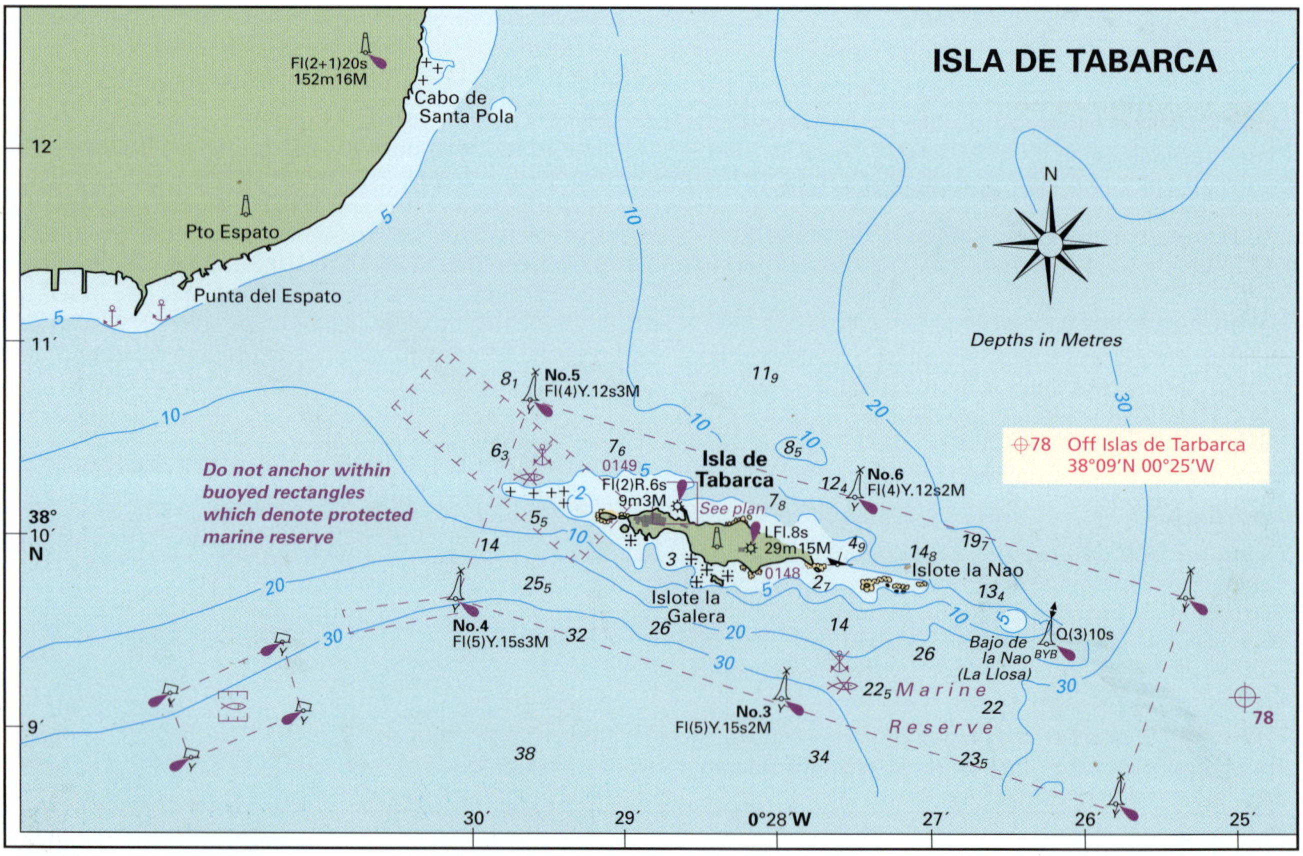

56. Puerto de Alicante

38°20'·3N 00°28'·9W

One of the largest ports in Spain which can be entered in any conditions. Two private marinas with 1,300 berths but space for visitors is limited in high season.

Charts

British Admiralty *469, 473, 1700.* Imray *M12*
French *7670.* Spanish *4722, 472A, 472*

⊕79 38°19'·35N 00°29'·1W

Lights

To the south

0152 **Cabo Santa Pola** Fl(2+1)20s152m16M Square white tower with metal superstructure 15m vis over 270° arc

0148 **Isla Tabarca** LFl.8s29m15M White round tower 14m

New Darsena Sur

0157.3 **Dique de Abrigo head** Fl(2+1)R.21s18m5M Red tower, green band 10m

0157.4 **Interior Jetty head** Fl(2)G.7s10m5M Green tower 4m

0157.43 **Dique de Abrigo centre** Fl.R.5s12m7M Red tower

0157.45 **Contradique head** Fl(2)R.7s8m3M Red tower 5m

New Fishing Harbour

0157.5 **East breakwater head** Fl(3)G.9s10m5M Green tower 8m

0157.7 **West breakwater head** Fl(3)R.9s7m3M Red tower on white base 6m

0157.9 **Interior jetty head** Fl(2+1)R.21s3m1M Metal post 2m

Old Harbour

0158 **Dique de Abrigo de Levante head** Fl.G.5s14m10M Green truncated tower 9m

0158.6 **Terminal granelles sólidos NE end** Fl(2)R.7s9m3M Red tower on white base 3m

0159 **Muelle 11** S corner Fl(2+1)R.14·5s8m3M Red tower, green band 6m

0159.3 **Muelle 11** N corner Fl(4)R.11s8m3M Red tower on white base 6m

0160 **Muelle A** SW corner Fl(2+1)R.14·5s8m3M Red metal column, green band 6m

0162 **Muelle de Poniente head** Fl.R.3s8m3M Red and white post 6m

0160.5 **Real Club jetty S head** Fl(2+1)R.21s4m1M Red post green band 3m

24510b(S) **Bifurcation Buoy** (just SE off new Dique Sur) Fl(2+1)R.21s3M Red, green, red tower

To the east

0166 **Cabo de las Huertas** 38°21'·2N 00°24'·3W Fl(5)19s38m14M White tower 9m

Port communications

Port VHF Ch 14, 20 ✆ +34 965 13 00 95
Marina VHF Ch 9 ✆ +34 965 21 36 00
Email recepcion@marinaalicante.com
www.marinaalicante.com
Real Club de Regatas ✆ +34 965 92 12 50
Email info@rcra.es www.rcra.es

Large city, marina centrally located

A large commercial and fishing port, good facilities for yachtsmen which have encroached into the former anchorage. Easy to enter and obtain shelter in almost any conditions.

The new fishing harbour has now been completed to the SW of the port with a conspicuous new breakwater with sheds behind it. This is not a harbour for yachts so do not approach it. However infilling and dredging is still going on between the

Alicante

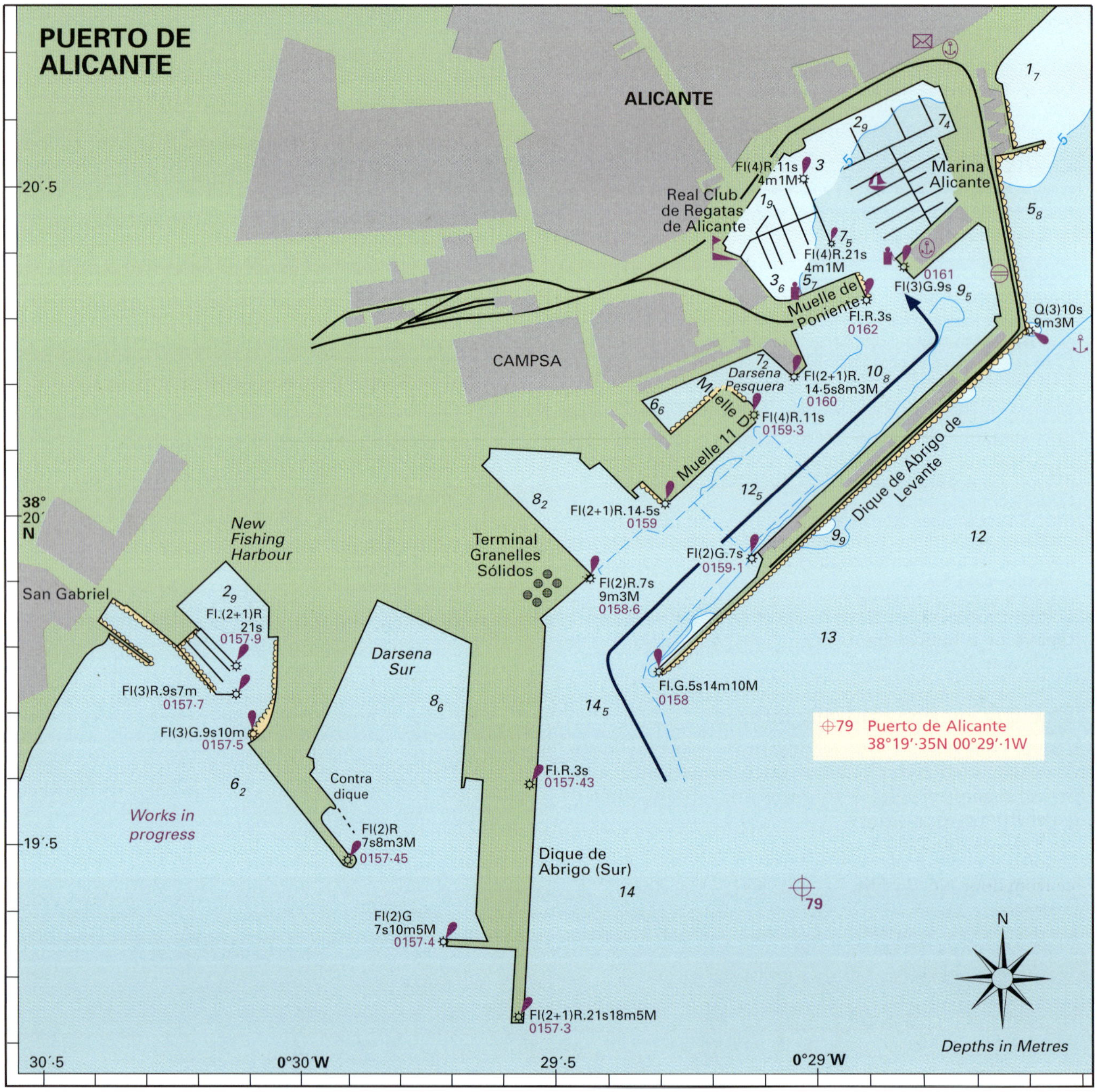

new breakwater and the Terminal Granelles Sólidos but the main quays and lights are now completed. There is a new bifurcation buoy just off the southern end of the Dique de Abrigo and all pleasure craft must leave this to port and proceed north to the old harbour.

Approach

From the south Round Cabo de Santa Pola, pass inside Isla de Tabarca and the hills behind the port topped by a castle will appear and be easily identified.

From the north Cabo de la Huerta is prominent with a whitish hill behind. Beyond it, three steep hills of a light yellow colour are noticeable.

GPS approach

Steer to ⊕79 from the southeastern quadrant and steer for the northern breakwater head (approximately 0·4M). Do not be tempted to steer for the new southern breakwater head which is now the main fishing harbour.

Entrance

Infilling work is going on to extend the Terminal Granelles Sólidos to the SW and to construct a new container harbour. A new *dique* has been constructed and there may be several buoys indicating the extent of the work. Keep well clear of this construction work. After rounding the Abrigo de Levante, follow it at 100m ignoring the first two entrances to port. The entrance to the inner harbour is the third gap. Keep clear of ships entering and leaving.

Berths

There are two marinas in the NE basin. Call Marina Alicante on VHF Ch 9 (or phone) and moor at the waiting berth just to the NE of the fuel berth, immediately to starboard on entering the marina. Take your documents to the office and arrange a berth. Spaces are limited but the marina does its best to accommodate visitors using privately owned berths. All berths have finger pontoons. Although busy and often full in summer, space is usually found in Marina Alicante, though it may be a longer berth than your yacht – and at a correspondingly higher price.

Alternatively, call Real Club de Regatas de Alicante and request a berth in their facilities on the W side of the marina basin. This is a private club and not particularly welcoming to visitors, but is nevertheless a good alternative if Marina Alicante is full.

Charges

High.

Facilities

Maximum length overall: Marina Alicante up to 60m Real Club de Regatas up to 40m.

Repairs of a limited nature can be undertaken. Contact Alicante Marine Services. The shipyard is prepared to slip, clean and paint yachts.

Two slipways in W corner of the inner harbour with capacity of up to 500 tonnes.

A number of cranes in the port with capacity of up to 30 tonnes.

Several chandlery shops in the town.

Water from taps on quays and pontoons.

220V AC supply points.

Gasoleo A and petrol.

Ice from door No. 2 of the ice factory in Dársena Pesquera or from club.

The Real Club de Regatas de Alicante has good facilities. It is both a social and a yacht club and an introduction may be required. Contact the secretary before using the club.

Many shops of all kinds and qualities but inconveniently placed for the marina. There is a good market about 1M into the city; use a No. 6, 7 or 8 bus.

Several launderettes some distance into the city.

TV satellite connections available for larger craft.

The Real Club de Regatas has moved to a new building over the slipway in the west corner of the inner harbour. Tripper boats now ply from the old position of the YC at the centre of the NW side of the inner harbour.

Locally

The city, founded by the Carthaginians and named Akraheuta, was the centre of the Punic empire. The Romans renamed it Lucentum from which the Moors derived Lekant and their successors, Alicante. It was obscured to British eyes until the early 18th century when it was assaulted by Sir John Leake and defended by General O'Mahoney; it became the seat of a British mercantile colony and was occupied by the British during the Peninsular War. More recently it was a Republican centre during the civil war; Primo de Rivera, founder of the Falange, was somewhat hurriedly executed in Alicante in 1936.

The festival, Foqueres de San Juan (St John's bonfires), on 24 June is worth attending. Good sandy beaches either side of the port. The beach to NE is the nearest.

Alicante is full of history along with wonderful elegant architecture, which has preserved it. Access to the castle on the hill overlooking the town is via a tunnel and lift sited close to the N end of the marina, along the main road running parallel to the beach. Well worth a visit, especially in the evening when it is cool and gives spectacular views over the town and marinas.

There are literally hundreds of street restaurants in town near the marinas with cheap local tapas and meals as well as tourist food, along with a number of top quality restaurants to the W of the town and some in the marina itself. Tapas bars abound across the road from the marina and are excellent value for money.

The town is 'humming' at night, with many bars, street magicians, musicians, street artists stalls selling just about anything, etc.

The main street becomes active around 9pm in summer when stalls are set up all along the wide pedestrian walkway running parallel to the sea. There is a lull around 10pm and nightlife begins in earnest at around midnight when thousands of

Alicante viewed from the castle N of the harbour *Graham Hutt*

Replica 18th-century naval galleon *Santísima Trinidad*. The most heavily armed ship of her day *Maria Kanayama*

people hit the bars. A very gregarious town and a popular nightspot for Spanish and foreign tourists alike. Unlike nightlife in Benedorm and Ibiza, these nights out are very much for the whole family. One of the most exciting and interesting places in Spain with something for everyone and far enough away from the marina to get a peaceful sleep aboard after a night on the town.

A local publication *What's on in Alicante* can be obtained from the tourist office along with piles of information on the location of museums the fortress, art galleries, churches, concerts, etc.

Communications

Major international airport – good for crew change. Rail service to Madrid. One terminal of the narrow gauge coast railway which runs a tourist excursion train as far as Dénia. Bus service along the coast. International airport (with connections to British provincial airports). Ferries to the Islas Baleares, Marseille and other ports.

✆ Area code 965. Taxi ✆ +34 965 25 25 11.
British Consulate Plaza Calvo Sotelo 1/2
Post: Apartado 564 ✆ +34 965 21 61 90, 21 60 22 .

⚓ ENSENADA DE ALBUFERETA
38°21′.2N 0°27′.8W

Anchorage in 3m sand in N corner of the Bahía de Alicante open E. Coast road with many houses and flats. Shops nearby.

L'Albufereta
38°21′N 00°28′W

Small, shallow dinghy harbour

A small artificial dinghy harbour with depths of less than a metre, little shelter and no facilities apart from a dinghy ramp and hardstanding. Real Club des Regates and some sailing schools use this harbour extensively.

L'Albufereta

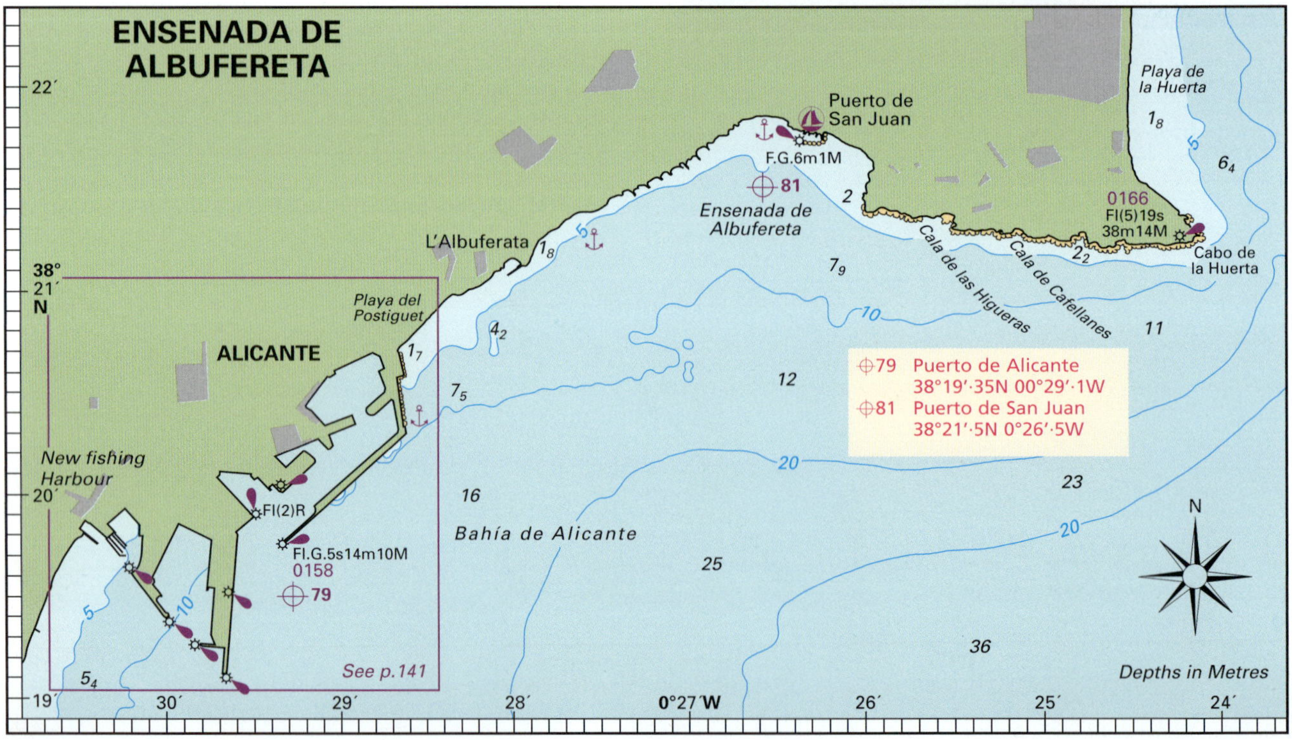

57. Puerto de San Juan (Club Náutico Costa Blanca)

38°21′·7N 00°26′·3W

A small private yacht club suitable for 230 yachts of 12m or less. Shallow in the entrance and few spaces available for visitors, especially in high season.

Charts

British Admiralty *469, 1700.* Imray *M12*
French *7670.* Spanish *472A, 472*

⊕81 38°21′·5N 00°26′·5W

Lights

0164 **Dique head** F.G.6m3M Green and white column 3m
0164.2 **Contradique head** F.R.5m1M Red and white column 3m

To the east

0166 **Cabo de la Huerta** Fl(5)19s38m14M White tower 9m
24685(S) **Buoy** 38°21′·3N 00°26′·2W Q(6)+LFl.15s4M ⯒ cardinal some 50m W of a submerged quay (under construction) off Puertoamor

Port communications

Club Náutico Costa Blanca VHF Ch 9 ☎ +34 965 15 44 91
Email info@cnacb.es
www.cnacb.es

Friendly but limited

A small popular yacht harbour with a very friendly *club náutico* which can handle up to 12m yachts but as it is very crowded, especially in summer, one must ring ahead to ascertain whether a berth is available. Although well sheltered by Cabo de la Huerta and normally with an easy approach and entrance, a heavy swell from the SSW could make the final stage difficult. Facilities for yachts are limited. Sandy beaches either side of the harbour.

Approach

From the south – see Alicante. The prominent Cabo de Santa Pola the off-lying Isla de Tabarca, the hills,

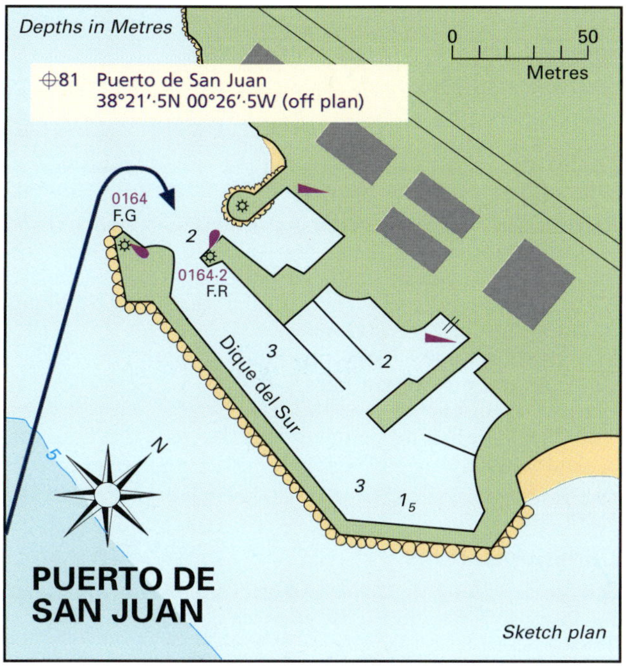

San Juan

town and port of Alicante are all easily recognised. The harbour is 3M NE of Puerto de Alicante and 2M to W of Cabo de la Huerta.

From the north After Villajoyosa the coast is low and sandy with many small seaside villages. A small range of coastal hills 8M to SW of Villajoyosa and a small peninsula, La Illeta, which has a harbour on its S side may be recognised. The low 'Punta del Río' has a number of high-rise buildings; Cabo de las Huertas is a low promontory with the Monte de las Matas (181m) just inland. Give it a ¼M berth as there is a submerged reef off it, then round Punta de la Cala and the harbour will open up 1½M to W.

GPS approach

Steer to ⊕81 from the southern quadrant and steer for the breakwater head (approximately 0·17M).

Anchorage in the approach

Anchor 200m to S of the harbour in 5m sand.

Entrance

Straightforward but look out for small craft.

Berths

Secure to a vacant berth just inside the entrance and ask at the clubhouse.

Facilities

Maximum length overall: 10m.
Slipway in N, centre and E of the harbour.
2-tonne semi-mobile crane on the central spur.
Water taps around harbour.
220V AC points around the harbour.
Club Náutico de San Juan beside the harbour with all normal facilities.
Several supermarkets nearby.

Communications

Bus service along the coast. ☎ Area code 965.

⚓ PLAYA DE LA HUERTA (PLATJA DE SAN JUAN)

38°21′·7N 0°24′·5W

Coastal anchorage open to E in 5m sand and weed. Road and houses along shore, sandy beach.

58. Puerto de Campello

38°25′·8N 00°23′·1W

A private marina with 474 berths surrounded by apartments and usually full in high season.

Charts

British Admiralty *1700.* Imray *M12*
French *7670.* Spanish *473*

⊕82 38°25′·6N 00°23′·0W

Lights

To the south
0166 **Cabo de las Huertas** Fl(5)19s38m14M White tower 9m
Harbour
0167 **Dique de Levante** Fl.G.3s8m5M Green rhombic (with hole) tower 5m
0167.2 **Contradique head** Fl(2)R.8s7m3M Red round concrete tower 4m

Port communications

Club Nautico de El Campello VHF Ch 9
✆ +34 965 63 34 00 *Email* info@cncampello.com
www.cncampello.com

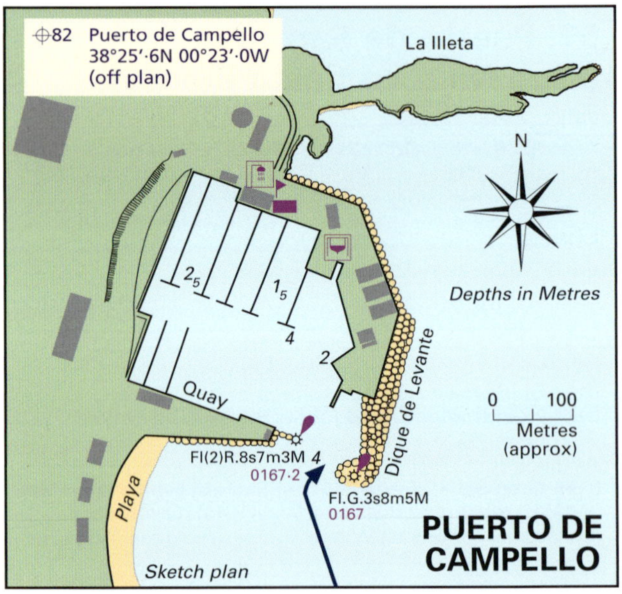

Small modern marina

Formerly a small fishing village and anchorage, now submerged in holiday homes and apartments. The harbour is easy to approach and enter. It has better facilities than several locally. Good shelter inside but swell enters with strong winds between SE and W. The caves, Cuevas de Canalobre, 10M inland, are of interest. Very good sandy beaches either side of the harbour. A pleasant town.

Approach

From the south The low promontory of Cabo de la Huerta, backed by Monte de las Matas (190m), is conspicuous. Give the headland ¼M berth as an underwater reef runs out SE-ly from it. The coast northwards is low, flat and dull with a long, sandy beach and seaside villages backed by high-rise buildings.

The (usually dry) mouth of the Río Montenegre (or de Castellá) is just S of Punta del Río which is low and flat but has a group of high-rise buildings. The harbour can be recognised by a grey/black tower block with red sun blinds on its SW side and an old tower with two creamy coloured high rise buildings to its NW.

Puerto de Campello

From the north The harbour and town of Villajoyosa are easily recognised. The coast to S is of broken cliffs with small coves and small hills inland. La Illeta is quite low and inconspicuous but the harbour can be recognised by the two creamy-coloured high-rise buildings to the NW of the old tower and harbour.

GPS approach

Steer to ⊕82 from the eastern quadrant and steer for the breakwater head (approximately 0·13M).

Anchorage in the approach

Anchor in 5m sand 100m to S of the entrance.

Entrance

Approach the harbour entrance on a NW heading and enter leaving the head of Dique de Levante at least 25m to starboard, or even more at night, as the *dique* sticks out a long way past the beacon, especially to the west.

Berths

Call office on Ch 9 or secure to a vacant berth and ask at the yacht club.

Facilities

Maximum length overall: 15m.
Electricians, radio, radar and engine mechanics, shipwright.
Slipway in NE corner of the harbour.
45-tonne travel-lift and covered dry storage (including a 'filing cabinet' for 200 motor boats).
Water taps on quays pontoons.
220V AC points on pontoons.
Gasoleo A and petrol.
The Club Náutico de Campello has showers, a restaurant, and launderette.
A few local shops with a supermarket a few hundred metres to the south.

Communications

Bus service along the coast and rail to Alicante and along the coast to Dénia in the N. ✆ Area code 965.
Taxi ✆ +34 965 63 02 11.

59. Puerto de Villajoyosa (Alcocó)

38°30'·4N 00°13'·1W

A fishing harbour but now given over to yachts, with a small yacht club with 330 berths up to 20m.

Charts

British Admiralty *1700.* Imray *M12*
French *7670.* Spanish *473, 4731*

⊕83 38°30'·2N 00°13'·3W

Lights

To the southwest

0166 **Cabo de la Huerta** Fl(5)19s38m14M White tower 9m

Harbour

0168 **Dique de Levante head** Fl.G.3s14m4M Green tower, white base 7m

0169 **Dique de Poniente head** Fl(2)R.6s7m1M Red octagonal tower, white base 6m

0168.5 **Espigón head** Fl(2)R.6s8m3M Red octagonal tower, white base 6m

To the east

0172 **Islote de Benidorm** Fl.5s60m6M White truncated pyramid 4m

Port communications

VHF Ch 9. ✆ +34 965 89 36 06 / +34 965 89 07 19
Email administracion@cnlavila.org/ deportes@cnlavila.org
www.cnlavila.org

Useful but sometimes uncomfortable

A fishing harbour now largely given over to yachts. Approach and entrance are easy but shelter is not very good, and with SE and S winds it can be uncomfortable. The harbour is sometimes oily and depths change with silting and dredging.

Approach

From the SW Cabo de la Huerta which has a conspicuous lighthouse is easily recognised as are the many high-rise buildings at Villajoyosa. A very large white tower block of flats, Cinco Torres (60m), lies just inland of this harbour.

From the NE Having rounded the long high rocky feature of Sierra Helada, the mass of high-rise buildings of Benidorm with its outlying Isla Benidorm are easily identified, together with the large white tower block of flats, Cinco Torres (60m), inland of this harbour.

GPS approach

Steer to ⊕83 from the southeastern quadrant and steer for the breakwater head (approximately 0·13M).

Anchorage in the approach

Anchor 200m to W of the head of Dique de Levante in 8m mud and weed.

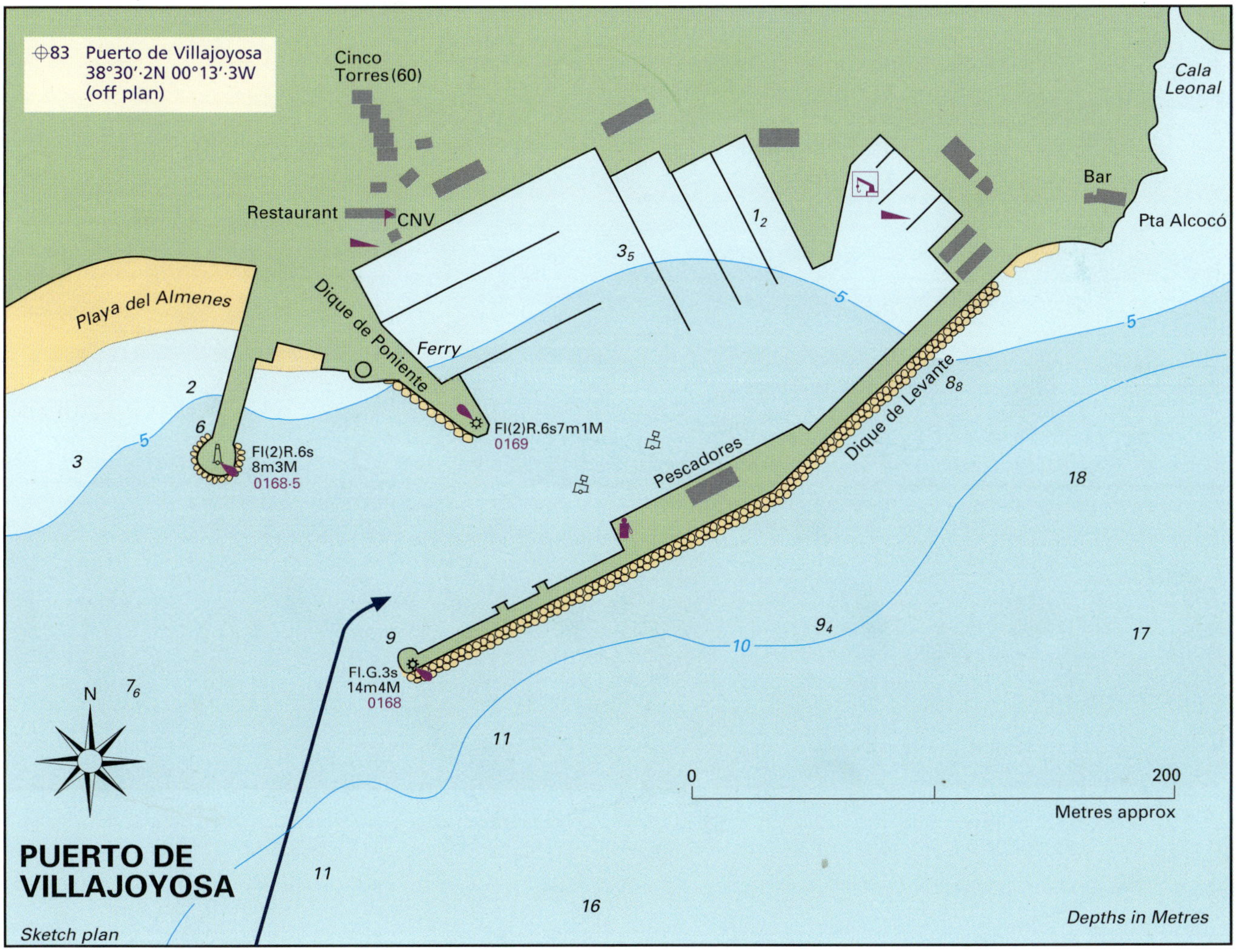

Entrance

Approach the entrance on a N course and round the head of Dique de Levante at 20m, passing between it and the artificial island with a light at the end of the submerged Espigón Antiarena on the north side of the entrance. The harbour tends to silt up and is periodically dredged and depths shown may not be correct. Keep clear of ferry berth near head of Dique de Poniente.

Berths

Secure to the pontoon just inside the Dique de Poniente and inquire at the yacht club for a more sheltered berth within.

Facilities

Maximum length overall: 20m.
Major repairs and engine work by the shipyard at the NE end of the harbour.
Slipway at the NE corner of the harbour, 100 tonnes and 3m.
35-tonne travel-hoist.
5- and 10-tonne cranes at the slipway.
Water taps on the Dique de Levante and pontoons.
220V AC points on pontoons.
Gasoleo A and petrol.
Club Náutico Alcocó-Villajoyosa.
A few small local shops but there are many in the town about 1M away.
Launderettes in town.

Locally

The old wall, ruined castle and fortified church in the town are interesting as is the Amadorio dam, some miles inland. About 24 to 31 July, there is a Christian feast in honour of the patron saint Sta Marta. Good beaches on either side of the harbour.

Communications

Buses and railway. ☎ Area code 965.
Taxi ☎ +34 965 89 00 24.

Villajoyosa

60. Puerto de Benidorm

38°32'N 00°08'W

Surprisingly for a huge tourist town, only a small fishing harbour exists with no room for visitors.

Charts

British Admiralty *1700*. Imray *M12*
French *7670*. Spanish *473, 4731*

⊕84 38°31'·9N 00°08'·2W

Lights

0172.5 **Dique de Abrigo head** Fl.G.3s8m5M White hut, green tower 3m
0172.7 **Interior Jetty head** Fl(3)G.7s5m1M Post 3m
0172.75 **Submerged jetty head** Fl.R.3s5m3M Post 3m
To the south
0172 **Islote de Benidorm** Fl.5s60m6M White truncated pyramid 4m

Port communications

VHF Ch 9. Club Náutico de Benidorm ✆ +34 965 85 30 67
Email info@cnbenidorm.com www.cnbenidorm.com

Tiny harbour

For such a huge developed town with so many foreign tourists, it is amazing that there is not a major marina at Benidorm. The small, old fishing harbour, consisting of one pier, one jetty and two pontoons, is now overwhelmed by one of the biggest tourist developments on the coast. It has minimal shelter. Approach and entrance are easy except in winds from S to SW, when it is impossible and the harbour untenable. The needs of yachts *per se* are not catered for but anchoring off is feasible and if any crew feels neglected, there is plenty of tourist bustle ashore. Long sandy beaches on either side of the harbour. There have been talks of building a large marina here for many years and it seems more likely now as this highly touristic area has grown into a huge township.

Approach

From the SW Follow the flat and rather monotonous coast from Villajoyosa towards the high massive rocky feature of Sierra Helada, which is seen from afar and stands beyond Benidorm. Islote Benidorm, a pyramid-shaped island, lies off the harbour. The small, white, rocky-cliffed Punta de Canfáli with houses and a blue-domed church on it lies just beyond the *dique*.

From the NE Round the massive bulk of Sierra Helada and the harbour will be found just beyond it, near the white, rocky-cliffed Punta de Canfáli and among a mass of high-rise buildings. A water-ski area with overhead tow lines on metal posts is laid out in the bay to E of Punta de Canfali.

GPS approach

Steer to ⊕84 from the southern quadrant and steer for the breakwater head (approximately 0·17M).

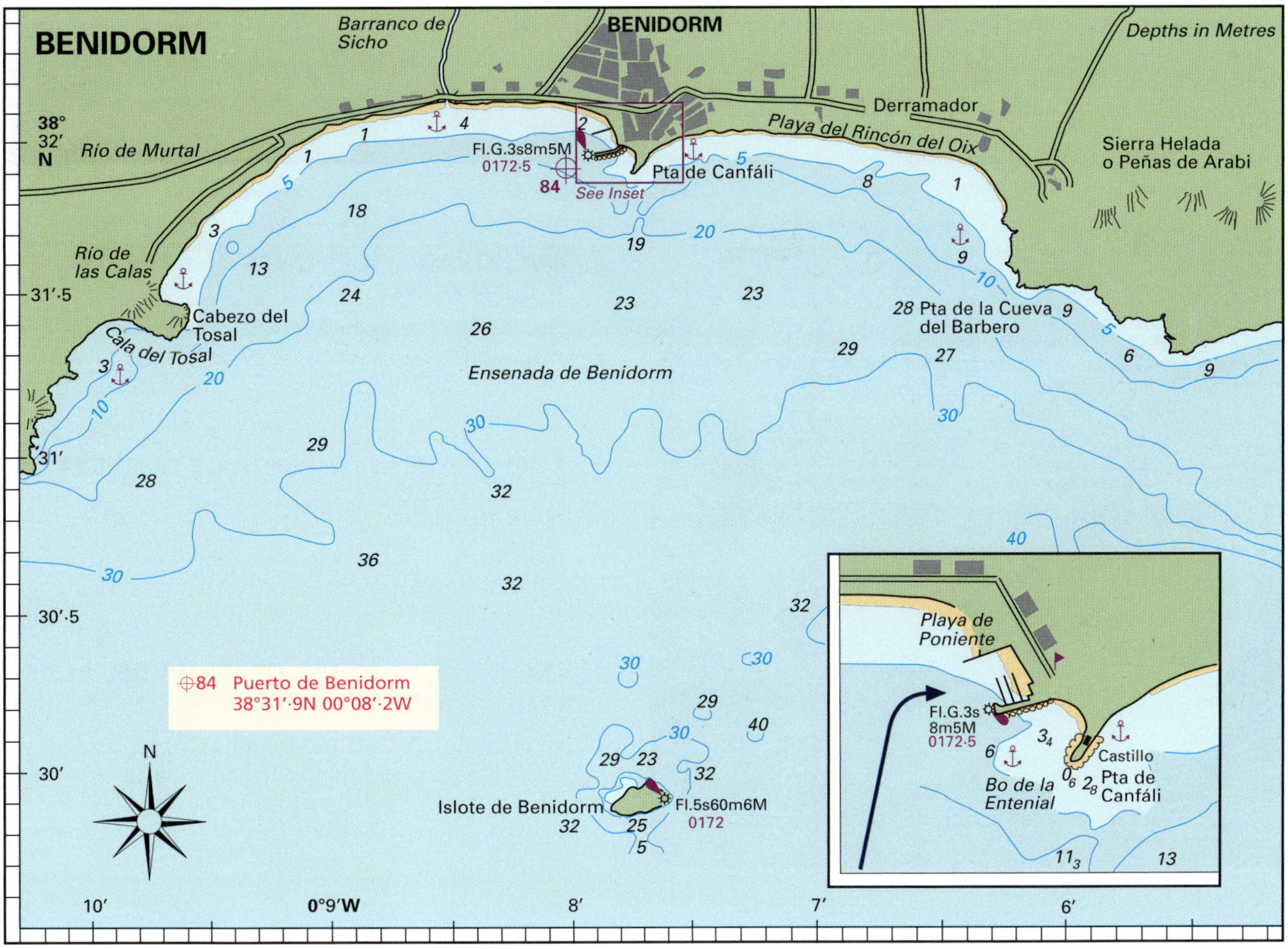

Benidorm harbour from SE

Anchorage in the approach

Anchor 150m to NW of the head of the *dique* in 6m sand.

Entrance

Approach the head of the *dique* on a N course; round it at 50m. Beware underwater debris closer to the *dique*.

Berths

A temporary berth may be found alongside the NW face of the *dique* but it is frequently used by ferries and fishing boats.

Anchorage

It is possible to anchor on either side of the *dique*, well clear of it, in about 6m sand.

Punta del Albir lighthouse from SE and first anchorage to NW

Facilities

Engine mechanics in town, mainly with experience in cars.
Hardstanding by the yacht club.
Chandler's shop in the town.
Water from tap near the root of the *dique*.
Many shops in the town and a market.
Club Náutico de Benidorm has a bar, lounge, restaurant, terrace and showers.
Several launderettes in town.

Communications

Bus, rail, taxis, car hire. ✆ Area code 96.

ENSENADA DE BENIDORM

Anchorage along the sandy beaches stretching between Cabezo del Tosal and Punta de la Escalata backed by massive high-rise buildings for package holidaymakers and open to S. Anchor in suitable depth offshore; sandy bottom.

⚓ CABEZO DEL TOSAL
38°31′·6N 0°09′·5W

There are anchorages N and S of this promontory, both open to the East. Anchor in 3m, sand.

Cabezo de Tosal, south anchorage from SW

⚓ ANCHORAGE E OF PUNTA DE CANFALI
38°32′N 0°07′·7W

Anchor in 3m sand open to S. Considerable holiday development ashore with skyscrapers. A water-ski circuit is established in this anchorage. Not recommended in summer for this reason.

⚓ ANCHORAGE W OF PUNTA DE LA CUEVA DEL BARBERO
38°31′·9N 0°06′·6W

A small anchorage open to S and swell from W. Road and development ashore, sand and shingle beach, bottom has rocky patches.

⚓ ANCHORAGES TO NW OF PUNTA DEL ALBIR
38°34′N 00°03′·1W

Three anchorages well protected except from N–NE by the Sierra Helada (438m). Sandy bottom with rocky patches. Down draughts from S–SW winds may be experienced. (See plan on page 149.)

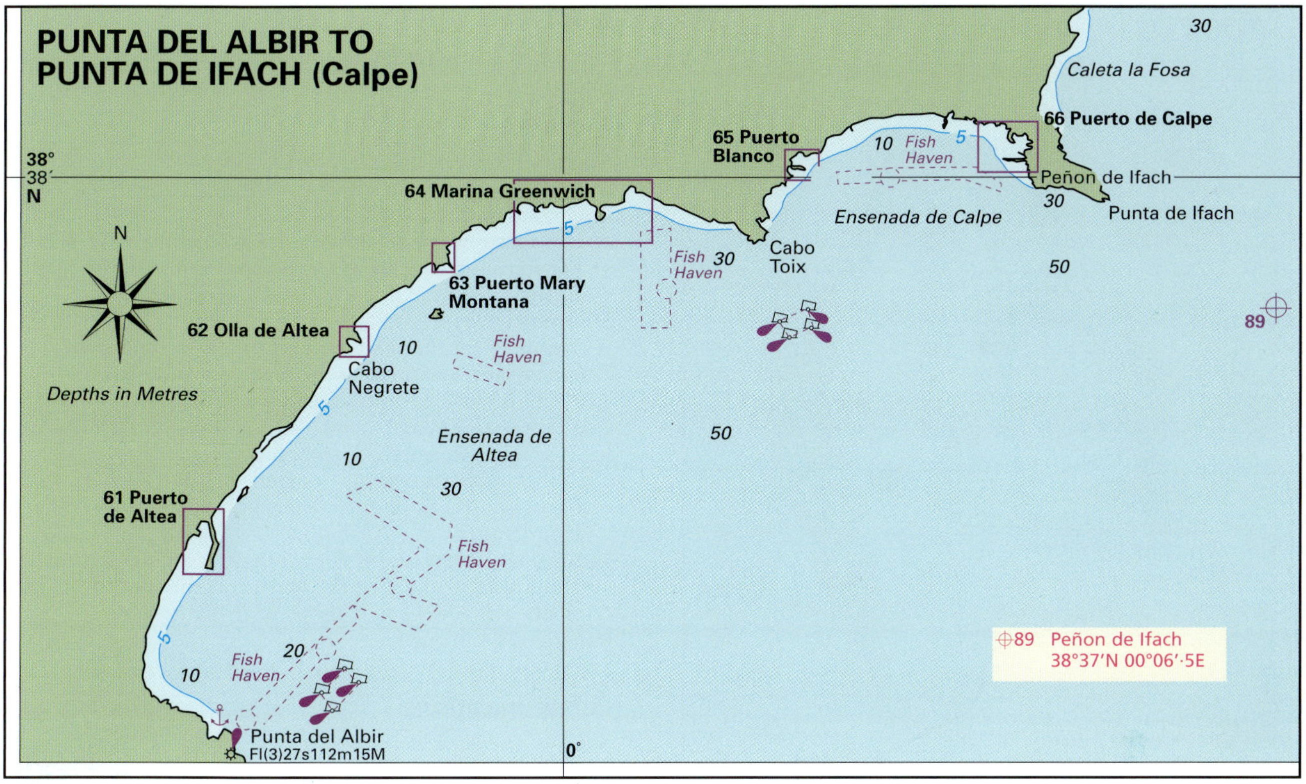

61. Puerto de Altea

38°35′·3N 00°03′·2W

A large and very safe marina with over 500 berths in the Club Nautico, and for a small number of vessels under 8m in Puerto Altea. Welcoming to visitors but prone to silting in the approaches, though frequently dredged.

Charts

British Admiralty *1700*. Imray *M12*
French *7670*. Spanish *473, 4732*

⊕85 38°35′·1N 00°03′·12W

Lights

To the south
0173.6 **Punta del Albir** Fl(3)27s112m15M
White tower on house 8m
Harbour
0174 **Dique de Levante head** Fl(3)G.9s12m5M
Green octagonal stone tower 6m
0174.2 **Dique de Poniente head** Fl(2)R.6s9m3M
Red octagonal tower 6m

Port communications

VHF Ch 9. Club Náutico de Altea
✆ +34 965 84 15 91
Email cnaltea@cnaltea.com www.cnaltea.com
Puerto de Altea ✆ +34 966 88 01 05

Excellent yacht harbour

Built near the place where Scipio landed and sacked the Greek colony of Honosca, Altea is a busy artificial fishing harbour with an excellent yacht facility and an easy approach. Shops are some distance away at the foot of the town which stands on a hill. The area is surrounded by high mountains which make it attractive. The old town on the top of the hill and its church are worth a visit. The village and castle at Guadalest some 9M inland is worth a visit. There are good sandy beaches on either side of this harbour.

Approach

From the SW Round the high-cliffed feature of Sierra Helada which has a conspicuous lighthouse on its NE end, Punta del Albir. From here the harbour walls will be seen and, beyond them, the church of Altea which stands on top of a small hill. The church has conspicuous blue domes.

From the NE The unique high, steep-sided peninsula of Ifach and the lower Cabo Toix are easily recognised. When rounded, the blue-domed church on the hilltop at Altea will be seen. The harbour walls will not be seen until much closer in.

GPS approach

Steer to ⊕85 from the southern quadrant and steer for the breakwater head (approximately 0·11M).

Anchorage in the approach

Anchor immediately S of the Dique de Poniente where a considerable amount of shelter can be gained from the Dique de Levante. Keep out of the way of speeding fishing boats using the harbour entrance. Alternatively, not so good, to NE of the Dique de Levante in 5m sand.

Entrance

Approach on a NW course and round the head of Dique de Levante at 20m. Enter the yacht harbour behind the Muelle Presidente. The harbour silts up and is frequently dredged which may change the depths. Watch for commercial traffic.

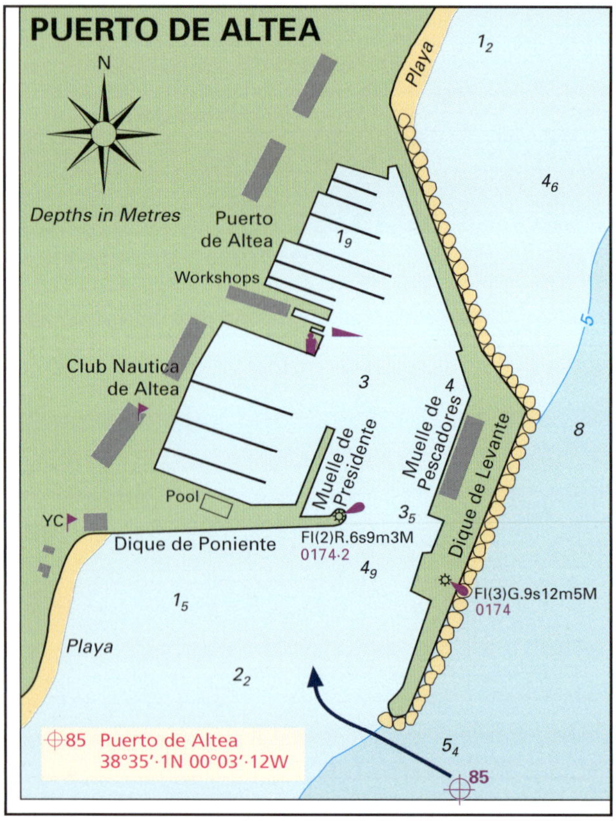

Berths

Secure to Muelle Presidente and ask at the yacht club on the SW corner of Dique Poniente for a berth.

Facilities

Maximum length overall: 23m.
Two shipyards for yacht repairs.
Engine mechanics.
A 100-tonne slipway; other slipways on the NW side of the harbour near head of the spur and root of Muelle Presidente.
30-tonne travel-hoist.
A chandlery on the seafront and others in the town.
Water taps on yacht harbour pontoons and quays.
220V and 380V AC on pontoons and quays.
Gasoleo A and petrol.
Ice is available near the yacht club.
Club Náutico de Altea, located on W side of yacht harbour, has a bar, restaurant, patio, showers and launderette.
Most of the shops and the local market are on or near the main road to the E of the church at the foot of the hill. There are a few small shops near the harbour.
Launderettes in town.
Swimming pool on Dique de Poniente.

Communications

Bus and rail services. ✆ Area code 965.
Taxi ✆ +34 965 84 02 36.

Puerto de Altea

62. Puerto de la Olla de Altea (El Portet)

38°36'·8N 00°01'·9W

A very small shallow harbour with only 36 berths for vessels under 9m. No room to accommodate visitors.

Charts

British Admiralty *1700.* Imray *M12*
French *7670.* Spanish *473, 4732*

Lights

0174·4 **Dique de Levante** Fl(4)G.11s7m1M Green round tower white base 4m
0174·6 **Dique de Poniente** Fl(4)R.11s7m3M Red round tower white base 4m

Port communications

✆ +34 965 84 06 97

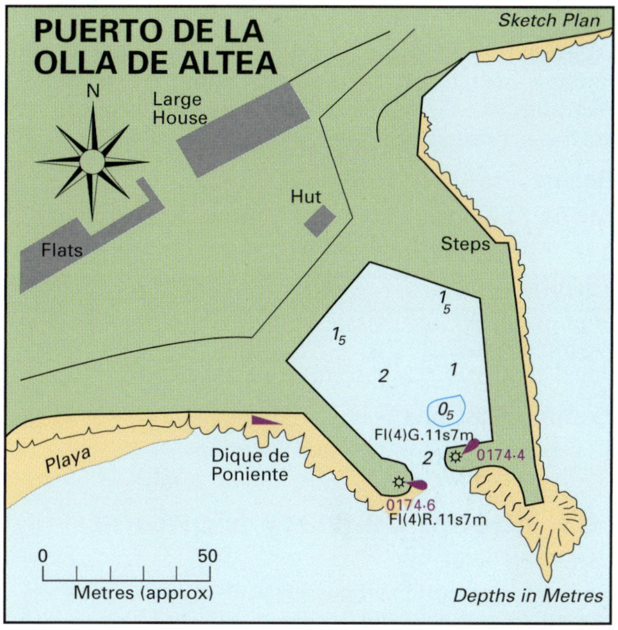

Minute harbour

This minute harbour is only suitable for day boats, dinghies and small yachts which can be hauled ashore in the event of bad weather. Approach and entrance present no problems in good weather but would be dangerous in heavy seas from E. Facilities ashore are limited and in the summer months it is very crowded. Small pebble beaches either side of the harbour. Large beach to S of Cabo Negrete.

Approach

From the south After the large high rocky mass of the Sierra Helada (Peñas de Arabi) (438m) pass outside Isla Mediana (Mitjana). Having cleared Punta del Albir, the town of Altea will be seen. It has a conspicuous church with two blue domes on top of a hill and its harbour lies to the S. Northwards of Altea harbour the coast should be given a 300m berth for ½M when Cabo Negrete will be identified by its rocky point and a large, white house in dark trees. There are rocks off the point. Olla del Altea lies 250m to N of this point and can be identified by a large private house behind the harbour.

From the north Round the prominent and steep-to Cabo Toix. Pass Puerto de Mascarat, which will be identified by its breakwaters and the smaller private harbour of Puerto de Marymontaña. Pass outside Islote and Isleta, two offshore islands, the latter with a shallow patch 0·2m inshore and having passed Isleta, go W towards the harbour. The large private house also shows up from this direction.

Anchorage in the approach

Anchor 250m to E of the harbour in 5m mud and stones.

Olla de Altea

Entrance

Approach the harbour on a W to NW heading and keep a watch on soundings. Enter on a NNW heading at slow speed; note shallow patch to starboard just inside the harbour.

Berths

Secure to quays to starboard, ground on slipways if a bilge keeler or haul out ashore.

Facilities

Slipways on W and N side of the harbour for day boats and dinghies.
Simple everyday requirements from local shops.

Communications

Rail and bus services. ✆ Area code 965.

63. Puerto de Mary Montaña

38°37′·5N 00°01′·1W

A charming private harbour but with no room for visitors except in an emergency.

Charts

British Admiralty *1700, 1701*. Imray *M12*
French *7670*. Spanish *473, 4732*

Lights

0174.8 **Dique de Levante head** Fl(3)G.9s9m3M
Green column on white hut 7m
0174.85 **Dique de Poniente head** Fl(3)R.9s9m1M
Red column on white hut 7m

Private harbour

An attractive private harbour, suitable for small and medium-sized yachts, belonging to a large estate and for use only as a harbour of refuge; it should not be entered without good reason. Facilities are limited to water and electricity. The main coast road lies 500m to NW from the harbour up a hill.

Approach

The approach is shallow. A shallow, rocky area lies to E of the harbour culminating in Islote, a small islet 350m to E–NE of the entrance. A larger rocky island, Isleta, lies 700m to S of the entrance with a reef stretching NW to the coast.

From the south From Altea which can be recognised by its harbour and the town on a hill, which is crowned by a church with two blue domes, the sandy coast runs in a N–NE direction and is backed by a range of hills. Cabo Negrete and the Puerto de la Olla de Altea will only be recognised if close to the shore. In the approach from this direction it is advisable to pass outside Isleta which lies 550m off the shore and then turn on to a N course and approach the harbour, sounding carefully with a lookout posted forward. From Isleta the harbour should be seen, backed by the rocky Montaña Bernia (1,129m) which is a pyramid shape. In the closer approach, the triple-arched gateway may be seen behind the harbour wall.

From the north Cabo Toix which is steep-to and the large harbour of Puerto Mascarat are easily recognised. Keep outside the 10m depth contour

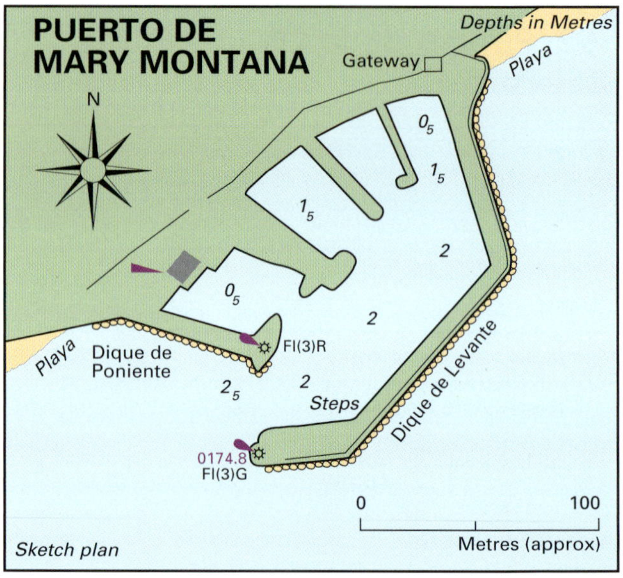

Sketch plan

which lies some 400m from the shore until 100m NE of Isleta. The harbour lies in a N direction and a direct approach can be made from here towards the entrance, sounding carefully and with a lookout forward.

Anchorage in the approach

The area near the harbour is of rock and the nearest suitable anchorage is in 5m sand 300m W of Isleta.

Entrance

Approach the entrance on a N course and enter on a NE heading.

Berths

Secure to the inner side of the Dique de Levante and report to the harbour official at the *caseta* by the gateway. If no one is to be found there to allocate a berth, proceed some 200/300m up the hill to a large house and report there.

Facilities

Water taps on all quays.
220V AC points on all quays.

Communications

Bus service along the main road and the coastal railway station at Olla de Altea.

Puerto de Mary Montaña

64. Marina Greenwich (Mascarat)

38°37'·7N 00°00'·3W

A large friendly marina right on the Greenwich meridian with 540 berths up to 30m in pleasant surroundings and welcoming to visitors.

Charts

British Admiralty *1700, 1701.* Imray *M12*
French *7670.* Spanish *473, 4732*

⊕86 38°37'·6N 00°00'·3E

Lights

0174.92 **Dique Sur W head** Fl(2)G.7s8m5M
Green round tower white base 6m
0174.9 **Dique Sur E head** Q(6)+LFl.15s10m3M
Black and yellow round tower 6m
0174.93 **Contradique head** Fl(2)R.7s8m1M
Red round tower, white base 6m

Port communications

VHF Ch 9. Port Office ✆ +34 965 84 22 00
Email marina@marinagreenwich.com
www.marinagreenwich.com

Convenient and pleasant marina

The harbour, interestingly lying on the Greenwich meridian, is surrounded by high rocky hills and has an attractive hinterland, worth visiting by car. There are now nine blocks of apartments behind the harbour against the cliffs. There are plans for the marina to be extended to accommodate additional berths (as there have been since 2000!) but this appears to be still way in the future. The harbour itself has good facilities. It becomes crowded in summer and it is prudent to book ahead. A small shingle beach to W of the harbour and a golf course nearby.

Approach

From the south Give the coast a 500m berth NE from Altea, which is easily identified by the church on top of the hill with two blue domes, to Puerto de Mascarat. Cabo Negrete and the small Puerto de la Olla de Altea are not conspicuous but the island of Isleta, which should be left to port, will be seen as will the Puerto de Mary Montaña and the small rocky islet of Islote. Approach the harbour entrance on N course.

From the north Round the unmistakable Punta Ifach (⊕89 38°37'N 00°06'·5W) and cross the Ensenada de Calpe. Puerto de Calpe will be seen NW of the Peñón de Ifach (332m). Cabo Toix, which is steep-to, is prominent and has high cliffs which slope up the higher ground inland. On rounding this point, part of the harbour breakwater will be seen. Punta Mascarat obscures the rest of the harbour when seen from this area. The harbour entrance is at the west end of the breakwater.

GPS approach

Steer to ⊕86 from the southeastern quadrant and steer for the breakwater head (approximately 0·13M).

Anchorage in the approach

Anchor in 5m sand between Punta de Mascarat and the E side of the harbour to suit prevalent wind.

Entrance

Approach the Dique Sur western end from the south quadrant, round it to starboard at 20m and steer east for the fuel quay, immediately to port on entering.

Berth

Secure to fuel quay and ask at the port control office.

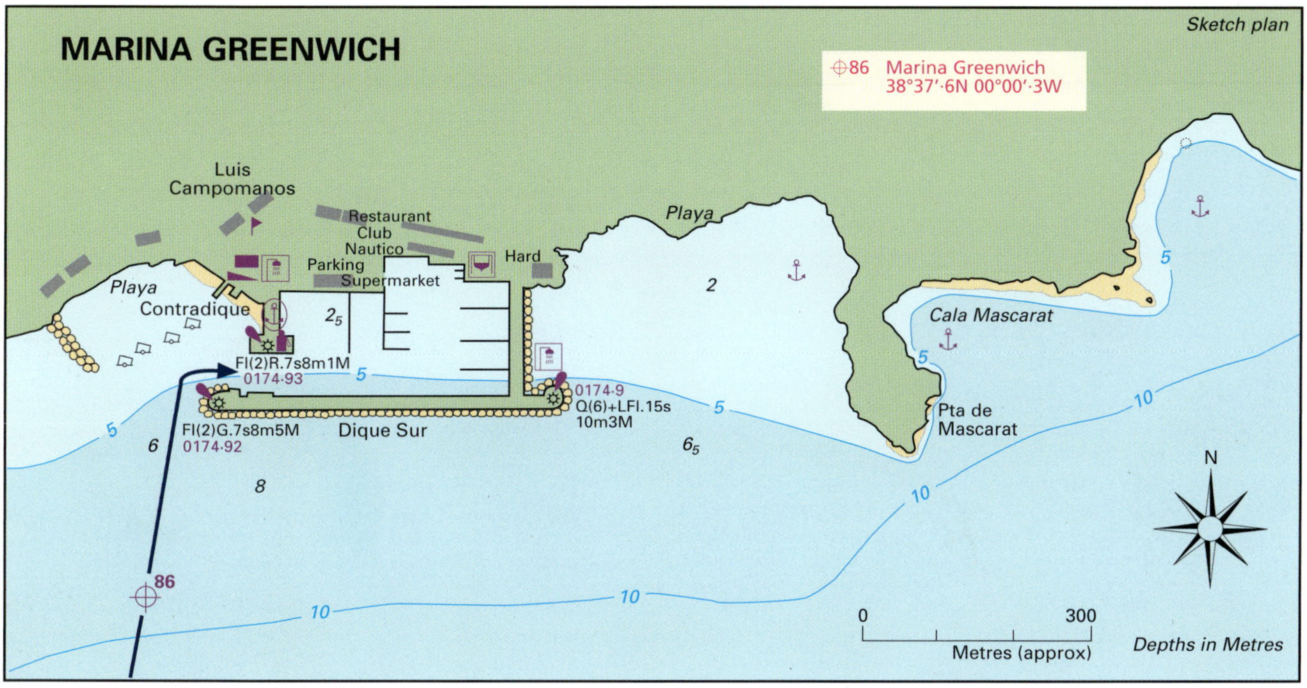

Marina Greenwich (Mascarat)

Facilities

Maximum length overall: 30m.
Engine mechanics and general repairs.
Crane.
50-tonne travel-hoist.
Chandlery behind the harbour.
Water taps on quays and pontoons.
Showers.
220/380V AC points on quays and pontoons.
Gasoleo A and petrol.
Ice on fuel quay.
Shops for everyday requirements and a supermarket behind the harbour.

Communications

Buses on main road above the harbour. Railway at Olla de Altea. ✆ Area code 965. Taxi ✆ +34 965 84 02 36.

⚓ PUNTA MASCARAT

38°37′·7N 0°00′·4E

Three anchorages in 5m sand and stone, one to W of Punta Mascarat, one to E and the third off the mouth of Barranco del Collada. By choosing the anchorage, the high cliffs can give protection except from S winds and there may be swell from SE or SW. The main road is at top of the cliffs.

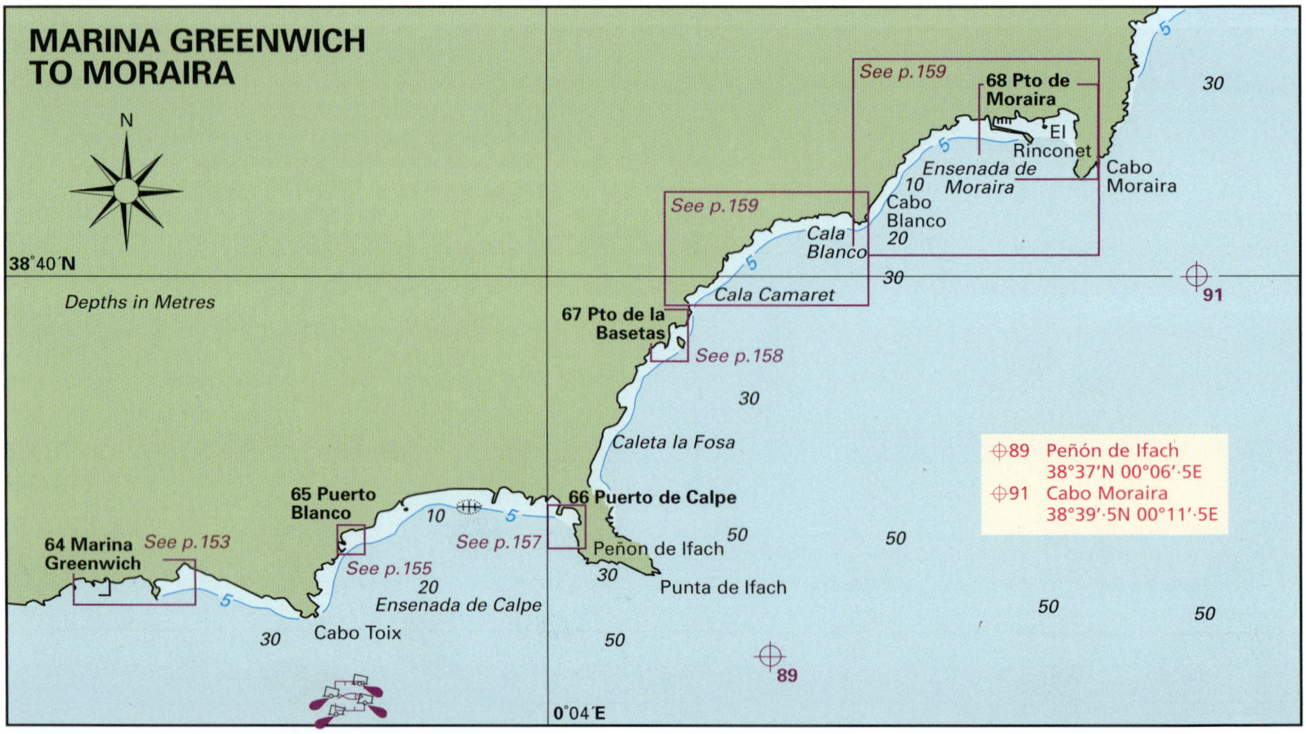

65. Puerto Blanco

38°38′·1N 00°02′·1E

A very small harbour with 112 berths up to 13m. No facilities or room for visitors.

Charts

British Admiralty *1700, 1701.* Imray *M12*
French *7670.* Spanish *473, 4732*

⊕87 38°38′·1N 00°02′·24E

Lights

0175 **E breakwater head** Fl.R.5s7m3M Red castellated tower 6m

Port communications

Try Ch 9. ✆ +34 965 83 18 60
Email administracion@puertoblanco.es
www.puertoblanco.es

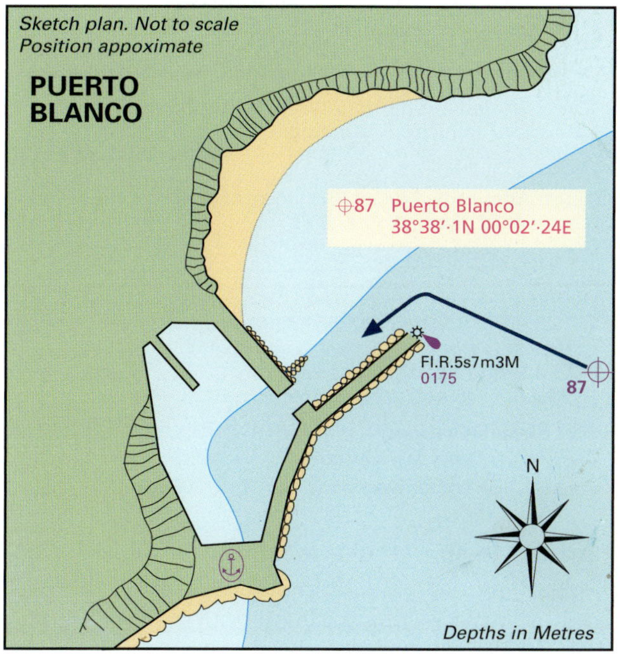

Small boat harbour

A small-boat harbour lying NNE of Cabo Toix and 800m W of Puerto de Calpe. It may be a useful alternative when Calpe is full but it may also be full itself. It has good shelter except in an easterly when there will be swell in the harbour. Facilities are limited. Some housing estates in the area.

Approach

From the SW From the conspicuous promontory of Punta de Albir (112m) the equally conspicuous Cabo Toix and Punta Ifach will be seen. The harbour lies on the E side of Cabo Toix which is steep-to.

From the NE From Cabo Moraira (⊕91 38°39′·5N 00°11′·5W) set course to round the conspicuous Punta Ifach (⊕89 38°37′N 00°06′·5W), then on to a W course towards Puerto Blanco which will be seen in the closer approach just to the N of Cabo Toix.

GPS approach

Steer to ⊕87 from the southeastern quadrant and then for the breakwater head (approximately 0·07M).

Entrance

Usually straightforward but may not be possible in a strong easterly.

Berths

Secure to a vacant berth and ask at the *capitanía*.

Charges

Medium.

Facilities

Engineer and workshop available.
Water taps on quay.
Supermarket ½ a mile away.

⚓ ENSENADA DE CALPE

38°38′·4N 0°03′·2E

The Ensenada de Calpe lies between Puerto Blanco and Calpe. Anchorage off sandy beach in 3–5m sand open E. Pay attention to unmarked wrecks off Playa del Bou and Playa del Almadrat. Road ashore with some apartment buildings.

Puerto Blanco

66. Puerto de Calpe

38°38′·2N 00°04′·2E

A very welcoming harbour with 264 berths with room for visitors, in nice surroundings.

Charts

British Admiralty *1700, 1701*. Imray *M12*
French *7670*. Spanish *473, 4732*

⊕88 38°38′·12N 00°03′·9E

Lights

0175.2 **Contradique head** Fl(4)R.10s8m3M
Truncated masonry tower, red top 4m
0175.4 **Dique head** Fl.G.4s13m5M
Masonry tower, green top 6m

Port communications

VHF Ch 9. ✆ +34 965 83 18 09
Email info@rcnc.es www.rcnc.es

Harbour in spectacular location

Located at the base of the spectacular Peñón de Ifach, the old fishing harbour, with a history going back to the Phoenicians, has been transformed by the construction of breakwaters, quays and pontoons for yachts. It is a busy harbour which can be approached and entered with ease. The shelter is good though a SW wind can bring swell into the harbour. It is worth visiting to admire the Peñón de Ifach; a climb from its NW side through a tunnel and along a perilous pathway to the top results in a spectacular view of the coast and a demonstration of the uncontrolled nature of high-rise and other commercial building. Good beaches either side of the harbour. Golf Club de Ifach nearby.

Approach

A dangerous wreck lies ½M to W of the harbour.

From SW having rounded the massive Sierra Helada, the Peñón de Ifach will be seen in the distance appearing as an island. Cabo Toix, another massive cape en route, is easy to identify.

From NE round Cabo de la Nao, high and prominent with a conspicuous lighthouse on top. Cabo Moraira, another prominent cape with a new yacht harbour to its W is also easy to recognise. The Peñón de Ifach can be seen from afar but appears as an island.

GPS approach

Steer to ⊕88 from the southwestern quadrant and steer for the breakwater head (approximately 0·12M).

Anchorage in the approaches

Anchor 100m to W of the head of the *contradique* in 5m sand or on the other side of Ifach in Cala de la Fosa, 5m sand and stone.

Entrance

Straightforward, but it is a bit tight inside and there may be some ship movements. With N winds, there can be strong gusts in the harbour from the Peñón de Ifach.

Berths

Call on Ch 9 and the marina office will respond with a *marinero* who will direct you to a berth. Visitors are usually berthed at the E side of the marina either side of the Club Nautico N/S pontoons. The marineros are on call during the night and always assist with berthing. There is surging with SW winds, which are frequent in the afternoons in summer.

Calpe and the Peñón de Ifach. Cabo Moraira in the distance

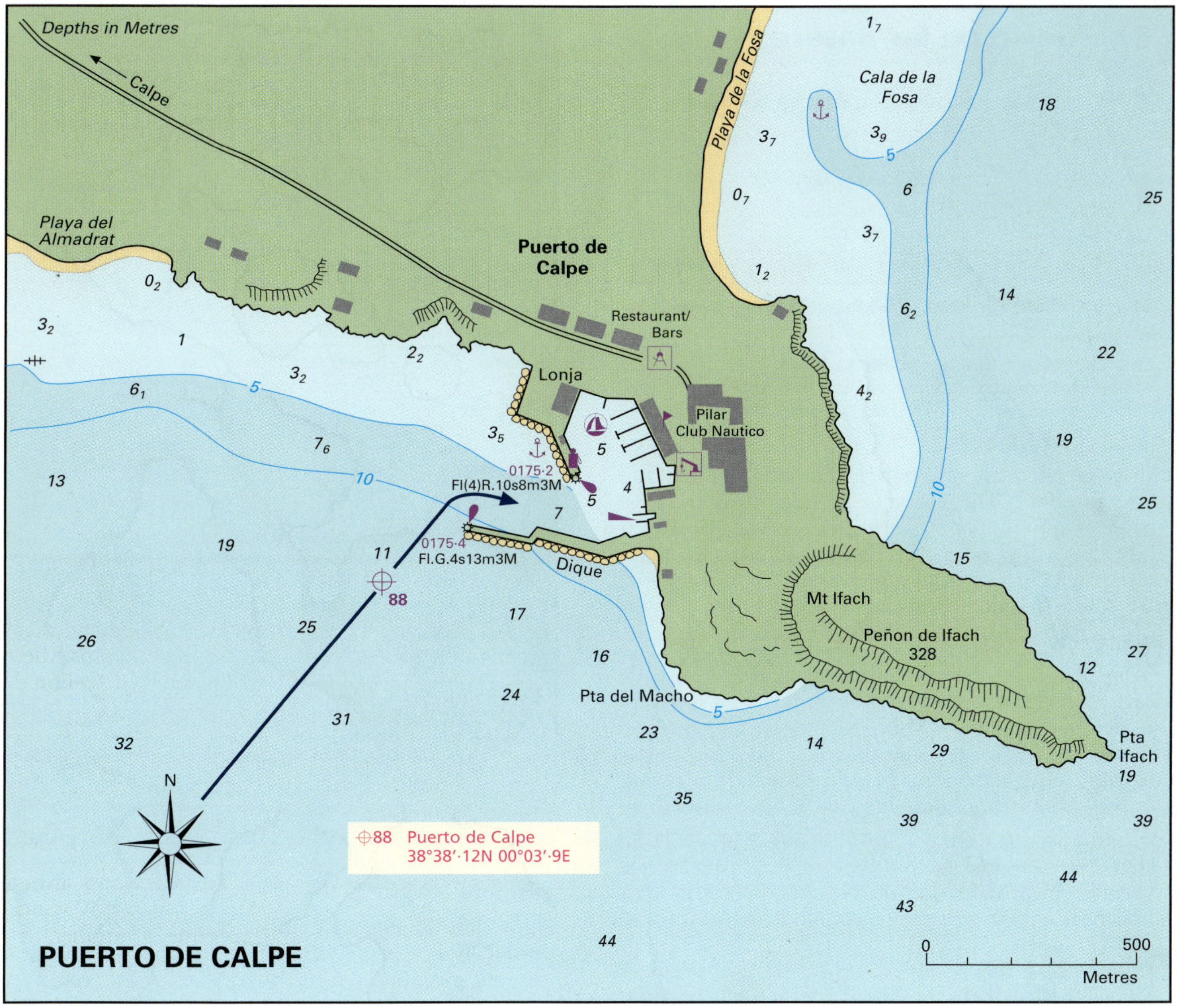

Charges

High.

Facilities

Maximum length overall: 30m.
The shipyard can carry out most repairs to hull and engines.
Other engine mechanics in the town.
Two slipways at the shipyard.
10-tonne crane.
Chandlery shop in the town and at the shipyard.
Water taps on pontoons but test it before filling tanks.
220V AC on pontoons.
Gasoleo A.
Ice on quay.
Club Náutico de Calpe with the usual facilities.
There are two supermarkets beyond the steps leading over the ridge behind the marina. More shops in Calpe about 1M away.
Launderette at the club house.

Locally

Calpe Marina is one of the most friendly and welcoming on the coast. At the extreme E of the marina is a very active sailing and diving school. Visitors with vessels 12m or less are berthed close to these schools on the inside of the N/S jetty. The activity presents no problems whatsoever.

There are two excellent restaurants in the marina, one run by the Royal Club Nautico de Calpe, serving excellent fare, at a reasonable price. The marina office is located close to the club restaurant a short walk through the boatyard.

Communications

Bus and rail services. ✆ Area code 965.

⚓ CALA DE LA FOSA (N of Peñon de Ifach)

38°38′·6N 0°04′·5E

Anchor off middle of Playa de la Fosa in 5m sand. Road and high-rise apartment buildings ashore. Open to E.

67. Puerto de les Basetes

38°39'·6N 00°05'·2E

A very small boat harbour for local motor vessels, with no room for visitors.

Charts

British Admiralty *1700, 1701.* Imray *M12*
French *7669.* Spanish *474*

Lights

0175.8 **Dique de Levante head** Fl(3)R.9s6m3M Red tower 3m
0175.9 **Contradique head** Fl(3)G.9s6m1M Green tower 3m

Port communications

VHF Ch 9. Port Office ✆ +34 965 83 12 13
Email info@cnlesbasetes.com www.cnlesbasetes.com

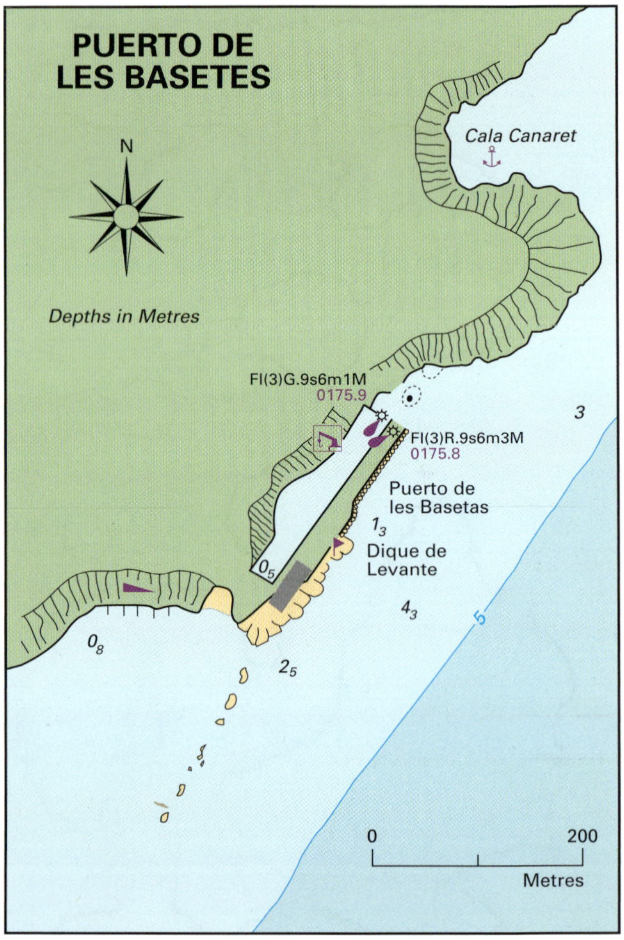

Small boat harbour

An attractive little harbour but for small yachts and dinghies only. The entrance is narrow and space inside is limited, not to say cramped. The sea wall is based on a line of rocks lying parallel to the shore within which quays have been built. La Cala 400m to S has a shingle beach.

Approach

From the south Round the unmistakable Peñón de Ifach (⊕89 38°37'N 00°06'·5W) (328m) which is steep-to. The harbour lies 2M N. A large tower on Cabo Blanco to NE is very conspicuous. The harbour is difficult to see until close in, when the harbour wall, with a small white house on it, will be identified.

From the north Round Cabo Moraira (⊕91 38°39'·5N 00°11'·5W) which is steep-to. Cross the Ensenada de Moraira in a SW direction closing the coast after 3M. Pass the large yacht harbour at Moraira and Cabo Blanco, which is steep-to but not very prominent; it has a sloping silhouette and a cliffed face on the E side. In the close approach, the harbour wall and a small white building on it will be seen.

Puerto de les Basetes

Entrance

Approach the entrance at the N end of the harbour on a NW-ly course, sounding and with a forward lookout posted. Go S of the small exposed rock and round the head of the Dique de Levante taking care of isolated rocky heads.

Berths

Secure to quay to port in a suitable gap and consult the *capitanía*.

Facilities

Slipways at the S end of the harbour.
Small hardstanding.
3-tonne crane.
Water from a yacht club tap.
220V AC in the Club.
Small yacht club.
Scuba school.

Communications

Bus service to Calpe on coast road behind harbour.
✆ Area code 965.

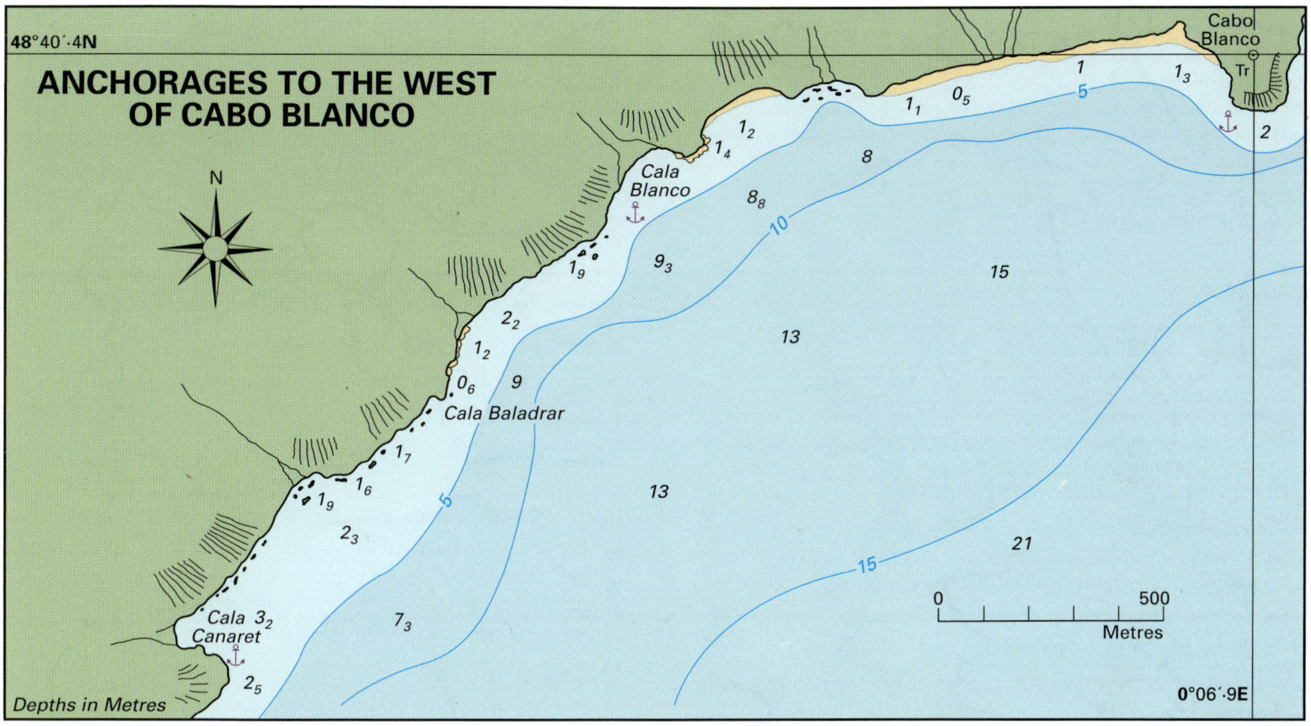

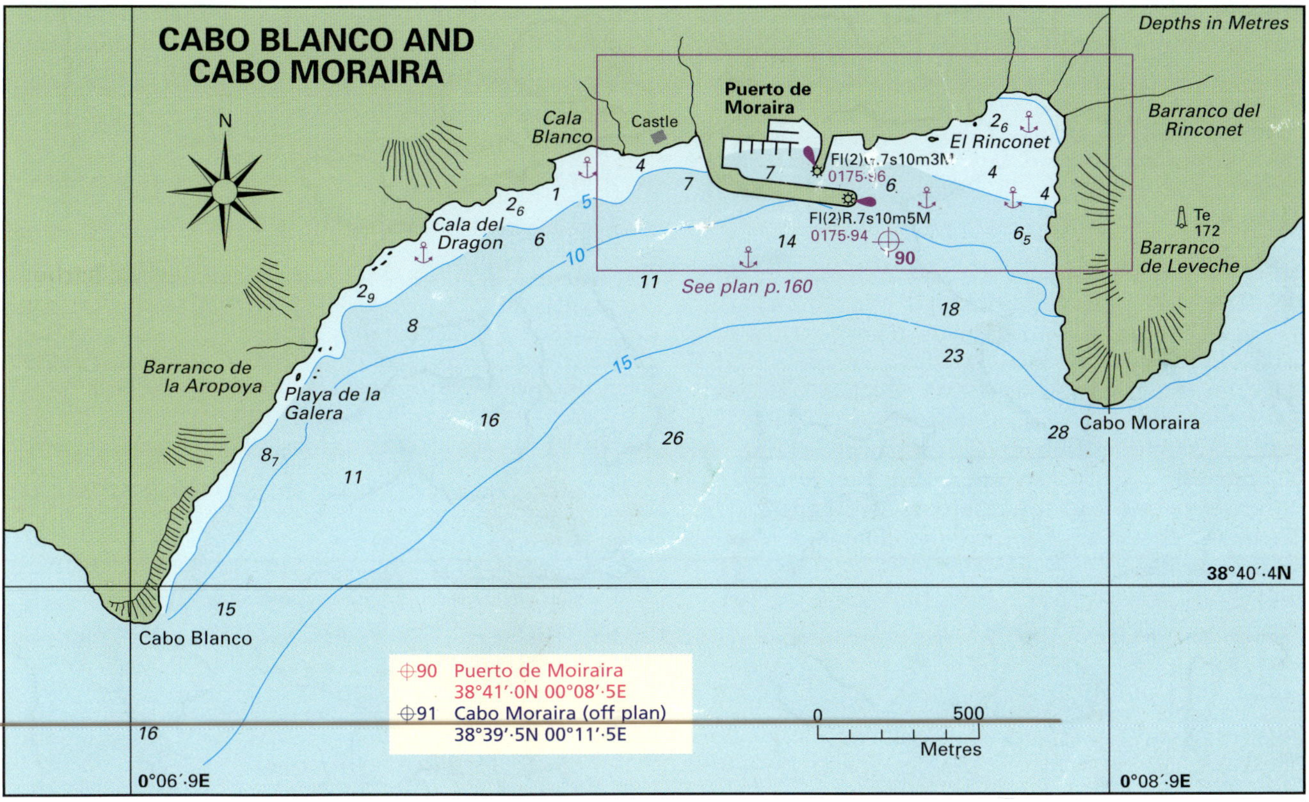

⚓ CALA CANARET, CALA BLANCO, CABO BLANCO

These anchorages should be used with care. There are submerged rocks which can usually be seen in the clear water. Rocks make poor holding in some areas. All wide open to the SE.

⚓ CALA DEL DRAGON

38°40′·9N 0°07′·3E

Anchorage off small sandy bay in 2·5m sand. Wide open to the SE. Road inland.
(May be buoyed off in summer.)

68. Puerto de Moraira

38°41'·1N 00°08'·3E

A large marina with 620 berths up to 25m, usually crowded in high season; easy to enter in most weathers.

Charts

British Admiralty *1700, 1701.* Imray *M12*
French *7669.* Spanish *474*

⊕90 38°41'·0N 00°08'·5E

Lights

0175.94 **Dique de Abrigo head** Fl(2)R.7s10m5M White round tower, red bands 6m
0175.96 **Contradique head** Fl(2)G.7s10m3M White round tower, green bands 6m
To the northeast
0176 **Cabo de la Nao** Fl.5s122m23M 049°-vis–190° White octagonal tower and house 20m
0179.2 **Inner jetty head** Fl(3)G.9s5m3M

Port communications

VHF Ch 9. ✆ +34 965 74 43 19
Email recepcion@cnmoraira.com www.cnmoraira.com

Modern pleasant resort

A large modern yacht harbour in an attractive setting, one of the easier harbours to enter in bad weather and well sheltered from wind and waves once inside. The new harbour takes up some of the old anchorage of the bay but the most sheltered part, which is more suitable for yachts, is still available.

Moraira is a useful point of departure for San Antonio-Abad in Ibiza, 55M. A climb to the Torre de Moraira is rewarded with a fantastic view of the coast. Sandy beach at El Rinconet. Golf Club de Ifach 4M.

Approach

There may be tuna nets in the bay.

From the south After Peñón de Ifach (⊕89 38°37'N 00°06'·5W) go NE-ly towards the prominent Cabo Moraira (⊕91 38°39'·5N 00°11'·5W) which is high, with steep cliffs and a tower on its summit (172m). The peak of Montaña Isabela (La Liorenza) (442m) lies behind. In the closer approach the houses of Moraira village and tower blocks will appear. The harbour lies just E of the semi-circular fort located near the village.

From the north From Cabo de la Nao (⊕100 38°44'N 00°16'W) which has high steep cliffs, the course is SW towards the prominent Cabo Moraira (⊕91 38°39'·5N 00°11'·5W), 172m with a tower on its summit. Cabo Moraira is steep-to. Round it on to a NW course towards the harbour which is then immediately visible.

GPS approach

Steer to ⊕90 from the southern quadrant and steer for the breakwater head (approximately 0·13M).

Anchorage in the approach

Anchor in the Ensenada del Rinconet (see below).

Berths

Make up on the fuel quay on the inner side of the *contradique* and ask at the *capitanía*. Note that all berths are privately owned so one should be prepared to be shifted around if staying for a few days. Some quays have rocky feet extending some distance. In summer, when it is very crowded, boats double-up alongside the Dique de Abrigo.

Charges

High. Note that the *club náutico* only permits a cumulative total of seven days berthing in the season for a visiting yacht after which temporary membership of the club has to be paid at the current weekly rate, in addition to the berthing charges.

Facilities

Maximum length overall: 30m.
Workshops.
Slipway in NE corner.
50-tonne travel-hoist.
10-tonne crane.
Chandlery shop beside the harbour and another in the village.
230/380V AC on pontoons.
Water taps on quays and pontoons but drinking water only on the two western pontoons and head of the *contradique*.
Showers.
Gasoleo A.
Butane Gasolinera de Benissa Monday–Friday 1200–1300.
Ice on fuel quay.
Club Náutico de Moraira.
Supermarket close by outside.
Shop at the N side of harbour and several in the village.

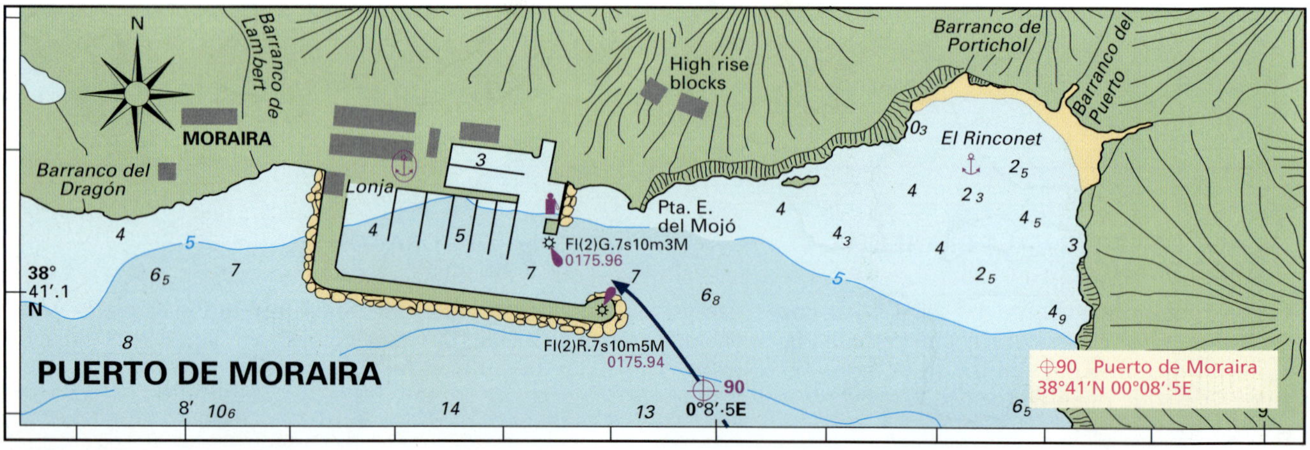

Moraira

Communications

Buses to Jávea and Calpe on coast road. Railway at Benisa. ✆ Area code 965.
Taxi ✆ +34 965 83 17 16 / 74 42 81.

⚓ EL RINCONET

38°41'·1N 0°08'·7E

Anchor according to depth, in sand up to 150m from the shore; sand, rock and weed beyond that. Open between S and SE. See plans on page 159 and 160.

El Rinconet

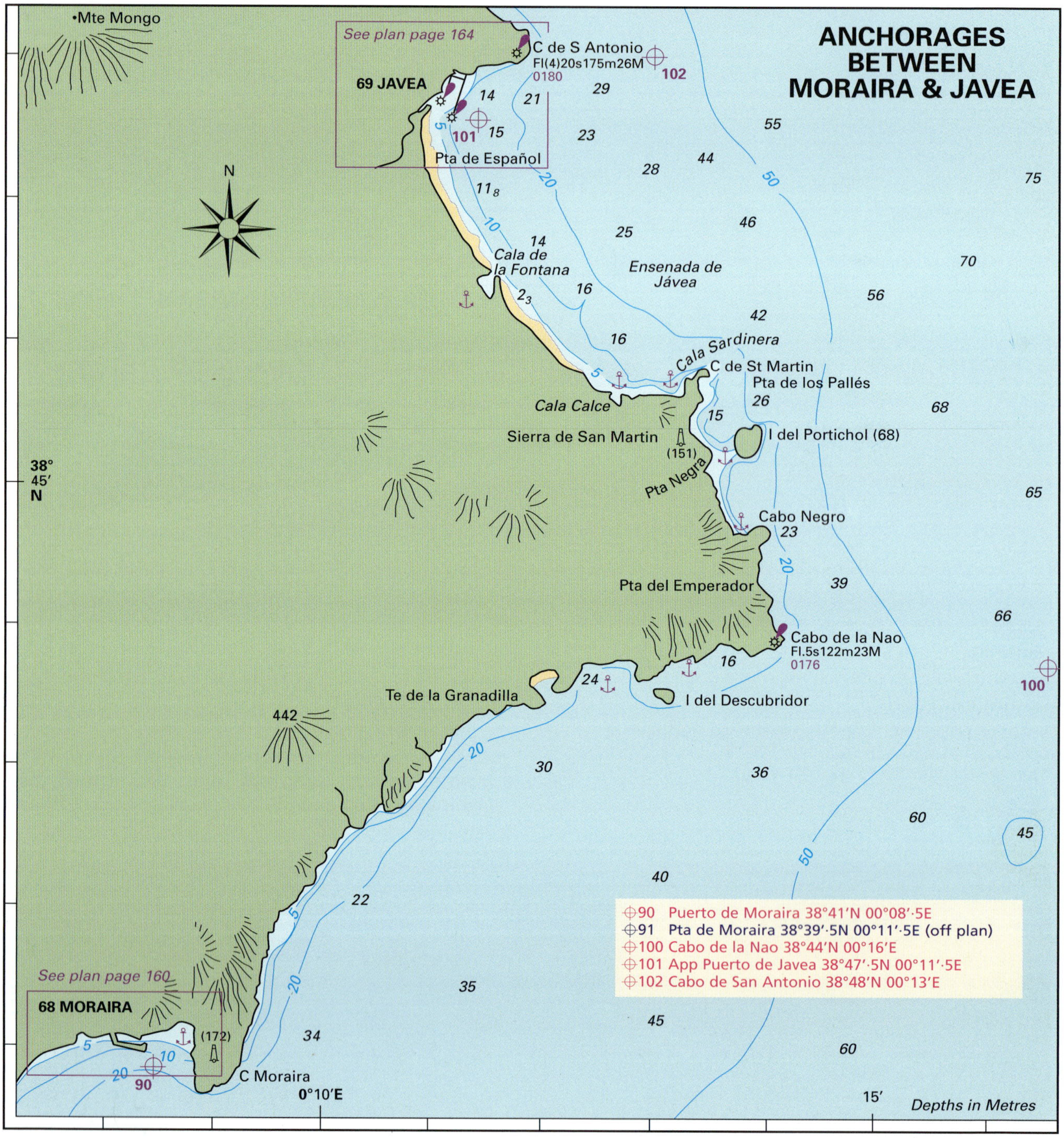

ANCHORAGES BETWEEN CABO MORAIRA AND JÁVEA

There are several interesting anchorages between Moraira and Jávea. Granadilla and Descubridor lie west of Cabo de la Nao. Details of the anchorages indicated to the north of Cabo de la Nao are provided in RCCPF *Mediterranean Spain: Costas Azahar, Dorada and Brava.* They all need to be treated with caution in terms of wind and swell conditions and because of submerged rocks inshore. Note that there is a traffic separation scheme (TSS) some nine miles ESE of Cabo de la Nao which should not seriously affect pleasure craft as they are generally closer to the point but be aware of its presence. In bad weather vessels using the TSS may be directed further inshore – skippers should be aware.

La Granadilla

Isla del Descubridor

⚓ LA GRANADILLA
38°43′·6N 00°12′E

Anchoring may be restricted by yellow buoys marking the swimming area. Beware submerged rocks near both sides of the entrance.

⚓ ISLA DEL DESCUBRIDOR
38°43′·5N 00°13′·1E

The island appears as a point. There are many submerged rocks.

Cabo de la Nao *Martin Walker*

Cabo de San Antonio to the E of Jávea – from the S

69. Puerto de Jávea

38°48′·9N 00°11′·2E

A large private busy marina with 380 berths up to 22m. Very few berths for visitors, who are made most unwelcome.

Charts

British Admiralty *1700, 1701.* Imray *M12*
French *7669, 7661.* Spanish *474, 4741*

⊕101 38°47′·5N 00°11′·5E 300°/0·3M to harbour

Lights

To the southeast
0176 **Cabo de la Nao** Fl.5s122m23M White octagonal tower and house 20m 049°-vis-190°
Harbour
0179 **Dique head** Fl.G.3s11m5M Green octagonal tower 6m
0179.2 **Inner jetty head** Fl(3)G.9s5m3M
0179.4 Contradique head Fl(2)R.6s9m3M Red tower 6m
To the northeast
0180 **Cabo de San Antonio** Fl(4)20s175m26M White tower and building 17m

Port communications

Club Nautico de Javea VHF Ch9 ✆ +34 965 79 10 25
Email info@cnjavea.net www.cnjavea.net

Warning

A traffic Control Zone lies 5M off Cabo de la Nao to the S and is relevant to yachts heading to/from the Baleares.

Javea Marina

From being one of the most pleasant friendly marinas on the coast in recent years, Javea is now crowded and repels visitors. Yachts are often turned away by rudely shouting *marineros*, even in severe weather when there are seemingly many berths vacant.

Approach

From the SE Round Cabo de San Martin which has several off-lying islets and, sometimes, tunny nets. The wide Ensenada de Jávea then opens up. The town stretches south and harbour is in the NW corner under the steep-sided mountain with abandoned windmills on the skyline.

From the NW Round Cabo de San Antonio (⊕102 38°48′N 00°13′W) which is a high, steep-sided, flat-topped promontory with a conspicuous lighthouse and signal station; follow round onto a SW course and the harbour wall will be seen in the closer approach.

From all directions the high pyramid-shaped Montaña Mongo, which stands to the W of the harbour, is very conspicuous.

Anchorage in the approach

Anchoring is prohibited S of the harbour; *see plan.*

Entrance

The breakwaters have stone feet and should be given a good 10m berth.

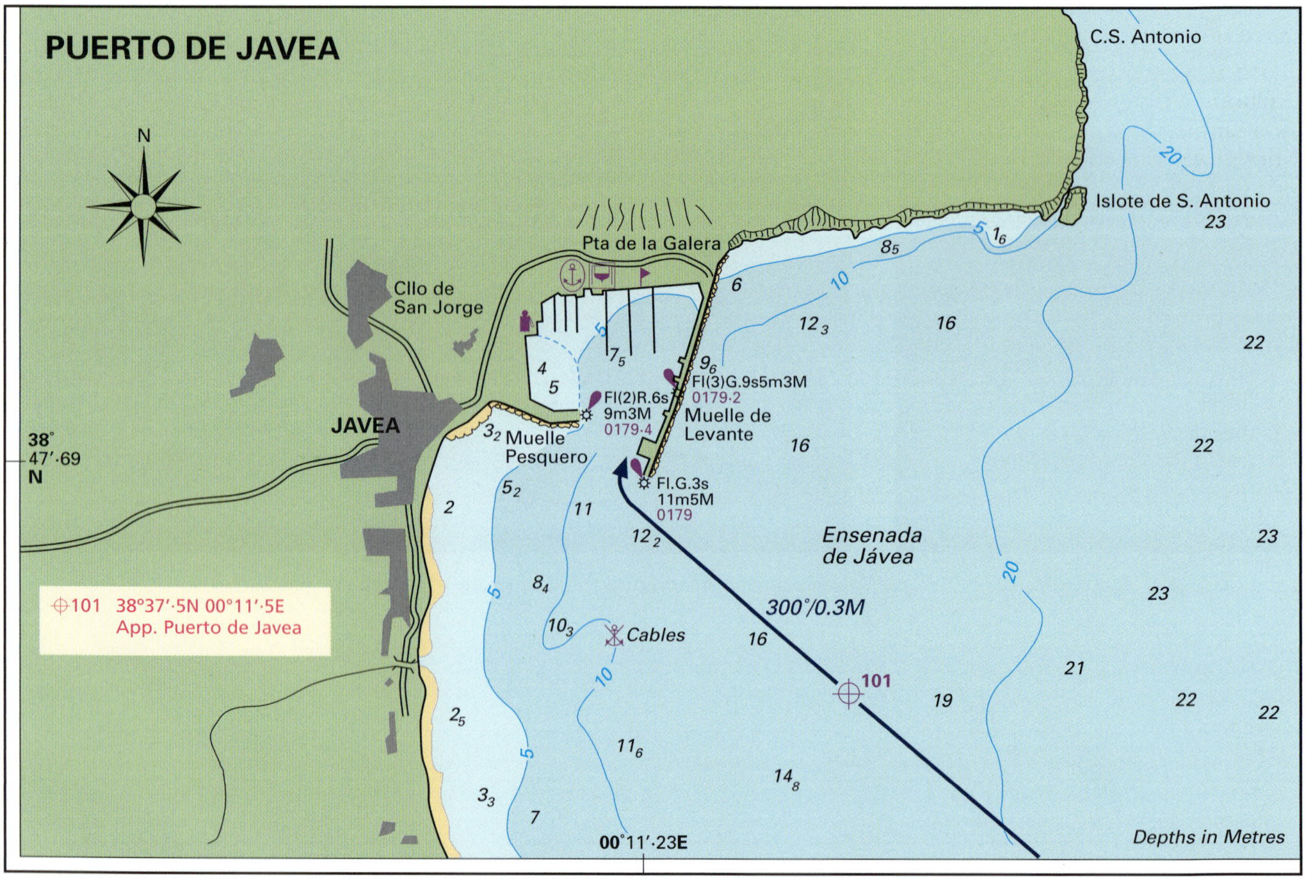

Puerto de Jávea

Berths

Berth stern-to the yacht club quay on the N side of harbour with anchor and trip-line from the bow or in a similar manner to a pontoon using the pick-up buoys. An alternative berth is sometimes available on the inner side of the *dique*, secured stern-to. There are underwater projecting rocky foundations to the *dique*: the three short spurs are in constant use.

Charges

High.

Facilities

Maximum length overall: 22m.
Limited hull and engine repairs.
Slipway to the W side of the yacht club.
65-tonne travel-lift and 6-tonne crane.
Water from a hose at the yacht club.
220v AC points at the yacht club.
Ice from the yacht club.
Gasoleo B only.
Club Náutico de Jávea with bar, restaurant, cabins, showers, swimming pool, etc.
Small shops and supermarket near the harbour, large supermarket, most shops, launderette and the market itself are in the town, about a mile away.

Locally

There are many caves in the area, some of which can only be visited by boat. The Gothic church at Jávea and the modern boat-shaped church near the harbour are both worth visiting. The view from the top of Cabo de San Antonio is good. There is a fine sandy beach about a mile south of the marina and a small pebbly one at the root of the Muelle de Levante.

Communications

Buses and railway in town. ✆ Area code 965.
Taxis ✆ +34 965 79 32 24.

70. Puerto de Dénia

38°50'·88N 00°07'·53E

A large safe port with three marinas and 1,360 berths up to 60m, a fishing harbour and berths for locals. Excellent departure point for the Baleares Islands.

Charts

British Admiralty *1515, 1700, 1701*. Imray *M12*
French *7669, 7661*. Spanish *474, 4741*

⊕103 38°50'·95N 00°07'·68E 228°/0·75M to harbour

Lights

To the southeast
0180 **Cabo de San Antonio** Fl(4)20s175m26M White tower and building 17m
Harbour
0184 **Dique Norte head** Fl(3)G.11s13m5M Green tower 7m
0185 **Dique Sur head** Fl(4)R.11s9m3M Red tower 7m
0186 Dir. Light 229° DFl.WRG.2·5s10m7M White column, black bands 8m 227°-G-228·5°-W-229·5°-R-231°
To the northwest
0198 **Cabo Cullera** Fl(3)20s28m25M White tower on house 16m
Note that between 0188 and 0188·5 there is a line of small red cylindrical buoys which must be left to port on entry.

Port communications

Real Club Nautica de Denia VHF Ch 9.
✆ +34 965 78 09 89 / +34 965 780945
Email info@cndenia.es www.cndenia.es
VHF Ch 9. Marina de Denia ✆ +34 966 42 43 07
Email mar@marinadedenia.com
www.marinadedenia.com
El Portet de Denia VHF Ch 9
✆ +34 966 42 66 75
Email info@marinaelportetdedenia.es
www.elportetdedenia.es

Commercial harbour with good marina facilities

A large fishing, ferry, commercial and yacht harbour continually in use since 600BC.

Several charter companies and diving schools operate from here, so supplies and spares are excellent. The oldest of the marinas is the Club Nautíco. This is primarily a members only club and is not very welcoming to transit visitors who are put on the uninviting isolated pontoons at the S of the marina.

Marina de Dénia – immediately to port as you enter the harbour – is where most visitors head. It has all facilities and a friendly staff.

Marina Portet is a very recent addition on the NW side of the harbour and much needed, since all marinas are full in peak season. There are also some small town quay berths in the NW of the harbour reserved for locals.

Approach

From the SE Round the high, steep-sided, flat-topped promontory of Cabo de San Antonio (⊕102 38°48'N 00°13'W) and follow the coast keeping a mile offshore to avoid shoals. In the closer approach, Castillo de Dénia will be seen on a small hill behind the harbour and the Dique del Norte. Do not cut the corner but make for a position 200m to NE of the head of this *dique*.

From the NW The low sandy coast is backed by high ranges of mountains. Montaña Mongo which lies behind this harbour, and the vertically faced Cabo de San Antonio which lies beyond it can be seen from afar. In the closer approach the Castillo de Dénia on its small hill and the long Dique del Norte will be seen. Keep at least 1M off the coast owing to shoals and make for a position 200m to NE of the head of Dique del Norte.

The head of the Dique del Norte has been washed away and underwater obstructions may still remain up to 100m to NE of the present visible head.

Anchorage in the approach

Anchor 300m to the E of the head of Dique del Norte in 7m sand.

Entrance

From at least 200m to NE, approach the entrance on a SW course, give the head of Dique del Norte 30m clearance and follow it in at this distance off.

Note If entering at night the leading lines have been replaced with a single directional tri-colour light on the front platform.

Berths

There are three marinas in the harbour. The Municipal Marina, at the NW end, is for small craft (<7m) only and it is for private berth holders only. The yacht club is still available for visiting yachts (call Real Club Náutico on Ch 9) but is expensive. There is a fairly new, and welcoming, marina immediately to port on entering (call Marina de Dénia on Ch 9 or phone) which has 400 berths and although further away from the town most provisions are now available on site.

Note There is a distinct difference in the welcome received between Real Club Nautico and the new Marina de Denia: the latter is very friendly and helpful.

At Real Club Nautico on a recent trip we were informed as the *marinero* left: 'Water and electricity on the jetty.' There sure was, but after washing down the decks and tasting it, the water turned out to be salt only! There is no provision for fresh water on the visitors pontoons, although the taps are standard marina fresh water fittings. Quite a shock if you happen to have filled your tanks and did not taste it first! It was pointed out later that there are notices: small faded stickers on some boxes at the end of the jetty: 'No Potable.' Certainly not something one would be looking out for. Fresh water can be purchased at the T end of one specified pontoon. The showers serving the visitors quays are also noticeably salty. (late summer 2013).

Charges

Medium; at the *club nautíco*, high.

Facilities

All ship work bar radar.
Two slipways, maximum 100 tonnes.
Cranes up to 12 tonnes. 70-tonne travel lift.
Chandler's shop behind the shipyard.

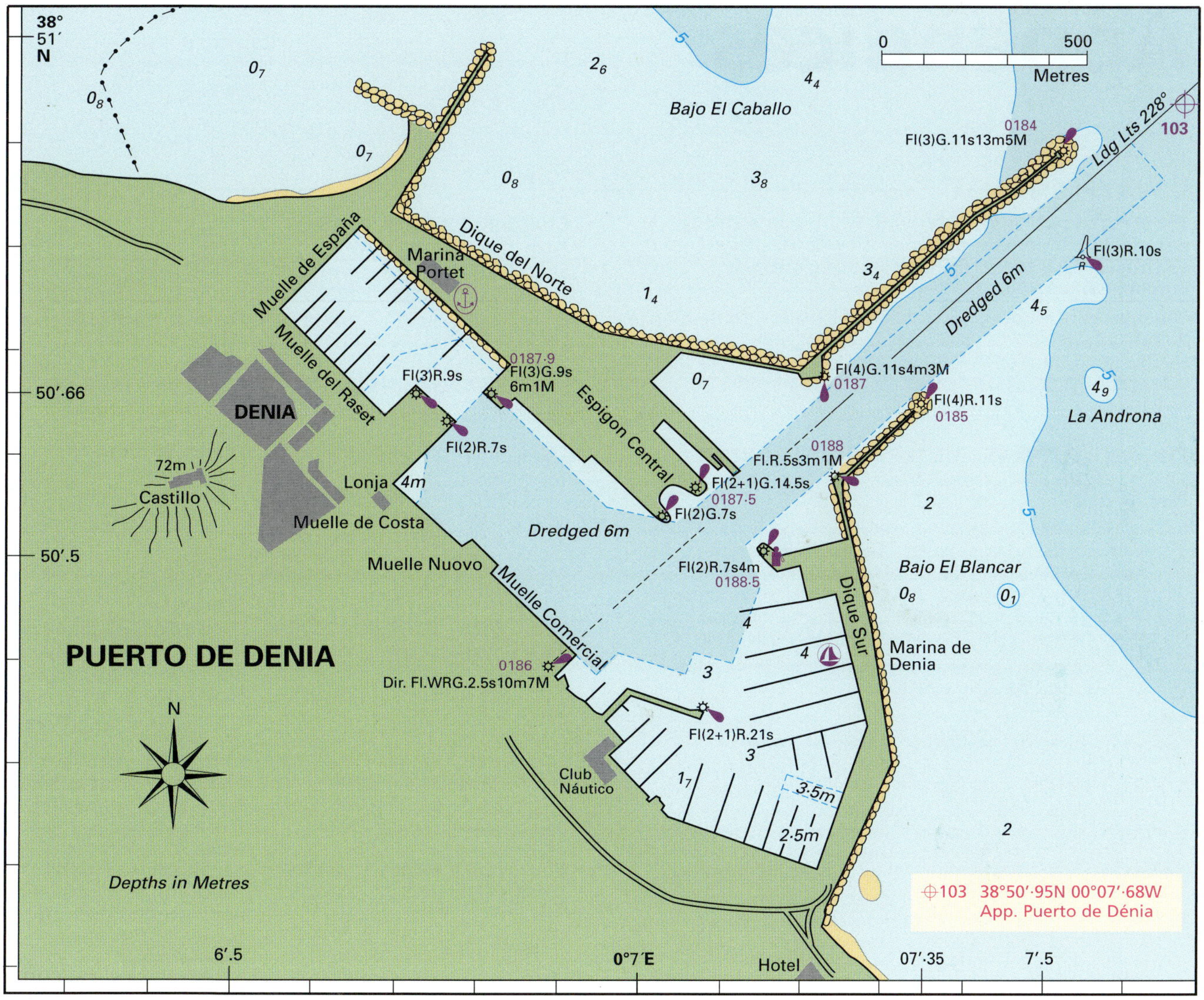

Water from taps around the yacht harbour and on the Muelle de Atraque.

Gasoleo A and petrol in the port and, for members only, the *club nautíco*.

Ice factory to the E of the Castillo de Dénia. Ice is also available from the yacht club.

The Real Club Náutico de Dénia has a large modern clubhouse with bar, lounge, restaurant, showers and so on. It is responsible for the S corner of the harbour. An introduction may be required.

A good range of shops in the town and an excellent market.

Launderettes in the town.

Locally

The port of Dénia is known to have been in use since at least 600BC when the Greeks invaded. The canal connecting the port across the shallows to deeper water ensures a calm within the port area whatever the weather – and winds can be very gusty around here. Sandy beaches are on either side of the port. Further yacht facilities are expected to be built as the plan is to make this the largest pleasure port in Europe.

The old town and surrounding area are attractive. A walk up to the castle takes a while but is very rewarding as it reveals spectacular views from the top. Steps right to the top have been well maintained through a wooded area and it is a pleasant walk with shade from the sun for much of the way.

Communications

Bus service. Dénia is one terminus of the coastal narrow gauge rail system. Ferries to Islas Baleares (new terminal 2008).

☏ Area code 965. Taxi ☏ +34 965 78 34 98.

Puerto de Dénia looking N

Appendices

I. WAYPOINT LIST

The WPs in **bold** form a series with which one is able to steer from off Gibraltar to Dénia. All WPs are derived from electronic charts to WGS84 from source material at European Datum 50.

The numerical sequence does not signify that a route may be safely selected from a coastal waypoint to harbour. Navigators must plot their own routes taking note of the numerous fish farms and other obstacles along this coastline.

Chapter I ENTRANCE TO THE MEDITERRANEAN

Port		Lat N	Long W	
	⊕1	36°03′·7	05°24′·4	Pta Carnero
1	⊕2	36°06′·95	05°25′·43	Algeciras approaches
	⊕3	36°06′·5	05°22′·7	Pta Europa west
2	⊕6	36°09′·5	05°22′·2	Marina Alcaidesa entrance
3	⊕4	36°08′	05°22′·3	Gibraltar South Mole
	⊕5	36°09′	05°22′·35	Gibraltar North Mole

Chapter II COSTA DEL SOL

Port		N	W	
	⊕11	**36°05′·5**	**05°20′**	**Pta Europa east**
4				Puerto de La Atunara
5	⊕12	36°17′	05°16′·2	Puerto de Sotogrande approaches
6	⊕13	36°21′·1	05°13′·6	Puerto de la Duquesa approaches
	⊕14	**36°22′·5**	**05°08′**	**SE of Pta de la Doncella**
7	⊕15	36°24′·65	05°09′·6	Estepona approaches
8	⊕16	36°28′·9	05°57′·4	Puerto de José Banús approaches
9	⊕17	36°30′·25	04°53′·55	Club Marbella
10	⊕18	36°30′·3	04°52′·6	App Bajadilla
11	⊕19	36°28′·8	04°44′·5	Cabo Pino approaches
	⊕20	**36°29′**	**04°38′**	**Pta de Calaburras**
12	⊕21	36°32′·6	04°36′·65	Puerto de Fuengirola approaches
13				Puerto de Punta Negra
14	⊕22	36°35′·5	04°30′·5	Puerto de Benalmádena approaches
15	⊕23	36°41′·7	04°25′·0	Puerto de Málaga approaches
	⊕24	**36°41′**	**04°20′·5**	**Puerto de el Candado**
16	⊕25	36°42′·8	04°20′·9	Puerto de el Candado approaches
17	⊕26	36°44′·7	04°04′·4	Puerto Caleta de Vélez
	⊕27	**36°42′**	**03°57′·4**	**Pta del Torrox**
	⊕28	**36°42′·5**	**03°44′**	**Pta de la Concepcion (Mona)**
18	⊕29	36°43′·7	03°43′·4	Marina del Este
19	⊕30	36°42′·7	03°30′·7	Puerto de Motril
	⊕31	**36°41′**	**03°28′**	**Cabo Sacratif**
20	⊕32	36°44′·25	03°01′·0	Puerto de Adra
21	⊕33	36°41′·65	02°48′·1	Puerto de Almerimar approaches
	⊕34	**36°37′·5**	**02°46′**	**SSE of Pta de las Entinas**
22	⊕35	36°45′·5	02°36′·15	Puerto de de Roquetas del Mar approaches
23	⊕36	36°48′·7	02°33′·8	Puerto de Aguadulce approaches
24	⊕37	36°49′·25	02°27′·75	Puerto de Almería approaches
	⊕38	**36°46′·5**	**02°25′·5**	**S of Pta del Río**
	⊕39	**36°41′**	**02°10′**	**Cabo de Gata**

Chapter III COSTA BLANCA

Port		N	W	
26	⊕50	36°45′·7	02°06′·2	Puerto de San José
	⊕51	**36°46′**	**02°02′**	**Pta de Loma Pelada**
	⊕52	**36°56′**	**01°52′·5**	**Pta de la Media Naranja**
27	⊕53	36°59′·2	01°53′·5	Puerto Pescaro de Carboneras
	⊕54	**37°10′·5**	**01°46′**	**Puerto de Garrucha**
28	⊕55	37°10′·5	01°48′·8	Puerto de Garrucha approaches
29/30	⊕56	37°14′·9	01°45′·7	Puerto de Villaricos approaches
31/32	⊕57	37°24′	01°34′·2	Aguilas approaches
	⊕58	**37°31′**	**01°17′·5**	**SE of Pta Negra**
33	⊕59	37°33′·3	01°16′·3	Puerto Deportivo de Mazarrón
34	⊕60	37°33′·9	01°15′·1	Puerto de Mazarrón approaches
35	⊕61	37°33′·5	01°00′	Puerto de Cartagena (outer)
35	⊕62	37°35′	00°58′·9	Puerto de Cartagena entrance (inner)
	⊕63	**37°32′**	**00°46′**	**SE of Cabo Negrete**
37	⊕64	37°37′·5	00°41′·8	Puerto de Cabo Palos approaches
	⊕65	**37°40′**	**00°35′·5**	**ENE of Islas Hormigas**
	⊕66	37 43′·2	00°43′·0	Mar Menor approaches (S)
	⊕67	37°44′	00°42′·8	Mar Menor approaches (N)
38	⊕68	37°45′	00°45′	Puerto de Tomás Maestre approaches (W)
47	⊕70	37°49′·2	00°44′·9	San Pedro del Pinatar
48	⊕71	37°51′·8	00°45′·3	Puerto de la Horadada approaches
49	⊕72	37°53′·8	00°44′·7	Puerto de Campoamor approaches
50	⊕73	37°54′·6	00°43′·7	Puerto de Cabo Roig approaches
	⊕74	**37°55′**	**00°41′**	**Cabo Roig**
51	⊕75	37°57′·5	00°41′·1	Torrevieja approaches
52	⊕76	38°06′·7	00°38′·0	Marina de las Dunas approaches
53	⊕77	38°10′·7	00°33′·9	Puerto de Santa Pola
	⊕78	**38°09′**	**00°25′**	**Off Islas de Tarbarca**
56	⊕79	38°19′·35	00°29′·1	Puerto de Alicante
	⊕80	**38°21′**	**00°22′·5**	**Cabo de la Huerta**
57	⊕81	38°21′·5	00°26′·5	Puerto de San Juan
58	⊕82	38°25′·6	00°23′·0	Puerto de Campello
59	⊕83	38°30′·2	00°13′·3	Puerto de Villajoyosa
60	⊕84	38°31′·9	00°08′·2	Puerto de Benidorm
61	⊕85	38°35′·1	00°03′·12	Puerto de Altea
64	⊕86	38°37′·6	00°00′·3	Marina Greenwich

Longitude W/E change

Port		N	E	
65	⊕87	38°38′·1	00°02′·24	Puerto Blanco approaches
66	⊕88	38°38′·12	00°03′·9	Puerto de Calpe approaches
	⊕89	**38°37′**	**00°06′·5**	**Peñon de Ifach**
68	⊕90	38°41′·0	00°08′·5	Puerto de Moraira approaches
	⊕91	**38°39′·5**	**00°11′·5**	**Cabo Moraira**
	⊕100	**38°44′**	**00°16′**	**Cabo de Nao**
69	⊕101	38°47′·5	00°11′·5	Puerto de Jávea approaches
	⊕102	**38°48′**	**00°13′**	**E Cabo San Antonio**
70	**⊕103**	**38°50′·88**	**00°07′·53**	**Puerto de Dénia**

II. CHARTS

Charts and other publications may be corrected annually by reference to the Admiralty *List of Lights and Fog Signals Volume D* (NP 77) and *E* (NP 78) or weekly via the Admiralty *Notices to Mariners*.

Obtaining charts

Imray Laurie Norie and Wilson, the publishers of *Costas del Sol & Blanca*, publish their own range of charts (see below) and are also sales agents for UKHO charts and publications. Order through **www.imray.com**

Up-to-date information on British Admiralty chart coverage for *Costas del Sol & Blanca* is available at **www.ukho.gov.uk**
where full details of chart schemes, titles and scales are given.

French (SHOM - Service Hydrographique et Océanographique de la Marine) charts, which offer more comprehensive coverage of the French speaking areas of North Africa, are listed at **www.shom.fr**

Note that SHOM chart numbers change and the SHOM website should be checked for the latest details.

Up-to-date list of sales agents for SHOM is available on their website.

The catalogue of Spanish charts which are good for the Strait of Gibraltar and the Spanish enclaves of Morocco may be seen at **www.armada.mde.es**

Chart agents

Before departure

Imray, British Admiralty and Spanish charts from
Imray Laurie Norie & Wilson Ltd,
Wych House, The Broadway, St Ives,
Cambs PE27 5BT
✆ 01480 462114, *Fax* 01480 496109
www.imray.com.

However in the case of Spanish charts, stocks held are limited and it may take some time to fill an order. It may be simpler to order directly with a credit card from

Instituto Hidrográfico de la Marina,
Pl.San Severiano, 3, DP 11007 Cádiz
✆ +34 956 59 94 12, *Fax* 25 85 48

Gibraltar

Gibraltar Chart Agency, 47 Irish Town, Gibraltar
✆ +350 200 76293
Email gibchartag@gibtelecom.net
www.gibchartagency.com

Spain (Algeciras)

SUISCA SL
Avda. Blas Infante, Centro Blas Local 1, 11201
Ageciras, Cádiz
✆ +34 902 220007
Email barcelona@suiscasl.com
www.suiscasl.com

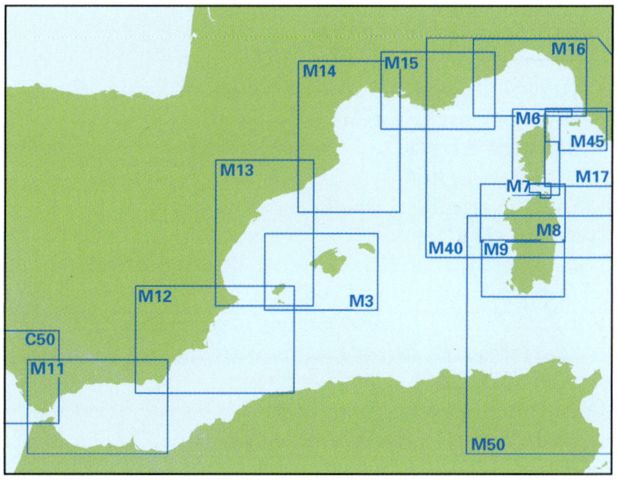

Imray charts

M3 **Islas Baleares – Formentera, Ibiza, Mallorca, Menorca**
1:350,000 WGS 84
Plans Puerto de Ibiza, Puerto Colom, Puerto de Palma, Puerto de Máhon, San Antonio, Ciudadela, Alcudia

M6 **Ile de Corse**
1:255,000 WGS 84
Plans Macinaggio, Bastia, Approaches to Calvi, Ajaccio, Approach to Propriano, Bonifacio, Îles Lavezzi

M7 **Bonifacio Strait**
1:65,000 WGS 84
Plans La Maddalena

M10 **Western Mediterranean – Gibraltar to the Ionian Sea**
1:2,750,000 WGS 84

M11 **Mediterranean Spain – Gibraltar to Cabo de Gata & Morocco**
1:440,000 WGS 84
Plans Strait of Gibraltar, Gibraltar, Ceuta, Almeria, Estepona, Puerto de Almerimar

M12 **Mediterranean Spain – Cabo de Gata to Denia & Ibiza**
1:500,000 WGS 84
Plans Mar Menor, Alicante, Dénia, Torrevieja, Altea, Villajoyosa

M13 **Mediterranean Spain – Dénia to Barcelona and Ibiza**
1:440,000 WGS 84
Plans Dénia, Tarragona, Valencia Harbour, Barcelona Harbour, San Antonio (Ibiza)

M14 **Mediterranean Spain & France – Barcelona to Bouches du Rhône**
1:440,000 WGS 84
Plans St-Cyprien-Plage, Puerto de l'Escala, Sète, Cap d'Agde, Roses, Palamos, Port Vendres, Barcelona Harbour, Barcelona Port Vell, Puerto Olímpico

M15 **Mediterranean France – Marseille to San Remo**
1:325,000 WGS 84
Plans Marseille Vieux-Port & Iles du Frioul, Iles d'Hyères, Golfe de St-Tropez, Golfe de La Napoule, Antibes, Nice, Rade de Villefranche & Cap Ferrat, Monaco

M16 **Ligurian Sea**
1:325,000 WGS 84
Plans San Remo, Approaches to Genoa, Golfo Marconi, Approaches to La Spezia, Viareggio, Approaches to Livorno, Livorno

APPENDIX

III. FURTHER READING

Many navigational publications are reprinted annually, in which case the latest edition should be carried. Others, including most cruising guides, are updated by means of supplements available from the publishers (web site www.imray.com).

ADMIRALTY PUBLICATIONS

NP 289 Leisure Maritime Communications (UK and the Mediterranean)
Mediterranean Pilot Vol I (NP 45) and Supplement covers the south and east coasts of Spain, the Islas Baleares, Sardinia, Sicily and the north coast of Africa
List of Lights and Fog Signals, Vol E (NP 78) (Mediterranean, Black and Red Seas)
List of Radio Signals
Vol 1, Part 1 (NP281/1) Coast Radio Stations (Europe, Africa and Asia)
Vol 2 (NP 282) Radio Navigational Aids, Electronic Position Fixing Systems and Radio Time Signals
Vol 3, Part 1 (NP 283/1) Radio Weather Services and Navigational Warnings (Europe, Africa and Asia)
Vol 4 (NP 284) Meteorological Observation Stations
Vol 5 (NP 285) Global Maritime Distress and Safety Systems (GMDSS)
Vol 6, Part 2 (NP 286/2) Vessel Traffic Services, Port Operations and Pilot Services (The Mediterranean, Africa and Asia)

YACHTSMEN'S GUIDES, ALMANACS, ETC.

English language

Mediterranean Almanac, Rod & Lu Heikell (Imray Laurie Norie & Wilson Ltd). A biennial almanac with second year supplement, packed with information. Particularly good value for yachts on passage when not every cruising guide is likely to be carried.
Mediterranean Cruising Handbook, Rod Heikell (Imray Laurie Norie & Wilson Ltd). Useful information on techniques such as berthing bow or stern-to, clothing, storing up etc. General information on cruising areas, passages etc.
Islas Baleares RCC Pilotage Foundation, 9th edition - Graham Hutt (Imray Laurie Norie & Wilson Ltd, 2011).
Mediterranean Spain – Costas del Azahar, Dorada and Brava, John Marchment (Imray Laurie Norie & Wilson Ltd).
North Africa, Graham Hutt (Imray Laurie Norie & Wilson Ltd). The only yachtsman's guide to the coast between the Strait of Gibraltar and Tunisia. Includes Atlantic Morocco.

Spanish

El Mercado Nautico (The Boat Market). A free newspaper published every two or three months and available from yacht clubs, marina offices etc. Written in Spanish, English and German it includes, amongst other things, a useful (though by no means comprehensive) listing of current marina prices.

French

Votre Livre de Bord – Méditerranée (Bloc Marine). French almanac covering the Mediterranean, including details of weather forecasts transmitted from France and Monaco. An English/French version is also published which translates some, though by no means all, the text. Published annually.

German

Spanische Mittelmeerküste, Wolf-Walter Ernst (Delius Klasing). Gibraltar to Valencia. Plans and aerial photos of harbours and anchorages.
Kreuzfahrten Westliches Mittelmeer, Peter Jurgilewitsch and Heiner Boehnecke (Delius Klasing). Harbour guide with photos and cruising notes.

Background

The Birth of Europe, Michael Andrew. A lastingly relevant comprehensive work with geological emphasis, which explains in simple terms how the Mediterranean and surrounding countries developed over the ages from 3000 BC.
The Great Sea: A Human History of the Mediterranean, David Abulafia.

Travel guides

Lonely Planet Guides (Books and e-books)
Andalucia
Spain
Morocco

IV. SPANISH GLOSSARY

The following limited glossary relates to the weather, the abbreviations to be found on Spanish charts and some words likely to be useful on entering port. For a list containing many words commonly used in connection with sailing, see Webb & Manton, *Yachtsman's Ten Language Dictionary* (Adlard Coles Nautical).

Weather

On the radio, if there is a storm warning the forecast starts *aviso temporal*. If, as usual, there is no storm warning, the forecast starts no *hay temporal*. Many words are similar to the English and their meanings can be guessed. The following may be less familiar:

Viento **Wind**
calma calm
ventolina light air
flojito light breeze
flojo gentle breeze
bonancible moderate breeze
fresquito fresh breeze
fresco strong breeze
frescachón near gale
temporal fuerte gale
temporal duro strong gale
temporal muy duro storm
borrasca violent storm
huracán, temporal
huracanado hurricane
tempestad, borrasca thunderstorm

El Cielo **The sky**
nube cloud
nubes altas, bajas high, low clouds
nubloso cloudy
cubierto covered, overcast
claro, despejado clear

Names of cloud types in Spanish are based on the same Latin words as the names used in English.

Visibilidad **Visibility**
buena good
regular moderate
mala poor
calima haze
neblina mist
bruma sea mist
niebla fog

Precipitación **Precipitation**
aguacero shower
llovizna drizzle
lluvia rain
aguanieve sleet
nieve snow
granizada hail

Sistemas del Tiempo **Weather Systems**
anticiclón anticyclone
depresión, borrasca depression
vaguada trough
cresta, dorsal ridge
cuna wedge
frente front
frio cold
cálido warm
ocluido occluded
bajando falling
subiendo rising

Lights and Charts – major terms and abbreviations

A	*amarilla*	yellow
Alt	*alternativa*	alternative
Ag Nv	*aguas navegables*	navigable waters
Ang	*angulo*	angle
Ant	*anterior*	anterior, earlier, forward
Apag	*apagado*	extinguished
Arrc	*arrecife*	reef
At	*atenuada*	attenuated
B	*blanca*	white
Ba	*bahía*	bay
	bajamar escorada	chart datum
Bal	*baliza*	buoy, beacon
Bal. E	*baliza elástica*	plastic (elastic) buoy
Bco	*banco*	bank
Bo	*bajo*	shoal, under, below, low
Boc	*bocina*	horn, trumpet
Br1	*babor*	port (ie. left)
C	*campana*	bell
card	*cardinal*	cardinal
Cañ	*cañon*	canyon
	boya de castillete	pillar buoy
cil	*cilíndrico*	cylindrical
C	*cabo*	cape
Cha	*chimenea*	chimney
Cno	*castillo*	castle
cón	*cónico*	conical
Ct	*centellante*	quick flashing (50-80/minute)
Ctl	*centellante interrumpida*	interrupted quick flashing
cuad	*cuadrangular*	quadrangular
D	*destello*	flash
Desap	*desaparecida*	disappeared
Dest	*destruida*	destroyed
	dique	breakwater, jetty
Dir	*direccional*	directional
DL	*destello largo*	long flash
E	*este*	east
edif	*edificio*	building
	ensenada	cove, inlet
Er	*estribor*	starboard
Est	*esférico*	spherical
Esp	*especial*	special
Est sñ	*estación de señales*	signal station
ext	*exterior*	exterior
Extr	*extremo*	end, head (of pier etc.)
F	*fija*	fixed
Fca	*fabrica*	factory
FD	*fija y destello*	fixed and flashing
FGpD	*fija y grupo de destellos*	fixed and group flashing
Flot	*flotador*	float
Fondn	*fondeadero*	anchorage
GpCt	*grupo de centellos*	group quick flashing
GpD	*grupo de destellos*	group flashing
GpOc	*grupo de ocultaciones*	group occulting
GpRp	*grupo de centellos rápidos*	group very quick flashing
hel	*helicoidales*	helicoidal
hor	*horizontal*	horizontal
Hund	*hundida*	submerged, sunk
I	*interrumpido*	interrupted
Igla	*iglesia*	church
Inf	*inferior*	inferior, lower
Intens	*intensificado*	intensified
Irreg	*irregular*	irregular
Iso	*isofase*	isophase
L	*luz*	light
La	*lateral*	lateral
	levante	eastern
M	*millas*	miles
Mte	*monte*	mountain
Mto	*monumento*	monument
N	*norte*	north

APPENDIX

Naut	*nautófono*	foghorn
NE	*nordeste*	northeast
No	*número*	number
NW	*noroeste*	northwest
Obst	*obstrucción*	obstruction
ocas	*ocasional*	occasional
oct	*octagonal*	octagonal
oc	*oculta*	obscured
Oc	*ocultatión sectores*	obscured sectors
Pe A	*peligro aislado*	isolated danger
	poniente	western
Post	*posterior*	posterior, later
Ppal	*principal*	principal
	prohibido	prohibited
Obston	*obstrucción*	obstruction
Prov	*provisional*	provisional
prom	*prominente*	prominent, conspicuous
Pta	*punta*	point
Pto,	*puerto*	port[1]
PTO	*puerto deportivo*	yacht harbour
	puerto pesquero	fishing harbour
	puerto de Marina de Guerra	naval harbour
R	*roja*	red
Ra	*estación radar*	radar station
Ra+	*radar + suffix*	radar + suffix (Ra Ref etc.)
RC	*radiofaro circular*	non-directional radiobeacon
RD	*radiofaro dirigido*	directional radiobeacon
rect	*rectangular*	rectangular
Ra	*rocas*	rocks
Rp	*centeneallante rápida*	very quick flashing (80-160/min)
Rpl	*cent. rápida interrumpida*	interrupted very quick flashing
RW	*radiofaro giratorio*	rotating radiobeacon
s	*sugundos*	seconds
S	*sur*	south
SE	*sudeste*	southeast
sil	*silencio*	silence
Silb	*silbato*	whistle
Sincro	*sincronizda con*	syncronized with
Sir	*sirena*	siren
son	*sonido*	sound, noise, report
Sto/a	*Santo, Santa*	Saint
SW	*sudoeste*	southwest
T	*temporal*	temporary
Te	*torre*	tower
trans	*transversal*	transversal
triang	*triangular*	triangular
troncoc	*troncocónico*	truncated cone
troncop	*troncopiramidal*	truncated pyramid
TSH	*antena de radio*	radio mast
TV	*antena de TV*	TV mast
U	*centellante ultra-rápida*	ultra quick flashing (+160/min)
UI	*cent. ultra-rápida interrumpido*	interrupted ultra quick flashing
V	*verde*	green
Vis	*visible*	visible
	vivero	shellfish raft or bed
W	*oeste*	west

[1] 'puerto' is applied to any landing place from a beach to a container port.

Ports and Harbours

a popa stern-to
a proa bows-to
abrigo shelter
al costado alongside
amarrar to moor
amarradero mooring
ancho breadth (see also manga)
anclar to anchor
botar to launch (a yacht)
boya de amarre mooring buoy
cabo warp, line (also cape)
calado draught
compuerta lock, basin
dársena dock, harbour
dique breakwater, jetty
escala ladder
escalera steps
esclusa lock
escollera jetty
eslora total length overall
espigón spur, spike, mole
fábrica factory
ferrocarril railway
fondear to anchor or moor
fondeadero anchorage
fondeo mooring buoy
fondo depth (bottom)
grua crane
guia mooring lazy-line (lit. guide)
nudo knot (ie. speed)
longitud length (see also eslora), longitude
lonja fish market (wholesale)
manga beam (ie. width)
muelle mole, jetty, quay
noray bollard
pantalán jetty, pontoon
parar to stop
pila estaca pile
pontón pontoon
práctico pilot (ie. pilot boat)
profundidad depth
rampa slipway
rompeolas breakwater
varadero slipway, hardstanding
varar to lift (a yacht)
vertedero (verto) spoil ground

Direction

babor port (ie. left)
estribor starboard
norte north
este east
sur south
oeste west

Phrases useful on arrival

Donde puedo amarrar?	Where can I moor?
A donde debo ir?	Where should I go?
Que es la profundidad?	What is the depth?
Que es su eslora Cuantos metros?	What is your length?
Para cuantas noches?	For how many nights?

Administration and stores

aceite oil (including engine oil)
aduana customs
agua potable drinking water
aseos toilet block
astillero shipyard
capitán de puerto harbourmaster
derechos dues, rights
duchas showers
dueño, propietario owner
efectos navales chandlery
electricidad electricity
gasoleo, diesel diesel
guardia civil police
hielo (cubitos) ice (cubes)
lavandería laundry
lavandería automática launderette
luz electricity (lit. light)
manguera hosepipe
parafina, petróleo, keroseno paraffin, kerosene
patrón skipper (not owner)
gasolina petrol
título certificate
velero sailmaker (also sailing ship)

V. CERTIFICATE OF COMPETENCE

1. Given below is a transcription of a statement made by the Counsellor for Transport at the Spanish Embassy, London in March 1996. It is directed towards citizens of the UK but doubtless the principles apply to other EU citizens. One implication is that in a particular circumstance (paragraph 2a below) a UK citizen does not need a Certificate of Competence during the first 90 days of his visit.
2. a. British citizens visiting Spain in charge of a UK registered pleasure boat flying the UK flag need only fulfil UK law.

   b. British citizens visiting Spain in charge of a Spanish registered pleasure boat flying the Spanish flag have one of two options:

   i. To obtain a Certificate of Competence issued by the Spanish authorities. See *Normas reguladore para la obtención de titulos para el gobierno de embarcaciones de recreo* issued by the Ministerio de Obras Publicas, Transportes y Medio Ambiente.

   ii. To have the Spanish equivalent of a UK certificate issued. The following equivalencies are used by the Spanish Maritime Administration:

   Yachtmaster Ocean *Capitan de Yate*
   Yachtmaster Offshore *Patron de Yate de altura*
   Coastal Skipper *Patron de Yate*
   Day Skipper *Patron de Yate embarcaciones de recreo*
   Helmsman Overseas* *Patron de embarcaciones de recreo restringido a motor*

   *The Spanish authorities have been informed that this certificate has been replaced by the International Certificate of Competence.
3. The catch to para 2(a) above is that, in common with other EU citizens, after 90 days a UK citizen is technically no longer a visitor, must apply for a *permiso de residencia* and must equip his boat to Spanish rules and licensing requirements.
   In practice the requirement to apply for a permiso de residencia does not appear to be enforced in the case of cruising yachtsmen who live aboard rather than ashore and are frequently on the move. By the same token, the requirement for a British skipper in charge of a UK registered pleasure boat flying the UK flag to carry a Certificate of Competence after their first 90 days in Spanish waters also appears to be waived. Many yachtsmen have reported cruising Spanish waters for extended periods with no documentation beyond that normally carried in the UK.
4. The RYA suggests the following technique to obtain an equivalent Spanish certificate:

   a. Obtain two photocopies of your passport

   b. Have them notarised by a Spanish notary

   c. Obtain a copy of the UK Certificate of Competence and send it to the Consular Department, The Foreign and Commonwealth Office, Clive House, Petty France, London SW1H 9DH, with a request that it be stamped with the Hague Stamp (this apparently validates the document). The FCO will probably charge a fee so it would be best to call the office first ✆ 020 7270 300.

   d. Have the stamped copy notarized by a UK notary.

   e. Send the lot to the Spanish Merchant Marine for the issue of the Spanish equivalent.

It may be both quicker and easier to take the Spanish examination.

VI. CERTIFICATE OF INSURANCE

It is necessary to carry a statement regarding insurance in Spanish.

The yacht insurance broker should provide this on request.

VII. CHARTER REGULATIONS

Any EU-flag yacht applying to charter in Spanish waters must be either VAT paid or exempt (the latter most commonly due to age). Non-EU flag vessels must have a valid Temporary Import Licence and may also have to conform to other regulations.

Applying for a charter licence can be a tortuous business. Firstly the Director General de Transportes at the Conselleria d'Obres Publiques i Ordenacio del Territori must be approached with a pre-authorisation application. This obtained, the application itself is sent to the *Capitanías Maritimas* together with ships' papers and proof of passenger insurance and registration as a commercial activity. A safety and seaworthiness inspection will be carried out. Finally a fiscal representative must be appointed and tax paid on revenue generated.

It will probably be simpler to make the application through one of the companies specialising in this type of work.

VIII. VALUE ADDED TAX

The Spanish phrase for Value Added Tax (VAT) is Impuesto sobre el valor añadido (IVA), levied at 21% in 2013. Note that for VAT purposes the Canaries, Gibraltar, the Channel Islands and the Isle of Man are outside the EU fiscal area.

Subject to certain exceptions, vessels in EU waters are liable for VAT. One exception is a boat registered outside the EU fiscal area and owned by a non EU citizen which remains in EU waters for less than six months.

For a boat built within the EU fiscal area after 1985 the following documents taken together will show VAT status:

a. An invoice listing VAT or receipt if available
b. Registration Certificate
c. Bill of Sale
d. For a boat built prior to 1985 the following documentation is required:
e. Evidence of age and of ownership. The full Registration Certificate will serve but the Small Ship Registry Certificate will not.

f. Evidence that it was moored in EU fiscal waters at midnight on 31 December 1992 or, in the case of Austrian, Finnish and Swedish waters, 31 December 1994.

Any boat purchased outside the EU by an EU resident is liable for VAT on import to the EU.

EU owners of boats built within the EU, exported by them and which were outside EU fiscal waters at the cut-off date may be entitled to Returned Goods Relief. In the latter case, HM Customs and Excise may be able to issue a 'tax opinion letter'. The office has no public counter but may be approached by letter or fax. The address is: HM Customs and Excise, Dover Yacht Unit, Parcel Post Depot, Charlton Green, Dover, Kent CT16 1EH ✆ 01304 224421. www.hmrc.gov.uk

All the rules change when a yacht is used commercially – most commonly for chartering. Note that, IVA is now charged on fuel for pleasure craft. As a result yachts cannot now obtain fuel at fishing ports and must get fuel at marina pumps (or in jerrycans from local garages).

IX. OFFICIAL ADDRESSES

Spanish embassies and consulates
London (Embassy)
39 Chesham Place, London SW1X 8SB
✆ 020 7235 5555
Email embespuk@mail.mae.es
London (Consulate)
20 Draycott Place, London SW3 2RZ
✆ 020 7589 8989
Email conspalon@mail.mae.es
Manchester
Suite 1a Brook House, 70 Spring Gardens, Manchester M2 2BQ ✆ 0161 236 1262/33
Edinburgh
63 North Castle Street, Edinburgh EH2 3LJ
✆ 0131 220 1843
Washington
2375 Pennsylvania Ave DC 20037
✆ +1 202 452 0100
New York
150 E 58th Street, New York, NY 10155
✆ +1 212 355 4080

Spanish national tourist offices
London
64 N Row, London W1K 7DE
✆ 020 7317 201
New York
666 Fifth Avenue, New York, NY 10103
✆ +1 212 265 8822
www.spain.info

British and American embassies in Madrid
British Embassy
Torre Espacio, Paseo de la Castellana 259D, 28046 Madrid
✆ +34 917 146 300
American Embassy
Calle Serrano 75, 28006 Madrid.
✆ +34 915 872 200

British Consulates
Alicante
British Consulate in Alicante, Edificio Espacio, Rambla Méndez Núñez 28-30, 6ta planta (6th floor), Alicante 03002
✆ +34 913 342 194
Barcelona
British Consulate-General, Edificio Torre de Barcelona, Avenida Diagonal 477-13, 08036 Barcelona
✆ 902 109 356 (in Spain)
✆ +34 917 146 403 (outside Spain)
Info.Consulate@fco.gov.uk
Málaga
British Consulate, Edificio Eurocom, Bloque Sur, Calle Mauricio Moro Pareto 2-2°, 29006 Málaga
✆ +34 902 109 356

X. DOCUMENTATION

It has been found useful to have the following list available for registering at each port or marina to be visited:

Nombre de yate (yacht's name)
Bandiera (flag)
Lista y folio (yacht's number)
Reg. bruto (registered tonnage)
Tipo (type of vessel)
Palos (number of masts)
Motor, Marca y potencia (engine make and capacity)
Eslor total (LOA)
Maga (beam)
Calado (draft)
Puerto base (home port)
Number cabinas (number of cabins)
Seguor (insurance company)
Proprietario (skipper)
Nacionalidad (nationality)
Telefono
Pasaporte
Tripulante y pasajero (passengers on board)
1. Nombre, nacionaldid, y pasaporte
2. Nombre, nacionalidad, y pasaporte etc.

Peñón de Ifach and Puerto de Calpe, looking south

Index